A TWENTIETH CENTURY JOB

by the same author

THREE TRAPPED TIGERS
INFANTE'S INFERNO
HOLY SMOKE
VIEW OF DAWN IN THE TROPICS

A Twentieth Century Job

G. Cabrera Infante

Translated from the Spanish
by Kenneth Hall and the author

faber and faber
LONDON · BOSTON

First published in Great Britain in 1991
by Faber and Faber Limited
3 Queen Square London WC1N 3AU
First published in Spanish
as *Un Oficio del Siglo XX* in 1963
by Ediciones R, Havana

Phototypeset by Intype, London
Printed in England by Clays Ltd, St Ives plc

A CIP record for this book is
available from the British Library

ISBN 0-571-16177-4

To the memory of Ricardo Vigón,
who loved the movies till the end

The author
wishes to thank
Marta Calvo
and Miriam Gómez
without whose co-operation
nothing would have been possible

To all those – audiences, producers, directors, the unmentioned critics, the writers whose quotations do not bear their names, to the wisdom of the elders, and, finally, to the folklore – that directly or indirectly collaborated in these labours of love for the cinema, won and lost . . . to all, once more, many thanks.

I suspect that I am, far more than not, in your own situation: deeply interested in moving pictures, considerably experienced from childhood on in watching them and thinking and talking about them, and totally, or almost totally, without experience or even much second-hand knowledge of how they are made. If I am broadly right in this assumption, we start on the same ground, and under the same handicaps, and I qualify to be here, if at all, only by two means. It is my business to conduct one end of a conversation, as an amateur critic among amateur critics. And I will be of use and interest only in so far as my amateur judgment is sound, stimulating, or illuminating.

James Agee in *Agee on Film*

Is there anything more illuminating than a film projector?

Chori Gelardino in conversation

This feeling of evanescence has always been with me as a critic; I feel I am fighting a rearguard action, for although each generation discovers anew the value of masterpieces, generations are never quite the same.

Cyril Connolly in *The Condemned Playground*

A boy never answers when they ask him what are you going to be when you grow up: 'I'm going to be a movie reviewer'.

François Truffaut interviewed

LELAND: Where's my notice? I've got to finish it!
BERNSTEIN: Mr Kane is finishing it.
LELAND: I suppose he's fixing it up.
BERNSTEIN: Mr Kane is finishing your piece the way you started it . . . He's writing a bad notice like you wanted it to be. I guess that'll show you.

Citizen Kane, 1940

Portrait of the critic as Cain

Devoured by my own resistance

Would it be a lot – Lot's lot – to say, if I said that this prologue is owed not so much to G. Cain's insistence that I write it as to my resistance to pleasing him? There's one thing for sure: any relationship is always a two-way passage. Between Cain and me (and not only my good manners, but his incommensurate egomania oblige me to put him in first place, in what he called top billing) there has always been the same violent exchange as between the hangman and his victim, Abelard and Heloise, coffee and milk: tradition unites us, folklore reunites us. But will history absolve me?

Cain's watershed

I knew Cain quite early: from his birth, in a word. I know from frank feminine frailties and certain early morning revelations that Cain rose, like Venus, fully grown from the water: his name came to his alter ego under the shower fully dressed. Since myth is frequently confused with religion, the sum of two syllables produced a near-miracle: a cinema critic would benefit from three thousand years of propaganda and the sibling sonority of a name.

Nobody is called Cain in Catholic countries or at least not in Spanish-speaking countries. That's the forbidden name, the name of a killer: the name of he who couldn't be his brother's keeper. That my friend was called Cain was due, I think, to the cinema. Others believed that he simply welded his first name to his last name and thus he raised Cain. Or perhaps it was his way of expressing his admiration not so much for Orson Welles as for Citizen Kane. *Be that as it may, Cain or Kane or Cane (as in sugar), the hard fact was that he was called Cain* * *– just as you can call me Job.*

Cain, is he the third man?

*By some deft legerdemain (atavism, Sigmund Freud, the Great Houdini?), Cain always liked the third person: his reviews adopted an impersonal tone from the beginning. ('*Da capo,*' as he loved to say, mixing music and the Mafia.) One day was revealed what was called by some connoisseur 'the limit': the opinions appeared in the mouth of a third man instead of the third person singular. 'The* cronista*' was*

** The bearer wanted his name to be followed always by an asterisk to give it – and him – the lustre of a small star.*

the one who saw the films: it was thus the cronista *who stated – and signed. At times the situation recalled that rhetorical figure called to put the blame on the lame. Other times, the critical atmosphere became unbreathable, because the* cronista *insisted on being – like God and King Philip II – everywhere.*

Who killed Hegel Valdés?

Asked about the third man, Cain said: 'You can say that it's a joke played on Herodotus's history. Or that it's a satire of social security systems. Or that it's borrowed from La peste.*' And he added, with the same rictus on his mouth that Billy the Kid had when he hurled a challenge: 'Take your pick.'*

One day the injury (or was it the insult?) arrived with anonymous alacrity. The note, which was signed by 'A fRieND' who surely was not one, said: 'caIn doEs noT WRiTE HIS cOlUMnS stOp. aNOther PERsoN wIth ThaT sAMe naME WRiTES THEm.' The intentions were as crooked as the letters.

I, for my part, tender a declaration which I can dispatch by a dialectical path: it can successively be hypothesis, thesis, and antithesis. Here it is: this history is not the truth nor is it a lie but quite the contrary.

The jawbone of Cain

There is a photo of G. (as we, his friends, called him; Caincito, women called him – there are other names but over them it's better to spread a subtle shroud of discretion and silence: they belong to intimacy) that shows him the way he was. He is shown smiling out loud – if the expression is allowed me and I don't believe there's anyone who dares deny me – and wearing dark glasses, on his head a hat and over his shoulders a poncho; he is framed by a clothes line with clothes on it and it is noon; far away, on a victrola, on a radio (the music has that sound of rain, of records raped by time and insistence) can be heard a song sad like the afternoon, what Ravel called a bolero. That is his spitting image: it only remains for him to speak. (And when he did he uttered le mot de Cambronne.*)*

Well then, it's all a lie: the likeness is a counterfeit. In the first place, Cain is not a Bolivian Indian as he seems to be in the picture. And the glasses are not dark, they're green. He has put them on to disguise his short sight and has succeeded: now he doesn't look shortsighted, he looks blind. He wears a hat on his head to prove that he has a head, but the hat is not a hat, it's a sombrero. (With his hat off, Cain looks like a pinhead.) The poncho on his back is actually a canvas by Wilfredo Lam that still has not been turned into a painting. Such an irresponsibility with a work of art (and I'm referring to the fact that Cain has thrown the cloth over his shoulders) is only proof of a savage scorn for art – thence his dedication to the movies. I have said that 'he is framed by a clothes line with clothes on it and it is noon' and I must confess a slight slackness on my part. The description is not truthful: it is afternoon. Do I have to add that such fantastic passion for disguises had led G. Cain to the most strange interludes? I think not: it would be wallowing in disgrace. Lastly, the first Cain was identified with a jawbone and he committed an evil irredeemable by mankind: he invented crime. The second Cain did an almost irreparable harm to the spectator: he thought that he had invented the cinema. But, as opposed to the original killer, our Cain believed that he could get away with murder.

Cain, canine, cynic

In the Dictionary of Omphalology, *these three words appear together. That's fine for our purposes. Often Cain has been described as a cynic. He, cynically, it is true, has responded: 'That may be because I go to the cinema a lot.' I confess that such a definition of a description does not please me – just as the description of a definition would not please me either.*

But Cain was willing to confess himself a dandy rather than a cynic – if he was really disposed to confession. He had on his desk an ironclad statuette whose head was missing. It was a fencer and this made the accident into a metaphysical occurrence. The fencer wore fine buskins, tight and smooth breeches that fell, nevertheless, in graceful folds. His blouse was open and it had a high collar: here ended his sartorial elegance. Our little hero had completely lost his head over something or other. He must have had a handsome head, with curly locks, medium sideburns and a handlebar moustache. But if his figure was elegant, his posture was more so: he had one foot stretched forward and the other set to manoeuvre; one of his hands gripped the sword correctly (it is a sword, not a rapier nor a sabre) behind the guard, while the other hand held, with detachment, almost the point of the steel (a stiletto?) and his little finger was laid out along the supple blade, honed as a razor. The whole figure was a symbol of the best of its time, of its sport. But the other fencer, a devious contender, had chopped off with one blow (the first and the last) the becoming head of our champion. The metal is iron, the sentiment irony.

'It's as if it were discovered,' he told me, 'that the Venus de Milo were knitting baby bootees.'

He recalled the difficult times of the Dictatorship, the messages from a policeman very *interested in the performing arts, censorship, and finally fear. He believed that the elegance of certain sentences, some few daring turns of phrase and almost direct allusions allowed him to confront destiny with weapons as effective as the sporting rapier or the fencing sword: the blunt épée. But the contender wielded an enormous sabre, capable of decapitating the most audacious as well as the pusillanimous. 'Machiavelli said,' said Cain, 'that the world belongs to cold spirits,' and continued; 'but cold spirits can end up as cold cuts before the enemy grinder.' I understood, I think, then. The dandy can remain calm, courteous, elegant, but that doesn't prevent the enemy from cutting his head off and making of him a most excellent corpse. Thus the small statuette acquired for him an allegorical and thereby exemplary meaning. Just like the Oscar. 'I call it Victory in Reverse Gear,' he told me. He terminated his monologue with a sentence, which, if not ambiguous, was at least obscure: 'Cynicism is the dandy's art of fencing.'*

Culpable erudition

If a black turtle was the emblem of the elegant Medici family (Cain, scholarly if not subtle, would add: 'Elegant, le gant, *got it?'), it is very probable that* Cine *inserted this fact in a review for a gangster film. Cain often liked to make a great erudite display. His erudition extended to saying that H. C. Robbins Landon was completing the total catalogue of the music of Haydn (which he must have done by now); that Chekhov met Tchaikovsky in St Petersburg in early December 1888 and they both wore fur coats; that the choice model of Delacroix was called Emilie Robert; that if jazz was born in the brothels of New Orleans, it was the order of the Secretary of the Navy, in 1917, closing them, that was the occasion for its diffusion and later development. He claimed that jazz originally meant to fuck – and then he hummed 'Potato Head Blues'. It seems to me that Cain encountered these facts in passing, in his chaotic and therefore Catholic readings. He inserted them in his reviews at the first occasion, whether they fitted or not. One day I told him so. His answer left me icy and so creamy that if I'd been made of tasty vanilla I wouldn't be here recounting this flavoured tale. By chance we were standing in the door of a kindergarten. He answered me with a quote he said was from Chesterton: 'After all, I believe that I won't hang myself today.'*

At times his erudition led him along a purple path. 'It would be a sick joke,' he would say, 'if Erostratus had not been called Erostratus at all.' Here he inserted a biography of his invention and terminated it with extreme prejudice: an old and infirm archaeologist travels alone from Ismir to the ancient seat of Ephesus. On the coast he finds a tumulus that is the tomb of Erostratus. No doubt about it. An inscription appears before his tired eyes: 'Erostratus was named . . .' As in a Monogram B-movie serial (and it is inevitable that Cain would make this reference to the movies), the wind erases the tenuous script and only the squalid scholar manages to read the long and confusing Ephesian name. Our serial scientist announces to the world that Erostratus was not named Erostratus but something else. There is a meeting of archaeologists, historians, erudites, and a few bored newspapermen to learn the new name of the ancient arsonist. The dusky discoverer begins to speak and, the instant he ends his anthropological peroration with the long-awaited phrase ('Erostratus was actually named . . .'), the same wind that erased the Linear B with the novice name of the arsonist, carries away the livid life of the archaeologist. Sick transit.

Cain's tongue is the language of the cinema

For centuries the theologians, the scholars of the Bible, the Talmudists and even Izzy and Mo and other immortal mortals struggled to understand the language of Adam. I cannot speak of Adam, because I did not know him. But I can speak of his descendant and the name is very apt. I can speak of how I spoke a lot with him: therefore, I must have spoken his language. It is thus that I can say with certainty that I spoke the idiom of Cain: Cain's tongue is the language of cinema. This idiotic idiom is also that of many of his friends. With all of them I spoke now and then and I seesaw that their language was also the language of the cinema. I know that I must give examples. As the trapper said, bear with me.

If Cain wanted to cut a long story short, he simply said 'I'll give you a synopsis.' When he was referring to an incident that occurred in a similar time and place, he identified it like this: 'In this sequence . . .' One 12th of October he was talking to me about the cinema (what else?) and someone came up and said: 'One day like today Columbus discovered America.' Cain interrupted the intruder violently: 'Don't bother me with that flashback!' On one occasion I visited his house and on arriving I surprised him framing me with his hands. I went in but Cain cut me off: 'Whoa! You're moving out of frame.' A dissolve and it was getting dark. I wanted to shed some light on the room and the conversation by opening the blinds. The tropical setting sun hit Cain squarely on the head and he shouted: 'You've just thrown 20,000 full-candles in my face!' (Of course this ejaculatory tone was almost in jest, since Cain always hated exclamation points and he was a quite sparing viewer and reviewer.)

L'avventura de Cain

Cain spoke about the cinema all the time and he, who could be called Lazy Soul, went off to cinemas that were truly off limits. He used to call those far away venues 'The site where Dad lost his vest' and the way he said Dad it sounded as if he really meant Adam. Did he mean where Adam lost his figleaf? Who knows. For he used to add: 'Your life vest is under your seat' and he pronounced vest closer to best. Was my life's best under my seat or near the aisle? Quién sabe. *Those expeditions were in fact to see a film that he had been pursuing for ages or he simply had missed, which by pronouncing it mist he never admitted that movies could pass him by.*

These were, as far as I know, his only adventures – which he called indentures, dentures for short. Ah caro Cain. *By showing what was closer to his soul, the screen, I want you to see some of his feelings.*

Cain and women

Cain often sang a song that goes like this:

I love ya, babe,
but before I'll be your dog,
I'll see you in your grave.

One time I asked him what he meant by that. 'Nothing,' he answered me, 'it's an old blues that the great Big Bill Broonzy sang.' I wonder if there wasn't something more back of his humming.

For a fictitious person Cain felt a very real attachment to women. When I reproached him that a lot of his section in Carteles *was dedicated to the cult of the pin-up girl, the chorine and the model, I thought his response would be a justification that could easily begin like this: 'It's the bait, hook and handle to get men, who, the surveys say, are enemies of my pages, to read me.' Or maybe: 'It's imposed on me by the publishers.' Or even: 'I have to eat, don't I?' But, on the contrary, Cain only said: 'I like them.' I didn't know right away if he were referring to his future photos, to the captions, or to both. Then he added: 'I like women.'*

So it was that the pages appeared decorated profusely with the most provocative women with the least quantity of clothing possible then. I think I see in this an haute bimboacy *and at the same time something that is very much like the perpetual hunger for fresh flesh that under-developed men have. A Third World War? Cain had another name for it: 'It's my cult of the occult,' he would say. 'Or rather my cult of the hidden person,' he would continue, completing the phrase after a pause that some spaced periods could refresh: '. . . the feminine person when she has nothing to hide. It is then persona grata. Heavenly bodies.'*

Curiouser and curiouser, Cain always went to movies alone. For this he also had an explanation: 'Women don't let you watch movies in peace,' he explained. 'It seems that the combination of the darkness, the music, and the so soft seats predisposes them to something quite different from a critical judgement: to erotic prejudice.' He winked. 'Give me a woman in the movies and I'll give you a movie star.'

I can say with certainty that Cain, rather than a fan of women, was a true amateur: he seemed to be eternally grateful to them that the female of the species had made his father eat the forbidden fruit of the tree of knowledge of good and evil. It is precisely this which allowed him to be a critic and, in a word, to exist.

Cain and the hoax

As everyone knows (and here we have an example of the fact that rhetoric is a method of cant: when one says 'As everyone knows . . .' it almost always means that few are the ones who know), hoax is an English word that has no translation. It means, first, fraud. But not only fraud, also literary deceit, innocent lie, canard, fraud, audacious and always imaginative falsification, and, lastly, Freud. Well now, Cain was a master of literary deceit, a craftsman of the not so innocent lie, a fan of the practical joke, a fanatic of the audacious and always imaginative falsification, and a con artist who planted the hoax, which he watered with his fecund wit and fertilized with his verbal brilliance, a random harvest in which he reaped not a few triumphs but abundant failures too. With Job's patience he gathered together his crop of inventions to delight those unhappy few whom he didn't bore with lies bigger than balloons and almost as full of hot air. Imitating Poe, following in the footsteps of Orson Welles, plagiarizing S. J. Perelman, stealing from Satie, borrowing from Marcel Schwob and robbing poor Borges blind, Cain annotated counterfeit bibliographies, made up original quotes, created new authors practically out of nothing, and came to adopt their texts with a signature in fashion – or out of fashion. Once, referring to the Marx brothers, he said that there was another triplet of comedians named the Engels brothers. Perhaps he was referring to the Ritz brothers, but this is doubtful. Rather than in a Freudian slip, one should believe in the Pavlovian hoax. On another occasion he invented a Hebrew actor of the Habimah called Menasha Troy.*

He even affirmed that the surname Pérez was of Scots origin and that its original spelling was MacPérez. Did you know that Arthur Miller put his name on an article that he never wrote? Only the facetious fact that it was a piece in eulogy of Marilyn Monroe and the beauty of the photos for which the caption text served, no more and no less, as a pretext, excuse the deceit.

There was nothing sacred for Cain when the hoax sickness attacked him: history, economy and geography were converted into pieces of a lame puzzle, which, once assembled, turned out to be a one leg pull. He recounted, for example, that once they pulled a pair of rabbits out of a hat in Australia. The rabbits, as is their wont, proliferated like rabbits. In ten years, millions of them were devastating the Australian desert. To stop the ravage of agriculture, the Government paid a dollar for each rabbit pelt. A particularly expert hunter called William Z. Williams eventually made a million Australian dollars in exchange for a million pelts. Since then this rabid rabbit hunter was known by the now legendary name of Bunny Bill.

Hyperbole, hypertrophy and even hypermetamorphosis (to use no

* I dispense with speaking of the monumental erotic iconography compiled by Cain, for obvious reasons. I will only quote two or three naughty names under each image: Amerigo Prepucci, Alexander's Ragtime Glans, Duns Scrotus, along with the more innocent ones: Herod's Diapers, Salami Where She Danced, Kid Pro-quo the boxer, the Sacher-Masoch Hotel and the Pequod Libet, a cheap ship: names that he threw overboard like second-hand mines. Let's see the sea at sea: Jean Paul Satire, Anaïs Pnin, Arthur Cunning Daily, Delius to rhyme with hedious, Sibelius to rhyme with tedious, Brahm's Bran for constipated composers, a writing block for writer's block: off with their hand! The Lady Squint, Princess Margerine, Ada Astra in The Way to the Stars, Piers Aspera in Flying Down to Cuba and, after the alcoholidays, a plaster cast of thousands. Brake a leg!

more than one page of the dictionary) served Cain to construct a dome of fantasies beneath which reality was seen through the hazy pane of his fabrications. He even came to forge Cuban facsimiles of the screen beauties and for a French Brigitte Bardot he substituted the Cuban B. B., he imported a fake Anita Ekberg from Old Havana, introduced a bogus Ingrid Bergman with a Panama hat and called her Panama Hattie. There was a moment in which he succeeded in placing in doubt the very existence of the prototype and almost affirmed that his imitations were actually the originals. Finally, at a banquet, in Matanzas, the Athens of Cuba as they say, he said, speaking of Hellenic culture, that Athens was the Matanzas of Greece.

So I think that it will be a long time before another cronista *so given to leg-pulling, so fallacious, so rich in lies, is born – if he is ever born again. If I had to think of his exact counterpart, I would not choose another name more fitting than George Washington: they were so different that they seemed to be twins.*

I remember Ricardo

It was I who introduced Ricardo Vigón to Cain, but as on other occasions it was Cain who became a true friend of Ricardo's. Three minutes after meeting him, it seemed as if they had known each other for years: as in radio, in friendship the short waves are the ones that travel longer. I don't say it like an order of merit stuck on the lapel of the memory of Cain: Cain like all mortals had two faces. This Janus Bifrons of critics made friends with the same easiness as he made enemies: if I spoke of short wave in friendship I should say as well that Cain made enemies with a high frequency.

I believe that it was the movies which united them with an umbilical cord of celluloid. If Ricardo had been called Abel they would not have been so brotherly. In the last years I saw little of Ricardo, whom I knew in the frenzied, innocent and lost days of the Ciné-Club, along with Germán Puig: those two alone battling against the hydra of indifference, provincialism and low-brow culture armed solely with enthusiasm. That is to say, gone away with their only god, the cinema. But Cain saw him often: he heard from him first in Paris, then Cannes, finally in Venice. Vigón spoke to him about the cinema with a new concept and Cain listened attentively. 'All that I know about cinema,' Cain confessed to me once, 'I owe to three persons: Ricardo Vigón, Germán Puig and Néstor Almendros. I put Vigón in first place,' he added, 'because it's to him that I owe most.'

I remember that once I went with Cain to a neighbourhood theatre in the sticks to see Mr Arkadin a third time. At the exit we met Ricardo with Jaime Soriano, another fan and friend of the cinema: this time a beatus in the quietus. (Soriano, more known in certain Havana intellectual circles as El Gallego, the relentless rapid reviewer, the only man who has given the cinema its due: he was capable of defiling a masterpiece in three lines.) Together we returned in my car and Cain and Ricardo never stopped parodying – with the amiable scorn with which one parodies a master – the melodrama in which Arkadin, a demented Marcel Proust, decides not to recover his past, but to investigate it, and as soon as his future son-in-law discovers his old friends, his former associates (Charlus is now Charlot), Arkadin eliminates them one by one through the simple art of murder. Arkadin is the last Faustian fascist of the cinema, just as Kane had been one of the first. Vigón, nevertheless, had carried the tragedy to the innocuous point of no return of farce and declared that a forthcoming film would reveal that Arkadin was the bearded lady in a circus: his secret is his sex. I can still hear how Cain and Vigón laughed in my little car, in the livid morning air, speeding along the road, 'shrouded in the luminous halo, in the barely transparent shroud of life'. I remember them both alive, which is how I want to remember them.

The death of Vigón was a rude blow for Cain: he barely survived him. I remember that he incessantly repeated, like Sartre after the death of Camus, with each new film: 'What would Ricardo say about this?' Cain often confessed that if he could understand almost before anyone what the Nouvelle Vague was about, it was because Vigón had done it before him. If he could appreciate regardless of all kinds of prejudices the quality of American movies, he declared, it was due to Vigón, who considered it the prime moviemaking moving machine in the world. If he glimpsed movie purity, if he could intuit 'the specific', as the academics say (the cinema does have them), he owed it, also, to Vigón. Thus it didn't surprise me when one day Cain said: 'I want to dedicate my book to the memory of Ricardo.' I was waiting for this. I believe that Ricardo Vigón, in spite of his suicidal modesty, wherever he may be, in heaven or in hell, in dust made dust and on the threshold of oblivion, anywhere between glory and the screen, will be there waiting for it too.

The book of Cain

It was his ancestors, the old artificers of the mythology of vengeance, who stirred Cain to write a book. 'If Daniel and Amos did it,' he told me one day, 'Why can't I?' He smiled in a way that I can only call anti-Gioconda: Cain always smiled out loud. 'I'll be a new Job,' he added. 'But this time it will be my readers who will show me their patience.' I can say with freakish frankness that he was not mistaken: I have had to hoard my patience with what Molière would not hesitate to call avarice, to be the first reader of the book of Cain.

Time present and time past passed and my decision passed over the deep blue sea of my doubts. I summoned Cain and asked him about the book. 'It's in your hands,' was his only answer. I didn't understand. 'I've written the book,' he said. 'So, it's all done now. Nothing more remains but a simple mechanical detail. With a certain technical pedantry, I'll tell you what the book needs: it only needs to be published. That's also called the final touch.' He tapped out some steps and I saw that he was carrying one of those paper bags that housewives call a paper bag. He deposited it on my desk with an effort that, I don't know why, seemed final. With his arms he made some signs of swimming and before plunging or rather dunking (me, my reality: Cain knew how to swim and keep his clothes dry) life *in the vast and well-known eternal ocean of all confusion, he smiled: it was the first time in his acidulous existence that I saw him truly smile, this extremist of affections who went from invective to eulogy with the speed of a thunderbolt and almost with its brilliance. Cain either was a morose moron or laughed with great guffaws that blazed a sonorous trail in the bush of his Cuban conversation. He smiled again, pulled back from the table to push forward the big bundle of papers, pages and published paraphernalia and then spoke:*

'This cherished varia was made by my wife.'

I imagined a new mother of Enoch (the Bible doesn't tell us her name and also passes over her genealogy: either the other Cain married a fictional woman or the flesh and blood woman who bore his sons was his sister: could our Cain also have committed incest?) counting the offspring of the new Cain as at the beginning, not long after the time when the Earth was formless and void. As at the beginning, I say, she counted the fruits of the trade, gathering harvest after harvest of reviews of all forms and colours, of columns of every order, pictures, photos, captions, phrases, slogans, saving them in those silos of memory called scrap-books.

I wanted to ask Cain again where the book was, but before I could pronounce his acid name, he said to me: 'There it is. You only need to select the critiques and submit them for publication.'

I would be lying if I said that I couldn't open my mouth: really I hadn't closed it at all: the mute O of astonishment didn't disappear from my face. I thought of Marilyn Monroe, I thought that successive spasms perhaps were the basis of her humid sex-appeal. Oh oh that oh! I also thought that by dint of struggling with Cain all my associations became moviewise. Still he added: 'I need a prologue,' with the same enunciation as if he had said: 'Dinner is served' or 'The night is moonlit and far away the stars are twinkling.'

I don't need to say that from that chaos of weekly openings in which mediocre movies were supplanted by rotten ones, I had to separate wit from chaff and select if not the most apt reviews, at least the least inept ones. I understood then – to embark on a line of thought that we can call Darwinian – that if man is descended from the ape, the critic must climb down from the sedulous ape. When I finished I discovered that on the way I had become more Homo but less sapient.

One day (a span of time had passed that only a watch without hands can measure) I showed the total tome to Cain. He reviewed the pages on which I copied, well-ordered, more than one chaotic critique and cast a glance through the pagination. At last he merely told me: 'I have written a wicked book but I feel as spotless as the lamb.' And he left.

It seemed to me an admirable quotation. A pity that Melville had said it first one hundred years before.

Next came the times charged with equal parts of leaden saturnism and tedium vitae in which I shut myself up in the shop. I approved designs in which happiness and sadness seemed to affirm or deny the existence of an author whom I knew to be as near and as far away as the music of a guitar: some chords, on touching the bass string, sounded in mourning, but there always stayed in the air the crystallized joy of the treble. His mind, unlike mine, was music and the mode was mysterioso. I inspected the variegated gamut of typefaces in search of those cursed cursives the printer's devil insisted Satanically on calling italics, claiming that Cain's book was written in roms. I burnt while the Romany fiddled in the shop. I recalled with melancholy late at night the verses of Surrey as all the girls went home, theirs not mine alas:

O happy dames, that may embrace
The frute of your delight . . .

The fortune of my pleasant choyce
Good Ladies, help to fill my morning voyce.

which Cain never heard because he never knew them: ah, at last some secret service.

Also there was the joy of meeting a gay desperado called Stymie Bold, wandering not far off, pursued by another dark rider named Sans Seriff. I found apposite the opposite analogy between those prairie dogs and the open spaces that Cain roamed on the screen. It was then I made up a wanted poster printed for bounty hunters in search of outlaws along the great divide:

REWARD

Five thousand metal molds
will be paid
to anyone who captures
dead or alive the outlaw

STYMIE BOLD

CAUTION!
ARMED AND DANGEROUS!
He is handy with lethal lead.

signed: SANS
COUNTY SERIFF

I corrected proofs with the tenacity and the efficiency that people often take for professionalism: I was a proofreader by trade, for a while, and I confess that this time I found as many errata in the book that could not be imputed to Cain as errors that were never made by the linotypists. I cursed my mission more than once and I charged as the culprit my bland and blundering heart. When the book was almost finished, I had already forgotten that I had to write these pages that you are reading now, dear reader. So it is that I had to undo what was done and I was castigated by every printer with the worst of curses: On you and yours, until the tenth generation, may there fall the black plague of misprints, transpositions, mixed family types (or miscegenation in the printer's shop) and my brow was marked with the cursed sign of Gutenberg. Look at it: e t a o i n r r r f f f f . . . .

The syndrome of Talmadge

Really I am happy that Cain disappeared before my work was finished: I fear that our friendship would have ended along with the book. I don't know why I imagine him with his quaint and curious volume of film lore in hand, as if weighing it, reading his reviews for the thousandth time, in his face what Carlos Clarens – another movie maniac – would call the syndrome of Talmadge *(or the last act of Norma). This mild medical expression had its origin in an anecdote from Hollywood at the beginning of the talkies. Norma Talmadge had just finished making her first sound film when suddenly she left the movies at the height of her fame, following the recommendations of her sister Constance, already retired. Constance Talmadge was alarmed by the criticisms of her sister's voice (she was the original Lina Lamont squeaking in* Singin' in the Rain*) and cabled her: 'Leave them,' referring to the Hollywood trash in the can, 'while you have beauty and fame, and thank God that Mama invested our money so well.' It was the time when they called the movies the silver screen and Constance never told a lie – except when they asked her age. Norma retired honourably and in silence, as a silent screen queen would. Her great moment, nevertheless, came three years later. A young film fan came up to ask for her autograph, while giving indications that at least he had not forgotten her. Norma made a grand gesture of dismissal with her right hand – shades of her divine shadow on the screen – and rebuffed the buff without even looking at him, 'Leave me alone, boy. I don't need you any more.'*

I have received a note: it must be from Cain

One day I receive a note: it is written on what Catullus called cacata carta, *so that the note not only denotes the urgency, but the fidelity to thought: Cain thinks even in the toilet.*

> *An idea has occurred to me: when you finish the book, put the first decent copy that the printer sends you in a lead casket of regular size which you have taken the precaution of making to measure.*

Bury the cask in a square yard of concrete ten yards deep; if you can make it three yards, then bury it seven yards deep. I've spoken with Oscar Hurtado, the poor man's Einstein, and he's told me that scientifically the cask can easily withstand an atomic explosion, as long as the exploding cone doesn't fall exactly on the lot marked with an X. According to him the lead cradle will make the book impervious to radiation and will leave it ready for perusal as soon as the capsule is opened. If my book succeeds in resisting the atomic bomb, the H-bomb and the neutron bomb (or the three of them) I'm sure that it will find readers – provided they can read after all. OH (Oscar Hurtado) says that the second capsule – the three by seven one – is much more effective because besides scientific security it will be under the protection of the cabala. Take measures to put in this missile to the future some issues of Lunes *and of the day's newspapers, the sports columns with chess problems and the recipes in the early show. Thus, besides literature, the chronicle of daily life and the magma of physical and sensual culture, that is, history, will accompany it. Please, don't forget that the casket must be made of lead. Tin, which is cheaper, won't do. Yours.*

The letter, of course, was signed, simply, 'G.' It also had a post scriptum:

PS H (Hurtado) says for you not to forget to put in my anti-bomb a copy of La Seiba *and to stick on the outside a decal of Rita Hayworth the way they did in World War Two. Thanks again.*

Second note from Cain

The next day I received another note – a pneumatique, *as Cain called it: 'air carrying air'. It said:*

Dear Max Brod: I have decided to leave everything in the hands of that scientific god, chance. Don't make a lead casket, forget the capsule: the atomic bomb will never happen. I've decided to imitate Claudius. According to the autobiography that Robert Graves did of him, Tiberius Claudius Drusus Nero *Germanicus,* Imperator, *thought: '. . . I shall not take the trouble to seal it (his book of memoirs) up in a casket (of lead): I shall merely leave it lying about. For my experience as a historian is that more documents survive by chance than by intention.' Although I don't have a god Apollo to take my book under his protection, I like this imperial disdain for science and, above all, for that midwife of the greatest assassin of all. The assassin, as you know, is time, the go-between, of course, is posterity. Yours, G.*

Third note from Cain

In the afternoon a third (as Cain said) preventive note arrived:

Dear Boswell: I've found a bit of Tacitus 'floating around'. Here's what the Roman historian says: '. . . A story that was the subject of every variety of misrepresentation, not only by those who then lived but likewise in succeeding times: so true is it that all transactions of pre-eminent importance are wrapt in doubt and obscurity; while some take for certain facts the most precarious hearsays, others turn facts into falsehood; and both are exaggerated by posterity.' Doesn't this seem to you a dulce *destiny for my book? Yours again, G.*

There was, as other times, a postscript:

PS Or should I say: our *book?*

Fourth and last note from Cain

On the third day, a fourth note came. It couldn't be from anyone but Cain:

Very dear Eckermann: I forgot to tell you yesterday that our friend Tacitus was referring in his peroration on the avatars of a chronicle, to a minor Caesarean intrigue: it is on account of that fact that I believe it to be a good destiny for a book to end up like the other twenty-eight tragedies of Aeschylus, all the 'truly great' poems of Alceus and the greater part of the verses of Sappho: literature converted into myth by vanishing. What greater glory for me than to have a future reader find bits and pieces of my book and on reading them, as on seeing the seven tragedies of Aeschylus, to think with a numb nostalgia (sigh) of what has been lost? Well then, my dear Max, the piece of the Annals *which I was citing yesterday has made me reflect on history and on her bed of Procrustes, time: she lies down, soft and sensual on top of time, but, woe to history if one of her limbs lasts longer and much worse still if she doesn't manage to fill up the vast bed. I truly truly [sic] believe that within 25,000 years – which* will *happen – all our present will be confused with our historic past and with our immediate future [he had put, bull's-eyes of the subconscious,* fruit *instead of* future*], in an infinite ocean of errors: history will fold in upon herself like a telescope and in that enormous accordion the facts that today stand out in some relief will disappear. The high reliefs, or the deep friezes, the 'historic monuments' that stand out in time with an obscene third dimension, will appear as a weak negative observable only as a transparency, in a confused, blurred vision. Print it! Thus Euclid and Euclides Candela will become one and the same person. We will be able to read in an encyclopedia (let's call it* Spacia *– to be pronounced specious) of the year 26,960 the following notice, which will by then not be at all astonishing: '*Euclides Candela *(323–1927 – BC or AD?), Greek mathematician. Wrote the column "Doric" in the Athenian newspaper* Agora. *In addition to numerous mathematical treatises he composed his eponymous editorial* Why a Roman?, *which analysed the increasing intrusion of Roman customs into Greece. He was the same who, in front of the Polygon (monument of the city of Colonus which copied the famous Pentagon, designed by the barbarian general Eisenoverius) told the Egyptian dictator Phuliensius Battista: "General, remember that there is no golden mean in geometry." The grounded greed of the tyrant put an end to the days of the geometer.' You're laughing, but it's no joke. It is very probable that our historical facts will be confused in the painstaking but fallible dispositions of the future historian, just as the multitude of facts telescoped in prehistory are fused for the modern archaeologist. Do we know anything today of the Wooden Age that must have existed before the Stone Age, our buffer for historical nothingness? In 25,000 years it will be very difficult to prove that James Joyce did not write* The Odyssey*; nor Homer,* Ulysses*; or that Virgilio Piñera was the author of the* Aeneid, *while Virgilius Maro wrote* Electra Garrigó, *a Roman tragedy; Edgar Kennedy, the Hal Roach comic, will be inseparable from Jack, his presidential brother; Igor Stavisky may be called a genius of the suite and swindle; Offenbach composed* The Art of the Parisian Fugue, *and Petronius Arbiter is nothing but a* Roman-à-clef. *William Shakespeare was a hack screenwriter for Globus Productions, Richard Strauss invented the waltz, to which Manuel de Falla responded with another pop tune, the mambo; Ravel wrote boleros; Sofonisba Angusciola painted today with the*

pseudonym of Georgia O'Keefe; Kafka, the dreamer of nightmares, Koffka, the sociologist, and Kupka, the non-objective painter, will be a single and indivisible person: the blasphemous Trinity; Michelangelo Antonioni painted a fresco (of which today, regrettably, are preserved no more than a reel or two) in the Cinecittà chapel, called L'Avventura, *which showed Adam looking for Eve with the help of the serpent among all the branches of the tree of knowledge; John Milton Proust composed a vast poem in seven volumes titled* In Search of Paradise Lost*: we do not possess today, lamentably, even a fragment of one of the seven books. And thus, in an archaic Arcadia, all our past history will be enclosed in what you and I can call anachronisms but what we will lament more: all the literature that we know as written, will pass, in an act of just vindication, once again into the folklore from which it came. Author, author!*

Concerning my book, once it's printed, busy yourself with leaving it to the planned hazard of the bookstores. My condolences, buddy.

G.

On the fourth day I received a simple note, which had the desperate resonance of a goodbye: rather than a letter, it was a postscript:

If you doubt that all is as I've described it, what do you want to bet it isn't? I'll see you in Oblivion.
Shake hands, rattle and roll, G.

A book whose very typography is wicked

Only a friend and among friends a brother and among brothers a twin brother and among twin brothers a Siamese twin: only a Siamese twin could have given himself to the task of completing this book. Hamlet could say to Laertes, in the promiscuous tomb of Ophelia: 'Woo't weep? Woo't fight? Woo't fast? Woo't tear thyself?/ Woo't drink up eisel? Eat a crocodile?/ I'll do't.' I can say to Hamlet, plunging as well into that capacious ditch where lay forever the beautiful and fair suicide: Do you want to pick a fight with me? Do you want to have some duck soup? Do you want to compile the book of Cain? Read it or just buy it and give it to a friend or to a foe, Dafoe.

This thirteenth labour of Hercules, this crusade after math, this quest for the Wooly Grail, this pursuit of the missing chord I have had to make alone and if I have come from the enterprise unscathed it is through an effort to survive superior to that old black thanatos which impelled me to accept an offer I couldn't refute. Like Stendhal, after having survived the crossing of the Berezina, I can say: 'I saved myself through force of will, since I saw many around me give up hope and die.' (Though there is no proof that Stendhal ever even saw the Berezina.)

I hope with good will to encounter some reader who will not cross this Berezina of ink, confronted with a book whose very design is depraved: those, the readers who abandon their hope, will die, I trust, of mortification.

Guilt and participation

My only alibi is a recurring conversation in which Cain asked me not only for the compilation of the book and this prologue, but also some notes that would precede every review: 'Self-criticism is the order of the day,' said Cain to me. I gathered (that's the verb) then that the only form of self-criticism which he permitted himself was eulogy: flattery will take you to the leader. The notes, then, would have to revise the reviews. So it was that many texts, patiently constructed, tumbled to earth with a single phrase of mine. My complicity was permeated by a vindictive spirit. A vendetta too close to poetic justice for comfort. If Cain had caused to burn with a flaming word more than one arduous effort on celluloid, I transformed the paper of his reviews into papier mâché.

The critique of the critical critiques

With time I have come to detest these reviews: I have of them not a just, but a hanging opinion. For years I was a forced reader of Cain. Not that I loved his column nor that the cinema interests me really (each day I like film reviews less: the more movies I see in colour, the more I understand my dog who is colour blind), but that I was a proofreader at the time when Cain was a critic. I know, I have said it before, but I will never tire of crying a lot like Lot: he never looked back. In the middle of my unsentimental journey I was forced to go into the savage jungle of his reviews. But I left it, fortunately, as spotless (to steal from Cain: stop thief!) as the lamb – but with less wool over my eyes. I lost it among my hates, pet or wild, because I detested Cain's gall, his elephantine pedantry, his perseverance in the organized crime of mendacity, his youth and unaltered ego. His constant referring to himself in the third person is no more than a clever disguise of his execrable egotism, not a reaction to it. Finally, his very job as a reviewer provided equal excuses for abhorrence as for admiration.

I believe that I ought to say as well that Cain could be generous: only largesse can explain his erudite's flourishes. If he was a pedant it was because he always wanted to give and hated to hoard knowledge as much as the prodigal hates the miser. His taste for the hermetic, his being obscure and in short his baroque art were not the particular fault of a petulant intelligence, but the excesses of being kind to strangers: he wanted to consider his reader as his equal. It was this form of intellectual democracy that led him to refuse always to think of the reader as an animal of an alien species or a member of an inferior race. 'The public doesn't understand,' they murmured. 'You only write for a coterie of friends,' they told him. 'Everything he does, he does to amuse himself,' they gossiped. Slander and libel were not strangers to him. But Cain knew more and better. Once when they raised their voice scandalized, he told me: 'Let them talk,' responding to my worries. 'I know that I'm on the right track because in my pages they'll find everything except that subtle form of disdain for the other: condescension.'

Was he right? Was he wrong? Leave him to heaven. As far as his reviews go, I'll try to establish a fair judgement – or at least, an objective one. Even before (or at least, at a pace with) the new European criticism, Cain had left in eternal discredit 'all the false reputations', as he called them. Carné, Duvivier, the English cinema were debunked by his Hermes ('Herpes, Hermes, who cares?', he used to say) with a fury, if not divine, then as just as Saint-Just's, though the guillotine loomed. Italian neorealism saw its decline at the time when Cain pointed it out. Maudits *masterpieces like* Kiss Me Deadly *or simply unnoticed ones like* Angel Face *found in him a sagacious and alert eye. Some great moments of the cinema, it's true, took him unawares. I refer to* Senso, *for example; or to* Madame de . . . *; or to* The Rules of the Game. *And many times he was incapable of seeing what there was behind the screen. I'm thinking of* The Wild One *by Laslo Benedek. Here he spoke of the more or less good acting by Brando and Marvin, of the photography on and off the mark, of the music, of the* tempo *of the movie taken from jazz. But he did not know how to raise the fine film of celluloid and discover that underneath the violence stood the philosophy of violence. (That is, fascism.) That beyond the taste for the sportive thuggery there was a sign of disconsolate fraud. Finally, he didn't see the poetry, the new poetry of movement and the vertigo,* *the crazed poetry of speed which is at the same time sensual frenzy and the irrational after Lautréaumont in the hazardous coincidence of a machine and of freedom on an American road: the vertiginous poetry of our century.*

If I single out this movie of no especial importance it is to uncover the moving mechanism of Cain, the one which permitted him to defend the unusual, because nobody had seen it before, or attack the respected, because it belonged to the wisdom of the public (and, why not? of the critics also) and he was incapable of recognizing that by way of escaping from a formula he despised, he had fallen into another formula because it was his own and he loved it. Thus when the real thing was where he wasn't expecting it, he was not capable of seeing it either. I told him this once and he answered me: 'A critic always suffers the occupational disease of attention,' he said and added: 'From seeing so much he ends up shortsighted: his spectacles aren't the symbol but a depraved sequel to the spectacle.'

I have tried as far as possible – that is, in a measure cut to human measure – to correct the squint, if not the critical myopia of Cain: when a review has seemed hopelessly long to me or boring, I have cut it; when there have been too many adjectives or too little clarity, I have subtracted and added; when an outstanding movie has had a review unworthy of its import, I have eliminated it. Almost always when this happens I declare it in a note. The notes also have the pretension of setting off each column in a categorical manner (or if not, on the flank) and of pointing out whatever is worthy of encomium. Sometimes I try to bring the review up to date, because I believe with Cyril Connolly (and it is for this reason that I have placed his opinion on time and criticism as one of the epigraphs) that nothing ages as much as that which lives, but that age leads inevitably to death: there is no column nearer to ruin than the one which seems most modern.

Cain's conversation was more phatic than vatic and yet I feel that although these notes of mine undermine him they are a vaticide more than a fratricide. The first Cain was no prophet either. Neither his brother nor his father were prophets. At the time God was the only prophet available and man carried the Jewish burden of being a prophecy. Cain was, yes, the first rebel and his protest, 'I am not my brother's keeper' was some sort of cry for freedom. It was, in fact, a constitution.

The absurd eating the absurd

These abhorrent pages seem no more to me than a symptom of the perversion of jobs. If the French Revolution brought us the end of artisanry, the revolutions of this century of revolutions will see the end of jobs. (But not of Job.) Now there is a science to study this anomaly called cybernetics. It is not for fun that I chose the epigraph by François Truffaut to begin the book. It's possible that some boy may still want to be a fireman when he grows up. Even if the fireproof asbestos and the faiblesse *of matches have practically finished off fires, boys will be boyish and there will be those who want to substitute for lead soldiers facsimiles of flesh and blood: they want to be generals when they grow up. There may even be others who intend to be surgeons or butchers, depending on their skill in disembowelling birds. Or perhaps, to enumerate, majordomos or*

aviators
bootblacks
divers
spies
undertakers
nuclear physicists
pawnbrokers
proofreaders
gymnasts
pimps
pirates (and the references come together because these professions pertain to the turgid legend of humankind) or even
Nobel laureates
surrealists
café operators
percolators
postmen who ring only once
pilots
co-pilots
Pilates
abstract panthers
ambassadors to the UN
secretaries general

secretaries
undersecretaries
secretary birds
abstract panters
s. j. perelmans
sotto voces
sostenuti
saties
apostles
apostates
opeds
cashiers
muralists
assassins in uniform
confidence men
and even mayors
mythomaniacs
functionaries
receptionists
Poes
poets laureate
poets
poetasters
unpublished poets
popes, a.
sons of popes
vice-presidents
aspirants
minotaurs
devoted spouses
bonapartists
d.j.s
bongo players
bookbinders
palmists
moonshiners
contrabassoonists
go-betweens
picassos
Jehovah's witnesses
brickmasons

writers
radio writers
sitcom writers
screen writers
CIA *agents*
rhinoceroses
hippopotami
monks lewis
adolphes saxes
panhandlers
major keys
heavy breathers
adoptive fathers
sons and lovers
buffaloes
buffalo bills
bills
illuminati
american express cards
cards
abstract pinters
trappists
rapists
aerialists
marsupials
moby dicks
peeping toms
bureaucrats
ticket takers
lapps
second lapps
box-office poisoners
valentinos
neonazis
cymbal players
pencil sharpeners
reflexologists
conductors (of trains)
conductors (of orchestras)
alexanders
ragtime bandits

romans-à-clef
negro spirituals
record players
hot jazzists
eunuchs
and of course the oldest profession

*But it's doubtful that there's a kid who dreams of being a cinema critic: the absurd never ends up absurd.**

A prologue after Bellerophon

Would that I could be for once Athena and yoke to the glorious laurel the feigned forehead of Cain. But I cannot do it because I am nothing more than an expendable mortal, with the sole gift of gab, a useless palaver that up to now has shown itself, like leeches, more harmful than beneficial. For me it would be very difficult (because to say impossible is to condemn any human effort to naught) to exalt Cain to the place that he merited – whatever this might be. Nevertheless, it is Homer who recalls: 'It is very easy for the deities who reside in the wide and horizontal ice to give glory to a mortal or to abuse him.'

Cain really should have asked the movie goddesses for this prologue and would have obtained a ticket to glory: by asking it of me he was certain that he could avoid foul play. Although perhaps I am a Cain for Cain. I'm afraid that this prologue may turn out to be a Bellerophontis Litterae. *I cannot dodge Cain's influence, which like the ghost of a writer haunts my dreams and even my daydreams: like Cain I must unveil the quote's source.*

Bellerophon was an ancient hero. Like Hamlet, he was sent to a king by another king with a letter asking that he be put to death: the first king was a too scrupulous host. In some manner known to the Dane too, Bellero succeeded in foiling the plot and the letter turned out useless, if not dangerous: it gave rise to a literary expression, Bellerophon's letter. Maybe this protracted prologue will be the death of Cain, but what if it were at the same time my own demise? Sait-on jamais?, *Cain might say, evoking shadows from the shadows.*

But it's true, one never knows. And now, double venom, to thy work.

* *I read, when the prologue is finished, a brutal confession which drags me into the maelstrom of all doubts. Former reviewer William K. Zinsser avowed: 'I am an American boy who grew up to realize one of the American dreams. I became a movie reviewer.'*

Carteles
1954–60

For five long years –
the extended duration of time
under duress has been
already noted by Bergson –
the readers of the magazine
Carteles *had to endure*
the critical
display made by Cain under the
umbrella of 'Cine'. With a
patience before which Job
seems frivolous
and Confucius
a desperado, the surviving
subscribers
waited every Wednesday
with a mixture of anguished
expectation and icy
indifference: will he show up
today too?, when are they
going to fire him?, this
man never sleeps? But Cain
pursued his readers with a
Montechristian zeal
and found them where they
least expected it: in a bus,
in the barbershop, in the
dentist's waiting room.
At the end, in a lustre
with less lustre than a lustre, Cain
had accomplished what he feared: he
had fewer readers than when he
began five years before.
These reviews, his collected papers,
will complete the siege – they
will assault the reader in the
last refuge: a book. Cain's body is his
complete works. This book has
been written, literally, over his
dead corpus.

this
is the first column by
cain
which seems to me
preserved
from time and tide

Martí in the Cinema

At last *La rosa blanca* (*The White Rose*) has been shown after a violent and hardly constructive polemic between apologists and detractors, which was maintained throughout the shooting of the film. *La rosa* has been sponsored by the Commission of the Centenary of the Apostle Martí. Directed by the Mexican Emilio Fernández and photographed by the Barcelonan-born Gabriel Figuéroa, it has over twenty actors of different nationalities, from the Mexican Roberto Cañedo to the Colombian Alicia Caro. But, at least theoretically, it is a Cuban movie.

It purports to be a film-biography of the life of José Martí. And here begin the reservations about the movie, which never should have been made. Because to make a biography of the Cid Campeador or of Robert Bruce – to cite no more than two dissimilar examples of liberators – is a feasible thing, since both are sufficiently far off in time to allow for an objective work and their subjects belong to legend, rather than to history. But to portray a man who died just before the turn of the century (1895) and whose grandchildren (one of them is the Hollywood actor Cesar Romero) are still living is an arduous enterprise from which one does not usually emerge unscathed.

Moreover, if the exact dimension of Martí has escaped all his biographers – utilizing the thousand tricks of writing –, how can one hope that it will be the cinema which will discover a man who was never a spectacle? Martí was not an audacious warrior, nor a picturesque hero, but a small man, withdrawn, a thinking machine who only communicated with his surroundings to fulminate with his flaming sword of words or to murmur some phrases of love and understanding for his neighbour. If there are lives to think of as impossible or to imagine as miraculous, one of them is Martí's. To make it tangible even if it be by the fleeting shadows of the cinema is like portraying conscience because Martí is the conscience of Cuba. That conscience – at times represented ingenuously but effectively as a gnome astride a shoulder – tells each Cuban, from schoolbooks or from overleaf in the almanac, how he is to be born, to live, and to die. As can be seen, the mistake was in the choosing.

The movie *La rosa blanca* has been made with every care. But that is not enough. It is necessary to have made not only a painstaking movie (which indeed it is), or a perfect one (which it is not), but also a moving one, which would revive in every believer the life, passion and death of Martí, but which would also move any stranger to identify with his life, to comprehend and venerate his passion for liberty and to mourn his death. There lie the greatest reservations about the film. In *La rosa blanca* all Martí is there, but Martí is missing. Absent in something less tangible than putting in his mouth the snippets of his prose that would fit well or following step by step his daily comings and goings. And the fact is that the movie has plenty of substance but lacks spirit. One sees José Martí struggle for an hour and fifty minutes and is never concerned with his anxieties. (There is a very mendacious American movie which could serve as an example: *Viva Zapata!*. Anyone with a passing knowledge of Mexican history knows that this Zapata is false from head to moustache to toe. But when he dies riddled with bullets, like a mad dog and Mexican, one feels what all Mexico must have felt when it heard the news. The spectator has been moved. This happens on very few occasions in *La rosa blanca*.)

Why? Because between being on guard against the historical errors (which there always are) and giving the movie a heroic tone, the personality of Martí has been impermeabilized to the point of an absolute dryness. A little less formal and historical rigour and a little more feeling would have been preferable. And at times veracity could have been achieved, without losing valid emotion. As in the scene of the march of the Spanish soldiers with his corpse. Wouldn't it have been more effective to drape it over a horse (as it was in reality), with the rain hitting the small lifeless body, than to parade it between a theatrical double file of soldiers with flaming torches? Furthermore, the psychological development of the character could have been truer and more accurate. Martí appears at times a violent man, quick to take the neighbour by the lapels. Or we see him fretting about liberty in the next shot, in which some poet friend of his from Mexico reminds us that 'the chains of his country will someday be chains of roses.'

Martí may have been a romantic, but one will never be able to allow the movie's insidious suggestion that the only thing that impeded him from throwing himself into the revolution was the love of one or two women. Martí may have been a singular man but was also a product of his people and of his time. The aforementioned either has been forgotten or sketched lightly in the film.

As far as its pacing, the movie offers the remarkable contrast of a copious succession of actions narrated with an overly slow rhythm. Perhaps this is because of the procedure of director Emilio Fernández, extending a brief nucleus of plot beyond the cellular horizon. This could be called an analysis. Now one is dealing with an exuberant biography, pregnant with facts and anecdotes which happened one after another and which demand constraint and the most difficult of processes: synthesis.

A final question remains to be asked: the original goal of *La rosa blanca* was to make known the exact image of Martí to the whole world – will it accomplish this satisfactorily, or will it be one more movie about one more patriot who once fought for the liberty of his land?

22 August 1954

The Greeks Hadn't a Word for It After All

Phryné, the Courtezan is a biography – you have to call it something – of the famous kept Thespian of love or of 500 years BC – whichever comes first. Here the lover of sculptor Praxiteles appears, more or less, as a pagan virgin. At more than two thousand years' remove, this film presents a Phryné pure of soul and generous (of body) against whom stands a conspiracy hatched by the elders of Athens. At the end – which is the real pretext for making the movie – there's occasion to enact the fabulous act of coactive disrobing, which winds up being the first strip-tease that history registers and man ogles. Ah Greek girls – but I cannot describe them! Please try?

14 November 1954

obviously,
cain ain't
seen
north by northwest *yet*

Perish, Peeper!

Rear Window is an amusing and excellent melodrama, in which an occasional voyeur doesn't content himself with seeing the bullfight from the barrera, but also tries to stick his pair of banderillas – to find himself corralled by the most dangerous bull of them all. Based on a story by Cornell Woolrich (otherwise called William Irish, his pseudonym more familiar to diggers of thrillers than his real name) seen on television some time back, the movie recounts, with a language no less visual by being complex, the fix in which a professional photographer finds himself negatively when, immobilized by a leg in a cast, he decides to play detective with a crime and its author hidden at the back of his field of vision. Introduced forcibly into the story are a masseuse-cum-amanuensis (Thelma Ritter) and a gorgeous society girl (Grace Kelly) in love with the elderly hero (James Stewart), the paralysed photographer who peers through the open windows of the neighbourhood for much more time than in the story, to present the most abnormal, subnormal and paranormal neighbours that can be collected in a block of New York's Greenwich Village. It's Greenwich mean time, folks! A female exhibitionist, a sexual paranoiac, an artist manqué, a left-handed pianist after Ravel, a zoophilic woman, a mild murderer and some Sunday sadists. Alfred Hitchcock (*Dial M for Murder* lately?) has fashioned a movie that is most moving without ceasing to show that recent inclination of the Master to enclose his cast of characters in a room to make them talk a lot while they move around very little. Carrying his tendency up the *tour de force*, Hitchcock has immobilized the central character in a stationary wheelchair and at the end – with clean legerdemain – turns his leg in a cast into two legs in the cast.

13 February 1955

Auschwitz, the Final Solution

The Last Stop (*Ostatni Etap*) is an extraordinary exposé of the tortures and killings of millions of human beings in the concentration camp of Auschwitz in Poland. More than a film, than a report, than a brief, it is a journal of the Dantesque dark night of the extermination policy of the Nazis. It is not a pretty movie, but it is a useful film, because it serves to remind the world of the ordeal – suffered by the Jews and with them, all those the Nazis considered not Aryan, that is to say, inferior – beyond human scope and imagination. The film is starkly realistic, but the spectator comes away with the impression that the horror he has witnessed is dramatic or melodramatic and not an atrocious *tranche de mort*.

The director Wanda Jakubowska (one of the few women directors in the world and perhaps the most powerful and hardened of them: she was an escapee from hell) has declared that in the movie she has avoided deliberately and consciously the total reconstruction of the Nazi infamy in Auschwitz: 'Because death and violence are not a spectacle. Contenting myself with suggesting through details, faces, incidents, the margin of the horrible.' The executions, the cremation, all the paraphernalia of the Final Solution are realized beyond sight and sound. One only sees the preparation of the death machine and the fearful choosing of the prisoners who proceed to be killed behind closed doors and afterward the smoke from the tall chimneys of the crematorium (a recent arrival inquires: 'What is that factory that's so busy?', and another responds in a casual tone: 'It's the oven'), smoking like the smokestacks of Averno.

Made on the very grounds of Auschwitz, using former *Schutz Staffels* from the *Lager*, collaborators, actresses and extras, who were themselves prisoners in the camp, the movie relates the short life, the passion covered with lice, sickness and hunger – and the sudden death of millions of female inmates enclosed in the women's section of the morbid mill of human lives that today is preserved as a true museum of horrors.

Made with a total disregard of formal worries, almost ignoring the middle to get to the end, with the objectivity and the economy that characterize great documentaries, the film moves one by its courageous starkness, to which the wobbly photography plus the imperfect sound lend an authenticity only comparable with that of *La Bataille du rail* or of *Roma, Città Aperta* and the other first samples of European neorealism. The only defects of the movie are its excesses: the women are too heroic and the Nazis too much cut from one black cloth instead of greys like baddies in a Western – they are portrayed without subtlety or nuances, without their wanton weaknesses, with the result that the latter fail to be as Herodic and the former as innocent as they really were.

The scene in which the French women march to the crematorium all singing *La Marseillaise* as one, without the least cracking in any of their voices, or the one in which the head of the camp runs to caress her little dog which whimpers upon hearing the terrifying cry of the women who are hunted by the SS, are not very convincing because grossly depicted: a paintbrush would have painted more exactly than the roller which was used.

Best terrible moments: the one in which several Nazis discuss the installation of a new crematorium that will permit the extermination of from forty to fifty thousand persons per day, and there is one of the group who dissents, adducing that it is for barbarians to think only of killing. Just when the spectator thinks that here, at last, is a human being, he must think again as the Nazi adds his modest proposal: to utilize the strongest inmates for forced labour, and to annihilate them later, when they aren't capable of any more work. Or the other evil instant in which a little girl runs smiling to recover her ball which has fallen at the feet of an SS man – he smiles at her, and then he returns the little girl to the file of hundreds of children and women who are marching towards the gas chambers.

27 February 1955

to do justice
to
garbo
has never been easy:
the cronista
was insulted,
vituperated,
scoffed at,
and cursed
by his readers:
later, nevertheless,
cain
was inclined to think
that after all
his readers
might be
right

Garbled Garbo

For *Anna Karenina* to be considered the most outstanding film of the week, twenty years after its original showing, could be due to two things: 1) that one is dealing with an exceptional movie, an immortal masterpiece; 2) that the other opening movies are really mediocre. The *quid* is much nearer to the second cause than to the first. One has here a desiccated version of the magnificent novel by Leo Tolstoy, in which appear many of the characters and some of the situations in the book, but from which is absent that ardent aura that differentiates the good from the truly great. A romantic air has been pumped into the film which distances it from any critical observation of the society of its time – the principal aim of the novel. The easiest anecdotes and a sketch of the plot line remain, but as in a fabric turned inside out: the threads can be observed distinctly, the yarn can be recognized, but in some way the cloth is not the same. Tolstoy, with a stuff of perennial quality, had fashioned a gown that could fit more than one woman well; Hollywood transformed it into a robe made to measure for Greta Garbo.

To her are due the greatest faults of the film, which suffers all the consequences of the star system, each scene to be thought out in terms of the star: by and for the Divine Greta. She shows here that if she was justly considered one of the most powerful personalities of the cinema, she was very far from having been an extraordinary actress. But despite the wan mannerisms of Garbo and the flatulent force of Basil Rathbone, the director Clarence Brown (*Intruder in the Dust*) succeeds in offering an example of sensitive control while completing a precise technical feat.

3 April 1955

A Star is Born Again

A Star Is Born is a musical tragicomedy and also the best movie in Cinemascope released up to now. It is in addition the vehicle for the return to the screen (after a long period of seclusion and a suicide attempt, followed by successful personal appearances in New York and London) of the singer and actress Judy Garland. The story is the same as that of a movie with the same title which won the Oscar in 1937, starring the now forgotten Janet Gaynor and the ever-present Fredric March. This time a movie star (James Mason) at the pinnacle of his fame, but a drunkard, discovers in an unknown girl (Garland) the makings of a star. He decides to help her and on the way loses what little remaining popularity drink has left him. When the new-born star (they have married and the actor is collecting unemployment) goes to receive the Oscar she has won, the drunken has-been husband interrupts her acceptance speech to beg pathetically for work. Not being Job he needs a job. From then on, the life of the star is a Calvary in which the cross of the husband weighs too much for her. Finally he decides to remove himself by way of a dive without surfacing in the conveniently nearby ocean. The blow morally topples the actress (a star is worn out), but in the last reel she recovers to announce to Hollywood and the whole wide world that she is the living portrait of the loyal self-denying wife.

With this sentimental plot plus some neurotic touches by Mason and a few more hysterical ones by Garland, the director George Cukor (*It Should Happen to You*) has made a musical which has a better story than most. That or a tragedy with melodies that linger on.

Begun as a modest production of little more than two million dollars, the filming of *A Star Is Born* went on (and on) for eleven months, pleasing the perfectionist spirit of Judy Garland and driving the executives at Warner to despair, as the budget blew up until it became a six million balloon. But it was well spent. Because never have the technical and artistic possibilities of Cinemascope been exploded and exploited to the maximum as in this movie. *A Star Is Born* seizes the opportunity to throw a scrutinizing critical gaze at many of the inner vices of the movie industry. And while this has gained for the movie the sympathy of uncertain sectors of the public, it has also won the certain enmity of many movie magnates. Even to preventing it from winning a single minor laurel at the Academy Awards.

All the weight of the film rests upon the minute minuet of Judy Garland's act from waif to wife, acting with what could be called 'controlled hypersensitivity' and singing with a better voice than ever. In spite of the fact that her figure, closer to the balloon than to the ballroom, prevents one (and two) from seeing her transform herself believably from a thin, timid timpanallier into the great lady of the screen. Nevertheless, the combination of acting, singing and dancing made her an easy Oscar winner, running out her competition (Grace Kelly) by more than a nose. (No quip intended.) Aside from the showmanship of Garland, the sober inebriation of James Mason and the fluid direction by Cukor, the most notable aspect of the movie is its perfectionist use of colour, thanks to the supervision of the photographer from *Vogue*, Hoyningen-Huene, whose visual good taste is also responsible for the colourful *The Adventures of Hajji Baba*. Rarely has the outsized canvas of Cinemascope been seen covered by the rich oil of a palette so lush (no pun intended) and so conscious that the theory of colours is something more than chasing rainbows.

24 April 1955

Documentary and Document Art

Memorias de un mexicano (*Memoirs of a Mexican Photographer*) is an extensive documentary (an hour and a half in length) and also the most valuable document that any country possesses of as turbulent a phase in its history as the Mexican Revolution. The movie spans from the earliest times of the dictatorship of Porfirio Díaz, at the end of the last century, to the seizing of power by Plutarco Elías Calles, in 1924, with an epilogue necessary to bring it to the present, using shots of all the presidents who succeeded Calles. Through the film marches the pompous and Frenchified court of Don Porfirio, and the old man himself, at once threatening and patriarchal, who governed Mexico for thirty years, until he was deposed by a triumphant revolution, led by Francisco Madero, who came to power thanks to the multiple rising of the generals Orozco, Villa and Zapata.

Then follows: the so-called *Decena trágica*, in which for ten bloody days chaos reigned in Mexico City, after the new pronouncement by those same leaders, Zapata, Villa and Orozco; the treason of Huerta, who having placated the rebels, instigated another counter-revolution; the treacherous shooting of President Madero and Vice-President Pino Suárez at the hands of Huerta; the successive rebellions of Carranza, Obregón, Villa, Zapata, and the other revolutionary generals; the death of Zapata, victim of an infamous ambush; the fall of Huerta and the rise of Carranza to power; the death of Villa, machine-gunned in the back in the middle of the city; the revolt of Obregón, who fought Carranza with the only arm left to him (he had lost the other in the fight); the flight and death of Carranza and election of Obregón to occupy the presidential chair, so coveted and more often than not empty; and finally, the election of Elías Calles and the return to the tumultuous and tortuous normality of politics as the only method to climb to power. Collaterally, the spectator witnesses the solitary death of the once all-powerful Don Porfirio, old and forgotten, in the Paris which, loving it so much, he wanted to graft on to Mexico; and the invasion of Veracruz by the marines on the pretext of defending American property threatened by the Revolution.

But the film is something more than a succession of historical postcards. It is a work of art. Militant and nationalist like most Mexican murals and almost as plastic, a quality that is very often sacrificed at the expense of that primary law of the newsreel: movement. The camera here possesses an extraordinary mobility and wanders over deserted streets, crowded plazas, cheering multitudes, threatening cavalrymen with wide-brimmed hats, double-breasted bullet-belts and rifles askew, salutes vehement partisans and flies over the dead of the Revolution like an apolitical vulture. At times (and this is a daring move for the times), it hops onto a train loaded with taciturn troops or with prattling politicians, and marches towards the barracks to be assaulted or stops at the next whistle stop, at the same time capturing with its single daltonic pupil the marvellous Mexican landscape.

The author of this fabulous feat is named Salvador Toscano Barragán and he was a small, elegant man, with a fine Mexican moustache. He was an engineering graduate. Toscanito, as his friends called him, was born in 1872 and after studying mathematics, optics, chemistry, and mineralogy, he decided one day that he had to rapidly get hold of a cinematographic camera. He had read in a newspaper that 'some Lumière Brothers' had just invented it in France. When the camera was in his hands – after a strange succession of setbacks that almost frustrated the attempt – Toscanito decided to photograph whatever he saw. He began to do this in 1897, so that when the Revolution began in 1910 he had more experience and skill than the professional photographers of the press.

With the aid of two assistants (a Mexican cinematographer says that they were more than two and even goes so far as to affirm that Toscanito did no more than co-ordinate the collective work of many photographers, out-Bradying Brady), Toscano Barragán covered over 500,000 square miles of the surface of Mexico, photographing uprisings, dead generals and live presidents with extraordinary vigour and valour, an exploit unsurpassed by any other newsreel unit in his time. On one occasion Victoriano Huerta, responsible for the assassination of Madero, ordered him to be arrested because he knew that he had taken certain compromising pictures. Toscanito found himself obliged to flee over the neighbouring roofs, escaping from a parlour situation – and a parlous one to boot. Shortly after the ascension of Calles to the presidency, sound displaced the silent cinema and Salvador Toscano Barragán decided that it was time to lower the weary eyelid of his camera. From then until his death, which found him blind in 1947, he never again placed his prodigious hand on a foot of virgin film.

Memorias de un mexicano is the fruit of the wondrous wanderings of Toscano and of the love of a daughter for the labour of her father. Carmen Toscano took on the wearying enterprise of reviewing and putting in order the 80,000 feet of film shot by her father at the end of 1947. It took her four years to choose and edit the negatives before converting them into the present movie. The film had so deteriorated that it was necessary to use gates of velvet so that the projector would not damage or wrinkle the negative. In the original scenes, the light was so variable that strips of film of similar brightness were carefully chosen and printed in pairs. This precision job, and the matching of the speed of the silent film with that of the sound film, was carried out using exact calculations to avoid the mechanical jerks which would have given the most solemn and serious scenes a ridiculous comic quality.

The new master negative was 33,000 feet long and its selection and preparation had cost 150,000 Mexican pesos, of which the government provided 91,000. But the money turned out to be insufficient anyway. Mrs Toscano keeps the rest of the footage in her house like a rare treasure of which every Mexican wants to obtain a frame – *even a small one*. Like the Florentines in the *Divine Comedy*, each family here has a relative in heaven or in hell – or travelling through purgatory at 24 frames per second.

8 May 1955

cain, by hurrying an
opinion,
committed one of his
most flagrant errors:
he declared all the
buildings of verona
to be baroque,
when in
verona actually there are romanesque
churches,
romanesque-gothic barracks,
gothic convents,
chapels of the late gothic,
palaces constructed
in the renaissance
style, but, alas,
not a single edifice that
can be called baroque

The Lovers of Verona

Romeo and Juliet is a princely edition of the work of the same name by William Shakespeare. Its virtues are many and visible; its defects are the same which all the earlier adaptations of Shakespeare have suffered. Because whoever said that Shakespeare was made measure for measure for the cinema showed that he neither knew what Shakespeare was nor did he know what film is. A London theatre critic (and a lover and intimate of the Shakespearean stage) has declared: '. . . the theatre of Shakespeare never offers visuality. It is a theatre that tends to capture and absorb the spirit, not the eye.' (And it happens that the cinema, in spite of sound, is an eminently visual project.) Another Shakespearean expert, the set designer Gordon Craig, held the view that the theatre of Shakespeare lost on the stage what it gained with reading: its metaphysical logos, its beautiful poetry.

Renato Castellani (forty-two years old, ex-engineer and one of the finest men of the new Italian cinema, director of *Due Soldi di Speranza*) has made *Romeo and Juliet* with a love more explicable in Stratford-upon-Avon than probable in Venice. For two years he worked on the film and the adaptation, which is also his, struggling with his deficient knowledge of English. Castellani not only directed the actors and supervised the work of the photographer, but watched over all the aspects that are involved in a film, from the costumes to the sets, including the hairstyles and the period music. So that *Romeo and Juliet* is almost a personal opus: on Castellani alone will be lavished the kudos or be heaped the ko's.

It had been said that Castellani has attempted to realize a neorealist Romeo and Juliet, inserting the classical tragedy into a realist format. Such a saw was confirmed by the fact that the principal actors were either quite unknown or not professionals at all. Susan Shentall, the youngest – she was then only nineteen – most beautiful, most naïve . . . and also most sensual of the Juliets since Elizabethan days (when all Juliets were just Jules), was an office girl discovered by Castellani in a London café. Romeo, Laurence Harvey (the impetuous Scots knight of *King Richard of the Crusades*), is a young actor of Lithuanian origin who up to then had only had small roles in insignificant English films. Harvey is also the youngest of the cinema Romeos, although, unfortunately, not the best. Another important character in the play, Prince Escalus, was entrusted to the writer Giovanni Rota and then dubbed into English.

But in spite of the non-professional actors and the real places, the intention of Castellani has been rather to encase the Renaissance tragedy in an exact environment and in a precise style as well. *Romeo and Juliet* is a baroque tragedy, the settings in which the action of the film transpires are baroque: the church of St Zeno, and the alleys of Verona, the Piazza del Campo, in Sienna, and the sumptuous Ca'd'Oro, in Venice. To capture the Renaissance atmosphere, costumes which copy exactly canvases of Filippo Lippi and Botticelli, and camera compositions which at times recall the masters of the high Renaissance have been pressed into service. As a *summum* of this pictorial preoccupation of Castellani it is sufficient to recall the scene in which Romeo has an interview with Friar Lawrence, filmed in the convent of San Francesco del Deserto, in which both whisper Shakespeare's lines, their heads resting against the famous mural of the *Annunciation*, by Fra Angelico.*

Romeo and Juliet, the film, is almost a work of art. Working against its ultimate perfection is the uneven ensemble acting – in which Sebastian Cabot offers a Capulet full of vigour and credibility, while Laurence Harvey is a stammering and weak Romeo who confuses the languid expression of the amorous with the pained face of the hungry. And that unsalvageable slowness, at times carried to blatant boredom, which all the movies based on works by Shakespeare produce. Another thing. The film runs from the initial chorus to the final words of mourning without any rhythm, fitting itself on occasion to the Shakespearean sounds. But most times the immortal lines seem obscure, unintelligible and opaque, while the movie progresses from canvas to canvas, superfluous but beautiful – for your eye only.

But in spite of its minor faults – and on account of them – *Romeo and Juliet* is one of the most handsome films that has passed through the screens of Havana in a long long time. Castellani knows how to instil into 'the tragedy of the star-crossed lovers' that innate plastic sense which is an Italian birthmark since the days when Correggio shouted: 'I also am a painter.' Its visual sensuality is a feast for the eyes, comparable to seeing the Gallery of the Uffizi animated or to sensing that *The Birth of Venus* is coming to life. A miracle owed to the English cinematographer Robert Krasker, who demonstrated anew all that can be gotten out of Technicolor, in the most pictorially perfect photography since he himself photographed *Henry V*. Both, director and photographer, have come together to record some marvellous visual cues, where Shakespeare only put 'Enter Romeo', '*Tacet* Nurse'. There's the scene of the masque ball in the House of Capulet, with the old galliard that recalls an air by Monteverdi and the Gothic masks peering from between the magnificent candelabra, while the tragic adolescents feel the initial call of their first and last love. A game of hands which say what their mouths barely dare to mutter, is one of the most memorable sequences of the modern cinema. In short: *Romeo and Juliet* is not Shakespeare, but never has Shakespeare been betrayed in a more splendid cause.

5 June 1955

* Cain trips two times over the same filmic rock: the scene was done in the studio, the fresco of the *Beato* was a fresh facsimile.

The Black Carmen

Carmen Jones is a modern (and Americanized) version of the well-known opera by Georges Bizet. Carmen (Dorothy Dandridge) is now a *mulata* – as fierce and avid for love as the gypsy of Prosper Mérimée – who works in a parachute factory, instead of the earlier cigar factory. Like the first Carmen, she places herself in the path of Joe (the Don José of the opera, played by Harry Belafonte), wraps him in her passion as in a mephitic mist and converts the good soldier into a defender and then an offender, not without first having abandoned him for the hurly, burly boxer Husky Miller (the bullfighter Escamillo of the opera), played by Joe Adams. At the end, and not a happy end, Joe kills Carmen who dies her bizarre Bizet death with an aria on her lovely lips.

The Mérimée story, now a classic of Romantic literature, has attracted the cinema since the silent days and nearly fifteen versions of the tragedy of the gypsy, the soldier and the strong man have been filmed, from a primitive version in silhouettes to the latest French realist version, including the hilarious spoof by Chaplin and another version in Technicolor, with Rita Hayworth contorting herself laughably around Glenn Ford and both being fools together in an unintended parody.

The new *Carmen* has its origin in a modernized version by that dynastic librettist Oscar Hammerstein II and was premièred on Broadway in 1944. Its action is displaced from the Spain of tambourines and bullrings to somewhere in the Deep South in wartime. The gypsies are now blacks, the romantic verses are converted into some sort of rhyming slang and the French music by Bizet has lost its Spanish twang and tone to sound like lightly coloured syncopations. If the opera lost body, density, it gained a realist credibility that the Spanish ear-rings, *traje de luces*, and pack of cards would never have gotten for it in this age of Kalmus.

Carmen Jones the film has gathered a young and apt cast of black actors and singers, who make of the movie the most exciting experiment with black performers made in Hollywood since the days of King Vidor's *Hallelujah!* (1929). Dorothy Dandridge is the most convincing of all Carmens, with more sound and French fury than Viviane Romance, as much sex appeal as Rita Hayworth and more dramatic talent than both put together. Harry Belafonte (folksinger, with Caribbean good looks, and with the acting approach of a coloured Brando) manages to believably convert Don José, a noble soldier, into a beast trapped by jealousy. Joe Adams – announcer, now singer – makes his

Husky Miller into a human being, pompous and punchy, but always more believable than the pompous Escamillo. The three, although they earn their living musically, do not sing here and have been dubbed by true singers since their voices did not reach the difficult tessitura of the score. Thanks to them and to the rest of their *Carmen* companions, the movie preserves an aura, ineluctable and fatal and at the same time full of gay and garish colour, which confers on it the doubly ambiguous atmosphere of a musical and a tragedy. It is a pity that the colour process and the costumes seem so shoddy and that the art director insisted on a crude realism which clashes with the artificial and stylized spectacle of a human being swearing eternal love or proffering a terrible death threat while his voice negotiates an aria. Furthermore, the speeches and the attitude of certain characters, in a spirit of parody of their Franco–Spanish originals, distract laughably from the ominous presence of Fate. Seeing these streets full of blacks, that multitude of dark skin packed everywhere and the cruelty of segregation and the despair and loneliness of knowing that one does not form a part of the place where one was born or one lives, the *cronista* thinks: Wouldn't that anguish be a more tragic subject than this paraphase of *Carmen*?

19 June 1955

the theme
of racism
escaped
cain:
gone with the wind *is*
also
a monument to the
segregation of the races

Still on its Feat

Gone with the Wind is the offering, again, sixteen years later, of what has been considered a classic of the talkies. The superproduction par excellence, *Gone with the Wind* has alarming statistics that still hold some of the early records. It was the most costly movie of its time, with a budget of almost four million dollars (really spent on the production, not on publicity); $50,000 was paid for the rights to the 1,037-page novel, with two and a half million copies sold and translated into more than fifteen languages; 1,500 candidates aspired to the role of Scarlett O'Hara (among them the young, delectable Susan Hayward) but the English actress Vivien Leigh finally got the coveted part, really for economic relief; 137,000 metres of negative film were shot, of which only 48,000 were printed, to give the film a monstrous length of four hours, minus ten minutes of intermission: a duration that is still only surpassed by *Birth of a Nation*, *Intolerance* and *Greed*, towers not of Babel but of silent celluloid; the city of Atlanta in the period of the Civil War was totally reconstructed in the studio and in the Atlanta fire sequence seven Technicolor cameras worked at a time; in a single scene 1,500 extras were used and that scene only lasts 50 seconds; finally, the movie got nine Oscars the year of its release. Such a labour of looking back in awe was not only that of the late director Victor Fleming but of the co-operation of several masked men to whom Fleming refused to give credit and whose names are still kept silent.* The movie stands like those ancient monuments which if they don't move by their architectonic might, nevertheless impose by their size.

At almost twenty years after the première *GWTW* retains much of its initial pull, although the added stereophonic sound and the new print for a panoramic screen fit it like a denture does a smile: fake and false. There is no doubt that *Gone with the Wind* is a classic of the cinema and one of the few modern American movies which deserve not a review in a magazine but a monograph. Although that might do no more than enumerate the thousands of feet of electric wire used or count the hours spent in shooting. The years, nevertheless, have left their mark on the once glorious Technicolor, which if it was a marvel then, today seems faded and muddy. But the sets are still magnificent and munificent, testifying that William Cameron Menzies (noted as one of the hidden directors) besides being an interesting director was a very gifted set designer.

In spite of the features worn by time, the anthological scenes of the burning of Atlanta, with the gigantic crane that holds the camera so it fills the screen with the thousands of wounded bodies fallen over the railroad tracks; the pan over the monumental colonial staircase, from which Scarlett discovers Rhett Butler; another crane shot over that

* A quote has it that George Cukor was called in to direct at the instance of Clark Gable, who considered him the best director around. But it seems that Cukor was responsible for the displacement of the axis towards the women. He was replaced, at the instance of Clark Gable, after doing all the work of preparation and the first shooting. Victor Fleming directed the film for nine weeks. Sam Wood for ten weeks. The admirable sequences of the fire and the other action scenes belong to several second unit directors and stunt men. How Fleming managed to get all the credit is one of the mysteries of the cinema.

same staircase when the outbreak of hostilities is announced; the startling pistol shot that the deserter gets in his face on the staircase of the manor in ruins; the fall of the pregnant Scarlett from the carpeted stairs (from which we know that three characteristic motives of the movie, and of the Southern aristocracy are: the love for the monumental and for staircases and for monumental staircases) have not gone with the wind of taste. Of course the movie retains as well the cheap air of soap opera, the pervading melodrama and the recurrence of death as a dramatic deus ex machine-gun.

3 July 1955

a masterwork
is
a masterwork:
despite
the efforts made by
the critic
to show it is

The Last Mystic

A squalid hand, almost transparent, writes with clear and monkish script: 'This is the story of a life without mystery.' Then, with the same modesty, the hand minutely relates the daily incidents of that life, but it also declares that 'he has accepted in his own life the constant presence of the divine.'

The hand belongs to a young rural priest of aspect at once calm and febrile, as if beneath the opaque cassock flowed a live trickle of spiritual quicksilver. The priest writes: he recounts his physical tribulations, the little that happens in the small parish, the veiled antagonism of the villagers. The priest describes: he reveals his anguish, the struggle to nourish his soul with spiritual bread, his forceful faith and the doubt which he has always suffered about the efficacy of prayers. The pages are filled with the priestly script, while the rural priest confesses his minute via dolorosa: the little girls who follow the cult make mockery of him with a wicked trickery which seems quite adult, he visits the fiefdom of the local Count and in turn is visited by the governess of the Count's daughter and by the grown-up daughter as well: he notes the dull rancour which one woman holds for the other and half understands the drama which has the castle as its stage: the Count's wife has found refuge in a small shrine since the death of her little son, the Count has adulterous relations with the governess, the daughter is aware of her father's philanderings: the mother also knows it but prefers to act as if she did not. The priest tries hard to make the Countess recover her faith, which she had buried with her son, also a waste. But the priest has scarcely said that he himself is ill.

The exhausting bicycle visits to the castle provoke spiritual seizures in the Countess and corporal crises in the priest. At times he suffers fainting spells and a cold sweat dampens his broad brow. Now he only nourishes himself with bread soaked in wine and his stomach pains sharpen. He takes advantage of a visit to a neighbouring priest, older than he, almost his counsellor, to visit the town doctor. The hardened physician – agnostic, hunter, cynic – recognizes in the little priest a stoic in a cassock. Their mutual sympathy and future friendship is broken brusquely – as brusque, as the coarse language of the doctor – by the latter's suicide while hunting.

In the midst of a Cartesian landscape of tired trees which rest their bare branches against the grey sky, the rural priest returns from the burial of the doctor to confront the last crisis of the Countess. After discussing transcendence, humility and love for God and being converted, she dies. The priest attends to the wake of his convert and, on the way back, suffers a fainting spell. When he recovers consciousness in the dark, he finds himself on the ground, his profile lighted by the lantern of one of the girls of the parish, the same one who had earlier made fun of him. The girl helps him to get on his feet and arranges for no one to see the priest in such a lamentable state. That would confirm the rumours of the villagers, who transform his infirmity into customary inebriation, in their gossip. On arriving home, the priest discovers that the viscous liquid which dampens his clothes is blood: he has vomited blood. He decides to depart for the nearby city to see a specialist.

In the city he learns that what he had believed to be tuberculosis is a stomach cancer, and now mortally wounded he seeks refuge in the house of a schoolmate from seminary, who has renounced his habit. Although he has decided not to die in the house of an apostate (the former seminarian has abandoned the spiritual life to 'attend to the development of his intellect'), death surprises him. Nevertheless in his diary there is a last entry, the script monstrously illegible, also deformed by cancer: the wayward sheep agrees to return to the flock.

That is the plot of the French film *Le Journal d'un Curé de Campagne* (*The Diary of a Country Priest*), directed by Robert Bresson.

Bresson is one of the revelations of the German occupation in France.

He has directed no more than three movies (*Les Anges du Péché*, *Les Dames du Bois de Boulogne*, and *Le Journal d'un Curé de Campagne*) and his name already appears in all the histories of the cinema. An uncredited dialogue writer and obscure screenwriter since 1934, he was revealed to the world of the cinema almost ten years later with *Les Anges du Péché*, the drama of a nun trying to convert a delinquent girl. When his virtues were counted, among them stood out narrative originality. There was also an introspective aura that was totally new. Another exceptional movie came to define such virtues two years later: *Les Dames du Bois de Boulogne*. Finally, his latest film, *Le Journal d'un Curé de Campagne*, placed Bresson, definitively, among the great creators of the world cinema. At present, Robert Bresson is working on a project quite unlike the preoccupations of his past films. It deals with Lancelot and the Knights of the Round Table.

Le Journal d'un Curé de Campagne is not a film, it is a cilice. Few movies are as anguished, as crushing, as desolating as this one. Its intention is to make the spectator suffer the spiritual tortures of the village priest, without recourse to description, never speaking of the sufferings in the soul of the priest, but placing the spectator between cassock and soul, next to the heart shrunken by the fear of God, agitated by the love of God, over the sick stomach, under the head hallucinating in faith, between red nausea and mystical ecstasy.

The movie is based on the novel of the same name by Georges Bernanos and is a successful attempt to reproduce the written word with faithful equivalents. Bresson deliberately rejected the passages in the novel which most lent themselves to be shot into a movie and stayed with the most aridly literary parts. With them he constructed a Christian temple, putting into images the words of the novelist, although with full intent he intercalated repeated graphic allusions to the act of writing a diary so that the movie would have the reiteration, the recurrence of the written reference that in the novel affected the form of a diary opened before the reader. In the final scene, when it would have been much easier to shoot the tomb of the poor priest and inscribe upon it a moving epitaph, he preferred to place on the screen a drawn cross, lighted very artificially and to keep it more than a prudent time, leaving in the spectator a profound mystical print. Some have accused it of being anti-cinema, but in the art of Bresson there is such a profound knowledge of film that he has permitted himself to reject the tired customary rhetoric to create a new time and space.

It is curious that the movie has seemed so lucid, so gripping for one who – like the *cronista* – has never felt an inclination towards theology and to whom the problems of spiritual transcendence are as alien and distant as outer space. Why? Because *Le Journal d'un Curé de Campagne* has ceased to speak a particular theological idiom but expresses itself in the universal idiom of art.

For the main roles, Bresson chose actors who had never appeared in films before. With the exception of Balpêtre, Nicole Ladmiral and Jean Riveyre, the other players in the movie are non-professional actors. From the malicious little girl to the Count's disquieting daughter, all are amateurs and appear in the movie because their faces or their particular mannerisms made them resemble the Bernanos characters. Among these one actor stands out from the rest of the cast, Claude Laydu, whom the public has had occasion to see in a similar part in a later movie, *La Guerra de Dios* (*God's War*). This hirsute, small, skinny actor, with a face that exudes a kind of angelic militance, is converted in *Le Journal* into what is the central character of the book: a mystic. That hypersensitized priest, sick, overwhelmed by humanity and anxiety to enclose Christian faith in a cornucopia, to go out in the world like a non-pagan Ceres, spreading hope, contrition and humility, is no more than that: the last of the mystics.

10 July 1955

Cain and Abel (and Freud and Kazan)

East of Eden is, possibly, one of the worst novels by John Steinbeck – and that's saying a lot. Long, fatiguing, loaded with rotund rhetoric and Biblical allusions interwoven with family confessions, in which the Hebrew tragedy of Cain and Abel (who in the book are called Cal and Aron) is related with an analytic sense borrowed from Freud. The book has been, nevertheless, a bestseller. Now the film version of the novel has been released and in three minutes short of two hours barely manages to transcribe a third part of the book. *East of Eden*, in spite of being loaded down with the sins of the novel, is an excellent movie. Filmed in Cinemascope and Warnercolor, the movie morosely, minutely permits its characters to reveal their tragedy. In a febrile, almost unreal, atmosphere, Cain learns that his mother Eve has busied herself with the selling of apples wholesale and he makes love to Abel's girlfriend. Then he kills his brother with a moral equivalent of the ass's jawbone. Later he almost kills Adam and behaves like a remake of the serpent. At the end nevertheless he is reconciled with the spoils of his father, thanks to the fact that his brother's bride-to-be is in possession of some psychological knowledge which, it is evident, escapes the Biblical context.

These dim spiritual aspects, however, are not an important part of the movie, but rather the formal brilliance with which Elia Kazan (*A Streetcar Named Desire*, *On the Waterfront*) has sewn his very new wineskin to hold an old rancid wine. Kazan, coming from the theatre, with his own ideas about acting, himself an actor, has developed a personal dramatic style which he has transmitted to his disciples (among them Marlon Brando and the players of *East of Eden*, Julie Harris and James Dean) and converted into his trademark. E.g.: an artificially awkward stance (on account of which Kazan has been called the master of the 'school of the acting hip'); interrupted, stammering monologues; cut-off dialogues where an actor steps on the words of the preceding player; mouthfuls mumbled from over the shoulder, while the actor walks away unconcerned with the camera; a clumsy limp hand which uselessly attempts to complete the lines which are less apt still; a painful sensation that the characters are trying to overcome a conflict in order to express themselves; and above all: violence, brutal frankness and striving for effect. All that Brando is. Also all that is good in *East of Eden*.

Here Kazan has kept the trappings of the Oedipal plot and the pseudo-Biblical epic characterization, without falling into the brilliant exhibition of tricks which he displayed in *On the Waterfront*. Besides he was able to conjure away the perils which this, his first encounter with colour (and, what is more important, with Cinemascope), presented him. With a concept similar but opposed to that of George Cukor in *A Star Is Born*, Kazan has not attempted to fill all the lateral space with figures or things, like the lazy decorator who hangs a picture on every empty wall and places a piece of furniture in every corner. But he tries, *hard*, to express by his objective use of the camera the subjective conflict of the characters. The meetings between Cain and Adam are viewed with the camera tilted, the scene of the break between father and son oscillates visually in a strange manner. When Cain confesses that he has killed Abel, the camera follows the swing in which he is rocking, with the rhythm of a pendulum and the chord of a pit. Or Cain sees Eve wrapped in a distant mist while he walks at her side and when he looks at Abel's girlfriend she also appears to him strangely diffused. Thus the triumphs that this film may win will not be shared by Kazan with the young Dean in his debut (too Brandoesque, too immature), nor with the excellent Julie Harris (though evidently badly cast physically), but with the capable Ted McCord (photographer of

Treasure of the Sierra Madre, *Belinda* and *The Glenn Miller Story*), who has accomplished one of the few really memorable jobs in colour that Cinemascope has produced in its short but confused reign.

18 September 1955

at times,
cain
was lucky
and ran into
four movies
which gave rise
to as many reviews
amusing
to write – or at least
to read

La Belle Epoque (*Pastel*)

French Can-Can is not a film. It is a splendid *panneau* of fin de siècle Paris, of an ideal time when the letters of the alphabet were not signs of destruction, but little pieces of some inoffensive jigsaw puzzle, where ladies who never worried about their figure but wore corsets under ostrich plumes, sipped absinthe with water and talked with fans not with fanatics to whisper a yes at once chaste and passionate or to proffer a sonorous threatening word: laudanum! The French of yesterday aided and abetted by the waltz taught the world their love for their time. The French of today assisted by the cinema infect the spectators with their longing for this belle époque. One of the first and most persistent viruses was *Le Silence est d'Or*, the memorable comedy by René Clair.

Now Jean Renoir (one of the true glories of the French cinema, son of Auguste, the impressionist painter, director of *The Marseillaise*, *La Grande Illusion*, *The River*) has just inoculated an entire finisecular bacterial flora into the public (ours) which longs less for the past than anything on earth. But, the reverse of Clair, Renoir does not look with nostalgia on the days of his childhood. For him the bowler hats, the boots and spats, the wide and long skirts, the little midinette, the can-can dancer, the chansonnier, the singers in vogue and even the princely suicides, are no more than plastic objects, figures from a mural of light, colours and rhythm, where his camera borrows from his August father the luminous, joyous brush. The whole film is no more than a pretext to flood the theatre with music and light. The plot, the anecdotes and the characters appear in the service of the can-can: *French Can-Can* is, in part, the apotheosis of the can-can. But it also offers the exquisite delight of animating the paintings of Renoir and Degas, and not only making it take on movement, but permitting us to hear the plastic music hidden in a spot of violent yellow or in the sonorous mauve shadow.

Welcome, *Welcome, Mr Marshall!*

Welcome, Mr Marshall! is the famed Spanish movie which has given all Europe so much to talk about. It is a satire about a quiet little town of La Mancha that is upset overnight by words from above that an American aid mission is to visit it. The whole town (from the shifty mayor, sly and deaf, to the impoverished farm labourers, including the kindly priest and the meddling neighbours) begins a campaign to make itself worthy of the promissory visitors. Not all the town, really. Because there is an old hidalgo – 'one of those with a skinny nag, etc., etc.' – who detests from the bottom of the dusty antique coffer which is his heart 'those Indians'. Perhaps because the Indians ate his conquistador ancestors, one by one, limb by limb. The best idea to dress up the town comes from a pair of cheap high-wire artists. But it is also the greatest humiliation for the stiff, proud Castilian character: the town is to disguise itself as Andalusian, wear their best waistcoats and boots and Cordoban hats and sing *coplas* and flirt among papier-mâché alleys under iron balconies of true makebelieve. The entire village is converted into an enormous set and all its inhabitants into the most gaudy *cantaores* in Old Castile.

But after all the rehearsals, petitions and hopes, the cortège of visitors passes rapid and deaf, in some fast cars of the latest model, totally closed, therefore blind. The town awakens from its sleep of reason to slam into the hard reality: Spain has continued in the same slumber for four hundred years. Nothing will change it, not even the generous and far-off Mr Marshall. The film is one of the best movies ever made in the history of the Spanish cinema. Although the vulgar situations, the gross jokes and the Italianate influence mar somewhat an effort memorable in every way.

An Island Called Buñuel

> *Robinson Crusoe*, like other films, was offered to me. I didn't like the book, but I liked the main character and I accepted him because there is in him a certain pureness of heart. More than anything, he is a man face to face with Nature . . . I tried to do some things that might have turned out interesting. I believe that something remains – some passages called surrealist and, apparently, incomprehensible, were cut . . . I made the film as I could. I wanted to portray loneliness above all, the anguish of a man deprived of human society. I also wanted to deal with the subject of love. I mean the absence of love or friendship, a man without association with man or woman. In the same way, I think that the relationship of Robinson and Friday remains clear in spite of the cuts: the relations between the 'superior' Anglo-Saxon and the 'inferior' Negro race. That is to say, at first Robinson, imbued with his own superiority, is distrustful, but at the end the two discover a great friendship.

Thus spoke Luis Buñuel to the French cinema magazine *Cahiers du Cinéma*. Earlier he had said that *The Adventures of Robinson Crusoe* was a movie where a man arrived at a desert isle and was confronted with the need of feeding himself. Both declarations could be the programme notes for this more than excellent adaptation of the perennial novel by Daniel Defoe. Buñuel has shadow-boxed with a classic and has won: he has himself raised his winning arm. The dual production (American and Mexican) seems to be the only movie agreeable to the senses made by the teratological director of *Un Chien Andalou*, without the poor dubbing and a certain formal coldness fogging the burnished mirror in which Buñuel has reflected the autobiography of Robinson Crusoe written by Daniel Defoe. But – what about Good Friday?

La Belle Epoque (Etching)

Casque d'or (*Golden Marie* – the title refers to the helmet of hair of the protagonist, a blonde prostitute) is for its maker, Jacques Becker (*Edouard et Caroline*, *Goupi Mains Rouges*), his most beloved film. By the *cronista* too, whose encounters with Becker extend from the days of the Ciné-Club of Havana, with the sordid *Goupi Mains Rouges* and the beautiful *Falbalas* (which makes poetry and almost magic of the world of fashion), to the deliciously domestic *Edouard et Caroline*, passing through the merry *Antoine et Antoinette*. This *Casque d'or* the *cronista* saw for the first time in New York, attracted by a promise of golden titles, especially by *The Golden Coach*, which actually turned out mediocre, pretentious and boring. *Casque* was, however, a revelation.

There are in the little story of the impossible love of a virile Parisian apache and a courtesan, romancing each other between the snares of a sordid story in the French fin de siècle underworld, enough poetry, a *tempo* as fitting as the times and a nostalgic and cadenced rhythm as in the initial waltz that the fated couple love to dance and dance to love in the hideout of the gang. Like Jean Renoir in *French Can-Can*, Becker has achieved a faithful portrait of fin de siècle Paris. But on this occasion it was not the amiable brush of the impressionists, but the steely burin of an engraver, describing the Parisian *bas-fonds* with the sound and the fury of a Goya of the *banlieux*. The tender romanticism of the love story does not prevent us from seeing – and showing – the fatal glitter, the deadly, imminent celerity of the guillotine slicing the head of the man, while the woman recalls for an instant that first waltz, now for the last time.

By a happy coincidence that repetition causes one to doubt it is a coincidence, Becker has been able to unite the photography, the sets and the costumes with the seductive acting of Serge Reggiani and Simone Signoret, the two lovers, in what is without doubt the best moment of their careers.

2 October 1955

on occasions,
the serious
movies
are more
hilarious
than the comedies:
the cinema,
which does not fear
ridicule,
convokes it.
cain
evokes it

The Empress's Cha-Cha-Cha

Theodora is the story – well, the fable with an immoral moral attached – of a kind of Sally Rand of the Eastern Empire: she with the fans. In the olden, bizarre Empire of Byzantium there are two parties – the *blues*, who are the hens at the top of the ladder, and the *greens*, those hens at the bottom – in complementary colours. To mix them, then, is in very bad taste. (As is well known the Byzantines had great visual flair.) The *greens*, using a terrifying weapon which the turbaned Turk never perused or used, force the emperor to cast a glance at theocratic Theodora and – hey presto! In less time than it takes to say Constantinople, the dancer is converted into a contrite, almost virginal empress: and with her green comes into vogue. But the *blues*, those singers who could hardly be said to lack ice water in their blue blood, conspire and start up with their Byzantine quarrels. A cruel civil war ensues which paints the neighbouring Black Sea the colour of mourning for ever. At the end, since there are always more good guys than bad, they win and Byzantium acquires a tacky but more peaceful blue-green hue.

23 October 1955

The Innocence of Alec Guinness

Father Brown is an English comedy that strings together several short stories by G. K. Chesterton, principally from *The Innocence of Father Brown*, in which this dour and daring little priest unravels the most murderous mysteries – and not exactly theological ones. Brown (Alec Guinness) encounters the criminal Flambeau (Peter Finch) and, the reverse of Don Quixote, he can say: 'We have run into the underworld.' Brown trades in his rosary for a magnifying glass and his chalice for a hot trail, and the confessions he hears don't cry out for pardon but for prison. At times the father has to step out of his priestly cassock. Other times he allies himself with foul flesh to arrive at the gist of the problem. Sometimes, he chases down innumerable false leads, but with the conviction that all roads lead to the solution or the absolution. A few times he loses his faith that the world can recover its state of original purity. That was before Eve committed the original punishable crime, aided and abetted by the first born criminal, the serpent.

In the movie, Father Brown is closer to a Don Camillo on the Thames than to the primitive conception of Chesterton: ingenuity plus intuition plus logic plus Good God equals smart sleuthing. Guinness plays the role with the scant sympathy Lutherans feel for Catholics, converting the candour of the father into the frank cunning of Brown. Be that as it may and thanks to a holy water-tight script – with a procession of gags and gangsters – and to agile and very good direction by Robert Hamer (*Kind Hearts and Coronets*), one must credit one more comedy on the balance sheet of the Anglican cinema. In making good comedies the English are always the first in church.

Snoring at the Bulls

The Magnificent Matador is a magnificent example of the *Art of Seeing a Bullfight Movie*: 'When the bull comes out of the pen, close your movie eyes. If you don't close them, Morpheus the matador will close them for you.'

20 November 1955

one of the
most
extravagant,
that is to say
dynamic
of the reviews by cain.
it is among my favourites,
because kiss me
is among my favourites

Spillana Macabra

The title alludes to a flower proliferating in American movies. The sower of the bad seed is named Michael (Mickey) Spillane and his best gardener answers to the name of Robert Aldrich. Together they have fertilized with sex, violence and sudden death one of the *fleurs maudites* of the Hollywood cinema of this year. Perhaps the most rare and perfect: the black dahlia of macabre poetry: *Kiss Me Deadly*. Run as an actioner at the beginning of October – with a gangster film which was the more fortunate for not being less mediocre – the *cronista* pursued it until he found it billed with *Hiroshima*, as if the latter were a presage of what would happen if the criminals in the former film had won. The treasure that the gangsters are looking for now is not gorgeous gold nor suave silver: it is an atom bomb. The scriptwriter A. I. Bezzerides (*Holiday for Sinners*, *Track of the Cat*) has transformed the common or garden gunmen of the novel into gangsters of the Atom

Age, and at the same time has tightened the action and eliminated whatever characters tended to unbalance it: that is, he has synthesized it.

On the other hand Aldrich, happy discovery of the Hecht–Lancaster company, director of grade B movies, creator of the audacious *Apache* and of the verist *Veracruz*, and the latest big talent in Hollywood, has disintegrated the script by Bezzerides and integrated it again. Using the camera as an aesthetic cyclotron, he has bombarded the absurd truculences of Spillane with inner action protons, megatons of baroque photography and electrons of movement and mobile actors: he has achieved – as the French magazine *Cahiers du Cinéma* so well said – the first film of the Age of the Atom.

The fauna of the underworld according to Spillane always had demanded a baroque treatment (*I, the Jury*) and theatrics (*The Long Wait*). Aldrich has magnified both demands and has succeeded in making a tortured movie, dramatically tangled, threatening and monstrous, like a gargoyle protruding in the night: the first great example of the modern movie Gothic since Orson Welles left Hollywood. Not since the days of *Lady from Shanghai* has there filed past the screen a collection of medieval creatures so tenebrous and well carved. *Kiss Me Deadly* is a triumph of direction: everything in it is controlled by the megalomaniacal will of Aldrich. The screenwriter moved the action from Victorian New York to motley Los Angeles and Aldrich readied himself to robe this city with a Gothic tunic, without resorting to abandoned amusement parks, cracked houses of mirrors, or monstrous mansions. Far from it. Down the steep streets and next to the secret sunny pools or in the palm-lined avenues strolls Mike Hammer avenging crime or refusing to take draft money. The camera shoots him from below, flattens him from above, frames him in the mean steps of Los Angeles, traps him in an angle of a staircase that is not a staircase any more but a seedy symbol, rests him again against the glass panes of a door and suddenly the door has a stained-glass panel with a heretic saint of the Middle Ages in the middle section. Later he is caged in a modern apartment and its pleasant fashionable features are converted into a Gothic play of sinister shadows.

For such a dubious deed Aldrich has counted on the complicity of Ernest Laszlo, one of the most capable painters in black and white left in Hollywood, and the incitement of the city of Los Angeles, cursed by the *film noir* and the novels of Raymond Chandler. Through it parade (and Laszlo portrays them in full face and profile) the most bestially born criminals of the movies: Albert Dekker, Jack Elam, Jack Lambert,

Paul Stewart, Percy Helton. With their mug shots (long and short) and dour dragnets for more exclusive prey, Aldrich has completed a case for the defence of Hollywood. Kiss it deadly for me.

All the Dead Japanese

Hiroshima has been accused of being *red* in the United States because it was produced under the auspices of the Union of Japanese Teachers, a union which was communist at the date of the film's shooting. But in the half-hour that is missing from the film (fifteen minutes cut by the Japanese censors: 'Too many horrors, hostility against North America, etc.'; another fifteen cut by the American censors for almost identical reasons) all the offences must have gone, because *Hiroshima* is largely directed against Japanese militarism and against the use of the bomb – although the movie says, of course, that the bomb was dropped by a B–29.

Despite the fact that the use of the atomic bomb against two Japanese cities seemed necessary in the midst of the sound and fury of the war, ten years have passed and the Japanese – and the Americans themselves – have taken it upon themselves to wash off the hideous stigma with which they were branded during the war. In two Hollywood movies, *Guadalcanal Diary* and *Back to Bataan*, the Japanese were tagged as monkeys whom one only had to shoot from the trees. It was said that the only good Japanese was a dead Japanese. Now they appear as what they always were: a human congregation, no better, but no worse either than any other people on earth. Hiroshima deserved the bomb no more than Thebes the plagues, Pompeii the eruption of Vesuvius or San Francisco the earthquake of 1906. But pink, yellow or black, *Hiroshima* is a powerful indictment of the last war and a timid demonstration of what any future war would be.

The film begins by showing the city bustling among ruins. A family takes up the daily task of sending the children to school; another concerns itself excessively with the nosebleed of one of its girls (later this scene will be multiplied, magnified in terrible contrast: thousands of children and women and men bleeding from the nose, bleeding from the eyes, bleeding from the mouth, bleeding from the pores: from all the orifices of the body), a soldier harangues the crowd, stops in the middle of a guttural speech and in an outburst typical for a Japanese actor, goes off like a robot and strikes a girl in the ranks whom he was addressing: she was not paying attention. There is an air raid alarm and life is interrupted, anguished. The alarm passes and life recovers its pace, perhaps with more vigour and perkiness. Suddenly, in the quiet morning, is heard the whine, like a bird that's a bad omen, of an airplane. 'Is it a B?' a teacher with her students, a group of workers, some girls, some soldiers on leave ask themselves. The response is an inferno. An explosion goes off and a city is transformed into a replica of a vision of the end of the world: Armageddon knocks on the doors: the bomb has burst: it's closer than you think and the film opens the sixth seal to say to the half-asleep spectator: 'Come and see.'

Will the seventh seal be opened?

Recreating skilfully by means of suggestions and metaphors the horror of the explosion (what really happened would be impossible to imitate and unendurable for the most hardened spectator), the director Sekigawa Hideo has achieved a Japanese replica of the circles described by Dante: except that Dante never was so Dantesque. Even in the midst of the chaos of the hecatomb, Sekigawa does not neglect the original plan and continues his actual attack against militarism and his paean to human solidarity. A general, *samurai* sword at his waist but burned to the eyelashes, inquires about his men insistently and the only answer is the vision of a wagon full of soldiers burning like a magnificent match. A scorched man tries to save his wife from the ruins of their house, but the fire holds him back. In the midst of the flames, the spectral screams of the woman beg him to find their son at school and take him to safety. The man initiates the search, among smoking derelicts, carbonized cadavers and ghoulish ghosts that flee to nowhere. A running soldier draws near, crazed, with a flag in his hand and cries out salutes to the Emperor. The man bows – order and hierarchy useless against chaos – and the soldier continues his demented race, howling salutes to the glory of the Son of the Rising Sun. Then a boy burned from head to foot confuses the man with his father, all in a torrential rain. Finally, the man finds his son, dead, among a group of wounded children. A three-year-old boy cries out that he is cold: the bomb has not only carried away his clothing, it has also torn off his skin. A bleeding teacher leads her students, holding hands, to the pier, where she and the girls disappear one by one under the water, in a scene of horrid beauty. A little girl cries out for her mother in the middle of the rain and the ruins and her cry is lost among the wails of pain of the wounded and the roar of destruction and death.

After this painful poem to Lot's wife, a cut takes the spectator seven years later to the city in the midst of reconstruction. And although the rest is anticlimax and pure visual palaver, it fulfils its purpose faultlessly, since without ceasing to oppose the war (another series of episodes show a boy earning his living selling skulls from the dead in the explosion; a young man abandons his position in a factory that begins to make grenades; some orphan boys ask an American soldier for chocolate; two lovers drift apart because she has been crippled by the bomb; a boy escaped from an orphanage returns to Hiroshima ready to work on its reconstruction) it is a magnificent magnificat to life: pestilences will come, plagues and wars, and death, and the sun will set and rise and man, like the earth, will abide.

27 November 1955

the decline
of zavattini (and
also
that of de sica)
was pointed out
ahead of his time
by cain

All is not Gold

L'Oro di Napoli (*The Gold of Naples*) is the latest movie of the didactic duo Vittorio de Sica–Cesarè Zavattini and, one must recognize right at the start, is not the best of either. It almost could be said that it is their worst (*Shoeshine*, *Bicycle Thieves*, *Miracle in Milan*, *Umberto D*) so far, if *Indiscretion of an American Wife* were not in between. But this time the director and the screenwriter are not left with the alibi of talking about the impositions of the studio system, filthy capitalists etc. In spite of the many limitations of working for an ambitious producer (Ponti–de Laurentiis), both selected the book to transfer to the screen and both chose the short stories that were to appear finally in the film. It is true that one of the producers (de Laurentiis) interposed his desire (orders) that his wife Silvana Mangano appear in it. It is true that the other producer (Ponti) declared that he would favour (orders) the inclusion of his protégée Sophia Loren in the cast. And it is known that both (Ponti and de Laurentiis) were in agreement (orders) on introducing into the film a positive, that is, optimistic, tale. All that (plus the massive mess of the Mangano–Loren rivalry, which has almost brought the producer to ruin and has separated the two partners for ever – or till the next movie) is not a great stumbling block. If one takes into account the obstacles which the Italian film-makers (who have begun to miss furiously the poorer but freer days of the early post-war period) encountered on their way: they are in heaven, that is, Naples.

The project of paying homage to Naples, his native city, is an old one with de Sica. Through his insistence he succeeded in convincing Zavattini, a more septentrional man, and both succeeded in convincing Giuseppe Marotta, a Neapolitan short-story writer who has handily managed to succeed the Sicilian Luigi Pirandello, to collaborate on the proposal. All were agreed that the Naples of the film would not be the Naples of pizza and *canzó*, of *Sole Mio* and *Torna a Sorrento*, which is the image of Naples that everyone has – including the Neapolitans. The film would approach reality by the shining path of the book and as Marotta says, 'the reality of the book is the reality of art', both notions which contradict somewhat the neorealist tenets (reality, nothing but reality) of which Zavattini has made himself God and de Sica the first prophet. Of the thirty-six stories which comprise *L'Oro di Napoli*, six were chosen, in a perfect division, and while Zavattini eliminated narration and Marotta added description, de Sica went off to his town to visit some relatives on the way to choose locations.

The film was finished but their difficulties had not yet ended. Its release passionately divided Italian critics. While some said that it was the best of the anthology movies, others declared that it was a step backwards taken by de Sica and Zavattini both. At the Cannes Festival the movie was received coldly but courteously. Meanwhile back in Naples, the preview created a small civil war. De Sica and Marotta – and also Zavattini – were accused of being liars, all three of being bad Italians and the first two (this, now, is graver) of being worse Neapolitans. The mayor of Naples said that de Sica had deceived him and that instead of the film to the greater glory of Naples which he had promised him he had come out with the same old song of *bons vivants*, pizza-sellers, adulterous women, corner studs, prostitutes and proud pimps, and he put de Sica next to writer Curzio Malaparte (spit and spat) as public enemy number one of Naples.

The *signore sindaco* ended by declaring: 'If de Sica comes around here again with a camera, I'll have him hung on a city lamppost.' What most pained the Neapolitans was that the film was called *L'Oro di Napoli* and showed under that title examples of the least golden paths of the city.

De Sica defended himself by saying in mellifluous tones: '*L'Oro di Napoli* is not wealth. No! *La pazienzia e la speranza sono il vero oro dei napoletani.*' Marotta said, in his defence: '*L'Oro di Napoli* is an inquiry, a documentary, if still a film on Naples, on a creative plane, an interpretation, a *ritráto di Napoli.*' Zavattini got out of the fix with almost Neapolitan grace: 'There are so many films to make in Naples,' he said, 'that their number is truly infinite, like all the living things of this world. And there are so many things to see in this city. (Sigh.)'

The polemic ended after the producers eliminated one of the stories, the one which least flattered the city – and lengthened the film to the detriment of its commercial *profitto.*

15 January 1956

remembering
summertime,
it is even
better
than
cain
said

A Single Summer of Serendipity

Summertime is the latest vehicle to carry Katherine Hepburn to the top: after seeing this movie one will not have to think much when the time comes to choose the best actress in Hollywood. She makes the film. Without her it would not exist. Without her and without Venice, of course. Katie is a mature tourist, thin of body and wide in soul, who arrives in Venice on vacation. The city gets under her skin, in one of the most beautiful colour pictures the cinema has produced, gotten by two forgotten ones: the Eastmancolor process and cinematographer Jack Hildyard.

The amber houses, the view of the isles, the bridges, the canals, the parsimonious gondolas and their erect, rhythmic *gondolièri*, the towers, the loveliness of the landscape, fill the woman with an exultant sentiment. At dusk, between the buzzing of the heat and the faraway and anonymous songs, the American secretary knows that a melancholy crisis will take the place of the early exaltation: it will keep her loneliness company. She decides to go off to town and this in Venice can only mean the Piazza San Marco. She sits down to watch the only inhabitants that Venice seems to have apart from the *gondolièri* passing by: the avid and tireless tourists (they look at everything without seeing anything) and the languid lovers, who do not see nor look at anything. By chance she meets a middle-aged Italian. He is good-looking, of course, and he changes her loneliness into confusion. The next day, when the American tourist goes shopping for antiques, the Italian antique dealer turns out to be the gentleman from the Piazza San Marco. The antique vase goes for a song into the hands of the Hepburn secretary, who at times seems too detached to be timid and at times too timid to be detached. But who offers a true portrait of certain Americans, whom their innate naïveté converts into grown-up children.

But the antique dealer (Rossano Brazzi, better employed here than in *Three Coins in the Fountain*, but still just a gigolo who courts American secretaries) has a rival. Katherine has met, in the street (in Venice all friendships are made in the street: it is painful to stay at home with such a beautiful city out there), another Italian, not as gallant or as well dressed, but quite as knowledgeable about women and what is more: about American women tourists. This specialist is an urchin of the canals (Gaetano Audiero), who like all Italian children of the post-war period is too adult for his own good. He is always selling something: fake Parker pens, ubiquitous company, unintelligible conversation, a not very literal translation of the wishes of his employer and an occasional porno postcard. As American secretaries might think Katie too pat, the Italians may find this boy too trite. But at the end both national groups will be reconciled in an eternal gesture of friendship: Gaetano ends up giving one of his fake pens to the *Americana*, as a memento and a farewell.

The story continues: Rossano and Hepburn fall madly in love: it is summer and it is Venice. But when she abandons her languid, lost ways and decides to quit being a secretary and become a woman on the make for a husband, she learns that Rossano has been already ensnared and Katherine feels what frustration and repressed desire are like. But (the Venetians, as everyone knows, are kin to Casanova) he gets her to accept his entreaties, love being another sporting occupation, like coming, say, to Venice to play tennis. Katie (who declares that being shy she has always wasted her visits 'because I didn't know when to go') this time manages to extricate herself from the arms of brazen Brazzi before it is too late too soon. She leaves on the same train on which she came, but things are not the same. On the platform Rossano waves in the air a gardenia that he could not bring Kate in time: a good Italian, he always has arrived too late.

Before the simple, sad and serene ending, which relates this film once more to *Indiscretion of an American Wife* – to the discredit of Zavattini and de Sica, who did not know how to handle a similar story with the gusto, the *savoir-faire* and the melancholy elegance with which David Lean has done it – other similar scenes take place in the piazza. The

English director (the same of *Brief Encounter*, etc.) has turned inside out, like a glove, the theatrical work of Arthur Laurents, *The Time of the Cuckoo*, without even the title making the cuckoo crumble. And as happens with certain fabrics, the reverse is more suggestive than the verse. With a very English vision of things and a particular concept of editing, Lean has fashioned, in this fashion, one of his best movies. The sense of humour that was missing from *Brief Encounter*, the flexibility that *The Passionate Friends* lacked (the former quality, thanks more than anything to the pair of silly sallying tourists created kindly by MacDonald Parke and Jean Rose; the second owed, like almost all the film, to Hepburn) are here. There is also its soft, sempiternal sentimentality, its too-late longing: a brave take of the sorrowful face of Hepburn, a faraway tune, a gardenia floating down the canal.

But the true *tour de force* of the film is that of Katherine Hepburn. With few words and less gestures she has shown the loneliness, the nostalgia, the love and the ultimate despair of the heroine, in a memorable and masterly performance, which surely will make her a competitor once again for an Oscar nomination and award. This gawky and resolute American lady, from the early 1930s to *The African Queen*, has made the nominators forget her scorn for conventions, her ferocious individualism and her temperament, and has been nominated almost every year. That is a perennial homage to her tremendous talent and her genuine beauty – like a gardenia floating down a canal in fact.

26 February 1956

The Knife of Damocles

The Big Knife is based on a play by the playwright Clifford Odets (writer and director of *None but the Lonely Heart*) and is a magnified image of a season in the hell of Hollywood. To reach better the solitary heart of the public, Odets has converted his hero into a film star popular with the teenagers, who, nevertheless, manages to be a domestic idealist. A half-way idealist, in fact, because his compromise between art and money has made him renounce his ideals in exchange for his deals. This alienates the star from his wife and creates in him a neurotic conflict when he finds himself forced to sign a new contract for seven years, now, this very minute. Here is where the drama and the film begin: the script has done nothing more than to stick to the play, scene by scene, speech for speech and exit after exit. To make it, the director Robert Aldrich (*Kiss Me Deadly*) not only required from adapter James Poe an adhesive script, but rehearsed his actors for more than two weeks on the same set (like Hitchcock in *Rope*) with camera and lights and sound.

Aldrich has succeeded in proposing a new riddle to the old Sphinx. Her answer has not been 'Guess . . .', but: 'Win and I'll devour you.' There are in the movie – as in the play – too many personal portraits and the caricature does not manage to make one forget the original: the gossip columnist, nosy and powerful, implacable in her job; the slavish and devoted press agent; the dramatic and iron-willed producer capable of anything because 'my film must go on', the attorney, peacemaker and skilled in shady sham; the righthand man, who is half way between a gofer and an executioner; the disillusioned and dipsomaniacal starlet; the adult adulteresses. They are all so much closer to their live replicas than a Madame Tussaud dummy.

Someone has pointed out that the play revolves around a moot point: the laws in California do not allow any actor to be signed for a period of more than five years. But it is not this that Aldrich pursues, but the argument that the cinema in general – and Hollywood in particular – deform the nature of those who serve them, as if a machine twisted its key screws. To make his point he has utilized a florid, flamboyant style, in which the camera of his favourite cinematographer (Ernest Laszlo) is like the shafts which pierce a soft St Sebastian. Aldrich has declared that his hero is a modern Faust and his statement proves that his style leans towards the Gothic style of *film noir* and it will not be long in creating a school for scoundrels. In *The Big Knife* he has subordinated style to the *tour de force* of using no more set than a drawing room furnished with the couch Freud first called hysteria. *The Big Knife* is the film that analyses the psyche of Hollywood. It is a pity that Odets – and Aldrich has not evaded it – dressed up his argument with the clothing of melodrama. No one conceives of a film producer muttering murder to achieve his goals. Why should he? He does not need it. He has another more persuasive force at hand. And less unlawful: money.

11 March 1956

this
review
almost
cost cain
his job:
bacardi and co.
felt themselves
alluded to –

their logo:
a bat

The Ghost Weekend

I'll Cry Tomorrow is the adaptation – apparently not very literal – of the bestselling biography of an alcoholic not anonymous who was a famous actress and singer, Lillian Roth. Miss Roth (the delectable Susan Hayward) reached stardom when she was barely an adolescent, ably guided by her mother (Jo Van Fleet) as one guides a soft robot. Her cybernetic career plus the death of her boyfriend – to whom she was married in real life – her alienation from her mother and the almost schizophrenic duality of being a highly unhappy person by day and having to fake a contagious happiness every night, led the singer to a dead end like a prison: only with bars on both sides.

Here there are two important facts doubly obscured by some dark hand hidden behind the camera: the illness which killed the boyfriend and the certain cause that leads the girlfriend to her marriage with a bottle of whisky instead. Alcoholism (like suicide) is a form of self-destruction at which one does not arrive suddenly, but by means of a long, tortuous process. With this first part of the movie – confusing, shapeless and not at all explicit – the spectator sits back to watch how a human being descends step by step the stairway to hell, until arriving at that base basement perennially wrapped in shadows, humid with alcohol, infrahuman, which the Americans have baptized with the apt and terrible name of skid row: the waiting room of delirium tremens. Roth lived in that exurb of derelicts sunk in the sombre sea of alcohol which each great American city has, the local Bowery.

Living among the real visions of men fallen to the threshold of hell, off-white zombies, and the unreal reality of roaches and bats – a famous distillery has seen to it that we all, sober and under the influence, equally see the chiropter – of delirium, she sank to prostitution to procure herself a drink. Rescued by her mother and back in New York, she escapes and attempts to commit suicide, but cannot. Incapable of destroying the container, she will eliminate the content: she finds refuge in a house that has some discreet initials on the door, AA. In the moral fortitude of Alcoholics Anonymous she succeeds in rehabilitating herself, after a Dantesque ordeal called cold turkey, the drying out. At the end, Lillian Roth narrates her voyage to and from hell on the television channels: a *tour* of DT on TV.

The movie is directed by Daniel Mann (*Come Back, Little Sheba*) with pitiless rhetoric, as if he were scrutinizing a bar with a microscope. Although at times he may pause to watch some pretty labels: the songs sung with her usual sexual power by the unchaste Susan Hayward. It is she – more than the certainly professional Eddie Albert and Van Fleet – whom one has to thank for this so effective effort to put on each bottle of rum a skull and crossbones warning.

15 April 1956

a reviewer used to say
that the worst
movies
made
the best
reviews: sometimes,
like now,
this is not
completely true

Mr Tati's Holiday

A mime passes through the wall of languages.

JEAN COCTEAU

The film
Monsieur Hulot's Holiday is an unusual film. Since the Marx Brothers released their swan song, an off-colour one, *A Night in Casablanca*, in 1946, the cinema has not seen such an accomplished example of creative sense in nonsense. Its author–director–actor, Jacques Tati, is a new genius of the comic cinema. *Cine*, who gave the word on Tati, said in an article on the cinema in New York, last October: 'The true gem of this Festival (the one given as a present to the author at the Museum of Modern Art) of International Film . . . was the French movie *Monsieur Hulot's Holiday* . . . [it] produces . . . the exact sensation of being in the presence of one of the masterworks of the comic cinema.' Today, seen again, *Monsieur Hulot* makes *Cine* feel happy to be able to claim that statement.

The author

Tati's real name is Jacques Taticheff and he is the son of Russian immigrants in France. In his youth he had been an all-round sportsman and a prominent soccer player. From that time many recall the imitations of the coach, the rival goalie and the funny fans that Tati used to do to the joy of his teammates. A little later Tati left behind half his name and all of soccer to dedicate himself to the stage. His new name was as well known in vaudeville as those of Fernandel or Bourvil. Unlike these men, Tati specialized in mimicry. Among his numbers was one in great favour with the public: the implacable imitation of a centaur – all horse.

From his performances at the Ritz he went on to make little shorts with René Clement, among them *Watch Your Left* and *The Postmen's School.* In those first efforts one could scarcely foresee the peculiarity of the art of Tati.

'But in spite of that,' says Tati, 'I was already the biggest comedian in France.'

No one, not even Fernandel, who is a tall man, could dispute his primacy. Jacques Tati is 6 feet 4.

Tati before Hulot

The first feature film by Tati was *Jour de Fête.* Based on the central idea of *The Postmen's School,* Tati told the tale of a tall postman during a national holiday. The hilarious adventures of a postman and his reluctant bicycle were used as pretext for an acute and thorough observation of the customs of the town dwellers. Some reviewers pointed out that his rigour in depicting town and customs diluted at times the humour of the incidents. But the film surprised the critics, who were aware of finding themselves, despite the few false notes, 'faced with a new sound'.

One of them said: 'The ballet-like style makes one think of René Clair, notably in the relations between François and the others, in the sequence of the greased pole, of the bumblebee, of the children's prank; in the very rhythm of the entrance of François on the scene, his crossings, his disappearances, his returns, the near suppression of speech, the great importance conceded to music . . .'

Tati carried these characteristics to their ultimate possibilities in *Monsieur Hulot's Holiday.*

Tati after Hulot

Hulot was a critical success in France, but was not as well received by the public as *Jour de Fête*. In the United States, on the other hand, the critics did not receive *Monsieur Hulot's Holiday* with the fervour of their French colleagues but as far as the box office was concerned it was a real hit: the foreign movie that made the most money that year. The favour of the public led a television network to import the comedy of Tati, which has no need of translators, and present it in a show called *The Great Spectacle*.

Just as the takings from *Jour de Fête* permitted Tati to make *Hulot*, the money from *Monsieur Hulot's Holiday* will permit Tati to make his next movie, now in the shooting stages. It is called *Mon Oncle* and according to Tati himself it will be 'a human comedy about the effects of a rustic sort of fellow visiting his brother's family'.

Tati in Hulot

Tati has said: 'The possibility of opening on to life and of revealing all its riches puts into play, to my way of thinking, the multiple uses of the cinema.' *Monsieur Hulot's Holiday* is the praxis of this theory.

More than anything, *Hulot* is pure cinema. The use which it makes of the image as a universal vehicle of laughter is uncanny. (In Cuba the film has been shown with a translation, in distracting subtitles, of the few dialogues of the characters who surround Hulot, who is always silent. In the original version these are no more than strictly background noises or the accidents of sound, a fact which the English version wisely understood, keeping the dialogues in French.) The rhythm of the action – so cinematic –, the use of sound and of music, elevate *Hulot* into a classic. Automatically this movie makes more than one pompous show into too literary or too stagey acts. The play is the sting.

When all is said and done, *Monsieur Hulot's Holiday* is a sociological treatise written by a humorist who has been able to understand that laughter is an exclusively human rictus.

Tati as a sociologist

Like Chaplin – to whom Tati owes more than many believe, but not precisely for the reasons that many think –, Jacques Tati is an observer of man, a sniper at life, who fires precise portraits of the individual strolling through his private life. In *Monsieur Hulot's Holiday* Tati observes, Tati relates. The beach is a sea-escape outside of time: a flight towards a brief space confined between two periods of life, before and after meaning nothing. During that time – as in any other feast, the carnival, for example – man tries to be someone else and only succeeds in being himself with emphasis. On this particular beach there is a good collection of samples for the sociologist with an amiable eye and a satirical mouth: the residents, the grumbling and grumpy waiter, always looking over the locals' shoulder. He is engaged in constant battle with owner and client alike. The owner is typically French and stingy but with a feeling that the customer might be right. He has the proportion or proper portion of everything from cheese to chateaubriand.

The invaders: the Englishwoman – a spinster perhaps – enthusiastic and sporting, the out-of-fashion vamp, still disguised as a silent screen siren, the couple made of ambulatory wife and solicitous but bored husband, the salesman whom the telephone pursues to the other side of time, the beach bum always exercising imaginary summer muscles, the spinster aunt so proper and the nubile niece, both beautiful, the retired commandant who deploys his vacations militarily, the innumerable, indefatigable, indecent kids, and, of course, Hulot. Hulot and his noisy, naughty petrolette: a midget car for a giant.

Hulot

Hulot is a born sportsman. His step leans lightly on the tip of his foot with a confident, even an optimistic trot and a brusque, almost rash slip of the ankle to strike a balance – thus he progresses. His personality is that of the timid man who attains to temerity. His acts tend to simplify human relations, and by that very means they complicate them awfully. Hulot is not a troublemaker like any one of the Marx Brothers, nor a maladjusted derelict like Chaplin, nor a daredevil *malgré lui* like Harold Lloyd: rather he is close to a cross between the inertia of Buster Keaton with the naïveté of Harry Langdon. He is a large Laurel to his own thin Hardy. He is foolhardy. Above all he is *sui generis* or perhaps *non pareil*. But I wouldn't send him to decorate a cake.

The influences

Much has been said about the rivers of influences that flow together in the humorous veins of Tati. Chaplin, Keaton, René Clair, and others besides have been spoken of, but if there is any influence on Hulot it is voluntary. Tati has chosen his teachers and they are Mack Sennett and the school of slapstick. In *Monsieur Hulot's Holiday* there are very few blows and no pies at all but one feels the sweep of the air displaced by the slaps and the aroma of French pastries. There is nevertheless an unnoticed influence: that of Steinberg and the cartoonists of *The New Yorker*. From them he has taken the calligraphy of his humour.

Tati is also a neoclassicist. His humour derives from the fathers of comedy; his carefree elegance, from the granddaddy of all comedians, Max Linder. Like Linder, he has arrived to fill the need in France for a Gallic comic. It has been worth the forty years' wait.

Gags and gaffes

Jacques Tati revindicates the gag in *Monsieur Hulot's Holiday*. That is the old comic recourse of the visual humour, the situation joke, the jest set. Here are some samples: a bus takes off crammed with passengers, the driver is about to turn the steering wheel and discovers with amazement that between the spokes is emerging the head of a small boy who hasn't found a seat; the salesman-at-large is swimming at the beach when he receives from the hotel the pressing news of his nth phone call and takes off instantly – to swim out to sea. Always working against himself, Tati enters a cemetery by mistake when he was actually heading for a picnic. A funeral is taking place and his car breaks down, Tati looks for the spare in despair and throws out of the boot a tyre smeared with oil. Fallen leaves stick to the tyre and when Tati picks it up, an errand-boy confuses it with a wreath. Tati dances in disguise with the woman he loves, but she is wearing an outfit so low-cut in the back, that the bashful pretender cannot put a hand behind her. He places instead a single finger on her neck strap. Tati's trademark is the gaffe and the guffaw.

From beginning to end, a masterwork

As before, better than before, one must say that from the slow foxtrot that opens the movie, until the bitter ending with the beach made into a desert (no sand castles but just sand) and Hulot deserted by the summer visitors who go back to the real time, *Monsieur Hulot's Holiday* is a masterwork of the comic cinema – and of the other kind as well.

29 April 1956

Divertimento Macabro

Ensayo de un crimen (*The Criminal Life of Archibaldo de la Cruz*) is the latest movie by Luis Buñuel to be shown here, although after this *Ensayo* Buñuel made two more movies, including one in France. In his Mexican phase Buñuel's *Ensayo* is the third *divertimento* which this director, who is a sublimated sadist, permits himself: the others are *Mexican Bus Ride* and *The Illusion Travels by Streetcar*. Of the trio, *The Criminal Life of Archibaldo de la Cruz* is without any doubt the best. It involves a grand joke on Freud's determinism – the infantile trauma which Viennese analysis has substituted for that old guilt complex of original sin.

Archibaldo (at that time Archibaldito – a spoiled brat) receives from his mother a music box and with it a story from his governess: the little box has magic powers and merely by starting it up anyone whom the owner of the music wishes can be killed. The days of the Mexican Revolution speed by and the boy, of course, hates his governess. In the street, shots are heard. The boy starts up the little box, a stray bullet enters through the window and kills the governess. The boy sees her on the floor, with a thin thread of blood oozing from her white neck and her soft thighs showing from under her skirt: he will grow up haunted by that image. One day (now Don Archibaldo) he runs into the little music box in an antique shop and automatically plans a series of murders against every beautiful woman who might get close to him. The murders are so perfect that no one ever suspects Archibaldo de la Cruz.

But one crucial detail is missing: Archibaldo (now Archibaldy) has never killed anyone: chance has committed his murders for him. With this thin anecdote borrowed from the play of the same name by playwright Rodolfo Usigli, *Ensayo de un crimen* gives Buñuel the chance to exercise those gifts sequestered from his days as a surrealist. Namely, masochistic surprise and the sadism of objects. Among many examples is the exquisite cremation of a mannequin which is an exact replica of actress Miroslava – who killed herself in real life only a few days after completion.

27 May 1956

1914: *Fin de Siècle*

Les Grandes Manoeuvres (*Summer Manoeuvres*) is the latest film by René Clair. *Manoeuvres* had its world première in Moscow. The next day the Soviet director Mikhail Romm published his review in the *Litteraturnaya Gazeta*. After showering Clair with proud praises he lamented the lightness of the subject, which was not roses. Clair retorted: 'Romm's article is generous and flattering. But we must understand each other with respect to the phrase *lightness of the subject*. For us, love is a very serious matter.' In that answer is the whole credo of René Clair and all of *Les Grandes Manoeuvres*.

The plot tells how an officer in the French army who has too much success with women makes a bet to seduce (he said conquer) any lady from the small town where his regiment is quartered; how he picks the woman out of a hat, courts her routinely, she rejects him and he falls in love out of pure spite, and how finally both find themselves involved in a passion which the bet almost makes into a tragedy. Very similar in its development to the solemn *Madame de* . . . and with a sense of rhythm that likens it to the masterpiece of Clair, *The Italian Straw Hat*, *Les Grandes Manoeuvres* is a vaudeville made seriously: as if they were performing a tragedy of impossible love in a burlesque house.

In its first part the film is lightly comic, slight, sarcastic, only to become a romantic drama later. In both parts, nevertheless, Clair manages to create an incisive portrait of those years immediately before the First World War, which have the same significance for him as the last years of the nineteenth century had for Jean Renoir: a belle époque. He shows that the fin de siècle took place in 1914. Slow at times, at others too schematic, René Clair has worked things out with the able help of Gérard Philippe and Michelle Morgan. More able and skilled than ever, Clair makes this his best film since *Le Silence est d'Or* (1946).

The film ends with the officer parading out on the way to the grand manoeuvre past the house of his lover, whom he has asked to open the French windows if she has decided to pardon his felony. The windows are closed. But can the reader imagine what a tragedy *Les Grandes Manoeuvres* would have been if it had had the ending that the producers did not allow Clair: the woman committing suicide from shame, from love and from grief. It is the maid who has opened the windows to let the gas out and the officer now passes by below, smiling, believing that the open windows say 'all is forgiven'.

cain,
cain,
why
do you afterglow?

Time v. Cinema

To speak – perhaps to write? – of *Casablanca* is like looking at an old photograph: there you are but somehow *that* is not you: in between there is memory, the time that went by and the renewed photofinish, its battle with time won – and lost. Time does not pass: you pass through time and as in a narrow hedge of brambles you leave your clothes and skin on the thorns too. In short, time is like the bank in roulette: it always wins. (It wins even when it loses.) And it has won against *Casablanca*. Is that obsolete, distant, almost ridiculous and surely false movie the one which you so lovingly remembered? Is the petulant part of Claude Rains the perfect portrayal of a gentleman in cynic's clothing that we treasured in our memory? And Humphrey Bogart, isn't he a caricature of what he pretends to be, with his immobile lip, his laconic utterances and his absurd existentialist gallantry? And isn't Paul Henreid ridiculous as the hero of the Resistance that they oblige him to be? Instead of conspiring underground and keeping himself hidden he devotes himself to conducting the *Marseillaise* in front of all the Germans, like a laughable apprentice of Leopold Stokowski? And what about Conrad Veidt, with his real German accent made into a phony one by the falseness of his role as a stupid Prussian gentleman? To the *cronista*'s questions, the reader can in turn ask: 'So, then, why the four points (the sign of excellence), what are they for?' They are for memory.

2 June 1956

An Avatar of Don Juan

Monsieur Ripois (*Knave of Hearts*) is a French–English co-production, which has as featuring players the most popular actor in France (Gérard Philippe) and two notable British actresses, one of them almost from the past (Valerie Hobson) and the other of the future (Joan Greenwood). The film itself is directed by a man who can be considered the most capable, technically speaking, of French directors: René Clément (*La Bataille du Rail*, *Jeux Interdits*). Based on the novel by the Frenchman Louis Hemon, entitled *Monsieur Ripois et Némesis*, it recounts the amorous adventures of a Parisian Don Juan in London: the exploits of a sniper of love.

Like a bourgeois Casanova, Ripois works in an office. Like every bureaucrat, he has no more than one job to do: putting on stamps. The office is run by a woman (Margaret Johnson) and she, very English, finds that Ripois does not put the English stamps on the English documents with the proper English correctness: rather with a negligent Latin abulia. Ripois, in turn, discovers that under the stiff 100 per cent wool double-breasted suit of the Englishwoman there are some soft, saucy legs and what is better: not English-made ones at all. Ripois, *très français*, decides to make love French-style to *l'anglaise*. Surreptitiously, he sends her a present: a flask of perfume – French perfume. Insidiously he takes the same tram as she does, although, English-like, he doesn't pay her fare. Skilfully he manages to move his wares into her house, she who is single of course. Perversely, once the conquest is completed in full, he withdraws to advance in a mask towards another stronghold to defeat. He takes leave of the Englishwoman French style, as the English say.

The next victim of this Landru of love, of this Jack a ripper of hearts, is a homely young girl (Greenwood), whom he knows – a knowledge that always abolishes chance – as always, from the tram. Ripois has been dismissed from his job and to console himself puts all his energy into taking this new love fort in a day: a Sunday on which, like all English Sundays, it rains. He succeeds. He leaves the girl with her heart (as they say) broken and all her illusions lost, and the spectator with the certainty that he has just seen one of the most beautiful film fragments of the European cinema. Next, please.

She is a prostitute (Germaine Montero), a French one, which in London is a trademark as guaranteed as English wool in Paris. Ripois finds himself hungry, dead tired, disheartened and for the first time – and this is a very well-observed trait of any Don Juan – he seeks out the paid company of a whore, the same kind he always rejected before. When she finds out that he doesn't have a cent, she doesn't throw him out to the street, but bathes him, feeds him, and puts him to bed. Ripois becomes what the French call (euphemistically) a *maquereau*. This short stint in the job of a paid consort will leave a trademark on Ripois – who, of course, is on the run again, this time, with enough money to pass himself off as a professor of French language. But he turns out as listless as a teacher as he has been vehement as a lover, though he has occasion to form an acquaintance with a rich lady (Hobson), who carries him to the altar in a Rolls-Royce. Ripois has told these adventures with very Gallic flavour and frankness to his wife's friend (Natasha Parry), with whom he pretends to be so in love that he attempts a fake suicide – so badly staged that it ends in a real near-fatal accident.

At the end of the film, Ripois is an invalid for life, taken around in a wheelchair by his wife and looking melancholically at every woman who passes by him, battered but not better, still a Don Juan, for whom his present hell was his past paradise: women.

cain
gores
garbo

Camille Coughs

Camille is the same banal tearjerker over which our mothers cried. But what saved it then from the soaked hanky, from the sigh and from the ridiculous, is what saves it from being forgotten twenty years later: the delicate, synthetic, able direction of George Cukor (*It Should Happen to You*, *A Star Is Born*) and the presence – sublime for many, impossible for others: an alien for the *cronista* – of Greta Garbo. The part of Marguérite Gautier is perfect for an actress with the face of Eleanora Duse and the tear glands of Libertad Lamarque. For Garbo – too tall and too strong, with a voice more imperious than clamorous, at times elegant like a Swedish peasant girl dressed by Dior, at others like a man in drag – it was not the appropriate role. If *Anna Christie* and *Queen Christina* permitted the talkies not to wound her mortally as they did her camera companion John Gilbert, movies like *Anna Karenina* and *Camille* put her in a situation so false and compromising that her retirement from movies was not long in coming. Garbo is, without any doubt, one of the most radiant, memorable personalities of the cinema: not only for her durable beauty, but also for that ambiguous quality of goddess and peasant, of feminine idiosyncrasy with trimmings of virago, which transformed her into a being as fascinating for the public as for Greta Gustafsson herself. Nowadays she sees herself on the screen and when referring to herself says: 'Look at her', 'See what she's doing.' In this film, Greta Garbo acted with supreme distaste before Robert Taylor. Nevertheless he has shown with time that he was just as perfect as a glamour-boy can be in such a role.

But in spite of her spite, *la* Garbo succeeded towards the end of the film – in the first part she merely limited herself to gurgling with her guttural laugh and to showing her long neck of a robust swan who dies hard. But beyond the cough and the falsely muted voice there is the mask of tragedy: the death of Marguérite is an affecting arpeggio and her fall has the silky mourning of a shroud.

17 June 1956

The Jester is Wild

The Court Jester is the latest movie that contains Danny Kaye. That's like saying: who's doing the containing? Kaye is now producer of his own laughs and has never been jokier. Together with his wife Sylvia Fine and the duo Frank–Panama he has made, in a single shot, two of his funniest movies. The first was *Knock on Wood*, the second is this act of royal buffoonery. The public will thank him for it, but Fox, Universal, Tony Curtis, Robert Taylor, James Mason and the Kids will be eternally ungrateful to him. With one gust of a guffaw Kaye has toppled all the cardboard castles, the tin soldiers, the sardonic villains, the Corsican brothers and even the dusty damsels, as if they were cards. To prove it, it would be only necessary for MGM and Paramount to put aside their differences and show *Quentin Durward* and *The Court Jester* back to back. One would be able to see that the latter is a perfect parody of the former. Or vice versa.

17 June 1956

cain
discovered
for the cuban public
that continent
in a map of the absurd:
ioneschia

Macabracadabra

MR SMITH: (*Still reading his paper*) Tsk, it says here that Bobby Watson died.

MRS SMITH: My God, the poor man! When did he die?

MR SMITH: Why do you pretend to be astonished? You know very well that he's been dead these past two years. Surely you remember that we attended his funeral a year and a half ago.

MRS SMITH: Oh yes, of course I do remember. I remembered it right away, but I don't understand why you yourself were so surprised to see it in the paper.

MR SMITH: It wasn't in the paper. It's been three years since his death was announced. I remembered it through an association of ideas.

MRS SMITH: What a pity! He was so well preserved.

from *The Bald Soprano*, by Eugène Ionesco

The Trouble with Harry is an unusual movie. It is also the best of the movies (in colour) of Alfred Hitchcock and along with *The Thirty-Nine Steps* and *Strangers on a Train* it forms the trinity of the macabre Hitchcockian humour: there is no abashed cadaver worse than a reluctant dead body.

Still amazed to see that Hollywood has permitted his insane Mona Lisa laugh to slip through the cracks – *The Sun Shines Bright*, *Beat the Devil*, and *The Night of the Hunter* also got past them – of a monolithic industry, the spectator attends a (triple) burial. And the (corresponding) exhumations. The victim is Harry, who has died (violently) in the nearby forest. He is discovered by a boy. The body has the serenity of a dummy and (almost) its very waxy aspect. The corpse is rediscovered by an (old) hunter, who has fired (three) shots, unerring all (for his age): one struck (an empty) can of beer, another a sign prohibiting hunting and fishing, and – the last? It killed Harry, believes (the senile) Nimrod. The cadaver (continues) catatonic. The old man decides to hide it, (but) the lonely place in the forest is transformed into a high street in the forest. There come the boy's mother, a (nearsighted) doctor, reader of (bucolic) poetry, a tramp, and a lady of (a certain) age. The first says: '(No!) It can't be! Harry! Harry – thank Providence – (the last of) Harry.' The second trips over the corpse, falls and (after getting up) ambles off. The third robs him of his lustrous moccasins and enjoys illustrious happiness. The last sees the old man bustling along (with the deceased) and says, 'Perhaps you would care to come over for (some) blueberry muffins and coffee later on?' And the venerable gentleman answers: 'I'll be there – with a clean shirt and a hungry face,' and renews his (mortuary) bustle and hustle.

Before proceeding with the (funereal) toil and making sure the cadaver remains unmoved, it is nigh well to cast a glance at the neighbours of the (vicinal) village.

(First) come first served. The boy Arnie is the son of (his) mom and has a (curious) sense of time: for him *today* is tomorrow, *yesterday* is today and *tomorrow* (is) yesterday. His mother answers a question about the (dead) man like this: 'Oh, him – (that's) my husband.' 'Yeah – when I saw him, he was dead.' 'Yeah – well, he looked exactly the same when he was alive, (except) he was vertical,' responds the (young) widow. The old man is a (retired) seaman: the lady a spinster. Besides them there is an old (grocer) lady who sells pictures by an (abstract) painter; her son (a cop) and the other (characters) already familiar: tramps, doctors, etc. The painter gets involved with the cop and the corpse because he (the dead body) ruined for him his still life in the countryside. From then on (nevertheless) he has to help out with the buryings and unburyings. These are as many as there are (guilty) consciences.

At the end, it is proved that the old man did (not) kill the man with a shot; (nor) the widow with a bottle, (nor) the spinster with a blow from her Cuban heel: Harry died a natural death. His (contrite) heart stopped and he lay down to die. Thus the group decides, having disinterred Harry, bathed him, washed (and pressed) his clothes, to put him in the way of the (morning) walk of the boy. 'Wouldn't it be nice if Arnie found him all over again? – then he'd run home and tell me, and then I'd phone Calvin Wiggs?' proposes the (young) widow. 'Yes – and Arnie could explain – quite clearly to Calvin – ' responds the painter. ' – That he found Harry – *tomorrow* – ' continues the (young) widow. 'You mean – *today* – ' (answers the painter.) 'But to Arnie – *tomorrow* is *yesterday*,' concludes the (good) mother.

With such elements – plus much influence by the Romanian–French playwright Eugène Ionesco on the part of scriptwriter John Michael Hayes (*Rear Window*), as we have (tried) to demonstrate (yesterday) – some literary, others technical – the film has remarkable photography (in Vistavision) by Bob Burks – and the (iron) cast – above all Edmund Gwenn as the old man, Mildred Natwick as the spinster and (especially) Shirley MacLaine, pretty and thin and lunatic in her debut (as the widow). The Old Man (Hitchcock) has composed an exotic farce, unique and (genially) boring, which is (like) a parody of his (most) well-made movies. For the first time Hitch does (not) let us see his (rolypoly) figure on the screen. Can such a thing be because the film is made up entirely of those (brief) encounters of insanity and the absurd interpolated into the mystery of a corpse with no body?

24 June 1956

first
bout
cain–bergman:
cain k.o.
in the first round

Woman and the Summer

Secrets of Women (*Kvinnors väntan*) is a Swedish film. Suffice it to say that there will be in it a free discussion of sex and a beautiful idolatry of summer: all the Swedish cinema is merely a Scandinavian version of

Le Déjeuner sur l'herbe, the once scandalous painting by Edouard Manet in which a woman – completely naked – enjoys, carefree, a picnic on the grass in the company of some fully attired gentlemen.

Secrets reveals how four women spend a Swedish summer evening. Three of them tell tales of intimacies while the fourth waits for a turn that never comes. The first story (played with a hieratic Nordic sensuality by Anita Björk) is an adulterous affair. Told with the lazy slowness of a daydream, the plot involves a clinging woman, an unemployed neighbour and a hysterical, suicidal husband. In the midst of it, Anita and her part-time lover hide out in a luminous little lodge by the sea. There, in some vague Freudian waves, they make love.

The next tale is a jolly adventure in which a married couple, now older, is reconciled from its squabbles in a stuck elevator. As in the physiological philosophy of D. H. Lawrence, an unusual way of making love becomes a bond of love. The last tale narrates with a complicated web of flashbacks within flashbacks the little obstetric odyssey of a pregnant woman (Maj-Britt Nilsson, she with a Latin beauty and of no relation to the May Britt of the Italian cinema). The whole story has a hallucinatory nightmare atmosphere. Daily objects gain such an absurd meaning that a simple sink is transformed into a fountain whose very drop-drop drips depraved. This rarefied aura achieves its absolute strangeness when the well-known can-can by Offenbach sounds like pure Schoenberg, in a Parisian party full of the phonetic fury that floods the useless conversation of a drunken idiot.

29 July 1956

Gone Fishing

The Naked Sea is a pretty title which serves to throw off the track anyone who thought that it was an amiable marine kaleidoscope. No, here is one of the most severe and truthful documentaries which have been made about fishing. Not long ago a short called *Tuna Clipper* was shown in Havana, which the *cronista* described – or should have described? – as a rough song to the work of men at sea. This long documentary is all that. But something else again. What in *Clipper* was pointed out by a sentence is here a paragraph, what before was a topic is now a treatise, and so *The Naked Sea* is a grand elegy on fishing, not as pure pleasure but as a hard way of life. From among the boiling blood of the hooked tunas, from their frenetic flapping of death, from their constant biting the bait, from being caught, from one and another and another and another flying over the deck, from the snap of the line on hitting the water, from the cry of the fisherman when pulling on the rod with all his might, from the sprinkling of the anchovies changed into trowelfuls of live bait, from the stern effort of the man who leads, from the swift cutting by the prow full speed ahead, from the eternal sea, always in surf and indifferent, immense, rises a song to man, to work, to life: a poem.

2 September 1956

Among the Zombies

Invasion of the Body Snatchers is a rara avis: a science fiction movie with a message for grown-ups. In Santa Mira there are people who don't recognize their own relatives: a niece says that her uncle is not her uncle: he has his distinctive look, his voice, his mannerisms, but something substantial has left him: his soul; and a little boy cries because his mother is not his mother: that is the plain truth for the child. The cases spread and the young town doctor (Kevin McCarthy, whom the *cronista* remembers well as the wayward son in *Death of a Salesman*) becomes intrigued but can come up with nothing better than sending his patients to the town's psychiatrist. But that night a writer friend sends for him and shows him something that he has on his pool table, which is not exactly a new cue stick: a dead body. But the dead body is not dead: it has features as if half made, as if it only lacked a scar here, a mole there, a wrinkle over there.

The hours pass and the corpse is transformed into the spitting image of the writer, who flees horrified to look for his friend. Next the doctor's girlfriend (Dana Wynter: beautiful, recently arrived from England, talented) also has her unfinished replica in the basement. The facsimiles, the doctor discovers, grow out of some gigantic pods, which open during the night and rob the nearest sleeper of his body cell by cell, in a brilliant adaptation of the Hindu theory of the karma. The doctor also discovers that the psychiatrist friend, the corner cop, the service station boy – the whole town, in a word, has changed into a pod. This seems laughable on paper, but on the screen it has the hideous clarity of a nightmare without waking dreamt by Kafka. The endless and silent pursuit of the hero puts *Invasion of the Body Snatchers* among the most harrowing movies which Hollywood has produced in a decade.

9 September 1956

on one occasion
cain said to me
that if
citizen kane *had not existed,*
mr arkadin *would be*
among the ten best
movies that he ever saw

The Acme of the Melodrama

Mr Arkadin (Confidential Report) is the masterpiece among all those movies about international intrigues. It is also the jewel in the *film noir*'s crown for the beheaded. Like everything that surrounds Orson Welles (whom the *cronista* considers the genuine genius of the American talkies) the movie surfaced suddenly in the murky waters of darkest mystery with the gurgling sounds of a drowning radio.

Mr Arkadin was born when Harry Lime was given mouth to ear resuscitation. Harry Lime was that turpid, turbid character who died in a sewer at the end of *The Third Man*. Slimy Lime reappeared on French radio. He was still a smuggler and an outlaw and a scoundrel and a magnetic man. One day there was a rival: a powerful magnate, with much more money and infinitely less scruples. His name was Arkadin. On the radio the tycoon's part was played by Frederic O'Brady, he who plays the drug addict in this *Arkadin*. It goes without saying that Welles kept for himself the Lime's share.

Arkadin started in 1954 and was finished at the end of 1955. Orson seemed to grant much importance to his new venture, considering that *Macbeth* was shot in twenty-one days. (Is the radio play the thing?) Actually this had to do with Welles, out of Hollywood, realizing at last one of his long-held dreams: a Gothic melodrama. He had tried it for the first time in *Journey into Fear*, a film which RKO took out of his hands to turn over to director Norman Foster. Foster is a mediocre but honourable man: he has informed the movie world that 'if the studio had let Orson do everything he planned in the script, *Journey into Fear* would be considered today an exceptional movie.' Welles had tried it again in *The Stranger* and especially in *Lady from Shanghai*, but always with a top dog from the studios looking over his shoulder, watching his work and going 'Teach, teach' through clenched teeth every time Welles let go the reins to unbridle his imagination. Finally, in *The Third Man* he was able to impose his efforts for a powerful realization and for a moving melodramatic sense of space and for a tortuous conception of the frame: *The Third Man* was a perfect specimen of the baroque cinema. But it was necessary to go further: to arrive at the virtual vertigo of the Gothic, at its demonism, at its obscure runic calligraphy by means of a curse and a quotation: *A powerful king said to a celebrated poet – What can I give you as a prize? and the astute poet responded: – Anything, Sire, but your secret.*

Orson Welles has said: 'Realism doesn't interest me. Newsreels are the worst enemy of the cinema as art. That is the material without interest. There is nothing easier than making a passerby on the street act in a movie. The most complicated thing is to make him come out of anonymity. It is with actors that one must make art . . . Realism and reality are quite different things . . . Realism does not exist.' He has therefore invented a reality, his reality. In *Arkadin* time and space do not coexist, space penetrates time and destroys it, and simultaneously creates a time of its own. When Welles sets up the camera next to the floor, behind a chair, on a gargoyle, in an aberrant close-up, he does not do it for pure visual trickery, for mere pyrotechnics: he is attempting to destroy space and create it anew.

Arkadin, like all the movies of Welles, interests one for the 'how it happens', not only for the 'what happens', so that the spectator goes from surprise to surprise. Not from the surprises that can jump out of a silk hat, but from the surprises of things that cease to be as they are without ceasing to be: a long familiar street which one morning is seen to be different, like a view through a mirror: all is there and all is lacking: there is nothing, nothing is lacking. *Arkadin* is an immense jack-in-the-box, a box of images, of cinema seen through the mirror of Welles.

From the beginning, with the presentation of the players in the style of the old serials (already with this introduction Welles has wanted to leave his film marked with the melodramatic stamp of the serials: *Mr Arkadin* is no more than that: the serial as seen by an intellectual) and the malingering, lingering music of Paul Misraki, the spectator finds his consciousness trapped by the screenplay and the film is like a gigantic cobweb, in which Welles, a bearded spider, weaves his plot of intrigues, deceits and lies. From then on the unexpected images succeed one another, as in a kaleidoscope of signs and like a brainteaser of clues. The truth rises up in fragments, is shattered, is recomposed and finally is discovered whole: the terrible secret of Arkadin is that he has no secrets. To sum up, finally, Welles guides the camera through a maze of images, through the genesis of every possible image: the labyrinth is the only guide to the mystery of art.

Welles, always a consummate director of actors and always accused of seeing himself in the mirror of the camera (like a Narcissus who looks at himself on the screen, reflected ad infinitum), has eliminated his person as a central persona: the centre of the film is its secret.

23 September 1956

it is evident
(here and everywhere)
that
h.
knows more
about movies than g.
ever knew

1 Hitch − 1 Arm = 2 × X

The Man Who Knew Too Much is a new version of an old movie by Alfred Hitchcock, with the same title, made in 1934. Why has Hitch hiked back to retrace his steps? 'Because no one has seen my other film in the United States,' he has explained, as if the US were the whole wide world. But there is another reason: old Hitch owned the copyright of the old title and that, plus his monumental emoluments as director–producer, make his honoraria ascend to a percentage that will guarantee him a cool million in less than a year. With which Hitch shows that he is the man who knows too much.

Now, ladies and gentlemen, the latest deadly somersault of the Great Al, without a net!, ladies and gentlemen, without a net but with a gross! (Drum roll and finally the crash of a clash of cymbals.) *A clash of cymbals changes for ever the destiny of a good American family.* The holy family travels through Morocco, but they spend all their time comparing it with Las Vegas. On the bus they meet a nice Frenchman (Daniel Gelin, showing that he is badly miscast), an ordinary gentle guy; but the mother (Doris Day, now a Hitchcock blonde) insists so much on how mysterious he is, that she ends up making him into a mystery. They also meet a very simple and friendly couple. Just as in the movies of Hitchcock one does not know who anyone is (unless one sees a fat man with jolly jowls: that one is Hitch), Gelin ends up dead in a most mysterious way and the recently met couple turn out to be a pair of dangerous criminals. Before dying, Gelin has confided a terrible secret to James Stewart: 'A man . . . a statesman . . . he is to be killed . . . assassinated . . . soon . . . very . . . soon . . . in London . . . Ambrose . . . Chapel . . .' That is what Stewart hears and of course he confuses the Ambrose Chapel with a harmless taxidermist, Ambrose Chappel, to achieve one of the funniest scenes in the film: a grotesque ballet danced by the employees at the taxidermy shop, animating the stuffed animals to escape the fury of the intruder. After a few attempts to rescue his son (who has been kidnapped to make the family keep quiet) comes a spectacular scene in the Albert Hall in which the 'Storm Cloud Cantata', by Arthur Benjamin, is used to commit and to avoid an assassination at the same time. Finally, a ridiculous scene in a well-known embassy, in which Doris Day belts out a song in an unpleasant caricature of herself.

The rest is pure corn. Never, since *To Catch a Thief*, did Hitchcock seem so trite, vacuous and repetitive. It made an American reviewer exclaim: 'It's time for Hitchcock to take a vacation.' The *cronista* thinks so too. Nevertheless scenes like the one which shows an accomplice of the assassins – a woman calmly following the concert with a score, in a macabre parody of the petulant music lover – who signals the moment for firing the shot so that it coincides with the cymbal clash, push the *cronista* to reconsider the initial agreement with his colleague: that sequence shows that a one-armed Hitchcock is still worth more than other directors with all the arms of Vishnu.

Pepino the Brief

Never Take No for an Answer is a Franciscan fable with an apodictic moral: if your pet gets sick, the best vet is the Pope.

Coke and the Cocotte

Razzia sur la Chnouff (Razzia) is a crime chronicle surrounded everywhere by crooks, except by one called 'ticket'. So this column will be written by the correspondent from *Cine* in Argot.

'Look, dis kid Jack Gabin is a swell guy: he won't do da shit nor da dust neither dat he's always flush with an' hot for bis'ness. And what happens, see, is dat dis guy he has a joint where he hawks soda an' stuff but he's got dis cashier doll, she only rings up da change an' besides she's a dash for cash an' da Jacko he's no dummy he pockets da change an' da slash: she's got it all an' to spare, an' bein' as she ain't greedy, well da Jack in the trade he tells her she should stay wid him an' she sticks an' don't ask for scratch, and da Jack who is hard and don't want to pass the payola, well he jus' gives her a place to flop, and clothes ta put on – but on her, less looks more. (The stuff ya learns with dis malarkey of French shows! And speakin' of French kissers – the other day I hear a bus jockey stops his rig an' sticks his nut outta da window an' sez to a two-wheeled job that was goin' along da street half-undressed: 'Babe, you're hotter'n a French movie!') As I was tellin' ya about dis cashier girl and da cashbox owner well dey got da romansin' goin' real hot, when da squad blows in an' commences to line 'em up, but bein' dat everyone t'rows out da rods an' da roscoes on da ground so da heat dey don't find nuthin' an' they cart da people off: den da girl dat sweeps da floor, she finds more iron dan in a foundry. Da Jack dey give him a rise in da precinct dat dey put on wid all da colors, but bein' as da movie's in black-n-white, well den youse can't see dem too good. So da Jack he gets a lil' kiss from da gal an' da slap on da backs of da other crooks who now were commencin' to be suspicious of him an' he starts to get to know all the little pushers an' pullers to see him up close an' when he's awready met up wid everyone an' knows how dere workin' it, how da dough's gettin' split an' da breaks too, well da real heat comes down from da real boss, da one who's half soul-saver. He turns chicken an' bein' dat he was awready way too yellow to turn yellow, since he tells dese guys dere tearin' up his house an' for them to split for a while an' hole up in da sticks and he'll come an' rescue him an' he sez to dis Jack and da Beano to tag along wid him. Da kid does it and dere leavin' when da dicks come to da country house an' surprise him an' in next to no time dey surprise da audience too, 'cause it turns out da bad guy was cool an' da Jack, he weren't yellow but blue jest like this: they reveal dat da Jack of all trades was a squeal, a stool or an informer.'

30 September 1956

i
also
liked this film

Don Giovanni without Mozart

Il seduttore is the third film on the Don Juan theme to be shown in Havana this year and is almost as perfect as its two predecessors. It is intriguing that the tale of the Burlador has been told by three different directors – two French and one Italian – more or less with a foreign tongue in cheek, but at the same time with a grimace half bitter, half acid, around the sutures of a laugh: that's satire. The fact is that since José Zorrilla wrote his immortal parody on the theme of the stony guest, Don Juan has been presented as a poor fellow hidden behind a stagy gesture and the petulance of his sex. The drama of Don Juan is that he knows women so well that he is really one of them: his sacred and profound knowledge is only an unacknowledged identity: a person only knows another by being that person: a dog's best friend is a dog. This wisdom of Don Juan is a fifth column in his character, a chink in his make-up: Don Juan is a man with cracks and through them comes the spectre of a woman. From the many interpretations of the myth one gathers that Don Juan, although he multiplies the activity which characterizes a man, is not a man. Nor is he a transvestite looking for his own skirts in those of others, as Doctor Marañón expounded. That is too easy. Don Juan is a sexual climber and the woman is a mountain: he conquers her because she is there.

The latest interpretations of Don Juan have masked him, transforming the lousy lover into a Mephistopheles in search of a Faust: first he was a lieutenant of dragoons stuck in the provinces: making love is part of military strategy; then, an expatriate who becomes a bum: love spells survival; now, he is a childish man, so immature that he is almost a girl: love is an eternal quest for one's mother, an Oedipus so complex that Jocasta is still growing up. In two words: delayed incest. Don Juan is a Casanova of scarce sense and much sex, who in the long run is conquered by his conquests. The film has hidden its Freudian couch with the Bergsonian blanket of laughter. Really it is a tragedy: Don Juan is a pitiable man, laughable, but depressing at the same time.

Alberto Sordi has grasped the meaning with an exactness more instinctive than intelligent. His Tenorio still blusters and shows himself to be an empty braggart, but he seems so down-to-earth now, that he has that unmistakable BO of the common man. Married to a woman who practically keeps him and spoils him like a mother, he lies around out of work, lies, plays tricks, seduces and believes he has conquered, when really he does not inspire passion but possession: he is the coin in the purse of a woman. At the end, after a climax more terrible than the supper scene with the Guest of Stone, Don Juan seems more tied to the umbilical cord of his wife's womb: playing on the beach, he is a boy again.

28 October 1956

this review
was as successful
as the film:
the success of
la strada
in cuba
was due to the success
of the review:
this is something that escapes me

The Road to Calvary

A novel is a mirror which walks along a high road.

STENDHAL

La Strada is what many attempt and few achieve: a poem. And a poem in the cinema is tantamount to a miracle. *La Strada* is a miracle.

La Strada is a road, the Italians say that it is a highway, but one knows that it is a road; a *camino real*, the same along which Tennessee Williams takes a walk with his ubiquitous Kilroy. But at times a road does not lead in any direction. Or to another road, and this one in turn leads to a dead end. Kilroy was born in a lavatory and got as far as the Parthenon: on both walls one reads *Kilroy was here*. *La Strada* is a road that was born at a stop on the way. Federico Fellini stopped one day on a highway and went into the nearby forest. He walked along and among the small, squalid pines he spotted a cart and next to it a couple of gypsies. Behind the pines he saw the folded tent of a circus. Beside the cart was an open hearth of three stones and from between the stones smoke was still wafting. Leaning towards the fire, the gypsies were eating soup from dented, dirty bowls. The woman was holding the dish with one hand and eating with the other; the man was eating with one hand and with the other kept his precarious balance as he squatted. Both were supping in silence and Fellini held his breath. They went on eating, always in silence. When they finished the woman stored both bowls in the creaky cart. They had not spoken a word. Thus was born *La Strada*.

La Strada is the story of the animal communion between a man and a woman. They are human beings but their understanding is primitive, pre-human. Between them runs a hidden current of silence, a neolithic empathy which unites them like a fossilized umbilical cord. The woman knows it: the man is oblivious. The man is named Zampanó but he could be called something else, even Adam. The woman is named Gelsomina and she is like her name: a jasmine. She is simple and yet marvellously complex like her flower's name, and although she cannot see the bee, she senses it. The man is torpid, turbid: through him one can see nothing: he is made of night. One day, many years later, after Gelsomina has died, she will come to him as the dawn and the man will leave his first human trace: a tear.

Zampanó is a circus strongman without a circus. He goes from town to town, from one piazza to another doing the only number that he knows: breaking the link of a chain by expanding his chest. Like every man of the circus, he needs a companion: like every male he needs a female. His last one has died and he returns to where he found her and repeats the transaction: for $15 he buys from the old village woman her remaining daughter, Gelsomina. This one is a simpleton, a friend of animals and of trees and of children, and like all abnormals she has a deep sensitivity. Zampanó takes her away. Soon her training begins: by force. Zampanó introduces her to his troglodyte's trailer – a wagon with two wheels pulled by a motorcycle. This is, at the same time, house, warehouse and transportation. He makes her his wife and, with blows from a staff, teaches her to play the trumpet and to announce his circus number with a theatrical pomposity: '*N'è arrivato Zampanó*.'

Zampanó is hard, Zampanó is cruel, Zampanó is Zampanó. But Gelsomina begins to love him. At first, she had abhorred him. She didn't hate him, because idiots don't hate: they simply abhor – they turn their noses up at what bothers them. Now, though, she loves him. But she suffers the loneliness of two in close company: Zampanó is indifferent to her existence. She matters less to him than one of the links in the chain which he breaks night after night at his circus. Zampanó, as always, is wrong: Gelsomina is his missing link, the one which by being broken will tighten the chain and will link him to mankind.

Gelsomina is a poet. They arrive at a town and she plants some tomatoes beside the road. They will go away tomorrow, but that creation by Gelsomina will remain: a tomato plant, a poem. Gelsomina listens to the humming of the telephone lines; she sings her favourite song to a sleeping Zampanó, late at night, on the imperfect trumpet; she talks to children; with calm clowning tries to entertain a boy sick with hydrocephalus; she gets confused in a procession and giddy in the church at the sight of the magnificent liturgy; she listens to the happy tunes of three musicians from nowhere who pass by on the way to nowhere. One night she drinks with Zampanó and feels pleased when he invites a laughing prostitute to their table. She is happy when someone beside her is happy, therefore she is always unhappy at Zampanó's side: Zampanó is not happy. But Zampanó goes off with the *putana* and leaves Gelsomina waiting, sitting on the sidewalk. An hour goes, two, and a pregnant mare passes by her side, slow, tired. The next day Gelsomina is still on the sidewalk and in the afternoon she finds Zampanó fallen in a ditch, drunk. They go.

In spite of Zampanó Gelsomina meets kind people on her way. One day she encounters a nun from a nearby convent, where both are spending the night. Zampanó takes advantage of the night to steal silver statues from the convent and Gelsomina reappears before the nuns weeping, truly pained. The little nun confesses to her: 'We never stay in one place long. So we don't attach ourselves too much to the things of the world.'

At a fair, Gelsomina finds a trapeze artist. He calls himself the 'Fool'. To Gelsomina he is an angel, not without something of a devil. By coincidence, Gelsomina and Zampanó and the 'Fool' work in the same circus. The 'Fool' pesters Zampanó constantly. He wilfully ruins his work. One night Zampanó is at his pretended arduous labour of breaking the chain. When he has almost made it, the 'Fool' breaks into the arena and says to him: 'Zampanó, you have a phone call.' It is the eternal struggle of the man who creeps against the man who flies, of the man attached to the ground against the man glued to the sky. Zampanó cannot take any more and chases the 'Fool' with a knife. He lands his tough hide in jail.

Meanwhile, the 'Fool' talks to Gelsomina and makes her understand that she is a human being. She complements the species as humanity completes her: the bells toll and ring for one and for all. Gelsomina thinks herself useless, unnecessary, but the 'Fool' teaches her that everything is useful: a tree, a cloud, a rock. It is here that the message of the film is clearest. Asked if the movie was Catholic, Fellini said the right thing: 'Only Franciscan.' The message of brotherhood, of facile pantheism – God is everywhere, even where He is not – moves Gelsomina and makes her comprehend that she is part of Zampanó as Zampanó is part of her. She waits for him at the gate of the jail and they leave.

On the road Zampanó runs into the 'Fool', who has suffered a mishap, and attacks him: he beats him, shatters his watch, splits his skull. As he goes away, he shouts to him: 'Let me catch you again, and you'll be sorry!' And the 'Fool', in his last clever comeback, mutters: 'How much more is there?' He looks with infinite sadness at his ruined watch and understands that his time is up. He dies. Zampanó disguises the casual crime, while Gelsomina howls with grief and with fright, like an animal before the evident mystery of death. They depart.

Gelsomina goes definitively mad and by doing so is transformed into Zampanó's conscience. She remembers the melody of the 'Fool' and calls for him, crying out loud. Zampanó can take no more and abandons her on a road, with her old trumpet by her side.

The years pass and one day Zampanó, older, more miserable, ridiculous in his weak act of strength, hears the song that Gelsomina used to sing and asks about her. 'She died, sir,' a little girl tells him. That night, Zampanó is thrown out like the trash from the bar he was prowling. Like all refuse, he ends up by the sea. There, on the beach, under the night sky, he listens to the deafening voice of silence and feels the heavy presence, like lead, of loneliness. He weeps: for the first time in his life he reveals that he is a human being.

As one can see, the film is also a message of redemption. It recalls, vaguely, the theme of *On the Waterfront:* the conversion of a brute to human faith; all men are brothers; 'Love thy neighbour as thyself.' It is here that the flaw appears in a beautiful, bitter and perfect film. Its characters are the poorest poor, almost pariahs. This subhuman being endures a hard, antipathetic life: to face it he has to make himself hard, antipathetic. His poverty, his misery – moral and physical – is not a human condition, it is a social imposition: the poor man is not poor because he wants to be, the brute is a brute in spite of himself. Can a simple conversion in almost divine terms redeem him from his anguished condition as a derelict? And those who have cast him there, those who have forced him into that life, will they be touched in their turn by grace and will they liberate him from his physical yoke, as he has been able to liberate himself from his spiritual chain? Those are questions which Fellini and the majority of Christians – 'My kingdom is not of this world' – not only do not answer, but which they barely put to themselves.

Nevertheless, *La Strada* is one of the most beautiful and perfect prayers of charity since the Sermon on the Mount was preached and another film as human, as rich in happiness, will be a long time coming, if it ever does.

Federico Fellini has constructed his movie like a cathedral: firm, monolithic, directed towards heaven. He took more than two years to prepare it and he matured his conception for ten years: he searched tirelessly for actors, locations and atmosphere; he sketched a story board and made good use of his skill as a cartoonist to draw a graphic draft of the physical characteristics of his puppets. From the music – composed by Nino Rota, in what is not only the marrow of the film, but one of the best movie scores from post-war Europe – to the costumes, including the acting, all has been supervised with the knowing eye of a master: the newest master of the Italian cinema.

Zampanó is played by Anthony Quinn with an understanding and a fervour belonging to a great actor. Fellini says, after pointing out Quinn's elegance, his Latin charm, and his exterior kindness, which made him too sympathetic to the public from the outset, spoiling the contrast with his final conversion: '. . . But if one had to choose from among professional actors I must recognize that Quinn, certainly, is the best suited to the not at all easy role.' The 'Fool' is played by Richard Basehart – another intelligent American actor – with a diabolical ambiguity, which makes him more like a latent homosexual than a wayward angel on an earthly mission. But the surprise within the surprise is Giuletta Masina, Fellini's wife, the fecund mother of *Europa 51*, who with a drum roll is transformed along with Maria Schell and Ingrid Bergman into the third of the trio of great European actresses of today. Her ridiculous get-up, her yellow wig and her set and game of popping eyes turn her into a cross between Charlie Chaplin and Harpo Marx: that is, into Harry Langdon. She has the sensitive delicateness of the first, the easygoing communicativeness and the sympathy for one's neighbour of the second, and the mimicry with a lack of IQ of the third. From all three she partakes of the genuine fibre of that histrionic nylon: the great film actor. It is she who holds the film in her feminine hands and confers on it the grace, the humanity and the infinite melancholy which is what woman has come to bring to the world.

La Strada has been considered an appendage of neorealism. It is no such thing. There is no relationship between this film and immediate reality – which is what neorealism aspires to, with the last term of its equation, the film-*enquete*, where the director is a kind of police–sociological–economic reporter and the actor a man who was lucky enough to pass by at the time of the poll – than that which, for example, *The Gold Rush* might have with the reality of the Klondike and the prospectors of the Yukon. If *La Strada* is like anything it is a Christian neosurrealism in which the old startling imagery, the aura of dream, the magic realism and the daily absurd are pressed into the service of love. But not of total love, full of the lust and the violence of carnal love as well as the spirituality of divine love, as Aragon, Eluard and Breton wanted. *La Strada* has almost neglected the former for the sake of the latter. So it is that Zampanó and Gelsomina seem like the two terms of an idea, as if Don Quixote were a single person composed of himself, Sancho Panza and Dulcinea.

11 November 1956

mm
doesn't mean
mm
but
marilyn monroe

The Wayward Waif

Bus Stop is a synthetic marvel. The play from which it comes has been destroyed by fire and still from its ashes the phoenix of a minor comedy has been reborn, as happy and hot as before. Better than before. In the play the bus stop was a terminal station but here it is an accident on the road. The real stop is for Marilyn Monroe, who if she is still one of the most turgid tarts of Hollywood, is also on the verge of joining the smartest set. Her version of the *chantoosi* of the West, who really deserves another name and whom a rude, naïve cowboy meets, is a prodigy of comic talent and of the discipline of a modest actress. These pages have already paid tribute to her beauty; now, they wish to offer it to what male readers know bulges least: her intelligence.

25 November 1956

Mexigenesis

Adán y Eva proves that the only punishment for original sin is the yawn.

2 December 1956

cain
ends his
second year
of life
in good form

The White Whale

Moby Dick is the third dip by the monstrous white whale of Herman Melville into the surfing waters of the cinema. The first time the book was brought to the screen was in 1926 with John Barrymore in the role of Captain Ahab: the film was called *The Sea Beast* and contained more molasses than Melville. The second time the whale had sound, but Ahab was the same Barrymore. This present version is at least more faithful to the book. Now John Huston has attempted a double task, superior to human fortitude: to do a screen version of that American classic and at the same time to experiment with colour. He has ended up both victor and vanquished.

He was a very uneven writer, but often he gave indications of a considerable force and originality.

NATHANIEL HAWTHORNE, in a preface to a book by Melville

The early years of Herman Melville never made anyone presume that he would become the most famous writer of the century in his country: he set a precedent in American literature, which Mark Twain, Sherwood Anderson, Ernest Hemingway, William Faulkner, Henry Miller would later repeat. Melville, who was born in 1819, escaped from his home very young and signed on with a cargo ship. He travelled through Europe and on the way back changed ships for a whaler. He deserted it too after a short time, in the latitude of the Marquesas Islands, under the protection of some cannibals. He was picked up by another boat which he proceeded to abandon. The ensuing years saw him a whaler, a stevedore, a mutineer, a prisoner, and finally a member of the United States Navy. In 1844 he returned to Boston for his discharge, collected his pay and in a symbolic gesture threw his uniform into the bay: he had broken with the sea forever. He was twenty-five years old.

He began to write and in a short time he published a novel that would make him famous, *Typee*, in which there appeared for the first time the subject which has been fodder, successively, for the famous writers Stevenson, Conrad, Somerset Maugham, for the fugitive painter Gauguin and the pomaded actor Jon Hall: the South Sea Islands. His friendship with Nathaniel Hawthorne, whose neighbour he was, was propitious for him: in a short time he astonished the latter with the thick draft of what seemed an interminable novel. It had as its title *The Whale*. Published in 1851 with the title of *Moby Dick*, the book had little success and Melville quit writing to become a customs inspector. At his death, thirty years later, he had not written anything more but three books of verse and a little novel which he left unpublished, *Billy Budd*. Ignored, *Moby Dick* let time go by over its cetacean's back, until in 1920 it was 'discovered' by an obscure critic. Since then it has been celebrated as 'the classic of American literature' and 'our only epic', by reviewers with 20/20 hindsight.

I have written a wicked book, but I feel as spotless as a lamb.

HERMAN MELVILLE, in a letter to Hawthorne

Melville once told Hawthorne that the true meaning of his book was contained in the oath, in the name of the Devil, which Captain Ahab drags out of his crew under the crossed harpoons, swaddling them in the maniacal pursuit of the albino whale: the book becomes, amid the threats of Ahab – 'the man who would be capable of buffeting the Sun if it insulted him' – an exact allegory of good and evil. But Melville took it upon himself to leave a new clue, capable of confusing all researchers even more. 'I fear,' he said once, 'that my book will be seen as a monstrous fable or still worse, and what is more detestable, as a sly and intolerable allegory.'

The theme of *Moby Dick* is the unhinged vengeance of a whaling man mutilated by a gigantic white whale, almost human in its astute cruelty. The book, like all parables since the Bible, can be enjoyed as an unusual adventure. The interminable annotations on whales which Melville makes, the chapters dedicated to the most minute recounting of the art of hunting them and its documentary nature, do nothing more than add a factual testimony and aid in understanding the environment which surrounds the paranoid Ahab. In its first hundred pages it has the tone of epic farce, which sets its tragicomic character. Like all the prose of Melville, *Moby Dick* is influenced by the Bible and by Shakespeare, and his characters seem like ancient prophets dedicated to a new trade. Nevertheless, through all the book there runs a mysterious and veiled allegorical note, which the author is not able to erase with his protests. The novel, in one way or another, has enormously influenced contemporary literature and this influence reaches from the nightmares of Tennessee Williams to *The Old Man and the Sea*.

But Jehovah had ordered a great fish to swallow Jonah.

BOOK OF JONAH

From its opening, with the stentorian sermon of Father Mapple, mounted on his pulpit which is the forecastle of a whaler, preaching about Jonah and his heretical attempt to escape the will of God by means of a boat and his punishment as food for whales, until the end in which the waiting whaler *Rachel*, like her namesake in the Bible, comes in search of the lost son of her captain and finds only Ishmael, the sole survivor of Ahab's ship, from the phrase the book opens with, that immortal line: 'Call me Ishmael,' so that the reader expects to meet an adventurer with no visible direction, like the Biblical character of the same name, until the last sentence – 'It was the devious-cruising *Rachel*, that in her retracing search after her missing children, only found another orphan' – there is a tacit attempt to liken the destiny of the *Pequod* to that of Jonah's boat, because the *Pequod* is also dedicated to a task foreign to the designs of God: pursuing with fury, with desire for vengeance, a creature of God, a whale.

What is a whale? The most formidable of all animals, an enormous mammal which lives in the sea: Ishmael has other information. 'Believe me, boy,' says Stubb, the second officer, to him: 'if God had wanted to be a fish he would have been a whale, believe me.' God is a whale, Ahab pursues the whale most worthy of being God, Moby Dick, the great white whale, with blue eyes, indestructible, avenger and judge at the same time. So? Ahab is a heretic, an enemy of God. Is it not madness which moves Ahab? Ahab has allied himself with the greatest enemy of divine reason, madness. And has he not invoked the powers of Satan in order to give chase to the whale?

Ahab will be destroyed. It was he who said: 'God is evil.'

Theologically the book is a blasphemy.

JOHN HUSTON

John Huston toyed with the idea of filming *Moby Dick* for years. He had thought that his father, Walter Huston, would be a perfect Ahab.

Then, after the death of his father, he shelved the project. Now, with the assistance of Ray Bradbury, more known for his fabling science fiction, he rewrote the script and chose an actor who would be a compromise between box office appeal and acting ability, Gregory Peck. Although Peck seems more like a Lincoln who has just lost the election than a crazed captain, his work is notable by any standard.

Huston, practically exiled from Hollywood, set himself up in Youghal, on the south coast of Ireland. This isolated Irish village would become the modern replica of New Bedford, the whaling port of the last century. There he constructed two and a half imitations of Moby (a facsimile served to impersonate an ordinary whale, conveniently painted grey), propelled electrically. It was a whale nearly 60 metres long, made of a special stuff and capable of swimming, submerging itself, biting a boat with its legendary crooked jaw and attacking a sailboat. But while it was tied to the pier a storm surprised it and it was lost. The shipwreck of the cardboard whale caused Huston more unpleasantness than the white whale did Ahab: the new replica cost six months of time and half-million dollars more. The half-whale was the tail, moved electrically and able to destroy a boat with one blow.

Moby Dick signals the return of Huston to Mother Warner, after having become a prodigal son, following the squabbles surrounding *Treasure of the Sierra Madre*. Motive? The fortune that Huston lost in the shooting and which he should get back at the box office. Now Huston has announced that his next film will be *Typee*. Author? Herman Melville. Producer? Warner Mothers.

In the filming of *Moby Dick*, Huston has attempted to innovate in colour photography. If the experiment had worked out, this film would mean the greatest contribution which has been made to the colour process since the engineer Kalmus perfected Technicolor. It has to do with the use of a double negative: one in more or less normal colours and another in black and white. Both negatives, being printed together, add a tone which enriches the texture and helps to create a turbid, torpid and oppressive atmosphere, eliminating the coloured pimpernels which gave Technicolor that look of a cosmetics advertisement. Unfortunately, the film only achieves a different palette at times and a sepia tint or a sombre black and white would have worked better.

Moby Dick is an excellent movie, but it is not a masterwork, like the book from which it comes. Huston has loaded the grim tints too much and has forgotten the whale of a humour of the original.

Furthermore, the film is reiterative and tiresome in its first part, only lightened by the formidable presence of Orson Welles, who has brought his Father Mapple to life with histrionics worthy of Lear. In the second part, nevertheless, the spirit of the book is present as the mephitic memory of the whale in the deranged mind of Ahab. After the scene in which Ahab watches the dead lookout fall and scrutinizes the waves that swallow him, the movie is flooded with the mystery of the book, as if they had opened a sluice in it and through it had seeped in the strange odour of mud which Moby Dick carries on his back. The dead calm cuts off the advance of the ship and the doubloon nailed by the captain on the mast becomes a double sun which insults him twice. The whale appears and disappears, surrounded by an ominous cloud of gulls, shrieking, menacing. Queequeg, the brotherly cannibal who is a master of the harpoon, sees death approaching and makes himself a quick coffin. Ahab does not sleep any more, flickering his eyelid sunken by a scar and eyeing the horizon, untiring. The whale appears and they give chase, but it is the whale who is the hunter: Ahab is imprisoned in the network of ropes and spent harpoons which cross the cetacean's back like the coordinates on the map of destiny and he sinks, sticking his incessant harpoon in the immaculate back of the whale. Moby Dick reappears and Ahab rises spectrally, still shaking his avenging arm like the clapper of a bell which tolls for the dearly departed: he is dead. The fury of the whale destroys everything and there only remains as a reminder the savage's coffin in the form of a boat and upon it, Ishmael, the young narrator.

This whole sequence has a visual grandeur that the book does not achieve despite the furiously baroque prose of Melville; and the whale takes on a hermetic aspect, beyond reason, swift and mortal like the Nautilus, the accursed submarine of Captain Nemo, another demented mariner, itself an infernal machine. Ray Bradbury has added to the moral fiction of Melville his wise, knowing dose of science fiction. But there remains as a precipitate of the omniscient divine presence the monstrous blue eye of the whale which stares at Ahab and recognizes him, moments before he destroys him. Is it an arbitrary occurrence that Bradbury and Huston have set the final encounter between Ahab and Moby Dick in its just terrain, in the joust of total destruction, in that site of which Melville never thought or knew, where the physical, moral and spiritual forces of the universe have met their Nemesis: on Bikini?

30 December 1956

cain
was as mistaken
about the

sense of visconti
as about the
sex of suso
in 'senso'

Denso

Senso (*The Wanton Countess*, Lux Film, Cofram) is a disappointing film. Received in Europe with much fanfare and considered by the main European critics as a masterpiece, the version shown now turns out to be little more than mediocre. If one considers that one of the most renowned critics in Italy, Guido Aristarco, goes as far as to consider it the 'best Italian movie of all time', the *cronista* can do no less than ask himself if the praise was addressed to the work or to its author.

The author, Luchino Visconti, is a curious personage of post-war Italy. Born in 1906, descendant of a renowned family of old nobility (said to be related to the last Dux), Visconti is a rare mixture of decadent nobleman and progressive citizen. A declared communist, he lives in a palatial mansion, framed by antiques and cubist paintings. Surrounded constantly by a cohort of adulators and admirers, he strolls along the bridges of Venice and the streets of Rome like a Mediterranean Oscar Wilde, not as brilliant but more restrained. With the looks of an actor from the times of the Caesars, Visconti has dedicated his money and his life to the theatre, first, and to the cinema, second. His theatrical preferences range from the *commedia dell'arte* and Goldoni to the modern American tragedy, and he has mounted extraordinary stagings of *La Locandiera*, *Tobacco Road* and *Death of a Salesman*. Attracted by the cinema, he renovated Italian films with *Ossessione*, a fraudulent version of *The Postman Always Rings Twice*, which in 1942 broke with the silly-sally comedies and the epics imposed by the Duce. Then he produced a neorealist film, *La Terra Trema*, dry and savage, like the Sicilian countryside in which it is set, but shot with a too evident artistic sense. *Bellissima* and *Senso* are his latest films. It has been said that he is the most famous director who has the least number of works. Of his titles none was known in Havana except a brief and mediocre tale from the film *Siamo Donne* (*We, Women*). A friend of the people, Visconti detests popularity and his scarce interviews with the press have been done with the top down, condescendingly, like the nobleman who lets himself be questioned by the commoner curious about lineage and family trees.

In 1953, Visconti and his collaborator, the screenwriter with the name of a tenor, Suso Cecchi d'Amico, offered to the producers of Lux Film a script called *The Wedding March*. The studios were not interested in the project, but they made them in turn the offer to produce a 'period movie'. Thus was born *Senso*, a version of a story by the fin de siècle author Camillo Boito, which in its early stages was going to be called *Summer Hurricane*, a name which Visconti rejected as vulgar. Visconti, as always, made the plot revolve around a certain scene. This was the one that had occurred to him one night at the opera. He was sitting in his familiar forward box at La Scala. From here he could contemplate the spectacle in all its splendour, but he could also see the exit and entrance of the singers and their transformation from beings of fiction into men of flesh and blood as soon as they passed beyond the visible scenery. It was then that Visconti glimpsed the dramatic possibilities there were in that simple game of fiction and reality, of its inconsistent living experience so similar to life. The idea is brilliant, but from the start it was marked with a stigma which would make of the film something as pompous and false as that which gave it its origin: the opera. Furthermore, the project would have an uneven trajectory before becoming reality on film.

Senso was intended as a grand film three hours long, in which the characters would slowly exude their personality without the need to explain themselves. The producers objected to the script and Visconti found himself forced to reduce the story to little more than an hour and a half, with the result that many characters – Marquis Ussoni, played by Massimo Girotti with an absolute insincerity; the lady companion of the countess, transformed into an enigmatic shadow by Rina Morelli (incidentally, both actors are discoveries and creations of Visconti) – had neither real logic nor dramatic truth and appeared and disappeared without any consequence, being incidental to plot development. The reduction of the script, moreover, is not only responsible for the fact that the character of Ussoni is little more than a reference in the dialogue and that his death catches the spectator unawares and he barely feels it – if he even manages to notice it in the hodgepodge of photos of the battle – but also guilty of the fact that the film starts out told in the first person by the central character, the Countess Serpieri, who ends up crazy. It is also responsible for an important incident (the handing over of the revolution's money on behalf of the countess to her lover, an enemy soldier, without the revolutionaries, inexplicably, charging her for her betrayal) being left unresolved, in the hope, seemingly, that it will be forgotten. Such faults are not the script's, they are the scriptwriter's: Visconti himself.

In the continuing story of the film's misfortunes, Visconti's favourite photographer, G. R. Aldo (the same as in *Umberto D*), was killed in a traffic accident, leaving the shooting unfinished. The English cinematographer Robert Krasker (*Romeo and Juliet*), who filled in for him, is the opposite in his cold perfection to the dynamic impressionism of Aldo. It is as if Titian had begun to paint a nude and Ingres had finished it. This is noticeable in the film: take a look at the scenes of the battle and those of the beautiful Villa Valmarana, and compare them with the final sequences and the interior scenes from the beginning: the first were photographed by Aldo, the latter by Krasker. Finally, Visconti was obliged to put up his own money to finish the unlucky venture.

Senso begins with a performance of *Il Trovatore*, that opera full of fatal plot twists and impossible vengeances, in which while the great guitar of the orchestra accompanies the singers on the stage, in the audience the theatrical spell is broken by the reality of the occupation of Venice by the Austrians and the resistance by the Venetians. But what seems about to be a long chronicle of the *Resorgimento* becomes a melodramatic novel of the loves (or is it amours?) of an Italian countess who loves her country, with a passion which she quickly transfers to an officer in the occupation army. The whole film is the narrative of the debasement and the infinite abjection with which the countess (played by Alida Valli in a pithy, passionate, and little less than masterly performance) lets herself be brought to that extreme form of human bondage which is a one-sided love affair.

Thus, the history of the third war of Italian liberation is no more than an immense backdrop for a dense, at times lucid, at times confused, tedious, false some sort of Grand Guignol opera which has sought out its music not in the fresh musical theatricality of Verdi but in the morbid lyricism of The Seventh Symphony by Bruckner. Nevertheless in spite of all its elaborate mounting, of the careful direction, half realist, half stagy, by Luchino Visconti, *Senso* has not achieved what a less spectacular film, *Jealousies*, shown obscurely and unnoticed, has decidedly attained: the pathetic, furious dramatic thrust of this form of Victorian tragedy, the Italian grand opera.

20 January 1957

Sick Heil

The Devil's General belongs to the stream of films with which the Germans are trying to wash away their sins of Nazism in a celluloid purgatory. But fortunately the film explains nothing, it simply expounds. Filmed in West Germany, *Des Teufels General* is a movie made with a perfection which recalls the German films before Nazism, those which brought to the cinema many of the characteristics which Hollywood later offered as its own: the mechanized brilliance, the clarity of the script, the sure and almost anonymous direction without ceasing to be extremely personal and a considerable display of skill. The movie has utilized a play by Carl Zuckmayer, a Jewish author whose play *Der Hauptmann von Köpenick* has been filmed by the silent and by the present German cinema. (Incidentally, the second version was directed by the same director as this film, Helmut Käutner.) Basing his work on a real incident, Zuckmayer, a refugee in the United States, took as a reference the case of General Ernst Udet, air ace of World War I and a bureaucrat in the Luftwaffe. Udet was a friend of Goering and died under obscure circumstances, which some hurried national honours – remember the later case of Rommel – made crystal clear. Whether or not General Udet formed part of a vast military conspiracy which beginning in 1933 tried to destroy Hitler, is difficult to know. But he does seem to have belonged to that clique of military men who at first saw Nazism as a resurrection of Pan-Germanism à la Bismarck. When they realized that it was in fact a chaotic and senseless totalitarianism, it was already too late.

Deceived or not, at any rate history sees them as yoked to the wagon of Nazism, even if books like *Das bittere Ende* may pretend that the 20th of July conspiracy was no more than the culmination of a process which not only included the eradication of Hitler and his entourage, but the return of Germany to humanity and to civilization. The General Harras of the film is a *bon vivant*, a drinker, almost a libertine, and although he detests the Nazis, he does not fail to fulfil effectively his part in the destructive apparatus of Nazism. 'He growls, drinks, chases women,' as a Gestapo agent in the movie says, but these are minor evils, because he does not stop being a good watchman over industry: to him falls the task of maintaining the technical efficiency of the airplane factories to which he has never added the adjective 'death-dealing'. '*Wir sind im Krieg*,' that old 'we are at war' is his answer. He is a *Krieger*, a warrior, a professional of war: he leaves the speculations to the politicians, to the moralists, and – lastly – to the philosophers. He has, nevertheless, an inopportune sense of humour. This does not please the Nazis: it is known that humour corrodes, destroys everything and if Hitler had an abstinence greater than his vegetarianism, it was that of an allergy to frivolity: he was a complete dictator and all dictators detest humour.

When they tell General Harras that the war in Russia is over with, that the Soviet regime is crumbling, that the democracies are rotten, that their morale is very low, he grumbles: 'Ribbentrop, 1921 vintage'; on one occasion when an SS officer proposes to him that he enter the Party, that he join them, because both detest 'the monocled ones', he belches and then adds: 'A good painter friend of mine, a good Berliner, used to say, "I cannot eat as much as I would like to vomit," where he said eat, I would say drink.' When the Gestapo comes to arrest him, early in the morning, he confesses to his host, a young lieutenant: 'Do you know what the difference is between Switzerland and Germany? In Switzerland anyone calling at this hour is always the milkman.'

The script – by the director Käutner and Georg Hurdalek – has left no traces of the play. If anything, it is *too* cinematic. As it is said that there are works of literature which are too literary, likewise one can be assured that *The Devil's General* turns out to be a film more cinematic than it should have been – it is a bit too keen to dazzle the spectator with pyrotechnics of images which are always interesting, but at times gratuitous. Fortunately, Käutner has been able not to add to the tree-climbing of the libretto a complicated photographic plot: the film has a very complex internal mechanics, but superficially it is very simple. With this he has demonstrated that he is the most able of post-war German directors in managing that particular form of polished realism which made *The Last Bridge* an interesting film, in spite of its compromise in pleasing both God and the devil. This time he has not had to please more than the devil, and *The Devil's General* is in all its first part, until the imprisonment of its hero, an experience as exciting as listening to the sluggish panting of the German generals registered on a tape recorder, owned by the Gestapo. In its second part, however, Käutner remains well on the side of the devil and the general dies in a manner too heroic for his Dionysiac life. It is as if Petronius had committed suicide by butting Roman heads with Nero.

3 February 1957

anastasia
and anastasia:
russian siamese twins

Anastasia in Pink

Anastasia (Twentieth Century–Fox) seems to be a phoenix which arose amid the cry of Fire! from a revolutionary officer in an obscure basement in Iekaterinburg in 1918. But the cinema has shown that, although its name may mean resurrection in Greek, *Anastasia* is a too-frequent phoenix; now two *Anastasias* have appeared simultaneously. Almost as many as the ones who invaded Central Europe soon after the coming of the Bolsheviks to power. So she has resurrected one time more than Jesus. This *Anastasia* – the American one: the public has divided the *Anastasias* in two: the American *Anastasia* and the German *Anastasia* – is glamorized, as if they had applied anaesthesia to the pain of the presumed princess for not being recognized as royal. In Cinemascope and colour, the film turns out to be a sentimental soap when it could well have been a black chronicle. Based on the play of the same name, relatively successful on Broadway, where an able American adaptation got rid of the weaknesses of the French original by Marcelle Maurette, *Anastasia* is the vehicle chosen for the return of Ingrid Bergman, triumphant, to Hollywood. It has been the return of an ex-sovereign disguised as a princess without a court. Accompanied by Helen Hayes, queen of the American stage for years, by Sacha Pitoëff, descendant of the famous stage dynasty, and by Yul Brynner, who has now been demoted from King of Siam to Russian prince, Bergman has achieved not only the recognition of the critics, but a welcome from the American public to one whom insidious press campaigns had shown as little less than a whore some years ago. The movie, understanding that the more unreal – and this does not mean less royal – Anastasia is, as a human being, the more credible she becomes as a myth, goes further than the play. It not only has Anastasia meet with her grandmother, the widowed empress – which never really happened – but has her flee with Prince Bunin, her tiresome tamer, converting the real love of Anastasia in the play, Doctor Serensky, into a voice with two lines, just like an untrusting fisherman. There is an old French adjective, lavish, which can be applied to this film. As long as to its correct meaning, downpour, one adds that sound which recalls the sumptuous silk, the velvet, and the noise of precious stones rattling together. At times the film is so gorgeous, so sensual, that the spectator believes that Anastasia will break out singing her reclamation of the Russian throne to music by Cole Porter.

Anastasia in Grey

Anastasia, the German one, is a film which suffers from a paradox: it is a documentary telling of a fiction. The movie narrates the *via crucis* of a woman who during the twenties tried to be recognized as the princess Anastasia by the remaining, scattered members of the Russian

Imperial family. Up to here the factual statement was correct. But the corollary is that the movie makes the reclamation of the presumed Anastasia its own and affirms that it is dealing with the authentic Anastasia Nikolayevna Romanov. That rhetorical figure is called wishful thinking. The flimsiest of logics indicates that Anastasia, like her parents and her brother, was shot in Iekaterinburg and that the alleged Anastasia is an imposter or a madwoman.

Even the director, Falk Harnack (a specialist in producing speedy facsimiles: he has already embittered director Pabst's life once with an accelerated version of the 20th of July conspiracy, and now has gotten the powerful Twentieth Century–Fox to set things up so hurriedly that they can première their *Anastasia* first, in a market which has proved to be as important for Hollywood as for Europe, that of Spanish America), found himself in narrow straits when he organized a symposium on the authenticity or falsity of the nobility of Frau Tchaikovsky or Anna Anderson. Documents concerning this woman's personality showed up which Harnack would have preferred to see burned. Consider some of the vital points of this history, one of the most astonishing cases of usurpation of identity on record.

Early one night on 17 February 1920 a woman who showed symptoms of asphyxiation, and appeared totally emaciated, was admitted to the Elizabeth Hospital in Berlin. According to what the police found out, the woman in question had been rescued by two men from the Landwehr canal, not far from the opera. She was not carrying an identity card, passport nor any other papers which might help identify her. She was wearing a dark, fringed skirt, a blouse of uncertain colour, cheap leather boots, wrinkled and torn, thick black stockings, covered with mud; around her shoulders she had on a peasant's shawl, secured by a safety-pin. She was about twenty years old and of delicate bearing. She was bony and was suffering from evident anaemia. Her body was worn out by work and blows. Several small scars crossed her face and a long furrow, narrow like that made by a bullet, ran the length of her skull. She was not examined gynaecologically. If she had been they would have found that she had been a mother. Attended with care, the patient refused to speak, much less to identify herself. She was christened the Unknown Woman. Every time the nurse would ask: '*Namen, Fräulein?*' she would turn towards the wall and cover her face with the sheet.

Persisting thus, after five weeks she was moved to the Daldorf Insane Asylum. There she was subjected to several interrogations. One turned out more fruitful than the others: the Germans were beginning to learn the art of making you talk. In the long litany of questions and answers there were one or two interesting points. When it was hinted to her that she could have been an unmarried mother, the sick woman became terribly angry. Then she complained that they were serving her breakfast at 6.30 and not at ten in the morning as she was accustomed. Finally she accused the employees of the hospital of treating her with too much familiarity: they were using the dubious '*du*' with her. One day one of the other sick women (who boasted of having sewn for the family of the Tsar) showed her a copy of the *Illustrierte Zeitung*, in which the possibility was broached that one of the Tsar's three daughters – Anastasia, Maria, and Tania – might be alive and a refugee in Germany. The sick seamstress let out a 'Eureka!' and cried out to her, as she gave her the newspaper: 'You are Anastasia, the Tsar's daughter!'

That was the beginning of the legend which has now resulted in an article in *Life*, in a French play and in two movies. The most immediate sources upon which the German film draws are two books by Gleb Botkin (who sponsored 'Anastasia' for a long time and is now legal counsellor for the old woman) called *The Royal Romanovs* and *The Woman Who Resurfaced*, and a book, *Anastasia, the Survivor of Iekaterinburg*, by one of the friends of the Daldorf amnesiac, Harriet von Rathless-Keilmann.

The film relates the details of the Anastasia dossier with a scrupulousness and a honesty worthy of a better cause, and thus achieves moments in which the movie seems more like a crusade on behalf of Madame Tchaikovsky than a mass entertainment to make money. Well photographed in black and white and efficiently directed, it relies on a deadening performance by Lilli Palmer who has managed to take all the punch out of an otherwise substantial role. Carelessly written and worse edited, *Anastasia* has two or three moments of emptiness and a marring anticlimax. Nevertheless, it manages to prove its doubtful thesis and the spectator leaves convinced that the old lady lost in the Black Forest is the last daughter of the Tsar.

But what the spectator may think is one thing and reality another. This arrived a few days ago in the form of a cable which was suspiciously opportune – or just inopportune:

> Bonn, 29 January (INS). The international mystery grown for four decades around a woman who claims to be the Grand Duchess Anastasia of Russia was cleared up today by a decision of a tribunal in West Berlin. Basing its decision on medical tests and an accumulation of statements taken over a thirty-year-period, the

tribunal affirms that Anna Anderson, fifty-seven years of age, is decidedly not the daughter of the Tsar.

10 February 1957

cain
did not tire
of talking to me
about this
film

The Gangster and the Artist

The Killing (United Artists) is a masterpiece. It is the apotheosis of the cinema of violence: from its beginnings with the inside views of a horse race, with its luminous and violently contrasting photography, its slashing music and its funereal vision of the deadly Percherons pulling out the starting gate, slow, their white manes in the wind with their air of dragging a hearse, the spectator is made aware that he is in the presence of an exceptional movie.

I

A man plays all the favourites for four different races, but he is not nervous. He is not a better or a bookie. In the bar of the racetrack he orders a beer and on the counter he leaves a paper with an address. The bartender picks it up. On one of the winning tickets he jots down the same address and pushes it over to one of the cashiers. The cashier notes down the address. Neither one is a crook. The fourth man is a policeman. All are in dire financial straits and they decide to join the plan of an ex-con to rob the racetrack. The first man, Marvin Unger (Jay C. Flippen), is a friend of the ex-con Johnny Clay (Sterling Hayden) and is the one to finance the heist. (In these times of capitalist high pressure, even to steal one must make an initial investment.) The waiter, Mike O'Reilly (Joe Sawyer), needs money for his sick wife, the cashier (Elisha Cook, Jun.) needs it for his fun-loving wife (Marie Windsor). The policeman (Ted de Corsia) spends on a car and on his mortgaged house much more than he earns.

The little cashier sees in the holdup a means of holding on to his almost fugitive wife. Although he has sworn not to reveal the plans to anyone, he cannot refuse her simplest demand. She in turn tells all about it to her lover, also a hoodlum (Vince Edwards). The robbery is brought off with an almost chronometric precision. At the time for sharing the take, the group waits in the ex-con's house. Someone knocks on the door. It is the lover of the cashier's wife, armed and accompanied by another gangster. The cashier, frightened and confused, fires at his rival, who, mortally wounded, discharges his machine gun at the group killing them all.

Johnny, the leader, on arriving at the house and realizing that something wrong has happened, takes off with the money as had been agreed. He tries to get away in a plane with his girl. At the airport the old suitcase that contains the money falls off the cart which is carrying it to the plane and flies open. The money is scattered by the plane's propellers and the thief is seized by two policemen who were guarding the airport. Vanquished, without offering resistance, crushed by the stupid accident that made him lose the money, he is taken away.

II

The movie owes its plot to several earlier films, especially to *The Asphalt Jungle* by John Huston. But its realization is its own and is indeed original. There are in it much subtlety of acting and some singular gifts of observation. Furthermore it is exempt from the pseudo-poetry that marred the Huston film. The poetry of violence and sombre tones of this film are legitimate. Here are some examples. When the wretched cashier tells his wife about the robbery, his bright eyes reveal their small, fearful pupils, while his gnarled hand covers his face before admitting that this is the day. The image of the Percherons leaving the starting gate is repeated again and again, like an ominous leitmotiv. During the robbery one hears the voice of the racetrack announcer in a litany, mixed with some fatal drumming, as if an ominous chorus were announcing the presence of foul Fate. The mask which the only robber wears is of a happy clown and while the money falls into the great bag which soon will contain two million dollars, the mask's mouth distends into a perennial smile, greedy and gloating and triumphant.

There are more signs of the presence of inexorable destiny: the suitcase which does not open, the badly trained little dog which will run out in front of the cart that is taking the money bag to the secure airplane, the chattering parrot which will witness the death of its mistress, the black parking attendant who offers a lucky horseshoe to the psychopathic killer (of the horse) who refuses it and is later killed, the money which is dispersed to the winds, like a Mosaic warning sign: 'Thou shalt not steal'; the fatal women: the leader's girlfriend, who accompanies him in his life of crime and bad luck, the wife of the cashier, unfaithful and inhuman, the invalid wife ignorant of the cruel fate of her husband.

III

The precision with which the robbery must be executed has provided the director Kubrick with the opportunity to play with time as the cinema of violence has rarely done. The movie opens with a narrator who if at the outset seems to be unnecessary is soon revealed to be most necessary. His voice is also the fatal chorus of the tragedy, at the same time as he informs the audience that the complex machinery of the assault has started running. On one occasion the movie jumps backwards, and the only indication which the average spectator has (the one who is not accustomed to paying much attention to what he sees) of what is happening, is that the narrator indicates to him with the scrupulousness of a timekeeper the time when each character fits into the clockwork of the heist. If he loses the thread of the hours, he is lost. That is the greatest risk which the robbers run, and the spectator runs it with them.

IV

As in the good old times, *The Killing* offers an extensive cast of supporting actors who are first class. Elisha Cook, Jun. as the cashier belittled by his wife, is a candidate for the best supporting performance of the year. Timothy Carey, with his sickly smile and his unintelligible speech, is a true psychopath. De Corsia, Sawyer and Flippen are credible and sincere. And the veteran wrestler Kola Kwariani is one of the most agreeable presences which the *cronista* has seen in a long time, with his shaved head and his monstrous wrestler's mien, which nevertheless radiates an innate elegance. Finally, Sterling Hayden brings off a difficult task: to give a different turn to a role which he has been assigned many times before. He was also a safecracker who was not exactly a safe cracker in *The Asphalt Jungle*.

V

Stanley Kubrick is the director of *The Killing*. He is a new name, but this is his third professional film. A photographer for *Look* magazine, he made his first film at twenty-one, with money from his father. His first professional film was *Fear and Desire*, whose cost he defrayed with $50,000 from his family. His second film, *Killer's Kiss*, has been received in Europe with applause and praise. Now, at twenty-seven he has just finished what can perhaps be considered one of the best gangster movies made in Hollywood in a decade, and which is the best film of the year up to today. Kubrick, who according to *Time* magazine looks like an undernourished Marlon Brando and who avows that he will make cheap and good movies, because the two are not incompatible, will not be a genius, the new Orson Welles, as he has been called, but there is no doubt that he is the most promising talent which Hollywood has today. We will have to watch him and eagerly await his future films. He looks able to produce more than one masterpiece.

17 February 1957

Tea for Two

Tea and Sympathy (Metro) is the expurgated version of a play as successful as it is mediocre. The play dealt with a problem as old as man but new in literature: homosexuality. It made of the conflict a mere trick with no treat, but the real conundrum of the drama was: who is the homosexual in the school – the professor or the student? Skilfully constructed and with an eternally sympathetic character, the black sheep which is actually the sacrificial lamb, *Tea and Sympathy* still could not hide three things:

a) Its dramatic structure, the affective triangle and the interrelations between the characters belonged to *Candida*, by Bernard Shaw and its motivation and plot too closely resembled for comfort those of *The Children's Hour*, and *Mädchen in Uniform*, all much earlier dramas.
b) It was crude.
c) It was hypocritical.

A brilliant staging by Elia Kazan and the performances of Deborah Kerr and John Kerr (no kin) made it famous in the United States and in the whole world. Hollywood could not miss an opportunity to squeeze what on Broadway – and now, as is apparent, off Broadway too – had been a juicy forbidden fruit. The work was purchased for almost a quarter of a million dollars and its author himself took the job of adapting it for the screen. But very soon the censors demonstrated that if a rara avis (the theme of homosexuality has been positively prohibited in Hollywood since the very beginnings of the industry and its occasional treatment is carried out by means of a complicated machinery of hints, which, at times, could convert a convicted and confessed uranist into 'a weak boy' (*A Streetcar Named Desire*), into a Jew murdered by anti-Semites (*Crossfire*) or, to take the cake, into two persons well-differentiated sexually and socially: in *Serenade* the 'protector' of the famous tenor is transformed – or is it transvested? – into a millionaire nymphomaniac and into a sharp music critic in a flat plot) could pass through its turnstile, they would take it upon themselves to adorn it with convenient feathers of another plumage.

The finished scripts were returned again and again by the Breen Office with alterations and recommendations that the director Vincente Minnelli (*Lust for Life*) refused again and again to accept. At last an honourable compromise was arrived at – which in Hollywood means a hypocritical caving in to the box office and social prejudices. The work has been mutilated, altered and prologued and epilogued in such a way that the accusations made against Tom Lee seem infinitely more slanderous than in the theatre (the boy is surprised, in the play, bathing nude with a pederast professor, and not sewing on a button with the professors' wives, as the film shows); that the adultery by the wife, full of tea and sympathy, of the professor is diminished by a final letter in which the good woman gets herself into a blind bind explaining to the boy that where she did what she did she didn't do what she didn't; and that the real sodomite, the professor, so athletic and manly, is not uncovered and accused by his wife (as in the play) but appears with flaccid flesh, wasted muscles, and an air of defeat: the final acceptance of his conflict, demonstrated through the expedient of showing him listening to 'classical music'! Which adds to 'classical music' – and its listeners and its players, of course – a new timbre of implying – and explaining – certain *deviations* in the sexual behaviour of the human male.

How is it then that the film turns out to be so excellent? Because, simply, Minnelli is a director of so much tact, so much talent, that he has been able to get around the obstacles with the skill of one who knows that 'handicap' means advantage as well as disadvantage. The crudities, the coarsenesses and a certain general bad taste from which the play suffered have been expurgated along with the three or four half-truths about the sexual conflicts of the American adolescent who studies in a boarding school. The American universities, in spite of the sports, the social activities and definite freedom, are no more than the modern version of the English boarding schools.

Similarly the hypocrisy in the play has disappeared, since if it passed for a diatribe against intolerance, in the movie the plot has been exposed for what it really is: a condemnation of calumny. If the boy in question had been a homosexual his ordeal would be justified. What has remained of the play appears clearly, without ceasing to be accusatory, and the marrow of the drama is enclosed in a capsule of good cinema which respects the theatre because it respects itself. The bridges between acts and some scenes that were trite and weak in the original, in the movie acquire an exemplary poetic strength. The confrontation between the vulgar waitress and the pulchritudinous lady; the scene in which Tom Lee tries to make love to the waitress and ends up with another failed attempt, that of suicide; the insane initiation of the novices is presented with an economy of melodrama and a comprehension of human relations that are the only poetry in a drama which is prosaic in spite of its poetic quotations, its love ballads and its wilted flowers.

The *cronista* recalls with supreme pleasure two moments, two transitions which are poetic instants: the woman has attempted futilely to hold back the boy from going to his date with the waitress because she knows that he is going to prove his manliness by destroying love. She appears at the window and looks towards the patio of the school, where, through some hedges and trees and the rain, there shines, in an inciting and malignant redness, the luminous sign of the café where the waitress works. The scene dissolves to another rain-streaked window where another woman, the waitress, closes the blind to initiate, once more almost in a mechanical caricature, the act of love which the conventions forbid to the first woman. The second instant surprises Tom Lee's roommate visiting the library in search of his friend. From down the empty hall, descending the grand staircase, rising from the room, from the phonograph comes some music, a piano piece, some Chopin, and the sound precedes the image of Tom listening in silence to the slow melody, next to the window, through which a crepuscular light bathes the scene. Those moments, of course, are not in the play. They could not have been. Not only because they are images of pure cinema, but because they prove that the true poet is named Minnelli.

20 February 1957

Triangle

Trapeze (Hecht–Lancaster; United Artists) is really another geometrical figure: a triangle. It is the myth of Icarus descending. A solo trapeze artist falls from the trapeze one night and becomes an invalid (the fallen Icarus). At the circus, of which Icarus is now a prop man, arrives a young acrobat. He is anxious to transform himself into a replica of the old flying trapeze artist, the only man in the world who could bring off the deadly triple somersault once. (Icarus has ascended to the level of Dedalus and there is a new Icarus to be taught how to fly.) Enclosed in the luminous labyrinth of the circus, Dedalus and Icarus try to best the Minotaur, who this time is not half bull and half man but all woman. The new Icarus learns the lessons of his master well and from the experience gained and suffered by the old Icarus, he is taught the dangers of flying too high. At the end, Icarus II flies alone and Dedalus vanquishes the Minotaur by letting himself be banished by it.

If this sounds too mythological there is another explanation at hand. *Trapeze* is no more than a revised and augmented version of *Variety*, a film which since its German original of 1925 has not ceased to incite facile facsimiles everywhere. The story of the two trapeze artists, who find themselves drawn apart like a chasm by a woman and settle their quarrel in the heights of the tent, has now been filmed in colour and with a cast (Burt Lancaster, Gina Lollobrigida, Tony Curtis) such as to attract to the old dark house every kind of spectator: of one sex, of the other and – of the other yet. But that is all. If the realization by the director Carol Reed (yes, the same man of *Odd Man Out* and *The Third Man*) is technically brilliant, it is very poor in imagination. Lancaster is at home on the trapeze, because he was a trapeze artist before becoming an actor. La Lollobrigida shows off her body at ease and at large, because she is really an exhibitionist: if she didn't charge the fabulous salary that she got in this film, she would still exhibit herself. The only legitimate surprise of the film is that Tony Curtis can act!

10 March 1957

at the end
of the review,
cain,
as always,
had been frank:
a timid censorship
converted his post coitum
into 'amorous lassitude',
which means
another thing altogether:
today i give back to the phrase
its purple original
sincerity

Streetcar Rival

Baby Doll (Warner) is the first comedy by Elia Kazan – and one hopes that it will not be the last. It is the second time that Kazan and Tennessee Williams have teamed up on the screen. Which can seem only too rare to the reader who may recall their previous association in *A Streetcar Named Desire*, a movie which many consider a masterwork.

'There you have it, it's all yours,' said the handsome man, smiling. 'Goodbye and good luck. Don't make many changes.' That was the farewell from Williams when Kazan left for the South to film *Baby Doll*. The message was not unusual. It is well known that frequently Kazan has totally changed Williams' works (the third act which Broadway saw in *Cat on a Hot Tin Roof* has very little to do with the first version that Williams wrote), to the point that it has always been said that if Tennessee Williams writes the plays of Tennessee Williams, Elia Kazan rewrites them. For another thing, *Baby Doll* was the first script by Williams written originally for the screen.*

Baby Doll Carson McCorkle Meighan is a young Southern wife: blonde, sensual and primitive, she has the beauty of a healthy animal. As she herself confesses: '. . . I never got past the fourth grade . . . I had a great deal of trouble with long division . . .' She is married to Archie Lee Meighan, a man who, to the economic problems of being totally ruined, adds a particular version of the morganatic marriage. If in morning-gift weddings the spouses must keep their prior state, here it is only one of them who after a year of marriage is just as before: Baby Doll. Williams works out the telling of this deferred wedding with a Boccaccian *savoir-faire*:

> BABY DOLL: Well – I told my daddy that I wasn't ready for marriage and – my daddy told Archie Lee that I wasn't ready for it. And – Archie Lee promised my daddy that he would wait until I was ready.
>
> SILVA: Then the marriage was postponed –?
>
> BABY DOLL: Oh no – not the weddin', (*Giggles*) we had the weddin'. My daddy gave me away.
>
> SILVA: But you said Archie Lee waited.
>
> BABY DOLL: Yeah, after the weddin' he waited.

* The screenplay comes from two plays by Williams, *Twenty-Seven Wagons Full of Cotton* and *The Unsatisfactory Supper*, which it in fact resembles very little. The idea of combining the two plays in one filmscript came from Kazan and both worked on the libretto. Kazan says: 'We worked so much on the script, without success at the beginning, that I came to contemplate with delight the idea that the husband riddles his wife with bullets at the end.'

SILVA: For what?
BABY DOLL: For me to be ready for marriage.
SILVA: How long did he have to wait?
BABY DOLL: Oh, he's still waitin'. We had an agreement though. I mean, I told him that – on my twentieth birthday, I'd be ready.
SILVA: That's tomorrow.
BABY DOLL: Mm-hm.
SILVA: And, uh, – are you – will you be ready?
BABY DOLL: (*Sigh*) – Well, that all depends.
SILVA: What on?
BABY DOLL: Whether or not the furniture comes back – I guess.
SILVA: Your husband sweats more'n any man I know and now I can understand why.

He who waits, Archie Lee, despairs though not in pairs. In order to recover his lost splendour, he sets fire to the brand new cotton gin of Silva Vacarro, a prosperous Sicilian who has set himself up in the neighbourhood. The rest of the film is devoted to watching how the vengeful Sicilian – a fine Mafioso – gets satisfaction by seducing the virgin wife. To settle their quarrel in bed? No, simply to drag out of her the confession that her husband was the arsonist. The husband on the instalment plan, however, learns that adultery has taken place and the film ends with a mad vaudeville chaste chase, which is an unusual thing indeed in the American cinema.

Baby Doll was made by Kazan with flawless technical mastery. Filmed almost entirely – that is to say eighty per cent of the shooting – in the little hamlet (444 inhabitants) of Benoit, in the state of Mississippi, no more than six professional actors appear in the movie. The rest are all inhabitants of Benoit, transformed into imitations of their own selves. Kazan faced not a few difficulties in the damp town. The most endearing of them was when the owner of a café decided to paint his establishment during the time that passed between the first visit by Kazan to the town and the shooting. It goes without saying that Kazan raised the roof high: the café had been chosen for its grimy and ramshackle look!

It is this aura of supreme physical and spiritual decay which permeates the movie. The roomy *ante bellum* mansion, desolate, inhabited only by rats, built in the middle of a field that seems more like the moors; the cotton gin that is falling to pieces; the grimy and toothless Negroes; the owner of the mansion; the young wife who sleeps in a cradle, with her thumb in her mouth; the husband who ambles through the house in pyjamas when it is already late in the day and whose only contact with his virgo-intacta wife is through a hole in the bedroom wall, which he himself has drilled so as to spy on her in her sleep; the old aunt, deaf, pale, a tenuous, evanescent figure whose only pleasure in life is visiting her sick lady friends in the hospital and eating for them the tidbits that other visitors give them, a caricature of Williams' woman in ruins: Blanche Dubois, thirty years after having been shut up in an asylum, still crazy and at the same time a denizen of a deluded vacuum chamber.

This affection for derelicts saves the film from the liking for decadence which threatens it. What Williams has called the charm of the 'ruined things which have the poetry of those things which people no longer living have lived next to' is reflected in the old ramshackle swing, in the corridor in ruins, in a dusty chandelier in the middle of a forgotten ballroom, in a Ford car destroyed by time, incapable of any motion, within which takes place one of the most beautiful and poetically achieved scenes of the film: Silva and Baby Doll find for the first time the sweet intimacy so propitious to love.

To make his movie Kazan has used Boris Kauffman (the photographer awarded for *On the Waterfront*), who has achieved a grey photography of a river delta countryside in mid-winter, filtered and perfect. Kazan has added to it the music of Kenyon Hopkins, which is at once evocative and mocking, satirical and bittersweet: pathetic. And he has collected an ensemble of actors who move around in the film as if the mock fictitious reality of the characters really belonged to them. Mildred Dunnock (the memorable mother in *Death of a Salesman*) has understood that she is the grandmother of Blanche Dubois this time and is capable of making one laugh and cry, alternately, to give the exact tone of tragicomedy that the film has. Her labour of love has been justly appreciated and she appears to be first in the running for this year's Oscar for Best Supporting Actress. It will be an injustice if she does not win. Karl Malden is an actor made to order for Kazan. His role as the quasi-cuckolded Archie Lee had been set aside for Spencer Tracy by Warners, but Kazan insisted on Malden and one has to bless his insistence: Malden is Archie Lee. In Silva Vacarro, Eli Wallach was hindered by his Jewish features from being a true Italian. But here, as in the stage version of *The Rose Tattoo*, he has managed to make up for it with an internal fire, with a vehemence which is definitively Sicilian.

The Baby Doll of Carroll Baker (a role that Warners wanted for Marilyn Monroe) is *Baby Doll* the film. As she goes, so goes the movie. If she is sensual (and she is sensual a lot) the movie *is* sensual. If she is comic, the movie becomes comic. If she is dramatic, the movie turns dramatic. Her début is one of the most impressive appearances that has been recorded in pictures. (She really débuted in *Giant*, but will always be remembered as a Kazan doll.) Doubtless she will have a long career, which it will be advisable to watch. A line from the film, one which will make her famous, demonstrates all her acting power. She had just come down from the room where Vacarro has taken a nap (Kazan and the Warners people assure us that nothing happened up there: only an innocent catnap), and in the midst of the sound and zoom of the husband who thinks himself betrayed, she whispers to Silva: 'I feel cool and rested, for the first time in my life. I feel that way, rested and cool,' and in her voice that line loses all carnal meaning to be transformed into the message of the neglected wife. Although no one in the audience might fail to think that it is the most poetic description of the *post coitum* made by the movies. It is this message which gives us the definitive key to the film: one has seen an American parody of *Lady Chatterley's Lover*.

17 March 1957

cain
was a man
who knew how to
emend
an error:
here he was already distinguishing
the sex
of suso

Enemies

Le Amiche (*The Friends*, Mercurio) is a *cronaca*. As at other times, the director Michelangelo Antonioni has performed a dissection – better: a vivisection – on that Italian upper middle class which, if he doesn't hate, at least he doesn't love. Also, as before, he has not used a searing firebrand but a frozen scalpel. 'Without indulgence and without cruelty' he describes the life of a little group of women who represent feminine life in an Italian city – Turin now. The women, it goes without saying, constitute a pretext for portraying a whole society. It is not a case of a scandalous denunciation through crime – as in *Processo a la Città*, a well-made film about a trial of secret crimes, suspiciously similar to the notorious Caso Montesi – or of an acid social chronicle – as in *Le infideli* – but of a painstaking (and this is the adjective to describe what has been called the Antonioni style) exposition of the smallest ups and downs of the human soul.

Actually, the girlfriends are not friends. A fact that Antonioni – and Pavese, because the movie is based on a short novel by the writer Cesare Pavese, a suicide, called *Among Women Alone* – is not the only one to have noted: women, contrary to everything that one would think, suffer an annoying incapacity to have girlfriends. A usual feminine declaration ('I'm no good at having girlfriends') seems to have guided the steps of the director in search of the tracks of the soul of woman. At a particular moment, the friends annoy each other and end up almost hating each other; the momentary link that united them – the novelty of the recent arrival of a woman, a fact that in women seems to have an almost mythic importance – is diluted in their memory, following death and tragedy.

Clelia is an independent woman. This can mean a hard look, a perpetual tailor-made suit, a doubtful reputation and feminism. Fortunately the woman is Eleonora Rossi Drago, one of the most sensual actresses of the Italian cinema, and Clelia turns out to be femininity plus business: a representative of high Roman fashion in Turin. Her arrival coincides with a touch of melodrama (melodrama is never lacking in the life of a woman): one of 'the friends' has tried to commit suicide. The motive? Political despair, bankruptcy, alienation or anguish? No, something more basic: love. By means of an inconsequential lady friend of the failed suicide, Clelia meets the other friends. Rosetta (Anna Maria Pancani) is the female of the species: she only lives for love. To a certain extent the rest are the same as her, except that in her love life she reaches a more frank level, an almost exhibitionist degree. Nene (Valentina Cortese) is the typical intellectual woman: untidy, unkempt, intense, with a subtle dominion over her painter husband and, of course, much more intelligent than he. Mariella (the Austrian Madeleine Fischer) is the most honest and also the most naïve: Clelia would naturally become intimate with her, but when she recognizes this it is too late: she has died. This time she has really committed suicide. And lastly there is Momina (the French actress Yvonne Fourneaux), a married woman, adulteress, go-between and pretentious and vain and egotistical: all this gamut of vices is spread over the most sexually attractive woman of the group. As always.

The girlfriends have boyfriends. Rosetta has a boyfriend, but her concept of love is purely sporting: for her a furtive kiss on the beach has as much meaning as yielding on the wedding night. Nene is married to a painter (Gabriele Ferzetti) who thinks he is the breath of fresh air of genius and only succeeds in convincing one that he has bad breath. Mariella loves the painter and he looks at himself like Narcissus in that mirror of love and it feeds his ego until it becomes obese. Momina permits the visits of a young architect (Franco Fabrizi), but also toys with the idea of going back to her husband: which does not stop her from showering warm attentions on both. Finally, the first, Clelia, who fled from love so as not to sacrifice her independence – the price in loneliness paid by all independent women, who are no more than solitary women – falls in love with the common assistant of the architect, an indecisive man, burdened with shyness. *Le Amiche* occupies itself wholly with weaving this yarn of yearning.

If the term 'intimist' fits any film it is this one by Antonioni. It begins with a pleasing view of Turin during summer, while one hears that definite variant of the Brazilian samba that they cultivate so much in Italy – one of whose models gave all its aural aura to *Terza Liceo*. The arrival of Clelia at the hotel, her encounter with her future friends, up to an incident as conducive to hysteria as suicide – still more in the feminine world – are treated with more coldness than coyness. Antonioni never engages himself: he only observes. If there is an analytical, objective author in the Italian cinema, it is he. His aspirations are confined to narrating facts with the dispassionate and distant prose – cinematic and, at times, poetic – of a trial proceedings. Passions do not move him. Neither does politics obfuscate him, nor do the tears of the sentimentalist cloud his vision. At times, his style is so cold that the spectator asks himself where such an accumulation of details without an apparent climax is leading. But with the sureness of a prosecuting attorney, this author expounds proof after proof until he wins the case. Once more – and definitively – Antonioni has proclaimed himself the prosecutor of the Italian grand bourgeoisie: the criminal has lost the trial.

Emotionally, the film revolves around four scenes. A brief picnic – half romantic, half intellectual – on a desolate beach, in the coldest autumn. A dinner, full of frustrations and desires, which ends in a futile fight. The confrontation between Clelia and her best friend, Momina, in a dress shop, on the occasion of its opening. The final scene of the film, in which Clelia waits futilely for her lover on the train. In the first scene, the group is formed. In the second, it is broken up. In the third, Clelia breaks the ties of friendship with the remaining member of the group. In the last one, she destroys her links with Turin and its ambience, leaving alone. On going away, she doesn't long for the group of friends but for the withdrawn lover who does not dare to face her for the last time.

Antonioni made *Le Amiche** in a space of two years. That's a lot for a movie without pretensions. Even in Italy. During the shooting Antonioni faced dire economic difficulties, and the project – which now was not a project but an unfinished picture – ran a grave risk of ending up in the files of forgotten films. On one happy occasion he ran into a producer who offered to finance the rest of the film, if he introduced some *reasonable* changes. 'Why don't we include a little dog spoiled by the girl that commits suicide?' the producer suggested. 'Then we make the little dog die too. Moving, no?' Antonioni felt so moved that the next scene of his film was shot six months later. After waiting for Rossi Drago to get her nose operated on for the seventh time – the seventh attempt through plastic surgery to improve her nasal appendix, which finally remained as before: unnoticed, because almost no one watches her nose – for Valentina Cortese to disentangle certain conjugal messes with a trip to London, and for Turin to have a similar look in spring to that of autumn – and after having obtained the help of a producer without a dog.

The film has, nevertheless, an astounding unity. Not only of style but photographically, dramatically, and aurally.

On the beach, over the misty sand, Mariella walks barefoot. From above, on a terrace, the friends observe her. 'Watch over Mariella,' Momina tells the unscrupulous Rosetta. To which she does not fail to respond: 'Let her kill herself alone.' The camera faces Mariella and her erratic steps along the sand, the prospects of the beach in mourning, the noise of the sea, convince her of her ultimate loneliness. In the tavern, the painter and the architect quarrel. The painter is jealous because his wife has had success with her ceramics and he has had none with his painting. After taking two or three punches, the painter leaves. His wife and her lover go to follow him. But Nene, always intelligent, yields the way to Mariella. In the street, Mariella hears from the lips of the painter something that shows his whole character: he needs no one, loves no one, needs nothing except himself, who loves himself. The declaration by the painter – uttered with a convincing conviction by

* Antonioni enlisted the co-operation of women for his interpretation of a woman's world. The script of the film was done in collaboration with the writers Suso Cecchi D'Amico and Alba de Céspedes. Cecchi is a longtime collaborator with the best Italian directors, among them the Visconti of *Senso*. In Italy, it is said that in *Le Amiche* the rigour is Antonioni's, the sensibility Suso Cecchi's and the mawkishness Céspedes'. Alba de Céspedes is a granddaughter of Carlos Manuel de Céspedes, the Cuban archpatriot, although she considers herself Italian and only knows Cuba as one more tourist once. A not very well-informed tourist, for certain.

Ferzetti, in one of the most disagreeable roles by a generally disagreeable actor – sends Mariella running through the dark alley and the night, while a pianola tune drowns out the mortal echo of her footsteps. The scene fades out to black and opens onto a luminous morning on the Po. With forensic technique Antonioni causes Mariella to be fished out dead from the river.

Clelia, embittered, sorrowful, returns to Rome. She waits to see her lover for the last time at the station. But he is there before her and always hidden, he has seen her pass by his side, take the train, come to the window, hoping to see him. In an almost ridiculous reaction, he hides behind a kiosk and from this risible watchtower observes the departure of the train, which starts out with Clelia at the window. The train leaves slowly with Clelia at the window. The train is lost from sight with Clelia still at the window. The soundtrack, very slowly, plays the same cloying samba from the beginning, full of nostalgia. The platform empties.

Here the spectator – or at least, the *cronista* – stays stuck to his seat, moved, convinced that he has seen not only the best film of Michelangelo Antonioni, but one of the most solid, unusual movies which has come from Europe in some time. This *cronaca* of mundane life, of the world of woman, has been seen with a man's eye, but with total empathy. Antonioni has shown this in the entire film: the men are contingent on woman. The reviewer, less skilled, has had recourse to a brief expedient: in the review the names of the women are repeated at tedious lengths, while the names of the men are no more than those of their professions.

24 March 1957

cain
confessed to me
having cried
at chaplin
(should we believe him?)

Dorado Eldorado

The Gold Rush (United Artists) is the key to Charles Chaplin. Perhaps the most perfect of his silent movies – don't forget that *City Lights* as well as *Modern Times*, in which Chaplin still refused to speak, were sound films – it has kept its comic qualities intact after thirty-two years. Now, Chaplin has given it a sound track and has added to it a subjective narrator (the narrator uses his voice so that the characters 'speak' through him) and has composed a brief score for it. 'Now' is 1942, when Chaplin decided to rerelease his old film. It happened like this: Chaplin showed his silent movie to some of his children's friends, and he counted the laughs that the oldest of his silent gags still had for the new generation. He reasoned that the rest of humanity might well think the same. For this new sally of the Tramp (whom he had already decided to leave behind, lost on the primrose path along which he disappears at the end of *Modern Times*), Chaplin chose his most perfect film, the one he considers his masterpiece, *The Gold Rush*.

The Gold Rush was selected some years back as the second of the ten masterworks of the cinema. *The Battleship Potemkin* came in before. The former film was the first of the great hits of Chaplin and his first feature film. None of his other movies has enjoyed the success which *The Gold Rush* had. The little fellow departed in search of gold and found it at the box office, in a buoyant America, enjoying the most fabulous economic boom of its history. It was 1925. Two years before, Chaplin made the only film in which he did not participate as an actor, *A Woman of Paris*. This time one is not dealing with a comedy but with a dour drama. The performer is Edna Purviance, Chaplin's favourite actress. *A Woman of Paris* introduced true psychological elements into the cinema, observed with a realist's eye: Chaplin stretched his affection for detail to the point that no one would recognize in him the easy-street comedian of the films by Mack Sennett, but rather the maniacal perfectionist Erich von Stroheim. (It is said that for one scene in a cabaret, Chaplin had a set with four walls built. In one of them he had had a hole drilled through which the camera peered with its monocle: in the scene, real waiters served a real meal to the rhythm of a real orchestra – which would not be heard in the film. Adolphe Menjou, sipping real champagne, looked out of the corner of his eye at the heroine like a true libertine.) Over the bitter and sour ending of *A Woman of Paris* – which he always regretted later – Chaplin superimposed the noisy humour of the little fellow who waddles through the snow with his impossibly big shoes, who suffers hunger and cold, who is confused with a tasty chicken and who ends up a millionaire: it is not strange that the film has a happy end. A reporter interviews the millionaire Chaplin, and for a photo he is made to wear again the beggar's uniform. But he falls down a staircase instead, as far as the third deck: there he bumps into his lost girlfriend. The reporter comments: 'Say – this will make a great story – and with a happy ending!' and Chaplin, now his own narrator, affirms: 'And so it was: a happy ending.'

It has been said that *The Gold Rush* is an autobiographical movie. To which one would have to add that all the cinema of Chaplin is autobiographical. *The Kid* is his infancy in the East End of London; *The Circus*, his beginnings in music hall by the hand of Karno, garrulous producer of pantomimes; *City Lights* is the rescue of many of his celebrated actresses, from anonymous obscurity to the hideous clarity of fame: not a few were blinded again; *Modern Times* is the individualist creator, trapped by an unending assembly line called Hollywood and being driven mad by it (Chaplin himself suffered a grave mental crisis once) and rescued by falling in love; *The Great Dictator* presents the little Jew with a moustache crushed by the Nazis, an image that Hitler, with the same moustache, would have enjoyed fitfully (*Monsieur Verdoux* in some ways escapes from this chart, perhaps because Orson Welles provided the story); *Limelight* is an admitted autobiography and a new version of *City Lights*, with the story of an old comic who no longer makes people laugh; to complete the sketch, Chaplin gave his clown a Spanish name, Calvero, in memory of his maternal grandmother. As one can see, it is not only Federico Fellini who supports his work with props from his life.

Like all the films of Chaplin, *The Gold Rush* is a madcap parody. Not only of adventure movies and of literature in a wild state as in Jack London but of the true tragedy of the search for gold by the countless prospectors of the Yukon, who risked life and limb in pursuit of a new El Dorado. To accentuate the similarities and thereby to split the difference, Chaplin begins his movie with a long thin line of men scaling a snowy mountain. With the laborious bustling of ants, the men show up dark against the snow, dwarfed by the mountain, mad under the sky – and the scene has nothing funny about it. But immediately an impossible precipice is seen ahead, and who comes up walking along the fearful and narrow ridge, risking his life by sheer ignorance? The Little Fellow, that's who. If on firm and sure ground he maintained a precarious balance, here he shows his scorn for danger by marching along as if on the widest avenue. But he does not fall. Miracles of gravity? Elie Faure, the art critic, has another theory: 'Hopping now on one foot, now on the other – those so sad and absurd feet – he represents the two poles of thought: one which is called conscience and the other desire. Hopping on one foot and the other, he seeks spiritual equilibrium, and after having found it for an instant he loses it immediately after . . .' Now the desire of Chaplin is to get rich from one day to the next and of course he doesn't have the remotest consciousness of the danger that he defies. Like Mr Magoo, another ineffable spirit, it is this innocence which saves him. Now it is no longer the instincts which preserve the species. In Chaplin's new species it will be its seraphic soul. If there is some drama in his life, it is that of the good man: his existence is badly tolerated by the wicked and he will never be understood. It is this which permits him to win in the end.

The Little Fellow arrives at a cabin. A wicked man inhabits it, but like Little Red Riding Hood, the Little Fellow doesn't see the danger and, at the wolf's mouth, only asks: Can I come in? The mean denizen of the cabin, a doer of iniquity, tries to hurl the Little Fellow into the snow and cold and hunger: to his death. But the elements are on the side of the Little Fellow: a strong wind prevents Chaplin from moving from his place. As much as he tries he doesn't succeed in advancing in his attempt – forced by the circumstances of a strong man – to abandon the cabin. When all is already lost, the elements vanquished by evil, avenging chance arrives. Another big man, but a good-hearted one, installs himself in the cabin and the Little Guy stays with him, the two opposing forces, good and evil, neutralized, equilibrium achieved.

The whole film is full of similar scenes, all of Chaplin is permeated by this primitive philosophy. But there is more. Chaplin has said: 'I have not tried to flatter the audience, but neither have I ever tried to impose silence on them.' He doles out the philosophy lesson, the critique of customs, and fills the film with guffaws: the sweet sap of laughter mixed with some salt tears. The romance of Chaplin is that form of solitary love which has even mortified someone as self-sufficient as Elvis Presley: the one-sided love affair. At a dance, the Little Fellow falls in love, at first sight, with the pretty, lissome Georgia. Georgia does not love the Little Fellow, she only makes fun of him gently, with affection. The Little Fellow asks for nothing more: his love is enough to cover the two: it is a wide sheet for a wedding bed with just one pillow. The sentimental scenes are managed with a kind of romantic detergent very near – or perhaps beyond – soap opera, and they show that Chaplin owes to Griffith everything that he does not owe to Max Linder and to Mack Sennett. Among the tears of weeping there are the tears of laughter and *The Gold Rush* is turned into one of the most complete pieces of humour which the cinema has given us.

Proofs:

a) The unforgettable scene of the dance of the rolls, one of the most beautiful from the silent days and a frank example of the poetry of movement.*

b) The slapstick or pure comic incident of the weapon which pursues the terrified non-belligerent: a shotgun obliges Chaplin to seek out the nearest refuge, while his two cabin-mates fight over the gun. But always the shotgun pursues Chaplin anxiously. The comedian will repeat this scene in *The Great Dictator*. On this occasion it is an animated cannonball.

c) Chaplin is dancing with Georgia. His pants fall down. He picks up an odd piece of rope and continues dancing. He notices that an enormous dog is slowing up his dance: the rope was holding the dog. Suddenly, a cat passes by . . .

d) Chaplin is earning a living shovelling snow. The snow that he removes from this door falls in front of the house next door. His clients grow. The snow keeps falling in front of the house next door. But now Chaplin doesn't dare advertise himself as a snow-sweeper: the house whose entrance the snow has covered is . . . the jail. (This scene was repeated with another reading in *City Lights* in the celebrated sequence of the street sweeper who has just finished cleaning up, irritated, the turds of a horse and now runs away after seeing with horror that down the street comes an elephant.)

e) Chaplin and his friend (brilliantly played by the late Mack Swain) are dying from hunger, on Thanksgiving Day to boot. For the dinner Chaplin only has one shoe, his right one. He has cooked it with culinary expertise and lovingly ladles the broth over it, as the most appetizing turkey. He serves it. Carefully he extracts the body of the boot and underneath there remain the nails, like the metallic spines of an unknown fish. Chaplin gobbles up the laces, which he has first rolled up on his fork, as if he were eating spaghetti. Now he sucks the nails with delight, like the bones of a tasty chicken.

f) His friend, still hungry, goes off his rocker and imagines the Little Fellow transformed into a hen ready for the oven. He chases him with his shotgun, but when he is just about to kill the hen, he sees that it is only the still starving Charlie.

g) And a long string of impractical jokes on which the best beads

* This new print of *The Gold Rush* was shown in widescreen format, so that the dance of the rolls could hardly be seen. This would have greatly bothered Chaplin, who always avoided close-ups, because 'in my work the expression of the hands and the legs counts as much as that of the face'.

are these: Chaplin takes a bent nail and holds it with his little finger so that Swain can snap it as if breaking the wishbone of a yardbird, to make a wish for providence; Chaplin buries the shotgun to keep his friend, whom he has not entirely been able to convince that he is not just a hen, from killing him; when he has buried it, he turns his back on it and throws snow on it with his feet, just like a hen; Chaplin pretends to be frozen so that any kind soul may feed him but when he is carried inside and he is given tea he instantly comes out of his stupor to pick up two or three extra lumps of sugar and thus be able to drink a too bitter tea; Chaplin is now a millionaire on board a ship when he comes up behind a man smoking a cigar, the man throws the cigar away and Chaplin, in spite of his rich clothes, from the force of habit cannot resist the impulse to pick up the butt and take a puff. All the life preservers on the ship have different names.

Finally, a new coat of paint on this old picture which has seemed to disturb many people: the narration. *The Gold Rush* is now narrated by Chaplin, and it is precisely this which transforms it into a key film: the one that truly shows what Charles Chaplin the author thinks about Charles Chaplin the character: what Chaplin thinks about Charlie. Now Chaplin has been transformed into a spectator of himself and thanks to the distance which time gives, has seen the raggedy rags bum from a lucid perspective. Here is what the *cronista* has seen about what Charles Chaplin has seen. The tramp is a poor wretch: this ultimate vision is contained in a single moment of the narration. Observing the dance scene as a narrator and describing it blow-by-blow from his choice seat near the trampled ego of the tramp in the corner, whose pants are about to fall down in patches, whose shoes are soleless, and who weighs less than 100 pounds thanks to hunger, Chaplin tells how Georgia, to show her utter contempt for Jack, has picked out the most deplorable-looking tramp in the dancehall . . . the Little Fellow, who can't believe his luck . . . Georgia, addressing herself to her boyfriend to pique him says: 'You see, I'm very careful whom I dance with' . . . The tramp is still a gentleman, like his pants come down in the world, but who keeps his anachronistic medieval customs and his costume in a society that is hostile and therefore cruel. Chaplin does repeat and repeat during the movie, each time he mentions the tramp, the phrase '*the poor little fellow*'. In that sentence there is nothing disparaging, or ironic, or reproachful. At most there is a faint hectoring meaning, which impels him to keep letting his character live in spite of the inclemency of the weather, of the time and of men. It is this survival more than a revival which definitively separates the Little Fellow from Don Quixote – and draws him near to the *déclassés* of the twentieth century, to the remnants of the old world in a brave new world, to an émigré from Victorian morality and bourgeois customs, to a character of another Charles, Charles Dickens.

14 April 1957

The Silence of the Sea

The World of Silence (Columbia) is the undersea world. This long documentary was made by Commander Jacques-Yves Cousteau, a man who has, without resorting to alchemy, been able to extract unheard-of treasures from the sea. Inventor of the aqualung (and also of a whole sea sport, skin-diving hunting), a laureate author, now Commander Cousteau takes advantage of the extraordinary visual force of the cinema to make a new exploration of his enormous ark. From it he not only extracts fish in abundance but what constitutes perhaps the most beautiful collection of photographs of the bottom of the sea. In motion.

Here are some samples of the treasure trove, if the word can faintly give an idea of what the eye sees: A tribe of porpoises swims at fantastic speed, never stopping their play. These mammals (which the film compares with dogs) zoom, swim, and plunge, in a strange competition of swimming and diving combined. The porpoises appear by the hundreds and soon the blue ocean turns mauve, a sea of crossing porpoises.

A group of sperm whales swims in a virgin sea and seems not to fear man. But it would have been better if they had: the boat collides with one of the cetaceans and a sperm whale pup is hacked to pieces by the propellers. With the mysterious urgency of mortally wounded animals, it swims to catch up with the flock and in its dying fit fills the sea with a too generous blood.

Attracted by the blood, sharks draw near. The sharks devour (with a bestiality which is beautiful because it is the salt of the sea and satanic at the same time) the sperm whale whole. They tear to pieces and triturate and then rend, rip, rift the tough hide and the soft flesh of the mammal – and they also have time to devour each other. The scene is possibly one of the most sadistic sequences of all French films – a cinema which not by chance comes from the same society as the sad de Sade.

An exploratory explosion brings to the surface fish by the hundreds. They die a slow, shallow death, in an almost human agony: the mouths with protruding lips, the blind popping eyes, the gills gaping like an unsuturable gash avidly seek a little water to absorb the oxygen.

A daring diver inspects a dead ship, tumbled on the bottom, and the perusal is transformed into the movie equivalent of what *The Sunken Cathedral* is in music, *The Marine Cemetery* in poetry, and 'After the Storm' in fiction.

Two divers towed by a strange, small submarine – evidently escaped from Jules Verne's Nautilus – do the most marvellous sightseeing man has dreamed. They traverse at fantastic speed the depths of the sea: the coral colonies, the abyssal fauna, the marine flora.

An endless parade of coloured fish and of coral formations uncovers for the spectator a new sense of colour: colour without sense. At those depths the dark turns the water black and hardly anything can be seen without the help of lights from outer space.

Regrettably, perhaps, the most beautiful sequence of the film (diverse divers descend to the bottom with their acetylene torches) is seen only momentarily. In spite of this sensual display, *The World of Silence* is a disappointing film: the sea is made of mystery. Cousteau, by revealing it, unveils it – and makes it disappear.

21 April 1957

Black into White

Mau Mau (United Artists) is a medium-length documentary, intended to present the famous African nationalists as a mob of murderers. The film, nevertheless, cannot keep a few truths from escaping through the cracks in the lies. The Mau Mau is not a terrorist sect from mere pleasure in bloodletting and killing (as neither have been the Cypriots or the Algerians), but an organized movement against English imperialism. Actually, it is a party, the African Union of Kenya, declared illegal by the English and reduced to a band of outlaws. Its chiefs – among them the formidable Jomo Kenyatta – are not barbarous natives, but politicians educated in Europe. The living conditions which the Africans are suffering (after all they are the true owners of Africa) are described in the film in a manner more wicked than naïve. The narrator says: 'In these lands there lived the Kikuyus, a tribe decimated by wars and epidemics. The English missionaries were the first to establish themselves in Africa; they brought religion and the colonizers converted that alien land into cultivated fields. Of course, with the tribal wars and epidemics eliminated, the Kikuyus proliferated, but the land did not increase . . . Some went off to the cities, where they yielded to vice and wantonness . . . They viewed with rancour the Asiatic and the prosperous white man [on the screen one sees an English couple, well dressed, which passes by some raggedy blacks lying on the ground], and their discontent was capitalized on by agitators . . .'

The rest of the film tells how the nationalist schools, the nationalist newspapers were closed and the nationalists imprisoned. A passing glance is also given to the birth of the Mau Mau and a disagreeable (and evidently faked) version of the terrorist oath is provided. Later scenes are shown of the perilous life of the English colonists and of the routing with tanks, machine guns and planes of the Mau Mau, currently armed only with machetes and spears. At the end, the necessity of bettering rather than battering of the native is recognized – once the terrorists have been liquidated. The film is no more than an outpost of propaganda (*Simba*, an English movie, and *Something of Value*, an American one, are to come soon) and of the continuation of the war on the African nationalists by other means. This lie will not be contradicted because the Mau Mau does not have parity of arms with the English: since it does not have tanks, machine guns and planes, it cannot make movies like this either.

21 April 1957

Yudoka

Seven Samurai (Shichinin no Samurai, Toho) is that rare thing in the cinema: the work of art in motion. Due to its primitive cruelty, its sporting sense of death and the dynamic energy of life, it is the perfect specimen of the *yudoka* film. One of the *pièces de résistance* of the postwar Japanese cinema, *Seven Samurai* is the costliest movie ever made in Japan – excepting *Teahouse of the August Moon*. Directed by Kurosawa Akira, the man who made *Rashomon*, it won a Silver Lion at the Venice Festival and has earned more money abroad than any other Japanese film, including *Rashomon* and *Gate of Hell*, two differently famous favourites.

The movie produced a small local war at the time of its Japanese release. Accused of committing an outrage against one of the staunchest institutions of the country, the military, and at the same time of breaking with the Shintoist cult of the hero, its foreign version was revised and censored. Originally the film did not end as it does now, with the samurai meekly leaving the village after having exterminated the bandits. In the original version the professional warriors who have remained alive decide to live off the village, taking their turn in exploiting the villagers. The moral is obvious and therefore dangerous. It is not convenient to ask the army for help to resolve the problems of the people. With that ending, the movie was bitter, despairing and true and what is more, an allegory of Japan, where militarism had consolidated the state, only to lead it later to the disaster of the war with the Americans and atomic destruction. To this reading were added others no less plausible. Kurosawa introduced elements of Zen Buddhism, the religion that dedicates one's forces to the achievement of the Good, by transforming the samurai (in Japanese the word means 'those who serve') into servants of a good cause – for a while.

The foreign version betrays the original intent but is more faithful to the nature of the characters, perhaps the most perfect of the film's elements. Each one of the characters is a microcosm, in himself. We find the aged samurai shaving himself like a bonze and serving two rice balls to a kidnapper: it is only a ruse with rice to trick and trap the kidnapper without endangering the child. This samurai is Shimada Kambei (splendidly, surely played by Shimura Takashi, who was the woodcutter in *Rashomon* and one of the noblest faces in world cinema) who enlists the seven samurai needed to defend the village, which at the beginning seemed on the verge of being destroyed and sacked by a horde of bandits.

One of the samurai is peaceable, quiet, good-humoured: he must surely have good digestion but he is the first to die. Another is a perfectionist with the sword, sharpening his skill every moment to kill – and to die. This time at least he dies for a good cause. Another is a young disciple, whom love draws away from a military career. But the most human of them all is the seventh samurai, a peasant who wants to make himself into a samurai and achieves his goal. This Shakespearean character – a mixture of sound and fury, of comedy and tragedy of errors – is the only one of the warriors who has a pathetic character. His stubborn attempt to elevate himself to the soldiers' caste is no more than a bold attempt to erase his miseries. Near the end the spectator learns that he is an orphan picked up from the ruins of war – a gesture that he courageously repeats with a child from the village.

Like every creator, Kurosawa has preferred to hide his critical hara-kiri dagger in the kimono of art – in this case of adventure. The film corresponds to what the Japanese call *sword films*, very similar in format to American Westerns. As such, *Seven Samurai* is one of the most entertaining movies of the year, with its constant action and its clipped rhythm. Here the internal dynamism of the Kabuki theatre is tied to the mobile plastic of cowboy movies. Kurosawa, who acknowledges the great influence of John Ford, has left behind the philosophical pretensions of *Rashomon* (which could be subtitled *In Search of Lost Truth* and which in spite of its medieval ambience was nothing more than the transposition of the Western ideas of Akutagawa Reinosuke, a writer not unlike Kafka) and has adopted a photography as audacious and bold at times as it is weak and imperfect at others. He has achieved a sensual, bright and violent movie, like the engravings from that sixteenth century in which the film takes place – and above all, hardly pretentious at all.

As it stands in its Western version, *Seven Samurai* does not betray its author. Kurosawa, born in 1910 and a former art student, joined Toho Studios as an errand boy, later becoming a screenwriter, assistant director and finally a director. Paradoxically, he achieved his greatest success with a rival company, the powerful Daiei. This studio produced *Rashomon* in 1950. A convinced socialist, Kurosawa's real ideas are contained in the final sentence which the old samurai addresses to the other surviving one, both turning their gaze towards the tombs of the fallen – four samurai, twenty villagers – and once again facing the toiling peasants: 'They have beaten us again. We have not . . . won. It was they who won.'

12 May 1957

Underdogs

Gervaise (Columbia) is an unpleasant film. Since the days of *Jeux Interdits* (*Forbidden Games*) the French cinema had not produced such a repellent, sordid opus. It is no accident that both have been directed by René Clément. But, watch out, it's also excellent.

It is an adaptation of *The Tavern*, by Emile Zola. In France *L'Assommoir* is one of the most popular of the novels by Zola and his first bestseller. It belongs to the series entitled *Rougon-Macquart, Natural and Social History of a Family Under the Second Empire*, and it was published in 1877. Written deliberately in the argot of the Paris *bas-fonds*, the novel is an indictment of alcoholism as well as a painstaking portrait of the lower depths. But in the mechanical world of the naturalist novel, facts follow a fatal sequence and the novel takes on a precise aura of Greek tragedy: from the outset one knows that Gervaise, a poor lame washerwoman, is condemned to catastrophe.

Gervaise has married (that is: she is the common-law wife of) Lantier, a libertine. The marriage does not last and Lantier leaves the street that is all sewer with a native product: a *petite putain*. Gervaise gets married, this time legitimately, to Coupeau, a roofer whom an accident makes first unemployed, then a drunk and finally, little short of a pederast.

Gervaise makes her way from her position as a washerwoman to installing herself briefly in her own laundry: the golden dream of every French worker of making himself into a bourgeois: from being a wage-earner she becomes a boss. She has set up the business with the money of Gouget, an ironmonger who is a good friend of her husband and who turns out to be the only decent person in the whole wide picture. Gouget is a worker conscious of his social position and proud of it. On one occasion he tells Poisson, the policeman friend of the Coupeaus, at a family dinner: 'Be content with what they give us? No sir, we'll take it!' The policeman contains himself 'because it's a dinner among friends'. But he cannot keep the character of Gouget from being revealed as of a noble integrity among so much malice.

Virginie, whom Gervaise had given a thrashing in the laundry, breaks into her domestic happiness – the single most famous scene in all the opulent work of Zola. Virginie is rancour and envy, but she is also *ananké*: she will weave the dragnet to trap the trusting Gervaise. It is she who brings Lantier back to the neighbourhood, who hatches the plot in which Gervaise loses her son and the love of Gouget, 'the only two decent things in my life'. Virginie would not have won if she had not been assisted by Coupeau, whom alcohol has degraded to the point of inviting Lantier to live with him. It is his fault (during one of his frequent drinking bouts he has vomited in the room and on the bed) that Gervaise is forced to sleep with her former lover, destroying for ever her escape routes from misery and greed.

At the end, drink corrodes Coupeau who lands in the asylum, crazed by absinthe, in a scene which is a real nightmare of frenzy, tremors and monstrous visions: the exact horror of delirium tremens.

The movie is made with the formal perfection which has made Clément, barely forty years old, the premier technician of the French cinema. Shot in Eastmancolor and then printed in black and white, it appears to be lighted in the spirit of the famous photographs by Nadar, the French daguerrotypist of the last century. Isolated objects – some badly shod and muddy feet, brutally bustling on the polished parquet of the Louvre Museum – acquire the plastic palpability, the brazen objective pathos of *Shoes with Laces* by Van Gogh. But this pictorial purism endows the film with a coldness, with a certain perfection which is unmistakably academic.

12 May 1957

A Poor Fascist

Difficult Years (Briguglio–Italia Films) is the best film by Luigi Zampa (*To Live in Peace*). Less solid than *City on Trial*, a misunderstood film, *Difficult Years* reflects the ideas of Zampa on life and movies. Unfortunately, poor photography and irregular sound keep the film some distance from the masterpiece it could have been. Based on a novella by Vitaliano Brancati, *The Old Man with Boots*, the movie recounts the unfortunate life of a poor municipal *funzionario*, whom the mayor forces to enrol in the Fascist Party and who is fired by none other than the mayor himself when the war ends, accused of being a fascist!

Piscinello (it means little fish) is *l'uomo qualunque*, the nobody who can be stepped on without leaving too much of a trace. Actually one has here a Chekhov character or better still, a Pirandello little fellow. It is not an accident that the film is set in Sicily, not even politically. It is precisely the south of Italy where fascism still has firm roots: in the Sicilian rocks, in the Neapolitan lava, in the end of the boot. Like every petty bourgeois, Piscinello's life revolves around the hearth. He has a wife – fat, fed on pasta. He has an elder son, his pet. He has a daughter: the type who gives you headaches, vehement, hot-blooded and given to love, without being very particular about her choices. He has, finally, twins, who like all twins are practically more of the same. He has – doesn't it go along with all the rest? – a harvest of sorrows.

It is 1932. In Cuba, Machado is weakening and tottering, but in Italy Mussolini is at his peak. It will not be long before his German disciple, Adolf, who copied his Roman salute, his goosestep, his taste for shirts of concealing colours but who showed a certain independence in his moustache, which he copied from Chaplin, will rise to power. In Rome the *Guardia Vecchia* parades omnipresent, omnipotent, omnibus. The victorious African campaigns are gestating behind the balconic jaws of the Duce. Soon forced volunteers for Spain and for Abyssinia will leave. Meanwhile, in Italy, the good people always oppose the dictators, now as in the times of the Caesars, behind closed doors.* Our anti-hero endures fascism. He finds himself forced to wear the uniform of the

* This does not seem to be totally true. It is known that both in Rome and in the north there was a strong opposition to Mussolini, first, and to the Nazis, later.

Old Guard and his wife – by means which are not very clear, although she may not exactly be a Venus – gets them to certify that her husband was one of the first fascists ever.

Time passes and Piscinello sees how his elder son is marching off to the front too frequently. First his son goes as a *spontaneo* to Abyssinia, then as a *voluntario* to Spain, later as a soldier to France, to Greece and finally to Russia. On his way back home, unscathed from so many missions, he is shot in the back by a German patrol, jealous that for the Italian soldier the war has ended. The *soldato* (played without much zest by Massimo Girotti) is evidently symbolic: this weary soldier, enrolled in bold or brazen adventures and finally betrayed, is every Italian soldier, the Italian people. Mussolini, from one speech to the next – with a voice suspiciously similar to that of Batista – sends oranges to Spain, the land of oranges. When Piscinello asks, they answer him: 'They're a kind that they don't have down there.' Indeed, one of the crates is accidentally broken and the oranges are changed, as if by dint of instant magic, into rifles. Meanwhile, the Italian people, prisoners in magnificent networks of railroads – 'dictators always perpetuate themselves in cement' – suffer privations. Hunger must be appeased with hymns and weariness with interminable parades. Then comes the debacle. Italian soldiers retreat in Spain, retreat in Abyssinia, retreat on the Russian front, retreat in the African desert, cross the Mediterranean on the run and seek refuge in the boot: they have lost the war. By cowardice? No, because Mussolini's war is not Italy's war.

The Americans arrive and the Germans leave. When they asked a French statesman, he gave an answer to which Italy can subscribe: 'Another war? Yes, we will endure it. What we cannot stand is another liberation.' The Americans restore order in Italy, supplanting the fascist chaos. As in the plays by Shakespeare, in which foreign soldiers always come to restore order, order is restored. The order is the old order. That is the same disorder. The mayor, a moron who is, of course, a fascist, continues as mayor. The civil servants will be the same. But there is a positive renovation, an almost decisive one. Piscinello is summoned by the *podestà*, who is now called *sindaco*. (Something has changed though: the titles: the first word was a fascist coinage, the second is democratic: the job is the same: mayor – but the occupation forces hope that under the spell of words things may change.)

In the presence of an American colonel the *sindaco* says to the wretched civilian: 'So you've been a fascist? And also in the *Guardia Vecchia*? Imagine that! You're fired. I'm sorry, but if you had been only a *plain* fascist . . .' Piscinello finds himself on the street without a job and old (the actor Umberto Spadaro reflects the years and the heartbreaks with a moving exactitude), his sons selling his old and hated (because he always hated fascism, for being brutal, blind and grandiloquent: the contrary thing to a common man) uniform. And the film ends on a bitter note. An American soldier, always concerned about having paid the right price and not knowing he's being cheated, a tourist showing underneath his uniform, asks him: '*Due mille lire*. Is that the price?' Piscinello responds fittingly: 'It cost me more than that.' Around him, however, the entire Italian people rejoices in the liberation.

2 June 1957

even
when
cain
exaggerates
he does it on tiptoe:
there are masterworks
of the cinema . . .
in spain

A Spanish Tragedy

Death of a Cyclist (Muerte de un ciclista, Suevia–Solfilm) is not only the best of the movies shown during the Week of Spanish Cinema, but it is the masterwork of the Spanish cinema.

The plot is the story of a passion, told in what Bardem calls 'the Stendhalian manner'. María José is a young lady of the 'best Madrid society'. Which doesn't prevent her from cheating on her husband Miguel, a rich industrialist, with her boyfriend from early youth, Juan, who is now a chairholder at the University, thanks to an old but efficiently pruned plant in Spain, the olive tree of nepotism. Juan and María José see each other in a hotel in the country. One day on the way back, they run over a cyclist. The cyclist is not instantly killed and Juan tries to help him, but María José stops him. Both of them leave and the cyclist dies. Now it is not an accident, but manslaughter.

This death looms over the life of María José and Juan like a sword hanging from a thread: the discovery of the truth is the thread of Ariadne by which the police will unravel the maze. Death unites them and at the same time separates them. They fear everything. They go so far as to plan the death of Rafa, an art critic who has climbed to the highest social circles thanks to his knack for finding the radius, the line that unites the circumference with its centre. Juan commits an injustice with one of his female students and comes to understand that his life, turned upside-down by this death, will only have meaning if he redeems himself by confession. This time not to a priest, but before the law. When María José sees that her world of luxury and pleasure will end abruptly in prison, she decides to eliminate the link between her freedom and her fear: her very lover. Juan dies in the same place where the cyclist died, but María José, drunk with freedom, commits hubris and a little later, destiny, disguised as another cyclist who literally crosses her path, sinks her in catastrophe. She dies.

This film, which looks like a Greek tragedy, is in fact a Spanish tragedy. It is revealed that Juan has been a convinced Falangist at some point in his life. Now, though, he is disgusted with everything. The only thing remaining to him from his illusions is the love of María José, and even that is clandestine.

María José only thinks of herself (and a word often heard in this portrait of Catholic Spain is the most anti-Christian word of all, egoism) and even her love is no more than a mirror in which she contemplates the admiration for her beauty. There is a scene that exactly represents this fine variation on a Pharisee theme. María José, with the meddlesome Rafa silenced by her husband, makes a date with her lover in church. She plans to win back the confidence of her husband without losing her lover. When she remembers the poor dead cyclist, it is to think of alms for the widow. (There is a similar scene in *Calle Mayor*, also by Bardem, in which the revellers, after leaving the whorehouse, comply with the town custom of throwing some coins at the virgin of the atrium, an automatic act of contrition.) While she speaks, inadvertently María José casts her offering in the nearby almoner mechanically, automatically, as if she were throwing coins into a slot machine and instead of the jackpot, she were hoping for divine indulgence. The fact is that Bardem has fully understood what the Marquis de Sade said about charity: it is a spurious means of quieting with money the claims that virtue makes on vice.

Miguel, the third part of this equilateral triangle, is a successful man and his success makes him almost *simpatico*: there is nothing more repulsive than a failure. He is a generous man in his way: he is inclined to forgive María José everything – except scandal. If they gave him a choice of a confederate for the worst crime, it would be silence.

Its characters make *Death of a Cyclist* a disagreeable film. The only sympathetic force is the students. It is only in them that Bardem sees generosity, nobility, courage. In the students and in a worker, a cyclist, who is the bringer of misfortune. Bardem is not mistaken. The scene of the student revolts prefigures the student demonstrations in Barcelona, which, indeed, landed Bardem in prison when he was filming *Calle Mayor*. The cyclist, contrary to the protagonists, does not flee from the sight of the deadly accident which he has caused. In the final shot of the movie, the desperate cyclist is about to flee. But he understands what his duty is. He turns half-way around. Far away he sees a light. He moves away, pedalling towards it, presumably in search of help. That is his lesson, which is also the lesson of Bardem: the workers and the students – the common man and his children – are the living forces of Spain. One will have to address oneself to all of them on the day that the last act of the Spanish tragedy is played out.

16 June 1957

the atheist
cain
(he didn't believe in
his grandfather)
moves towards
metaphysics

The Infinite Being

The Incredible Shrinking Man (Universal), once you get past the first hearty laugh at the thought of an evident joke, the unsanforized man,* produces only nervous laughs. This modest film (it only cost $400,000: a bagatelle . . . for Hollywood) and successful (in the United States it has already made some four million dollars) is one of the most striking movies which the *cronista* has seen. To be exact: the most hair-raising since the release of *Invasion of the Body Snatchers*.

A man, in no way extraordinary, is transformed into a phenomenon of atrocious mien by means of an infernal machine (the A-bomb) and a domestic discovery (DDT). The man has been exposed to an atomic cloud on a day's outing and later is sprayed inadvertently by a fumigator. The radiations invert the vital process and produce a malignant anti-cancer: the man begins to shrink. With this simple chilling plot, Universal has hit upon a transcendent and, in more ways than one, metaphysical theme. The man becomes news and he suffers

* Cain always made fun of advertising slogans. *To sanforize* is a verb invented by a textile maker which meant that its products (pants, in this case) were protected from water shrinkage by a special process.

from that illness whose contagion is so sought after at first and which is shunned with disgust when one suffers from it: notoriety. Later a grave maladjustment to a world which is that of those bigger than he assaults him. Paradoxically an adult is given a dose of his own medicine: those who are smaller don't know what's good for them. Next he becomes a sideshow freak and finds momentary happiness in the love (his wife has stayed behind in the world of normal people) of a midget from an amusement park. Soon, though, he is a dwarf to the dwarf and the man takes refuge in a silly little doll's house that his wife builds for him in the living room. One day his wife goes out and the man is attacked by his cat, which causes him to fall into the dark basement. When she comes back, his wife believes that her husband has been devoured by the cat and she mourns him.

It is here that the ultimate solitude begins and that the man suffers his third metamorphosis: his world is now the pitiless wild world, full of death and violence, of the beasts and the insects. Hollywood, as if in passing, visits a land which monsters of the mind like Kafka and the surrealists have inhabited before. But the ordeal doesn't stop there. The little man struggles for his existence with an insensate courage that would move old man Darwin. A matchbox is his dwelling, a needle a defensive weapon, a match a terrible torch. There are the enemies: the space between two slats of a beer crate is an abyss, a step of the staircase, Everest, a spider, the most colossal and perverse adversary. One day the man finds that the world of the insects is too big for him too: now the metallic mesh that was a prison is an escape route. Grown smaller he finds – at last – the truth. It is this terrible truth (although the whole film is irreproachably realized) which puts *The Incredible Shrinking Man* in an exceptional category. The minute man senses (and can communicate it even to an atheist like the *cronista*) what faith is. What for the common man is the absurd in life and the immensity of the cosmos, is for this uncommon one the infinite microcosm – and he feels equally alone. Then a Cartesian thought comes to save him: 'Yes, smaller than the smallest, I meant something too. *To God, there is no zero.*

23 June 1957

The Black, Heart of Africa

Something of Value (Metro) is a hypocritical film – which, as happens many times in art, does not stop it from being excellent. Based on the novel *Something of Value* (a bestseller by journalist Robert Ruark, called 'a Hemingway diving in a tub of blood'), the movie does not accumulate horrors and lies against the Mau Mau – it does something worse. It tries to reconcile the conqueror and the conquered in a formula of compromise which is not very far from the mendacious ending of *Giant*: the black child will be reared next to the white child and hate will be erased by time. It happens that the lie is a by-product of hypocrisy: the latter will never be the solution to the African problem, while one of the parties maintains the other in shocking servitude. Before explaining this premise, it is good to offer the facts of the problem – in this case the imperialist problem.

In 1888, the IBEA (Imperial British East Africa) Company obtained from the Sultan of Zanzibar what was known as the Protectorate of East Africa and which in 1920 became a Crown Colony. The colonizers – English, of course – were of the same spirit as Sir Cecil Rhodes, 'trusting always in the right of the English race to govern the world'. At present Kenya has four million inhabitants, of which only 35,000 are white. Nevertheless, the whites control the government, the parliament, the courts and all the important posts, whether state ones or not. Thus when a character in the film is amazed and declares: 'What are we supposed to do, pack up and get out because their grandfathers were here first? I was born here too! This is my country . . .', one has to answer him: 'But some are born masters and others are born slaves.' And although the discrimination does not reach the horrid degree of their neighbours the colonists of South Africa ('Africa for the *Africanders*', was the motto of Malan), there is a declaration by H. G. Wells which it is fitting to quote. Wells reveals the dismemberment of Africa with a single sentence: 'In a quarter of a century the partition of Africa was completed.' Describing the East India Company (like the IBEA), he says: '. . . a quasi-independent state – a state, however, with a marked disposition to send wealth westward.' That is to England. And finally he formulates a denunciation of the European activities in Africa: 'No European power has perfectly clean hands,' says Wells, 'in this matter.' Wells, who was very English, really meant: England's hands are like Lady Macbeth's hands: they are stained with blood, blood that no propaganda can wash away.

In this context one must recall the annihilation of the Matabeles by Rhodes, which suggested that in his famous quotation 'evangelization and percentages', he could, at a pinch, have substituted a lethal term for the first word. Miró says, in his *Libro de Sigüenza*: 'Don't you know that there were civilized men, Europeans, true Europeans, who in order to find out the range of their rifles lined up seven blacks in a row and pierced the seven human backs?' These examples could justify, in part, the violence of the Mau Mau, although terrorism may not be the most effective political weapon. But there is more. In the early fifties, the governor of the protectorate of Kenya, the predecessor of Sir Evelyn Baring, declared illegal the African Union Party of Kenya, put its president, Famel Odede, in prison, closed the party's schools and persecuted its members. It was then that the Mau Mau was born. A terrorist organization which took advantage of the habitual discontent and a recent levy on huts (the English always unleash revolutions with levies: remember the Boston Tea Party, 1776) to initiate its war of expulsion and extermination. The *pangas* (native machetes), night assaults and the killing of women, children and old people were the trademark of the Mau Mau, which was not a barbarous and savage organization: in it there were doctors, lawyers, writers and politicians as astute as Jomo Kenyatta.

Of course the organization could not convince the backward indigenous masses by means of dialectics and it took advantage of ancestral fear and the influence of the witch doctors to achieve its ends. But brilliant strategists (among them Dedan Kimathi, whom the book and the movie try to imitate with their Kimani wa Karanja, and the fabled General China) soon emerged and the English had to acknowledge that the Kikuyus knew how to wage guerrilla wars effectively. Finally, the Europeans with tremendously superior resources succeeded in subduing the rebel uprising, although to do this it was necessary to destroy entire villages and resort to mass extermination. Two operations, Operation Anvil and Operation Broom, levelled the black suburb of Nairobi, where they even used bulldozers to knock down the huts of straw, wood and cardboard.

All this Ruark heard from others and he suffered a lamentable confusion – a very American one, for that matter – in that the only thing visible in his book was the violence, the blood and the injustice – just justice as far as Ruark was concerned. The producer, Richard Brooks (*The Blackboard Jungle*), removed from the book its clichéd situations and its stereotyped characters (the white hunter, the evil white man, the good white man, the bad black man, the good black man, the jungle, Africa, love for the land, sex) and put in all that there is in Brooks as a writer, to come up with a reasonable script, still violent, but less dehumanized. The director Brooks went off to Africa, stocked up with good actors from California and England, took the best ones there are in Africa and has come up with an effective, tense but fatally flawed film. Occasionally Brooks the writer writes some trite but true lines ('Kimani's guilty of only one thing, Captain – guilty of having been born black'); he also explains certain things.

The Mau Mau also has its origin in the fact that the English transformed the habitat of the Kikuyu. They converted the blacks into slaves in their own home, and destroyed their old ideals and beliefs. Tradition and the respect that formed the backbone of the family and the Kikuyu clan, strongly centred on the patriarchate and respect for the elders, were ended, making fun of the old people, treating them like dogs in the presence of their children, etc.

But Brooks also entertains: aided by beautiful photography by Russell Harlan, hindered by the monotonic music of Miklos Rosza, helped by the fine supporting performances of Wendy Hiller, Ken Renard (Karanja, the father of Kimani) and Juano Hernández, hindered by Rock Hudson (he has the defect of saying his lines as if he were an actress and not an actor), Sidney Poitier (Actor's Studio darkest Africa) and Dana Wynter (was she mad or was she sane?, did she love her husband or did she detest him?, did the Mau Mau exist for her or was it just a black pigment of her deranged mind?).

Throughout *Something of Value* the impression remains that this is a film in which good and bad people – black or white – dispute over injustices or justices and not, above all, over a system of exploitation of the native by the European. For the final line of the film, the words of an old imperialist, Winston Churchill: 'The problems of East Africa are the problems of the world,' one must substitute another declaration by the Mau Mau leader in the film: 'The whole coloured world burns with the fever of revolt, with the fire for freedom.' This means Africa. But it also means Asia, Oceania and, above all, America.

21 July 1957

cain
dying of laughter,
told me once:
'there are only
three
really
funny faces
in the cinema:
ben turpin's
and harpo's
and totó's'

Cops and Robbers (*Guardie e ladri*, Cofram) is exemplary. Without being a work of wonder of the cinema, it is free from pretensions and it manages to entertain while imparting a simple lesson of coexistence – which goes beyond the simple idea that a simple person may come up with: cops and robbers should appreciate each other, because certainly the same doings, right or wrong, put food on the table for both. That, of course, is not the point. The real *quid* of the matter is expounded by the plot with an impeccable felicity. Sposito is a careless cat burglar: he lets himself be picked up by someone he robbed. Pursued, the thief attempts one of the most absurd getaways in the movies, which still works because his pursuers are as incompetent as he is. Breathless from chasing the burglar, the cop begs him to give himself up: '*Maledetto!*', he was shouting moments before with typical Italian rhetoric. 'Don't you see that you've robbed an American? You jerk, what will they say about us!' When at the end, cop and robber fall, worn out with fatigue, it is the beginning of a beautiful friendship. Which doesn't stop the robber from escaping with a trick in which some handcuffs with a long chain, a bathroom and bellyache are involved: a trio that by grace of grace convert the gross into the graceful.

Now the policeman is the one pursued, since the robbed American thinks that they were in cahoots and reports it to the cop's superiors. So as not to lose his job, the agent called Buttons becomes an Italian copycat of Father Brown. Candour is replaced here by a useless suspiciousness. Agent Buttons tries everything: everlasting vigilance, enveloping friendship, deceitful courtship and he is seen in the impossible role of a sheep in wolf's clothing. In his zeal to apprehend Sposito he sets himself up as the guardian angel of the thief's family, and they believe he is an angelic creature. At the end, as the policeman is not very far from this seraphic portrait, he almost lets the thief go free. But in a gesture of good Chaplinesque slapstick, it is the crook who drags the agent to the commissioner's office so he won't lose his job.

The movie is ably directed by that dubious duo Steno and Monicelli. It was not meant to last long, predestined by its origins: Mario Monicelli was a philosophy professor in a *lizeo* and Steno – real name, Stefano Vanzina – a journalist, writer, and then screenwriter. They also produced *Le Infideli* but the partnership has now definitely been dissolved. The screenplay was written by Pietro Tellini, with a perfectly constructed, richly embellished, wisely balanced script. Nevertheless the success of the film is due to its principal actors, Totó and Aldo

Fabrizi. Everyone knows that Fabrizi is no favourite of the *cronista*, but this time the actor has contained his hippolike histrionics and nourished his acting with a whole wealth of the vernacular. The true *vedette*, though, is Totó, whom *Cine* saw (with not very good eyes one must say) for the first time in *Man, Beast and Virtue*. Totó – real name, Antonio de Curtis-Gagliardi, is a vaudevillian, a nobleman with a proven title, a truly picturesque figure and the leading comedian in Italy – with his famished figure, his prognathous profile and his facial fugue, in which his eyes go one way while his generous nose takes a detour and his jaw is a lantern in search of a Diogenes. Totó has that rare expressiveness that makes him a great actor in a true vernacular vein. He indeed is this bitter, amusing, sad film.

4 August 1957

Obscure Desertions

The Rebels (*Gli sbandati*, Mercurio) is an *opera d'essordio*, a début. Not, in this case, by a beautiful actress or a promising actor, but a director. The film is from top to bottom the work of a single man. That man is named Francesco Maselli. (It would be better to say a boy because Maselli finished this his first movie before becoming twenty-three.)

The movie (which was at first going to be called *The End of the Summer* and which has been filmed almost entirely in the beautiful villa of Toscanini, in Crema) is no more than a negative solution – that is, negative for the character – of the dilemma of Oedipus. When Andrés goes off with his mother on the way to security and wealth and leaves behind Lucía and all that she means of risk and chance, he really abandons love and the human condition.

There is a short detective story by Q. Patrick in which a son, to free himself from his mother-ivy, decides to kill her, spurred on by his ivy-lover. The murder will take place at night on the nearby mountain. Mother, son and lover – the three persons of the verb 'to love' – go up the steep slope. Before the chasm there is a slight moment of confusion. A body falls into the abyss and the moon illuminates the survivors. All the horror of the story is contained in that moment: the son chose to kill his lover: the mother-ivy has won. So it happens in *The Rebels*.

Maselli was making documentaries at the age of sixteen. Then he worked as a screenwriter along with Michelangelo Antonioni – one of his most perceptible influences – and met Zavattini, who persuaded him to help on an episode of *Amore in Città*, a useless neorealist experiment. The episode in question, written by Zavattini, was based on a factual account from police files and was called *The Story of Catherine*. It turned out to be the best in the film. This was enough to convince the producers to back the sad story of the adolescent aristocrat and the fleeing *fanciulla*: a sad story, because essentially *The Rebels* is a love story. To his credit, Maselli, almost made to order by Zavattini, the high priest of *neorealismo*, has understood that if the story of a poor man who loses his bicycle is moving, so is that of the rich boy who abandons the love of his life, his only fortune too. In its way *Gli sbandati* is an implacable film.

The war is a distant memory in the country house in which the countess has sheltered her son and his two friends. Not long ago Badoglio's peace treaty was signed and now Italy is occupied by the Allies and the Germans. The boys are enjoying themselves. Andrés has his collection of jazz records and the pool table in the basement and the occasional outings to the country and to the beach with Isabel. Like him she is an aristocrat who is vacationing away the war. Andrés is undecided: no, cowardly, rather. He fears his mother almost irrationally, he also fears disorder. Coinciding with the sudden departure of his mother, some refugees from the city appear in the region. They are poor people and the haybarn is home enough for them. Among the refugees comes a young woman, in whom misery has erased every trace of youth. She is Lucía.

Andrés and Lucía get to know each other. Although they are the same age, poverty has tempered the character of the woman, who has the hardness, the decisiveness and the courage which the young man lacks. Lucía and Andrés fall in love. Love gives Andrés courage enough to break off with Isabel, who now seems vain and voluble to him.

Not far from the villa, a convoy of Italian soldiers captured by the Germans stops. Some soldiers escape but they are pursued. The prisoners seek refuge in the house. Andrés, persuaded by Lucía and his friend Carlos (one of the few positive persons in the film: the rich boy who throws in his lot with that of the humble and the poor) in an absurd gesture hides the deserters in the country house. Faced with death and desperation, Andrés believes he has grown up. For another thing his cousin Ferruccio (who has that born horror of the crowd which cost more than one noble his life and who is besides an effeminate character) decides to go and warn the Germans, who lose no time in besieging the country house. That night a multitude of things happen in Andrés's life. Lucía is his, he decides to leave with the refugees and join the rebels in the nearby hills, he hits his cousin, the squealer, with an unknown energy, he knows death up close: his life has changed that night. But the day comes and the shadows are defined. With the morning his mother arrives, who in a spectacular rescue – a characteristic one – has brought a German colonel to save her son's life. Andrés now has two paths. At the end of one is Lucía: life and death, love and his own realization. At the end of the other is his mother: the security of the maternal bosom, weakness and infinite abjection. He chooses his mother.

The final sequence of the film is pathetic. Lucía leaves with Carlos and the prisoners, pursued by the Germans. Andrés takes refuge in his mother's car, in which the German colonel and his cousin are riding. In the distance some reports are heard. Andrés, his mouth wide open, only emits some low cries as of a newborn. The prisoners succeed in tricking the Germans, although they leave behind two dead. A German soldier turns one of the bodies over with his boot and discovers that it is a woman: Lucía.

Maselli has visualized his film with hard eyes. His apprenticeship with Antonioni has helped him to offer the intimacy of the characters without the least sentimentality. The portrait of Andrés – an autobiographical character, no doubt – is demolishing and effective: it is the portrait of a cowardly soul. In the background are the other figures, seen in passing, but with clarity and lucidity. From Zavattini he has learnt the knack of creating immediate reality. One single moment – the long agony of a wounded young soldier – has more conviction than many true-to-life films with their vigil of cold sweat, agonized breathing, death rattles and then death. In this wise manner a new talent has emerged – Maselli will belong to the latest generation of Italian film-makers.

18 August 1957

cain
believed in
generosity:
therefore
he was a pedant

Americans in Paris

Funny Face (Paramount) is the most brilliant musical, visually speaking, in the whole history of the musical. But its virtues are graphic rather than cinematographic: all its richness, its originality resides on the surface. Plastically, it is a masterwork. As a musical (as cinema, simply) it ranks very far below not only *An American in Paris* but also *On the Town* or *The Band Wagon*, panned but, to be just, a turkish delight. But, let's face it, *Funny Face* is a marvellous experience.

As in any self-respecting musical, the story is, to steal an adjective from Françoise Sagan, banal. An American photographer from a fashion magazine discovers, in a very Hollywood happenstance, a bookworm Cinderella: a girl of innumerable possibilities as a model practically buried among books: she works in a bookstore in New York's Montparnasse, Greenwich Village. The corny kernel of the story is carrying the beautiful girl to the Greenwich Village of Paris, Montparnasse, and making a model out of her. The solution is love: that panacea of every plot for the movies. The model and the photographer end up loving each other for life and all the difficulties are smoothed out for ever and ever. The lovebirds fade away poetically in a fragile raft on a French rivulet and the audience is left with the tag: 'And they lived happily . . . till the end of time.' In this case till the end of the reel.

The movie begins with a few titles – the credits – which have all the promise of sophistication, good taste and visual sense. On an opaque glass lightly is seen the face, all eyes, of Audrey Hepburn. After her follows a succession of formless forms in which a negative image with another in colour are combined and the titles are put together very much like the way the American fashion magazines – feminine or masculine: *Vogue*, *Harper's Bazaar*, *Esquire* – display their graphic wares. This is not strange because the technical adviser and title designer is Richard Avedon, one of the three best fashion photographers in the world. There's more: it's been said that the hero of the film, the Dick Avery of Fred Astaire, is patterned after Avedon and his amazing ability to convert a woman of flesh and blood into a translucent clothes rack. From the opening credits to the last scene, the whole film is dominated by Avedon and his photographic sense – which is not always as cinematic as one would wish, but which is always beautiful.

Audrey Hepburn (here more a photographable object than an actress which, it seems, will be her definitive destiny, as could be seen from *War and Peace*) lets herself be framed by a changing and fetching Paris. She descends the grandiose staircase of L'Opéra and moments before the photo immobilizes her for ever, the spectator enjoys the fleeting vision of tulles and gauzy silks flowing among multicoloured and stiff uniforms. She pretends to buy some balloons, under an insistent Parisian rain and from the grey death-rattles of the afternoon and the

Prussian blue of her dress, the orange, green, yellow balloons escape against the leaden sky and glow insistently before the dazzled spectator. The model waves goodbye and takes the train and the photographer takes in that goodbye along with the steam of the engine and the melancholy of the desolate, dressy figure on the platform. The girl is at the entrance to the Louvre, hidden behind the gigantic decapitated Niké, and she emerges from between the muddy winged victory and the grand staircase, wrapped in red chiffon, descending the stairs with the air of a feminine victory over art. The model is the true beauty, the other woman, the Greek one with wings, is a ruin: her beauty is that of yearning and desire. Now, to cap it all like the great designers, the girl is dressed as a bride, in the background there is a chapel, among willows and further back, a river. The scene is viewed in a tenuous and diffuse fog, like that of the pictures by Monet the landscape has been idealized and the model is in her perfect frame.

These scenes – not isolated, but set within the context – explain why the successes of *Funny Face* are almost all plastic. The director Stanley Donen has let himself be carried away by the mastery of Avedon and has rendered captivated homage to the art of colour photography, neglecting the art of photography in motion. This after all one must celebrate more than lament: the film is still a perfect example of visual entertainment. Besides, Donen has done the impossible to distance himself from his masters. That is, from Minnelly* and from Kelly.

Donen (come from Broadway as a choreographer, then assistant director for MGM and disciple of Vincente Minnelly, co-director with Gene Kelly of *On the Town* and *Singin' in the Rain*, director of *Seven Brides for Seven Brothers*) was lined up for his masterwork in *Funny Face*. On no other occasion had he been seen so preoccupied with achieving a movie at once living and perfect: a classic. Paramount permitted him any formal experiment, provided that he would let the possibilities of exact colouring of the Vistavision system be seen. He had as a dancer the veteran Fred Astaire, the antipodes of Gene Kelly as far as choreographic conception. (In passing it must be said that Astaire, a favourite of *Cine*'s, this time appears definitively defeated by age.) The pair were completed by Audrey Hepburn, who united her grace and her ability as an actress with the knowledge gathered from her time as a ballet dancer. The movie was filmed at a cost of more than three million and was able to count on the natural settings most resembling a set of Paris: the city of Paris.

* I've never understood the Cainite joke of calling Minnelli Minnelly. Could it be a dig at Vincente?

The story of this Cinderella is also the story of a bunch of Americans in Paris. This is risky, due to a too direct winning antecedent – which Donen does not wish to recall. But Paris has changed after a few years and now it is not painters who have recently come to the Left Bank, nor failed musicians who wander among charming little old ladies and fascinating rhythmic shopgirls. It is rather the most prominent members of a prominent fashion magazine who come to take the city as a background for the promotion of a new model. The model for her part is more intellectual than physical, and she only comes to the City of Light to meet Professor Flostre, 'the apostle of Empathism'. Donen avoids the tender affections of Minnelly and eludes the sporting trepidations of Gene Kelly (a mixture of Nijinsky and Doug Fairbanks), doling out his ample sense of caricature – which does not prevent him on more than one occasion from confusing Astaire by teaching him choreographic elements imported directly from some other earlier movie by his masters. For example, the dance by Astaire under Audrey's window is an unsatisfactory mixture of a parody of *Romeo and Juliet* with the caricaturing pantomimes of O'Connor in *Singin' in the Rain* – in his coarse imitation of a bullfight.

At times, the caricature is on the mark. In the initial scenes one of those fashion magazine directors and the whole recherché American press are satirized, with their occasional phrases in French and their luminous ideas for La Ville Lumière. (One of the pillars of the movie is, without a doubt, Kay Thompson, who arrives to drag off Astaire with her mature vitality, repeating what Jack Buchanan already did in *The Band Wagon*.) In *la pièce de résistance* of the movie, the caricature is almost genial. Audrey Hepburn visits an existentialist cave where everyone is very preoccupied with suffering, feeling indifferent, filled with boredom and ennui: in one word existing. In the background an orchestra so absurd that their most normal music is a bass player who places his bull fiddler horizontally, tries to play jazz and all that he comes up with is concrete music produced by inconcrete means. The den is full of smoke and depravation. Audrey tries to explain her philosophy with movement. All in a movie of pure cinematic creation: the lighting, the music and the dance join to produce something very similar to the final ballet of *An American in Paris* (there, it's been said!) without its pretensions to pictorial reproductions: a new caricature of good taste. But this does not last, because caricature cannot produce (if the librettist will pardon me) *empathy*, but sympathy from those ingenious and so superficial things.

8 September 1957

Welcome, Señor Berlanga

Calabuch (Ideal) is, up to now, the best comedy of the year. But it is also something more: *Calabuch* covers a lot of ground. Beneath its facile exterior full of funny incidents there are complex cross-references of inside information. The Spanish cinema is the lasso in which to catch the conscience of the country. First *Welcome, Mr Marshall!*, then *Death of a Cyclist* and now *Calabuch* (and in a certain smaller way *Calle Mayor*) contribute with raspberries called *trompetillas* – the trumpet reduced to the major modes of humour – of Jericho, a cheery echo to josh the tumbling great wall. One single example of this film is enough. The lovers escape for their honeymoon on a boat. The boat has been christened *Hope* with the crooked calligraphy that the village's Sunday painter has devised. The moment to christen her arrives and, to the strains of the hymn of Falange, the priest gets ready to sprinkle the vessel with holy water. The water falls on the letters and the sign is effaced. Hope has evaporated to heaven with the holy water and to the strains of the anthem of Franco.

The story is the escape of an elderly atomic scientist to the calm Calabuch, a lost village in Spain. The hamlet is actually a fortress occupied by the commoners of yesteryear who nowadays form one big family. There one finds the minutest garrison of the Civil Guard, a priest, a lighthouse keeper, the mayor plus the local smuggler. The only thing the Sergeant of the Guard does is to put a lookout on a prominent rock and to make a few villagers, disguised as centurions for the annual staging of the Passion, do their drill around the rock. The smuggler plays the trumpet in the town band and is a habitual guest in the local jail (whose only cell has a broken lock) so that he comes and goes at will. The lighthouse keeper plays chess by phone with the priest, who cheats. Not only that, when the priest loses he comes to the lighthouse to shout abuse at the keeper. The mayor is a selfish town-dweller whose only concern is the state of his townhouse. All the mischief that is done is done by the smuggler and one of his confederates: none other than the boyfriend of the sergeant's daughter.

When there is a film showing (during one of them there is a jolly joke on the official Spanish newsreel, that small wonder of tedium in dulldrum that is rightly called the *No-Do* to rhyme with the dodo) the smuggler, who doubles as the projectionist, takes advantage of the dark to sneak in his latest loot, which he is keeping in the church. On moonlit nights the sergeant's daughter and her *novio* see each other clearly but clandestinely. Still, the whole town lives a happy and quiet life that seems to be a medieval encystment in our modern world and perhaps is a reflection of another greater cyst: Spanish life.

To this ideal village arrives the sage of the atomic age George A. Hamilton, whom the whole town will soon know by the shorter and more familiar name of Jorge. Hamilton is escaping from the atomic bomb, from the sonic boom and frenzy of a world on the road to destruction to find refuge in the quaint Calabuch, with its faint feuds and its semblance of a formal family of the sixteenth century preserved in the formaldehyde of the *dolce far niente*. Jorge also sleeps in the jail and is taken for a senile sidekick of the smuggler. But little by little the villagers come to love him as the town's own. There he helps cosy Calabuch to win a skyrocket competition. You see, he has not forgotten his expertise as a physicist and builds a marvellous and impossible missile. He lives as one with the tranquil town, until one day his hiding in the cache of Calabuch is discovered and a foreign fleet comes for him. The old man goes off saddened, leaving behind the town (and the spectator) with the taste of a great lost friendship and the rediscovery of the purest humanity.

All this has served Berlanga to construct a series of scenes which, if they give the film an almost episodic character, still bring it close on the one hand to honest English humour and on the other to honourable Italian neorealism, without ceasing to be the most Spanish movie ever seen by human eyes.

Jorge goes to night school and solves a problem of apples and greedy boys by means of complicated equations – to arrive at the same solution as the illiterate moron who by his side solves it on his fingers. Five. In the immoveable feast of the town's patron saint he sees an ambulatory bullfighter – who walks his bull alongside him. And the spectator has the opportunity to enjoy the most hilarious parody of the *fiesta brava* since Cantinflas bloodily caricatured it in *Bloodless and Sandless*. He plays the church organ on the occasion of a wedding and discovers (without giving it too much importance) that the bad sounds of the harmonium are due to the smuggler's American cigarettes hidden in its belly. The adventures of Jorge produce the smiles in this comedy but the villagers offer the laughs (heading the excellent cast, very justly, is Juan Calvo) with their frank (or is it freak?) decisions. The noisiest: nearing the end they decide to defend Jorge's property (which now belongs to the town and not to science) battling with lances and staves and stones and rusty shotguns against . . . a fleet.

It is a pity that technical carelessness and excessive confidence in the raw material prevent Berlanga from obtaining the masterwork to which he is destined and from which he has fallen short by a step: a laughing *paso doble*. Or Spanish twostep.

6 October 1957

cain
always believed
that his father's
problems
were not
the serpent's
fault, but
eve's

On Matrimony

The Bachelor Party (UA) tries to prove that matrimony really is a martyrmony and it manages this so effectively that, at the end, the film, frightened by its own audacity, attempts a happy ending which makes the spectator, this time the actor (because one has here an Aristotelian film) even unhappier. In a free metaphor, the movie extends the love tragedy of Romeo and Juliet to the point of transforming it into a drama of passion: Montague and Capulet are reconciled and Romeo and Juliet get married. They will end up killing each other, but for quite different motives and it will not be a double suicide this time but a mutual murder: matrimony, so the film says, is the tomb of love.

The film begins with a view of Stuyvesant Town, a brick structure in New York composed of several buildings and very similar to a workers' phalanstery. The massive, monotonous construction houses hundreds of people, but it is only two of them who interest us. Charlie and Helen Samson have just answered that odious reveille: the alarm clock. They are a couple like so many others in New York, with nothing to distinguish them except that our attention is fixed on them. Exactly the same as with the amoeba which falls on the slide, its importance is lent it by the microscope. The woman gets up ready to go, but the man remains half-asleep, sitting up in bed in a pose that makes him look a lot like *The Thinker* by Rodin except for two things: he is wearing pyjamas and he is not thinking. He is simply bored in his dopey drowsiness. The woman is now talking on the telephone to her mother and tells her a bit of news enough to make her husband fully wake up: she is pregnant.

The wife is excited at the prospect but the husband isn't. 'He is not excited,' says the author. 'If he feels anything it is unhappiness.' For this couple the unwanted child is a domestic drama. The bundle of joy disappears before the daily agony of an already strained budget and is transformed into the nightmare that lurks behind every dream. The woman doesn't much want to have a child either, but after all is said and done she is a woman: that is, a model for a mother.

'Listen, you don't have to pretend you're excited about the baby coming,' she says to her husband, after telling her mother about it. 'I had some bad days before telling her. I said: "Oh boy, that's all we need, a baby." Then I said to myself: "If I'm having a baby, I'm having a baby and that's all there is to it." I began to like the idea. We're going to have a family, Charlie.' Charlie goes off to work and as soon as he leaves the ghost of the past begins to pursue him. His lost bachelor days appear in the form of a young man who makes a pass at an unknown woman in the subway, in the colleague at work who is late because he spends his life on a perennial spree, in the bachelor party, to which he at first refuses to go and which he later attends, in the blue movie that he watches with his friends, in the escape to an artists' gathering and in his rapid conquest of a pseudo-intellectual partisan. At the end of the day the husband nevertheless knows that he has made a journey to the end of the night.

On the train, disturbed by the proximity of the passenger making a pass at his travelling companion, Charlie and a friend from work, also married, recall their bachelor days. An insignificant joke produces a disproportionate laugh and Kenneth, the friend, ends the story with a phrase that is at once a complaint and a reproach: 'Yeah, it was a lot of fun in those days.' They pass away.

In the office the presence of Eddie, the only bachelor of the group (his other office pal will get married the next Sunday: it is for him that they will throw the bachelor party that gives the film its title), puts the married men in an invidious (or envious) position. Eddie can come to work late, since it doesn't bother him if they fire him and he comes in late because he has spent the night with a striking blonde or with a brawling brunette or with a very hot redhead. 'I get real jealous of Eddie sometimes,' says Walter, the oldest of the group. 'He's as free as a bird. Did you ever see that convertible he's got?'

The real stag party begins when Charlie, in search of his lost time, decides to attend. Dinner starts in that amiable, civilized and ingenuously amusing tone that characterizes gatherings of two or three Americans to drink or eat. There are some jokey gifts and more than one joke as a gift. The party goes on when, on the way to Eddie's house, the group runs into what the author Paddy Chayefsky calls (and he himself declares 'for mysterious personal reasons') the existentialist girl, who guides them to another party in Greenwich Village. No one goes in. The party seen from outside looks like a Roman bacchanal celebrated in a Bona Dea mystery room, but Charlie gets a dubious invitation from the so-called existentialist. From there they go on to the late show of what are called blue movies and which should really be called rabbit punches to love, on account of the sordidness and cruelty with which they disguise an act so simple and pure in nature.

After more alcohol and talking and walking and frolics which seem more like a regression to childhood than the easy, sassy recall of adolescence, the group comes up with an idea that is purely childish in its intention of identifying masculinity with a familiarity with carnal commerce: Arnold, the groom, is compelled to seek the company of a prostitute. But the party is falling apart now. One of the participants goes home to his family, another gets lost in the night. He leaves pursued by his fears of a mortal illness from which he is suffering and whose recent discovery will not let him live in peace. The rest – Charlie, the hero, Eddie, the bachelor, and Arnold the groom – sneak into that party in the Village, to discover that the pretended saturnalia is only a trip to boredom, loneliness and blatant pedantry. At daybreak, Charlie, after dropping Arnold off at home and into the arms of his fiancée, returns home urged on by a violent longing – which is more credible within the psychology of the character than in the real context of daily life.

By the end of the film, nevertheless, Charlie – and the spectator with him: and it is this which the median moviegoer will not forgive the film: that it throws his vices in his face and obliges him to recognize them as his own: on account of this it is doubtful that *The Bachelor Party* will be the success that its importance as a social document and its values as a film deserve – has uncovered one by one the many veils of the human soul in that brief crazy dance that is life. Walter is not wounded unto death, he is actually a walking corpse. His daily worries at work and his too facile humour only serve to hide reality: he is a failure. At forty-five he is only a not at all indispensable bookkeeper in an ordinary firm – failure of his dreams of success through money –; the depressing blue movies still excite him, although he may hide it – failure of sexuality –; his daughter is little less than a juvenile delinquent and his wife a demented nullity – failure of his family life. His whole life is useless, his colophon is *nada*. And at the most depressing moment of the film, that poor man starts to talk about his days of glory, how he was the most brilliant student of his class. 'Everybody thought I was going to be the first Catholic to be President,' he recalls bitterly. 'Where did it all go? Where did it all go?'

Kenneth, the most balanced of the group, sticks to his family, because he fears the return of the season in that private hell when he had no job and got drunk every night. 'It was rough,' he declares, 'and I used to go out every night and get loaded and pick up any girl that would look at me – and I mean *any* . . .' Eddie, the happy bachelor, is really a desolate soul who fears loneliness more than the company of the devil. When the group is breaking up at dawn, he still wants to continue the revel. Someone tells him, Charlie maybe: 'Don't you ever want to go home?' And he answers: 'What do I wanna go home for? I read all the papers.' Arnold, the groom, who started the night with the noble prospects of a nice marriage and a happy honeymoon, has suffered a cruel change. At the end, he is a poor drunk trying to help his ego, condemned to confinement for life, to make its way through the bars of the inhibition that alcohol has filed down. In an intimate moment he belches to confess to Charlie that he doesn't know why he's getting married, that he doesn't love his bride to be, that he doesn't like her, that he hasn't even looked at her very closely. She is a distant cousin, a widow, whom his mother and her parents have dumped on him. Still more: Arnold confesses himself to be a virgin and confesses as well the fear inspired in him by that dour, demanding woman. During the encounter with the prostitute, fear keeps him from speaking and it is Charlie who gets him out of the jam, and takes him away. Now early in the morning he has decided to break the engagement and cancel the wedding: Arnold who started off as a groom satisfied with being born, ends the night a complete ruin: the bachelor party has really been a farewell to celibacy.

To sum up, the casual acquaintances are shown to be as unexpectedly unfortunate as the old friends. The existentialist is just a poor girl who thinks she is an intellectual and is only disloyal competition for the earlier whore: she exchanges love for a counterfeit coin. After starting up a rapid and informative conversation which is actually a monologue, she lets herself be kissed by the recent arrival on one condition. 'Just say you love me,' she begs. 'Just say you love me – you don't have to mean it.' When she sets a date with him is when she reveals her true tragedy, not the fake one that she's been telling up to now. For that no more than a few sentences are needed: 'There's a little bar . . . I'll meet you there in half an hour. Promise me you'll wait, because I can't stand being alone at night.' She is another Eddie.

This daring, conniving and brutally depressing film was written by Paddy Chayefsky (*Marty*, *The Catered Affair*) with a steel-pointed pencil. Or with a grinder for human flesh. The film is daring because rarely has Hollywood risked touching on so many taboos without receiving the curse of the tribe. In *The Bachelor Party* there is poverty and misery; abortion is talked about and it is partially considered; male virginity is declared and prostitution is shown; an obscene film session is attended and is commented on. (Here there is a joke which made the *cronista* laugh, for obvious reasons: at an apparently effective shot, someone in the group says: '[I] think the *Daily News* gave this one four stars.') And homosexuality and its relationship to the intellectual milieu are shown, momentarily. These scandalous sketches are drawn not by a sensation-seeking brush but by a naturalist burin. Rather one would have to say neonaturalist, because Chayefsky does not make the minute description of the ugly side of the human face an end, instead it is a means to prove his thesis. But one speaks of neorealism because without the existence of Italian neorealism this *Bachelor Party* would never have taken place. Furthermore the uncanny ear for the most private and hidden conversations makes all the dialogue seem as if it were a stenographic transcription of daily life.

But there is a point which is lacking: *The Bachelor Party* is a film without poetry. The sole mention of daily toils and tribulations does not have enough poetic charge to sustain a work of art – and *The Bachelor Party* is far from a work of art. If it is masterly, that is because it sums up a whole genre and brings to an end a whole heap of failed attempts and of never-fulfilled intentions, and it has fallen far from a work of art. Chayefsky has forgotten that the first law of film is movement and that before the word, in the cinema at least, was the action. Denunciations, however necessary, do not always find a place in museums.

13 October 1957

The Slippers of the Rose

The Red Shoes (Rank), at its opening, almost cost the *cronista* the friendship of an old classmate. Months after the première the *cronista* – the *cronista* was not then the *cronista* – still hadn't seen the film, because he had against it an old prejudice produced by intellectual snobbery. It was something too popular and by an antithesis of demagoguery the public was always wrong – and by opposing . . . But the day arrived when the film reached the *cronista* who was not a *cronista*. Surprise! Where there should have been catering to the worst vices of the box office, there was honesty. Where there should have been bad taste and prodigality there were the best of tastes and an exemplary economy of means for a magnificent production. Where there should have been boredom and flatness there was lightness and brilliance. Finally, where there should have been that which the snobs call 'arty' and which is to art what the bead is to the pearl, there was the nearest thing to true art that the commercial cinema can produce. The face of the adolescent *cronista* not yet the *cronista* lit up. 'I like it,' he said and decided that it was the best English film he had seen that year, including *Hamlet*, which he always considered a sample of what must not happen to Shakespeare in the cinema and anyway Shakespeare is what must not happen in the cinema. Time passed and other similar films (even the authors of *The Red Shoes* got out the carbon paper and they turned out an impossible copy not a dream) passed by his eyes and he kept considering the concoction of ballet, romance, fantasy melodrama, and *roman à clef* as the pleasantest drink.

Now the past has come back, as Proust would have said. *The Red Shoes* has remained a near-classic. It has been one of the English movies which has made the most money (in New York alone, on its release, it stayed fully booked 108 weeks: a record) and got three votes for the European selection of the ten best films of all time. A director as skilled as King Vidor put it in sixth place in his private selection, the three votes equalled it to *L'Atalante*, *The Cabinet of Dr Caligari*, *Grapes of Wrath*, *Modern Times*, Pudovkin's *Mother*, *Our Daily Bread* and *The End of St Petersburg*. Finally, the *cronista*, on the way to maturity, now thought that when the public prefers one thing with so much persistence it is because there is something tasty there: eternal truths, universal principles or direct appeals, and also that (for something extra) the customer is always right. Besides, there was still its weighty position on the lists.

But the second viewing of the shoes has caught them faded. The red shoes of yesteryear are pink today. *Ecce* cinema. The classics of yesterday are the antiques of today: the successes of the past are the present laughingstock. In the cinema ten years is a life in prison. Nevertheless, with the first impression fraying (due to the fact that Technicolor is a colour system that improves daily and a masterwork rapidly becomes a work in progress) on the screen *The Red Shoes* still have some of their original colour. With this second viewing a decade later and also taking recall into account (someone very wise said one day that criticism was no more than the telling of a first impression) the *cronista* now attempts a commentary.

The Red Shoes begins with an affectionate barb (and that is one of the characteristics of the film: the polished quip, the satire that doesn't do much harm) at the English melomaniacs and ballet buffs. The critique doesn't go deeper than the amiable anecdote with a sting (the balletomane who scorns music to the point of not being able to tell Beethoven's Ninth from the *Circus Polka* but who, when she spots the fabled impresario hidden in his box, almost falls from the gallery), the sentimental tale (the young conservatory student who recognizes in the score by his old teacher, that is being premièred that night, too many bars from a composition of his that he left with the conductor to grade), and the complacent observation (the noble lady who invites the mysterious impresario with a calling card and scrutinizes his reaction with her opera glasses, her back turned to the other spectacle). Later comes the double decker of a young ballerina who loves the ballet more than life, of the young composer who loves life, music and the ballerina in that order but scorns the ballet, and the catalyst of both, the impresario who loves only ballet and hates everything else, including music, the composer and life. But the ballerina becomes the exception to the rule. Love intrudes and Cupid's arrow becomes a dagger in the back of the impresario, to shorten him to an imp. Now the ballerina loves love more than the ballet, and the composer and the impresario drive her to madness and suicide. The film ends with the posthumous homage of the company. Since there is an impresario in the house the homage is truly spectacular: the ballet is danced as if the ghost of the ballerina were wearing the red shoes.

The screenplay is the exacting and firm backbone of the film. Craftily built, in little more than two hours the script relates its simple story with an abundance of details at times and with a precise sense of synthesis when necessary. Life on stage and backstage (and three-fourths of the film happens behind the curtains) is observed with a remarkable exactitude. (For Roger Manvell, the English critic, this is the British film that best portrays the show before the curtain rises.) The relation between music and dance is accentuated so as to eliminate from the spectator the idea (shared at times by the *cronista*) that the ballet is no more than gymnastics with background music fit to tell a fairy tale. The brief biography of the impresario (which though the authors may not wish it has to be lined up with the life of Sergei Diaghilev, the iron-clad taskmaster behind the Ballet Russe and the renaissance of the ballet at the beginning of the century) is told with wit. The one truly objectionable item is the melodramatic ending, which only a need for a jolt to the public can badly explain.

The movie, among its darings, shows what relative time is about. The ascent of the ballerina to the villa on the Riviera in which the impresario stays takes an amount of time drawn out by a long dissolve. The return of the prima ballerina who left the ballet for marriage is told in a flash: the impresario gets his lawyer to induce the ballerina to meet up with him somewhere. The impresario is unusually seen watching a fashion show. A lapdog barks. The impresario turns around to see the owner of the dog coming towards him: the runaway ballerina. 'Ah, my dear Boris, what a pleasant surprise!' she exclaims. Cut to the ballerina now dancing again her great success, *Les Sylphides*. This skit is told in less time than that employed by the first leading ballerina in going up the monumental staircase.

La pièce de résistance, the long central ballet that gives the film its title, is a good example of the linking of ballet to the cinema, not long before the Americans attempted the same thing precisely in *An American in Paris*: the creation of a film language that would render the ballet the same service as did the stage conventions in the past. (Here one should mention the influence, in their turn, of the American musicals and all the sympathy that the film shows for the canons of Hollywood, in their agility, freshness and showmanship.) The ballerina passes from one setting to another, eliminating as she dances the impossible barrier of space and creating a different, unique space: she dances with a newspaper that comes to life until it is transformed into her partner, strolls through desolate places, climbs a cliff and dances next to a thundering sea: it is the applause for her performance. Time has also been licked.

The end of the film, given its mawkishness, is brought off with dramatic severity by Anton Walbrook; in the same way that the ballerina of the film is brought to life by Moira Shearer (herself a ballerina in real life), with maximum choreographic veracity. Both successes are the successes of four: of these two players and of the directors, two of them, Michael Powell and Emeric Pressburger.

Powell and Pressburger (the ones who had the recent fiasco, *Pursuit of the Graf Spee*, and the hit *The Elusive Pimpernel*, the movie that the *cronista* considers the acme of entertainment), the fantasy, fabulous, fantastic duo came up in *The Red Shoes* with a success that perhaps they will never repeat again. They combined too many contrary elements for their repetition to produce the same phenomenon without contradicting the laws of alchemy: Powell and Pressburger obviously do not have the philosopher's stone of movie-making.

10 November 1957

Looking the Blind Goddess in the Eye

Twelve Angry Men (UA) arrives with a certain aftertaste of anti-climax, when several lesser films (among them, *Perfect Strangers*) have appropriated not only its content but also its form. But it is the best of all, *And Justice Was Done* included. Their common antecedent, though, still remains the most effective indictment of the institution of the jury. This is called *Verdict of Twelve*, the novel by the English writer Raymond Postgate. What confers on *Verdict* its supremacy is a materialist honesty in the investigation of the personal motives of each juror, which reaches the wise decision that their conscience is no more than a result of their daily life and not an immanent entity. Thus the book begins with an assertion by Marx: 'It is not the conscience of men that determines their existence, but on the contrary their social existence determines their conscience.' *Twelve Angry Men* does not investigate the life of each member of the jury, it lets their decision spring from the personality of each one.

The foreman of the jury (this does not mean that he is the most capable: usually the first who was selected by lot is chosen as head of a jury if the other jurors are in agreement and if the defence attorney and the prosecutor admit him) is a middle-aged man, with maturity and a sense of organization, but uncultured. He is the football coach in a high school. Juror number two is a small bank clerk with a voice smaller still. Juror number three is emotionally the most complex and it is not by chance that it is he who most wants to send the defendant to the electric chair. Juror number four is the one who never sweats: on the hot summer afternoon the rest of the jury sooner or later suffer from the oppressive heat, but juror number four remains as well-groomed as at first: his high social position does not permit him to sweat. Juror number five is a mechanic who lives in the same grimy slum as the accused. Juror number six is also a humble man: he is a house painter and shows the respect for the elderly and the innate good manners of all artisans. The seventh juror has no other passion than baseball and his only concern is getting to the ball game on time. Juror number eight is the dissident: the man who doubts. He is also an architect. The ninth juror is an old retiree. Juror number ten is the owner of a garage and has a cold. Juror number eleven is a well-educated immigrant, a watchmaker, possibly Jewish. The last juror is an advertising man: in spite of his flashy clothes he is the dullest of the jury members. The spectator will know these men not by their deeds, but by their words: little by little, according to how they stand before the dilemma (and for some of them it is not even a dilemma) of whether the accused is guilty or not.

The movie, before the camera goes into the jury room, lets us see for a moment the face of the accused, by turns impassive and petrified with fear: he is very young and dark-skinned. He is a juvenile delinquent and he is probably Italian or Armenian or Puerto Rican. This fact does not seem very important at first, but later it will be seen to what extent his body has almost been destroyed on account of the colour of his skin.

From this moment on the camera installs itself next to the table around which the twelve men are to argue whether the accused deserves the death penalty or not (there can be no other punishment for him: it will be all or nothing; he has been accused of first-degree murder) and it leaves the room only with the verdict. In reality, the film is a trial by jury. This is not carried out in the courtroom but in the back room of the jury. Here the calm persistence of juror number eight serves as a defence attorney for the prisoner. Only sick rancour, insurmountable prejudices, righteousness and vainglory are his prosecutor.

When on the first vote all condemn the accused, except juror number eight, an extra-legal battle begins between the man who permits himself the luxury of doubt and the rest of the jury, which doesn't stop to think that behind its thumbs-down there are frivolity, flightiness, lack of humanity, racism and even lurking psychosis. Juror number eight doesn't believe that the accused is innocent, but he doubts he's guilty and grants him the benefit of the doubt. The juror with the cold insists on convincing the dissenter: '. . . He's one of those,' he explains and reveals his racism. Juror number three also wants – better, he is anxious – to see the prisoner punished. In the course of the discussion he relates his conflict with a wayward son. At the end, asking that the accused be condemned, he tears up his son's photo and all are convinced that juror number three has transferred the hatred he has for his own son on to the accused. The fourth juror is not prejudiced and is not a sick person, but rather a methodical man who thinks he is slightly superior to all. For him the issue is imparting justice and he sticks with an inhuman logic to the depositions of the witnesses. He is one of the most intractable of the contrary jurors due to his impassiveness. At the end, nevertheless, his judgement is felled, by a fact perhaps too gimmicky, too miraculous, and which is one of the few flaws in the plot. One of the old jurors, the first who supports juror number eight in his demand for acquittal, notices that the woman witness had some marks on her nose, next to her eyes, though she was not wearing glasses. The witness, who claimed to have seen the boy kill his father, had not been able to see the crime clearly and had in fact been awakened by the noise of the murder. Though she had said that she had seen the killing being committed she was really lying when she affirmed that she recognized the killer.

When the trial has ended in absolution, the jurors leave one by one by different routes, in the rainy afternoon, and only the old juror stops to ask the architect his name: justice has seen in spite of being blindfolded.

The film was made in New York by one of the fresh batch of directors who come from television and from Broadway, and there is in it something new and vital that points to the absence of the tutelage of Hollywood. The film shows a cult of true democracy (at times it reaches frank socialism when it makes the workers and the artist the serene and noble men and leaves the villain roles for the bourgeois) and the need for justice without sermons. The sending out of an important message by means of the cinema and the rejection of banality and crass commercialism make *Twelve Angry Men* an adult and brave film; although this may not make it a model movie, with its total dependence on the word and its form cloistered and crammed with static and long-held close-ups that betray its origins in television.

For this jammed session of justice, the movie relies on a dozen excellent actors. It would be better to say almost a dozen, because Lee J. Cobb, with his stock of howls, shrieks and roars, and his vitiated Actor's Studio acting, transforms all his scenes into an analyst's delight. The only thing lacking is to ask for the nearest straitjacket for actors. Cobb, the day before yesterday a good actor, has corrupted himself to the extent of turning himself into one of the worst good actors in Hollywood, only surpassed in this rapid decline by Rod Steiger: his acting makes of his part a case for the prosecution. From the always excellent Henry Fonda to the icy E. G. Marshall (the failed father in *The Bachelor Party*), from Ed Begley's congested racist to Jack Warden's naïve sports fan, all play their roles with a dynamic and a good acting taste which are astonishing. But the prize is won by old Joseph Sweeney. (Perhaps the reader may recall him as the evil brutal butler of *The Man in the Grey Flannel Suit*.) With his vinegary face and his mean mien, Sweeney (as the punctilious and fastidiously honest old man) manages to make his playing a source of sympathy. At the end the spectator leaves convinced that the prisoner owes his acquittal more to Sweeney than to Fonda, even though the latter has been his legitimate defender all the way.

As much as a writer's film (the script is by Reginald Rose, who took it to movies from his own television play), *Twelve Angry Men* is a director's film. The recently arrived Sydney Lumet (this is his first film) has completed an impressive job in which the sure handling of the actors has as much importance as the exactness of the cutting. Lumet, who is the son of a famous Jewish actor, was a stage actor at five, but soon abandoned acting for directing. As he says, 'There is something not very worthy in being an actor. Being an actor is fine when you're a kid, but when you're a man, it is an unseemly trade.' Curious words for a man who knows his way with actors so well.

17 November 1957

Nondescript
manuscript
found in
a bottle . . .

... of milk

I went to see Cain once in his den and we talked dentures. He was not in this time so I had to do with a composite of the latest conversations – that is many monologues. A biographer of my ilk might pay heed but not respect. Cain is lucky I'm dead tired: ruins won't find me moved by impavid rather than avid. I can attest that Cain never wore a figleaf: he didn't even wear briefs and went to bed in the raw as befits a film buff. His lovemaking, albeit incestuous, was sporadic, even rare. You see (a phrase he used to distraction) he was afraid that every woman might turn out to be Mother Eve. Only half in jest he claimed that he hated all Eves, including Christmas Eve. He would rather be profane than profound. Ideas, he said, belong in the deep, where any pearl-hunter might find them. Profane on the other hand could lead you anywhere, even to profanity.

He talked a lot of baroque actors. Of course Welles (whom he always called Arson or Awesome Welles) was the greatest exponent of the mode but not démodé. *So was James Cagney. So was Edward G. Robinson who was for him the greatest actor on the screen. A great stage actor like Laurence Olivier was a classic going for baroque. 'What about actresses?' I dared ask. Bette Davis, he said, was the greatest of them all. But so was Barbara Stanwyck, a baroque pearl. He also loved, strangely, Elsa Lanchester, who got it (got what?) from Charles Laughton, broke and baroque, a real tour de farceur.*

He hated Truman Capote (whom he called Harry Truman Capote) when he asked for a movie to be pruned down. 'You know instantly,' he said, 'it is a literary man who's talking, not a film-maker, least of all a moviegoer. We always want more not less. Otherwise how could anybody explain the remake, the sequel and the series. It is the light fandango – and the crowd keeps asking for more!'

He admired Clark Gable, a linear actor if there ever was one. But apparently he admired Gable as a leading man who wore his dentures well. So did Brian Donlevy, one of his favourite villains. Donlevy wore a double denture in his master scene in The Glass Key, *where he vigorously brushed his teeth in front of a mirror, talked to one of his minions and smiled like a lone shark out of the foam. Of dentures and adventures. I asked him point blank if he wore dentures. 'Yes,' he said, tight-lipped, 'but only when I smile.' I was surprised that he forgot supporting actors like Walter Brennan and Douglas Fowley who played their dentures like a mouth organ. He was too busy smiling.*

Talking about this book, he called his collected dicta When Scopes Collide. *But he didn't want to talk about it. Not now. Instead he insisted on digressing about his love life. It wasn't boring but it simply had no bearing on the reality of the book. He said that love was, 'Either odd or odious if you're a spectator in a platonic cave. In darkest love you always carry a torch but you still cannot see. In love I am what the French call* de trop *but pronounced the trap.'*

He said, 'Let me put it this way', and he put it this way: 'Dining with Claire Voyant I could see clearly what her craving was. "Your appetit, ma petite," *I said, "is* très grand, grosso modo." *Then I noticed that she wore a Jello ribbon around her mouth. Needless to say I sent her packing.* Amour *and swift.'*

Once when I came to visit (with *he always insisted) he protested, 'Beware, the condition of my parlour is parlous.' He looked gaunt, almost emaciated. When I told him, he claimed he went up and down the streets on his elevator shoes. 'It's quite uplifting,' he assured me. 'The best cure for depression, believe me.' He claimed that there was no prohibition without a depression. 'When I tread on forbidden ground, first I'm sorry, then I'm sore and it all becomes sorry wrong member.'*

He still collected (or concocted) extraordinary names for ordinary people. This included busybodies and nobodies and even dead bodies. He went over his roll call with a mouthful of pastiches de menthe. Phileas Fogg did pass par Proust, a name he sometimes pronounced Prowst. Now there was one Robert Rubato, a pianist whose repertoire was all Chopin. Champagne he loved and claimed that in a toast he always shouted 'Proust!' That was his prosit. He called my job Cream and Publish. (He referred of course to this book.) Then in a quantum leap he said that Esther Williams should end her life with a water pistol. He labelled his art Pop! He told me of his visit with ('Let's leave the with without, will you?') Egisto Tango, a Joplinesque pianist. He sat at his piano to tear the score to pieces. He called the result 'Trois pièces en forme de désespoir'. *Then he asked me, 'Satiesfied?'*

His muse (almost his tenth plus temptation) had him, 'head over Cuban heels'. He added, 'I'm incurably traumatic!' Apparently she was sad and sentimental, or so he mused over his muse. 'A tear ductile girl. She always takes tissue of what I say. But I never, ever harmed her. All I'm guilty of is resisting a cardiac arrest.' It was his intention to create a club called Anonymous Anonymous. For unknown women who write love letters and then forget. He didn't really look desperate but he cried out: 'My life is, like my whisky, on the rocks!' Suddenly he became philosophical, or what he called the ballroom couple Philo and Sophie, to compete with Veloz and Yolanda. 'Hindsight is to judgement what nostalgia is to feeling. I'm desperate not disparate. But I'm more willing to make hay than to make sense.'

Sometimes, though, he made sense. Shakespeare apparently described the movies most aptly: 'It's all fortune and men's eyes.' But he came back to love, which for him was closer to murder than hate is. 'Love is just a Sargasso Sea of condoms with all lovers swimming in semen.' He stated that his days, like fingers in winter, were numbed. 'So you do the writing while I go down to buy the morning-after papers.' When he came back he told me that there were by the news-stand three very serious black men waiting for the bus. 'I took a good look at the second grave nigger.' I didn't laugh. He shouted:

'You lack, Jack.'

Then he went on into some sort of foul frenzy of recollections:

'Her tits were as cold as cold cream, her nipples were beauty spots and her cleavage was a soft chasm or rather an abyss in search of a nun.'

'What's this, pulp fiction?'

'No, just a trip. I've arrived at the last station in life, Extreme Junction.'

I kept mum, my lips were sealed and all that chat about secrets in the confessional. He winked.

'You should write all this down for me. After all the Holy Ghost wrote speeches for Jesus.'

But then he went back to base. Aping Victor Mature (one of his favourite stars) in Shanghai Gesture *he said, 'I was born in a bournous.' But the way he pronounced it sounded as if he were born in Borneo, which made him an orang-utan. As he always was in trouble with foreign languages, he wrote it* orang utang, *which means in Malaysian 'man in debt' – an impertinent pertinent description if there ever was one.*

Still in a bournous he told me stories out of The Arabian Knights. *He called them parables. 'There were two princes,' he intoned as in Rimsky-Korsakov's 'She Heard a Sad Story', 'and both were called Oman. One was cruel and vicious, the other saintly and kind. They were known as Good Oman and Bad Oman.' He said that his favourite actress for the role of the princess was Debra K. Dabra. I told him that he probably meant Debra Paget and he said that if he had meant Debra Paget he would have said Debra Paget. End of the story.*

Once I found him shadow-boxing according to the rules of Queensberry. He was then in the middle of one of his many feuds and he claimed to have spent a night among diatribes. He was saved from catastrophe by a mere feline line along which he moved like a cat burglar. His philosophy of life had become very simple by now and he wanted to deal only in ideals. His opponent seemed to be an idealer who played his ideas close to his chest. 'Some of his criticism,' he confided, 'reminds me of the rich man who hacked his two sons to pieces, effectively splitting heirs.' Apparently he shaved every morning with an Occam razor. 'Then there is Wilde and there is Wilder. One is an Oscar, the other wins them.' But he claimed that he always talked tongue in cheek: 'I have a terrible nostalgia in my wisdom tooth.'

On the other hand, when he was happy it was like throwing a party – as he sometimes did. His idea of a romp was to drop chorines into a swimming pool. Or going to a night club where he assured us there were angels waiting in the wings. A million angels could well gather on his springboard to allusions, for he didn't have a swimming pool and therefore no chlorine was handy: it was all sheer make believe with words, his mirrors. Once he lifted his shirtsleeve slightly above the wrist to show off what I thought was a Cartier. 'This is my night watch,' he said. 'It's a 24–carat Rembrandt made in Holland. It not only tells the time but warns you about the weather – which is perfectly useless in the tropics. Regrettably there's no gold watch to perfection.' He believed in perfection.

That's perhaps why he dared rewrite Antony's speech to the populace. It began like this: 'A fine Roman, my friends, is he,' to end: 'This is a fine Roman.' You see, he brought Caesar back alive.

Rondel of requests

The rondel of requests is a litany. Every day I said to Cain: 'Your book isn't finished. I've written the prologue, I've written the notes and yet it isn't finished.' He answered me: 'No, it isn't finished and it won't be finished in 500 or 600 years. The Shvedchikovs come and go, but art always endures.' I couldn't get another word out of him. The most he said was: 'What would Marcel Proofs say about this?'

One borrowed day, apparently bored, he asked me: 'What do you want from me?' I told him the book was lame, a stump, that it was lacking a spine. 'Then, what it needs is an osteopath,' was his answer. But I knew my requests had pierced his hermetic spirit and through the chinks of persuasion the light of doubt was percolating in. At least (or was it at last?), he asked me: 'You think so?' While I nodded, nearly napping, he said to me, 'What can we do?' My answer could not help but be philosophical too: 'Nobody knows.' He looked at me from head to toe, then from toe to head, then from right to left and finally said: 'This is a Huxleyan eye exercise.'

What is it you want, kid?

Our discussions lasted longer than a jamming session at the United Nations. Cain didn't give in, I didn't cave in. As things go so things went. But one had to arrive at an accord: peace is an extension of wartime politics. Finally, one day, Cain faced me down: 'What is it you want, kid?' Almost out of breath (I had run after him all afternoon), I couldn't answer him that day. The next day I told him: 'As we were saying yesterday . . .' and I stood there paralysed: 'What was it we were saying yesterday?' Cain helped me out: 'We were talking about what was lacking on my book. You were saying that it was a Doric column.' 'Doric, no,' I cut him off. 'Dorsal.' 'Fine. Doric, dorsal, who cares? Let's say Doris Day.' 'As you like,' I told him. 'But the book has to be finished.' 'Why finish it? If Schubert had finished his Unfinished Symphony *it wouldn't have been called by that name.' I stood there thinking about those words which if they were not wise, had to be plain stupid. Like Doctor John H. Watson faced with Holmes's power of analysis, I said to myself: 'Must this man do these things?'*

What Dottie wants

A referee with a reefer, Dag Hammarskjöld (he dead), even Petronius Arbiter would have declared a draw. If they're waiting for me, I'll never throw in the towel: vomiting the towel is bad form. Even on someone else's towel. I warned Cain: 'The book is obscure.' 'It's because it's night-time,' he answered me. We turned on the light and saw that the book was still turbid and confused. 'It has to be enkindled,' I said. 'Look, pal,' Cain assured me, 'don't worry about darkness at noon or the dead of night. They used to tell Perelman that the first thing a humorist should do was not to worry whether they understood his jokes or not.' I interrupted him: 'But you're not a humorist.' 'Neither are you,' he retorted: he always retorted, 'and still you spend endless days on that joke about what my book needs most.' 'Yes,' I said, 'because it's true that the book is missing something.' He stopped to think. Then I committed an error that I will not forgive myself for as long as I live – for in death it's unlikely I'll be able to. 'And who said that to Perelman?' Cain looked me straight in the eye, at both eyes:

'Well, I believe it was Dorothy Parker or Dorothy Sayers. Or maybe it was Dorothy Lamour.'

And now – the Duo! Groucho Marx and Engels Bert Humperdinck!

God could rest on a Sunday, but I on Sunday morning, Saturday at night, Monday in the conticinius, Tuesday about the diluculus, Wednesday at vespers, Thursday nel pomeriggio, *Friday, p.m., which is barely the same, Saturday* dans l'après-midi d'un fan, *which also adds up to the same thing, and Sunday death in the afternoon at the bullfights, which is not the same thing, because always at five sharp it occurs to Ignacio Sánchez Mejía to drop dead, and I don't want to see the blood of Saint Ignatius on the sand, much less running towards the beach in a viscous red pool: that is to say and in a simpler way, that every day I had to follow Cain with the same old song: 'Peter Lorre, camelots, bars from Mars, Pepsi-Coke, Orange Leduc, Ave Caesar Morituri Salutaris,' singing along the way, up and down along the aisles at the movies until I found him in his usual seat and asked him again: 'What is truth?', which translated from dem Zen Buddhism means: 'Life is but an empty dream and things are not what they seam.' It was then that we had to go together to the gents, during the intermission, after seeing* Blemished Butterflies, *on a programme that included* The End of St Petersburg *(or* Son of Khan*) and while Cain was betting against Eliphas Levi to see who could piss faster further, I read an inscription on the wall that must have been signed by Kit Marlow:*

> *'Fuck for free.*
> *Have horse, will travel.'*

Dors of perception

Sunday night I was reading in L'Europeo *an article signed by one Nick McIavelly in which he related the wayward adventures of Rod Steiger and Diana Dors in her house in Rome, and which had the same name (the article, not Diana's house) as my epigraph, when I thought I was too much into this movie madness (by day looking for Cain among the shadows, by night writing raves and correcting galleys: as lousy as you can be with the book of Cain) and that my perception was beginning to not be able to distinguish when I was seeing a movie that resembled life and when I was watching life resemble a movie. I decided to read something else, leave Diana in her* putiferio *(which in Italian means mess and not what you, Ramón Navarro, imagine, nor what you thought, Barrymore Brothers and if you insist on watching me with those lascivious eyes, I promise you I'll slice them to bits – and that's exactly why baloney fears the grinder even in Aleppo once . . .) and occupy myself with more serious reading.*

(And so to bad. I had bought two or three capital books or I had spent much capital on two or three books I bought, I don't know which. But among them there were some on physics, on metaphysics, on 'pataphysics – please, an apostrophe before the word, to avoid being made a pun of – with titles that promised the gift of the Spirit and Ebony too.) Manual of the Good Plumber *by Manuel de Falla (a pirated Chilean edition of the same book has a double play on the cover:* Manuel of the Good Plumber *by Manual de Falla);* The Book of Tea *by Jeremy Lipton;* Murder as a Fine Art *by Thomas de Quincey (no relation to the English author: it is, evidently, a mere coincidence);* Some Arnold Schoenberg at 70 mph *by Mercedes Benz;* Illustrated Bilingual Spanish Dictionary, *by Manuel de Falla;* Did Adolf Hitler Die?, *by John Birch;* Is There Any Sex After Life?, *by D. A. Sade;* My Metaphysical Adventures, *by A. M. Zhdanov;* Make an H-bomb in Your Own Backyard, *by Lord Bertrand Russell;* A Lesbian in Lesbos, *by Francis L. Spellman, and – last but not least –* Let Boys Be Boys, *by Oscar Wilde. As sometimes happens, when faced with such a random harvest of titles the prospective reader is overcome with selective paralysis and he ends up like Buridan's ass: hay and water are his double diet.*

Submerged in the deep waters of my doubts I was, thinking what book to take to bed with me, then picking up a quaint and curious volume of forgotten lords, when the phone rang. It didn't take me much time to recognize the tone that was saying, incessantly: 'Hello?, hullo? hallo?' It was not my master's voice but myself. At the other end there was only the silence of Bell. I was about to hang up when I heard the mocking voice of Cain saying 'I called you my friend to ask you a trite, banal and silly question.' 'Go ahead,' I said more weary than wary. 'Why being in general and not nothingness instead?' 'What!' I almost shouted. 'Why is that column necessary?' 'What column?', I asked thinking that Cain had perhaps started to dabble in architecture. 'Which column would it be? The dorsal fin you were talking about.' 'Ah,' I said returning from between faith and terror. 'It's indeed very necessary. The book needs an aesthetic marrow.'

I could hear the silence of the sea and see Vercors on the other shore with a tape recorder, taking down each silent wave, the quiet undertow, the tranquil tides. 'I can't do aesthetics,' Cain said in my ear. 'Leave that to Bazin and Boileau and Buffon. Render unto Little Caesar what is Caesar's and unto Caesar what is God's Little Acre. That rhetorical figure is called materialism, buddy. No, I can't do it. Not now and not in 964 years either, if I lived to call myself Methuselah.' I insisted for a while. 'It's that the book is chaotic and needs vertebrae,' I told him. 'You're not making sense but orthopaedic metaphors,' Cain told me, still on the phone. 'What does it matter if it's chaotic? Look at Ulysses.' I looked at Ulysses: at that moment he was about to be transformed into a swine in Circe's arms. I was about to shout at him: 'That woman is going to give you a roasting!' But Cain interrupted me: 'Not that Ulysses, stupid. I'm talking about Ulysses underlined. The one by Joyce.' I shut my mouth. I was going to shut the door too, when Cain spoke again: 'Now I know you're going to say that I ain't no Joyce. Who's telling you I'm not? This could only be cleared up by Joyce's widow and since she's dead now, there you are and here I am, the man who is a book without a spine.'

I insisted still more. I held fast for forty-eight hours. The black from Cienfuegos, the strongest man on the docks, was in front of me and was gripping my hand. So that lookers-on would not think of a love affair, I tried to wrestle with him. Now I had spent a day and a night wrestling and my arm was forming an angle with his arm while the table was our hypotenuse. This was a triangle, rather. What a solid side the Negro had! Finally, just when I was about to be checkmated, I managed to tickle the Negro with my bishop and I defeated him.

Cain's arm must have gotten worn out from holding up the receiver. He resigned the game and said to me: 'Fine, Philidor. What do I have to say?' 'One moment,' I cut him off, 'one moment, my friend. They're going to say I'm writing the book for you. You have to know what you have to say.' 'Well,' he told me, 'no aesthetics please. When I'm named Aristotle I'll write a poetics. In the meantime I can make my selection of the best movies . . .' 'Great,' I shouted. 'The ten best movies of all time. Now I'm seeing it in neon above the title: The Ten Best Movies of All Time! G. Cain will bring 'em back alive!'

Cain let my imagination fly like a kite and then with the soft razor of his aloofness he cut the thread of my fantasies. 'Lay off, Barnum,' he said. 'They aren't going to be the ten best anythings of all the any things. I'm simply going to choose the movies that I've liked the most or those that have seemed the best to me since I've been seeing movies move. And it won't be ten. Maybe it'll be three or nine or sixty-nine.'

'Perfect!' I said. 'We'll be able to advertise them like this: The best movies that I have seen, *by G. Cain.' 'As you like,' he told me. 'I believe in the almighty Cinema, the rest is advertising. That rest I leave in your hands.' 'Many thanks,' I said to him. 'Listen, Togare,'* he said at last. 'You'll have to come by my house to pick up the list. If I'm not in, I'll leave it in a visible place.' I limped, with the phone in my hand, like Walter Brennan, I pushed my rummy cap over to one side and said to Humphrey Bogart who was at my side: 'OK Boss.'*

The Dead Sea reels

I arrived now at Cain's house at the ungodly hour when I usually visited him: three in the morning (I knew it because someplace they were playing the waltz 'Three in the Morning'). This Darkula of film reviews sleeps mornings and then gets up, goes in the bathroom, leaves the bathroom and goes in the moviehouse: sometimes he forgets to put on his clothes and goes into the moviehouse naked. So the early morning is the only time to pay him a visit. I did. I knocked, like Lot, lots of times and when I was leaving, disappointed, I saw that the door was ajar. I came in and was already about to shout 'Anybody home?', when I saw light in his study. I went in, I saw, I took note. There was the familiar wall full of photos: Marilyn Monroe naked on her calendar, Marilyn Monroe dressed in Some Like It Hot *(that is, almost naked), Marilyn Monroe, like the Venus by Sacher–Masoch, lined in furs (that is, almost dressed) during the shooting of* Bus Stop. *On the south wall, apart but not separate, there was a photo of Hedy Lamarr all milk and ebony not as the brown native who whispered 'I'm Tondelayo' to launch a thousand jeers. Next to it there was a photo of – Lo and Bea Hold, the twins! Also an engraving of William Wilson, who had married Lo's lot. Wilson, or it so transpired, which is not difficult in Havana, was a dubbing actor. Cain claimed that he loved him like a long lost brother. Or so he said. He also loved Lo but apparently he had Bea in his bonnet. These are permutations I never quite understood. Cain was the man with a thousand facets but no diamond he, rather a demon. There was a still from* Underworld, *by Von Sternberg; a photo of Chekhov with his dogs in Yalta, another of Sartre, dedicated: 'To Cain who has proved that hell is the other spectators': JPS; a photo of Ignacio Piñeiro, illustrious singer of* sones, *and another of Luis Buñuel; a photo of Neruda, dedicated as well: 'Let the* cronista *awake!*

* He referred to the famous but obscure tiger tamer from Hungary.

Extravagarily, Pablo Neruda'; and a photo of Ricardo Vigón; photos of several Cuban poets, on account of which I mention none so as not to have to mention them all; an icon of St Barbara, with a sign over it that says: 'To remember me by when it thunders,' a precarious decal of Stendhal who seems more like Uncle Tom, the impassive mandarin of the Chinese charade, a map of the nine places to hide in case of nuclear war; and, in the middle of it all, as if presiding over the chaos, a photo of G. Cain in which one can see that he has just come out from seeing a movie. Desperation succeeds euphoria and stupidity supplants intelligence in a dramatic unveiling, not to say a revelatory trance.

On his worktable there are Aspern's papers and more papers by Cain, old Cahiers du Cinéma, *a dictionary, more papers, newspapers, endpapers, clippings, pencils, the electricity bill (exorbitant), an ashtray, a box of matches with an inscription:* 'The phoenix will be reborn from its cold ashes'; *and dominating this horizontal orb of idiocies with the point of his sporting sword, the decapitated fencer whom I pictured in the* Portrait.

I looked around in that precious garbage dump and found some other curious things (an order of peremptory eviction, a letter that began, 'Dear Mr Cain: I am an avid reader of your reviews and I think they're the best thing I've ever read. I'm three years old and since I was one . . .'; another letter that began similarly: 'I read your reviews every week and they seem to me the best in the world. I'm in a fix too, could you lend me $5?'; a letter in a fatally feminine hand on pink paper: 'Cain dear, last night when you left me I couldn't shut my eyes as the pink bandaids you stuck on my eyelids weren't any good . . .', there followed other revelations of the brutal, beastly sadism of my friend (who once declared, 'Machismo is my gizmo') and I put it away in my pocket to read it at home; there was a bill from the Chinese laundry (in Chinese) that at first I thought was a poem by Ezra Pound and other papers of no importance) but I could not find my Dead Sea reel.

I checked the library not without noting down in my wanderings for a Jew some books, at random: Rhythm, *by Ojino-Knaus;* Jazz, Jazzmen and Their Problems, *by André Hodeir;* Dogma and Ritual of High Magic, *by Eliphas Levi; the complete works of Freud, a huge biography of Freud, other books on Freud by the disciples of Freud, by the daughter of Freud, by the enemies of Freud;* The Prophet Armed *and* The Prophet Unarmed, *by Isaac Deutscher; the complete works of Machiavelli; the complete works of Stendhal, of Shakespeare, of Maupassant, of Chekhov, of Gogol, of Hemingway, of Machado de Assis, of Tolstoy, of Lorca and Larra; and among many other complete works, my complete works; the* Ubu Roi, *of course; a Catholic version of the Bible and a Protestant one; the Selected Novels by Raymond Chandler; and some movie books that I didn't want to jot down; jazz records next to the library and on top of a beaten-up record player, with records by Beny Moré, Fredy, the* Descargas Cubanas, *the* danzón *records of Odilio Urfé (not related to Odilon Redon) and some records of more serious but more boring music: a deluxe edition of the Nine Symphonies by Beethoven, some Schoenberg, Tchaikovsky, Stravinsky, Mahler, Vivaldi, Bach, Manfredini, Albinoni, etc.*

I didn't find my reels there either. Not even a player piano roll. What Orson Welles would call, 'Ah, pianola!' I left.

The manuscript surfaces from the deep

When I was closing the door, I looked down at the frame disappearing into the floor and saw some empty milk bottles. A piece of paper was sticking out of one of the bottles and I thought it was a message to the milkman. Out of sheer curiosity I drew near to read it. It said in big letters Idiot, *in smaller letters,* Dostoevsky*: it was my message to García: Cain was blowing where he wished. It went like this, handwritten in ink:*

Dear Gertrudestein: it is truly lamentable that in one man there are at the same time my Heminge and my Condell. But fine. Those are the risks of being called William Shakespeare in your own time. I leave you my manuscript in a milk bottle so that it will be easier or perhaps harder for you to find it. Also so that the milkman will learn of these dire decisions: I am a democratic writer and I don't believe in secret writings. Also to prevent, in case some important concept slips out of me, your stealing it from me as at other times. It will be impeded by the suspicion that the milkman knows. Thus I will assure myself that you'll be my Lucretius – if one day I become your Epicurus.

The door is open, in case you want to read this note in cool comfort. The air conditioning is on, so are the lights. Enter.

You have insisted that I put my funny vertebrae on the dorsal spine of the book – it will not be my fault if the autobiography of my immodest person that you're completing, suffers a slipped disc one day. You can, then, call the orthopaedist in the house. He already knows. There go those critical bones of content.

During the time when I was the cronista *I often received rare requests. Some of them requested my silence. Others, more just or more in the spirit of a* tricoteuse *simply asked for my head. Often they wanted to know who was the better actor, Marlon Brando or Rin-tin-tin, and if it was true that Signe Hasso always used a wig on the set; and on one occasion a reader, anonymous but equally anxious, asked if Marilyn Monroe was a natural blonde and believed that I surely must know, 'because I suppose you have* those *photos of her'. He didn't say more but he didn't have to. Many asked me for a list of the 'best films of all time'. This is impossible, of course. Or at least, it's imbecile. Now an intelligent person like you (I cannot risk the dishonour of having an idiot for biographer) makes me the same request. I suppose that there is in this a kind of comatose curiosity. I cannot throw on my narrow shoulders a responsibility which when push comes to shove is utterly irresponsible. I would be an Atlas who cheats: the globe on my back is hollow and helium fills it. The only thing I can do on your behalf is to recall the movies that I've seen and then think about those that I've liked the most or about those which had the most importance – for me. And run the risk of forgetting the one that I've liked the most or the one I consider the most important.*

But fine, there's no way out: it's this list or a collection of arty idiocies. Maybe some day, in the holograph of my testament, I'll leave you a collection of reflections and recollections, with just one condition: that you consider them notes for a book that you must promise me never to publish. Something along the lines of the Pensées *of a doubtful Pascal. Blaise can be blessed or full of bliss.*

Now no more hesitations by the sea, by the sea, by the seaside: into the water, hook, line and sinker to deceive some unwary fish. As Hamlet's ghost says, List, o list!

I consider that the cinema (the cinema-for-me, *that is: if not it would be another person who would be setting down these damned considerations) began with the talkies. The rest is pre-history, paintings in a cave, quartz axes. The silent cinema placed emphasis on the image by defect, not by aesthetic calculation, in the same way that the gestures of a conversation behind a window reflect a different image. Both lack sound: that is, total reality. For another thing, I've always felt like I'm in the museum when I see a silent movie. And the cinema is precisely the opposite of museums. I say this not to ask for indulgence but to lay down the cards I used to play close to my chest. Without further ado (about nothing) here's the list. Each title is followed by a line that is meant to be explanatory but also definitive:*

1. Citizen Kane *by Orson Welles: the cinema finds its limiting date: from here on it all will be bw or aw – that is, before Welles or after Welles.*
2. Monsieur Verdoux *by Charles Chaplin: the only truly Marxist film that the cinema has given us and also the bitterest of them all.*
3. Ivan the Terrible *by Sergei M. Eisenstein: the* great *Stalinist film, an epitome of terror and total power.*
4. Monsieur Hulot's Holiday *by Jacques Tati: a treatise on ontology of being-in-order-to-laugh.*
5. Vertigo *by Alfred Hitchcock: the apologia of love, the first surrealist movie.*
6. Les Quatre Cents Coups *by François Truffaut: to the screen by the primrose path to growing-up pains.*
7. Bicycle Thieves *by Vittorio de Sica: the only neorealist sample that permits exegesis: taken allegorically it is not very far from the metaphysics of evil in Melville.*
8. The Diary of a Country Priest *by Robert Bresson: cinema at the service of theological anguish.*
9. El *by Luis Buñuel: a great master pulls Freud's whiskers and shows him all the good that paranoia can do.*
10. Ugetsu *by Mizoguchi Kenji: if there exists that which is called the poetry of images, here is its paragon.*
11. Pather Panchali *by Satyajit Ray: when neorealism arrives in India and is fused with Buddhism: a contemplative film.*
12. L'Avventura *by Michelangelo Antonioni: the memorable moment in which the cinema says to the novel: Move over, sister. I can tell a story too.*

As I believe in movie genres, as I believe in literary genres, I must include a sample of the Western, of the cinema of violence, of the musical, of the comedy: the genres that the cinema took from a certain pulp and pop literature and transformed into art by dint of poetic intuition:

THE WESTERN Rio Bravo *by Howard Hawks (or* Red River *by Howard Hawks; or* My Darling Clementine *by John Ford): Homer would have written the same epics if he had had to make movies.*

CINEMA OF VIOLENCE I Am a Fugitive from a Chain Gang *by Mervyn LeRoy (or* Scarface *by Howard Hawks, or* Public Enemy *by William A. Wellman): social denunciation carried out with a nihilist violence.*

MUSICALS An American in Paris *by Vincente Minnelli (or* Singin' in the Rain *by Stanley Donen and Gene Kelly, or* The Band Wagon *by Vincente Minnelli): the apotheosis of joy and movement: the dance taken as a sportive occasion.*

COMEDY City Lights *by Charles Chaplin (or* Duck Soup *by the Marx Brothers, or* Some Like It Hot *by Billy Wilder): slapstick made classic.*

Some films that do not appear here – I'm referring to A Bout de Souffle *by Jean-Luc Godard, and to* Hiroshima, mon amour, *by Alain Resnais – represent the future possibilities of the cinema and the obtaining of a pure precipitate from the cinema of the past, respectively. But I believe that because of their very originality, they are films more to be studied, analysed, copied than to be seen over and over again.* A Bout de Souffle *is, for its part, the least academic example of an art that by being art now has its established academia.* Hiroshima, mon amour *successfully explores the graphic possibilities, the texture of the screen.*

Well now, buddy-boy, it's over: it is a beautiful two-headed baby. If you guys take good care of him and part his hair down the middle, you'll be able to exhibit it in a circus.

It would not be just, nevertheless, if I did not speak of some silent films that have seemed extraordinary to me, in spite of the noticeable absence of sound. Pre-history must come before history, but it is tethered to her by the umbilical cord of culture.

To my mind there are three great silent films, great because of their enormous influence. They are: The Great Train Robbery *(1903), by Edwin S. Porter, which not only gave us Hollywood* and the Western but also The Birth of a Nation, the movies of William S. Hart (that is, of Thomas H. Ince), the serials of Tom Mix, Buck Jones, Hopalong Cassidy and the Z Series from Monogram, and also the gangster films and the whole American social cinema from Intolerance to The Salt of the Earth;

The Battleship Potemkin (1925), by Sergei M. Eisenstein, which gave rise to the Soviet cinema until The Fall of Berlin, the Nazi documentary with the masterworks of Leni Riefenstahl (after Walter Rüttmann), Olympia and Nuremberg Rally, the so-called engagé cinema with L'Espoir by André Malraux, an antecedent of Roma, Città Aperta and Paisà, the following neorealism of de Sica–Zavattini, and the agrarian, regional cinema of Fernández–Figueroa; and

Un Chien Andalou (1928), by Buñuel–Dalí, a film that makes the marvellous penetrate the cinema and that, by being followed up with L'Age d'Or creates by spontaneous generation all the cinema of Luis Buñuel, influences the technique of the latent shock that Alfred Hitchcock calls suspense and which is the embryonic cell of his cinema, the cinema of Ingmar Bergman, influenced by the surrealist aesthetic of negation, the Rossellini after Stromboli, which is more moving than the earlier Rossellini, and lastly the whole Nouvelle Vague, influenced by surrealism, by poetic nihilism and critical paranoia, by Buñuel, by Hitchcock, by Rossellini and by Bergman as well.

Of these three films perhaps the least original is the one which seems to be the most, The Battleship Potemkin. I confess also that it is the one that most preserves its first impact as a political mural and a historical document. Un Chien Andalou is a deliberate and calculating film, but to the marvellous-real of the cinema it was able to add the marvellous-oneiric and a violent sense of the visual metaphor: this anarchist, nadaist film is one of the indubitable, durable masterworks of the cinema. Porter had no idea of what he was doing when he made The Great Train Robbery. It is possible that in all the history of the cinema there is no film more original and new, even though its elements are taken from the cheap, sensationalist pulp press of the era and from yellow journalism. With The Great Train Robbery, Porter brought to the spectator for the first time, the movies: in a wild state, it is true, but there were all the possibilities realized later in Citizen Kane.

There are some films that still preserve their original beauty or *their primitive grandeur and that in spite of the absence of sound have moved me every time I have seen them. Here is a list of them:*

The Birth of a Nation *(1914–15) by D. W. Griffith*
Intolerance *(1915–16) by D. W. Griffith*
The Immigrant *(1917) by Charles Chaplin*
The Cabinet of Dr Caligari *(1919) by Robert Wiene*
Greed *(1924) by Erich O. von Stroheim*
Entr'acte *(1924) by René Clair*
The Last Laugh *(1924) by F. W. Murnau*
The Gold Rush *(1924) by Charles Chaplin*
Dura Lex *(1926) by Lev V. Kuleshov*
Sunrise *(1927) by F. W. Murnau*
The Passion of Joan of Arc *(1927–8) by Carl Theodor Dreyer*
Arsenal *(1929) by Aleksandr Dovzhenko*
Tabu *(1929–31) by Flaherty–Murnau*

As you see, this list of thirteen, fifteen or sixteen films is so arbitrary that it must be a classic. It is transparent that Chaplin, Murnau and Griffith dominate the entire silent cinema with their talent. If you put the two lists together you will see that Chaplin comes out the winner, to be exalted as the greatest genius of the cinema – if you will permit me this super superlative. After him come Murnau, Eisenstein, Griffith (allowing for the parentheses) Howard Hawks and Vincente Minnelli! Orson Welles could have been represented as well by The Magnificent Ambersons *and* Mr Arkadin, *but it was not to be, alas! Well, here you have your/my lists. Take them to a statistician and obtain whatever averages you like. I can add, to heap confusion on chaos, that there is a film that I like better than any other and which does not appear on the list. Its title is . . .*

If you wish add that it is the film that I've seen the most times and that I would see it again even if my life were to end like that of Oedipus: in blindness, but also in happiness: now I will only have the memory of it.

Nothing else remains for me to say, except to ask: What would Gregory La Cava say about all this?

Always your Alicetoklas,
G. Cain

No, I am not the bible of the cinema

This was the manuscript found by me in a bottle (of milk) at the door of the house of Cain. I release it as I found it. Where some spaced full stops and an asterisk appear, I could read nothing: the milk or perhaps the water in the milk (who can trust his milkman?) has blurred the ink and the name of the film in question was illegible. It seemed to me that it said Kiss Me Deadly *or* Touch of Evil *or maybe* La mesera del café del puerto *by the immortal Juan Orol. But I'm not sure: I couldn't decipher it. Is there among the readers some graphologist, a graphomaniac or maybe a gramophone? Even a druggist would do. While I wait smoking for the revealer of the crabby writings of Cain, I release these critical digests for the Socrates Press. Perhaps some may think that this is an apocryphal gospel, but there will be no Council of Trent for this final codex. Cain has died and his disciples not only denied him, but helped in his crucifixion: the apostles played the sure hand and preferred to be apostates.*

Another thing. It is good to kill all hopes all at once and know that no one will take these topsy torpid digressions as the Holy Bible of the movies.

the love of cain
for todd (michael)
and todd-ao,
for de mille
and for big women
(cain was the first
lover – platonic of
course –
of anita ekberg)
is nothing more
than a proof of
his taste for
the monumental

The Second Time Around

Around the World in Eighty Days (Todd–UA) presents a problem to the *cronista* which is at the same time a problem for the expecting spectator. It is a masterwork, but one doesn't know of exactly what kind. It is not a fantasy nor an adventure movie nor a musical nor a comedy nor a tragedy nor a global documentary nor an action film nor a psychological drama nor a detective thriller, nor a romantic soap opera – and nevertheless it is all those things at once. First and foremost it is a superb travelogue, with the Jules Verne book of the same title as a Baedeker. Here comes the plot. Its extended latitude (from the prime meridian at Greenwich back to Greenwich, passing through the looking glass of the International Date Line) permits it to make a showy catalogue of stars. The mean time becomes generous space.

Fogg of London

The movie begins with some formal notes by the commentator Edward R. Murrow who tries to pinpoint the 'phenomenon that you are about to see' (the Todd-AO process) and the film properly. Murrow chooses as point of departure and counterpoint of arrival an old, charming and masterly film by Georges Méliès, *The Voyage to the Moon*. At the end, with the credits designed by Saul Bass in what might be a summary of the film, the spectator grabs that *Around the World in Eighty Days* is sandwiched between a primitive and delicious *baguette* and a modern and sophisticated white bread that instead of surrounding ham actors and cheesecake they set up for a competition between candid camera and true poetry.

Then there appears the fleeting and powerful sight of a missile with a mission. Finally (and now without any warning) London is seen on any day in 1872. Since it is a day like others, the Baedeker shows a bedecked band as it passes by playing *Rule Britannia!* From an adjacent alley appears a cyclist riding an enormous and primitive bicycle: it is Passepartout, the skeleton key that is to serve the second hero as a passport to life and to adventure. Passepartout is looking for work and finds it in the house of Phileas Fogg, 100 per cent Englishman. Colourless, odourless and punctual, Fogg takes breakfast at eight twenty-four. 'Not at eight-twenty five nor at eight twenty-three.' The water in Fogg's bath must come up to the height of one foot, three and a quarter inches: 'No less, no more.' His toast must be at a temperature of 83 degrees . . . Fahrenheit: 'No more, no less.' Perelman says (it is S. J. Perelman,* all wit and whimsy, who has reduced Verne to verbal slapstick) in his synopsis. 'On arriving at the Reform Club (Fogg), stops and automatically takes out his pocket watch from his fob and looks up. By his expression we know that this gesture confirms the punctuality of Big Ben.'

This boring Briton, who has caused his compatriot the director

* Cain thought at first that Perelman was a Jesuit. He had seen his name on an index – Perelman, S. J.

Michael Anderson to say that he is an 'umbrella that travels', finds himself involved in a wager as a result of his petulant nature. Suddenly he is required to go around the world in . . . eighty days! 'Impossible . . . !' 'Fantastic!' 'Ridiculous!', say his club companions, Trevor Howard, Ronald Squire, Robert Morley and Finlay Currie, of no relation to the actors with the same names. (It is, evidently, a coincidence.) But Fogg is a man who would rather travel than eat and vice versa and he undertakes the long voyage instantly. It is only necessary for him to say to his valet: 'We're leaving for the Continent in ten minutes . . . around the world . . . Now, reassemble your faculties and start packing!'

They leave for France. In Paris they meet up with a coachman very like Fernandel, with a passerby who absurdly resembles Martine Carol (there is something that identifies her as the anti-Martine Carol: she is fully dressed) and a travel agent exactly like Charles Boyer, only aged. The travel agent tells Passepartout about the eleven thousand wonders and about the same amount of virgins bathing in the seven seas. But on getting to the natives of Bali he stops. 'But no, women of Bali cannot be described,' says Boyer's double with a sigh. With a bigger sigh, Passepartout begs: 'Please, try!'

To Fogg's discontent, they learn that an avalanche has obstructed the tunnel that links France with Italy and they cannot go through. Boyer the agent has a solution: he will rent them a coquettish balloon, he owns it, called 'La Coquette'. 'Are you quite sure, sir, this is not just, eh, Gallic braggadocio?' asks Fogg dubiously. 'Monsieur, you are now addressing,' says Boyer, as full of confidence as the balloon is of air – and almost as puffed up, 'the second most celebrated balloonist in Europe.' 'And who is the first?' asks Fogg. Boyer answers: 'He is not available. He was, uh, buried last Tuesday.' Nevertheless, they leave by balloon. Passepartout remembers that he has left the gas on in London. 'No matter,' his employer calms him down, 'it will continue to burn – at your expense.' Later, Passepartout, always the gentleman's gentleman, with a valet step picks snow from an Alpine peak and serves iced champagne to his master.

And the trek goes on – through the seven seas and the five continents with these two minor magellans as a couple of vaudeville comedians. Fogg never despairing nor troubled, much less defeated; Passepartout always ingenious and as able as his label claims and as loyal. The perfect pair of the domestic English ideal: the gentleman and his servant: Holmes and Watson, Pickwick and his valet. This duo is joined by another English institution: a policeman, who suspects that Fogg is the author of the robbery at the Bank of England. Now the trio travels through Africa, Asia and Oceania, and finally the wide screen of the United States and back to London. Where, because of the police, they arrive too late to win the bet. But as always, Passepartout saves the day and the night at the movies: this time helped by the 180th meridian.

Passepartout (Part Two)

On this second viewing of *Around the World in Eighty Days* (the first was reviewed 27 October last), the film wins and loses. The version shown in Havana looks smaller than the one seen in New York, because now the Todd-AO process is seen reduced almost to the proportions of Cinemascope but it keeps its sonorous opulence. It has gained anyway because the distortions of the image are barely noticeable and the sensation of width and depth is still there. The *cronista* believes that the sound has all the disadvantages that music lovers suffer who court high fidelity: by hearing the noises one ceases to hear the music. The endtale with its innumerable figures and caricatures is the best part of this monster film of four hours' projection time that revives the old silent intermission: the credits are a movie in themselves, although one can't deny that they form part of the show.

Some of the excursions that are actually incursions (the appearance of José Greco and his troupe, for example) are seen to be gratuitous. But others, like the cameos of great stars, are shown to be full of humour once the surprise has passed of seeing Peter Lorre as a seaman, Marlene Dietrich showing off her legs for a second, Frank Sinatra turning his back on the audience like a pianist with bad manners and George Raft in his true-to-life role: bouncer in the Vernian equivalent of a gambling casino. On the other hand, the scenes of visual flair (the balloon trip, the train that travels through half of India, the handcart transformed into an inland sailboat to cross the American prairie) keep their initial extraordinary beauty. For another thing, among the farrago of dancers, bullfighters, elephants, balloons, elections, Indian temples, Japanese temples and the ubiquity of Cantinflas (here funnier than before), are noticeable the mockery, the self-caricature to which Anderson subjected the character of Phileas Fogg, 'the walking umbrella'.

'England, Your England'

'Some critic may possibly look back and say one day that Mike Todd's *Around the World in Eighty Days* is one of the best British films the Americans have ever made. When that happens, I'll be the first to shake his hand. For though I may be biased – after all I directed the picture –

I can think of no better propaganda for Britain than *Around the World.*' These words come from Michael Anderson (*The Dam Busters*), the English director of Todd's movie, who has been transformed overnight into one of the leading English directors. Perhaps the best review of the film is provided by Anderson himself, when, speaking of the 'English umbrella that travels', he says that Passepartout represents the joy of living. Asked which one of the characters he liked most, he replied immediately: 'Can there be any doubt? The second, the fantasizing Passepartout.' The character of Cantinflas is the force of America (or of the Latin races) in the face of old Europe. It is well that it be Cantinflas, a Mexican, who has played it, because the Americans are also somewhat sons of these tired Englishmen. The dichotomy of the film appears in that Anderson (or Perelman or Mike Todd or whoever), while he loves Passepartout, has not dared to hate Fogg, really a detestable man.

Todd is God

Whoever has known Michael Todd must be surprised that he has made of this monster film not a monstrous thing but something as graceful as a prancing elephant. He copied the idea of filming the Verne book from Orson Welles, who had already done it on stage, but all the rest is his – the final credits, fine and sophisticated, as well. This confirms the *cronista*'s contention that the cinema is a new art that demands new artists. A musician, a novelist – the novelist more than anyone –, even a painter have to nourish their work on a culture, a tradition, and on intelligence plus talent. A film-maker, no. He can be an intrepid illiterate and achieve a masterwork based on intuition, pluck and what Napoleon knew formed seventy-five per cent of any victorious army: money, money and money.

5 January 1958

The Demagogue

A Face in the Crowd (Warner), as a movie, is some distance from the masterwork; but as an indictment, it is one of the documents for the future historian of the American twentieth century. Even as a testimony, the film tries to bite off more than it can chew. Nevertheless, it manages to get in two or three good bites: the nemesis of the demagogue, television, advertising, American fascism, collective hysteria and, what is more, the cult of the depraved personality.

In the late thirties there was buried, with a naïveté peculiar to the pre-war period, a 'time capsule', in the United States. It was a missile-like tube – prefiguring the ICBM – in which letters, books, bits of films and other documents were sent to an erratic Columbus who might want to find out what the American world was like before the great catastrophe. (The nightmare of the atomic bomb was not even dreamed of.) Among the dour data that were lacking (the suicides from the Depression, the flaming crosses of the KKK, panaceas in pills) one missed especially *Citizen Kane*.

This film was a veiled biography of one of the four facets of the American spirit: the tycoon: the powerful lord, the smiler with a knife under the capitalist cloak, the new baron with a right of first flower over thought, rapist of all virgin ideas, champion of right-wing causes and imperialism. The man who boasted of having started a war in order to have his reporters write about it (precisely the war between Spain and the United States, which continued our own), a tireless worker and the boss of bosses: William Randolph Hearst, *homo americanus*. To his make and likeness all the rest were cut (Morgan, Rockefeller, Mellon) and all wanted to escalate him: he seemed the Everest of success.

Welles, nevertheless, with the pinprick of a movie, had deflated him. The same vigour with which Hearst's standard-bearers protested (Louella Parsons for one) showed that he had hit the bull's-eye: the colossus was a weak man, his shield was the shell of an oyster, a museum armour: inside there was nothing but emptiness. That was the life of the all-powerful man turned to dust and ashes and silence. In the capsule there was another witness to the American Age declared missing: the social climber, the nobody transformed into a dictator of public opinion: I give you Lonesome Rhodes. Reversing Kane he would 'sell' a loneliness that he never suffered.

It is curious that the American popular heroes have turned out to be, each in his own manner, reactionary soldiers. Teddy Roosevelt, first, stayed one step away from tyranny through the sporting sense he had of life. He was a Buffalo Bill of politics and he did not know how – or did not want – to make himself into a dictator: he would have been the first dictator of the American empire, recently erected. But his political certitude was very far from the democratic perspectives that Walt Whitman so naïvely saw in the near future. Huey Long, the boss of Louisiana, was a declared fascist. Only his assassination and one or two political mistakes (or as Kazan says: the absence of a broadcasting medium like TV) interrupted the rise and rise to power of one who would have easily been the Mussolini of New Orleans.

Nearer to us, Senator Joseph McCarthy kept for three years (almost a presidential term) a whole nation half fascinated, half terrified, waiting for that mendacious opportunist to decide who had the right to life, work and freedom and who deserved calumny, prison and scorn. A couple of errors in calculation (a tell-tale whisper given in front of the television camera to one of his beadles, too), the fear of his former associates and his lack of political intelligence plus Providence in the form of a duodenal ulcer, nervous upsets and, lastly, a knee cancer liberated the world from the third threat.

Fortunately the fourth threat is only fiction. Lonesome Rhodes is a singing tramp. He is 'discovered' by a backyard intellectual and overnight is transformed into an American hero – thanks to 'coast to coast' television. He is an ignorant redneck, a libertine and a climber who does his job with the easy nature of the *arriviste*. He displays a tremendous force of conviction that drags the masses to appreciate or repudiate what he orders them to, more than anything because he is primus inter pares. With an all-embracing strength he 'sells' mattresses, a tonic (here the movie seizes the opportunity to poke a demolishing satire at television, which in its race for gain sells trash to an eager audience by convincing them that the worst is the best by dint of repetition. The movie definitely convinces the *cronista* of one of its points: if it is harmful that the scientists have given in to the military as makers of instruments of destruction and death, a thousand times worse is the alliance of the psychologists with the publicity people to search and destroy the free will of human beings – and not only by means of the subliminal ad) which is no more than aspirin and sugar, and a political candidate, who is the 'last of the isolationists'.

That is what the 'conscience' of Rhodes says. She is the pseudo-intellectual lady who discovered him. The response from General Haynesworth, sponsor of the programme with the tonic is: 'Oh, that's what those left-wing New York papers say.' He is referring after all to the *Times*, to the *Herald Tribune* and to the *Post*, as leftist as *Izvestia* can be right. When this 'general' tries to make of Lonesome a force of the majority of the people, he defends his concept of an iron-fisted leader thus: 'But my study of history has convinced me that in every strong and healthy society from the Egyptians on, the mass had to be guided with a strong hand by a responsible élite. Let us not forget, in TV, we have the greatest instrument for mass persuasion in the history of the world . . . But Lonesome Rhodes could be made into an influence – a wielder of opinion – an institution positively sacred to his country, like the Washington Monument . . .' Rhodes succeeds in 'selling' the public his candidate and almost has in his hands a position that seems right out of *1984*: Secretary of National Morality or rather Morals.

Earlier he has married a seventeen-year-old girlie who has won, in Baton Rouge, a baton-twirling contest, 'that American art'. Now he finds out that his wife is cheating on him with his associate and he can't fire him because the man has fifty-one per cent of the stock. Furious he yells at his wife: 'You don't own fifty-one per cent of the stock. You're fired! . . . You'll get your money every week as long as you stay in Arkansas . . .' Suddenly, his world seems to fall apart. His discoverer, more out of spite than conviction, causes the *Lonesome Rhodes Show* to stay on the air when the star believes he's off, and so the public learns of the real scorn that this illiterate demagogue has for them. His friends, his sponsor, the candidate, all desert him and the end catches a lonely Lonesome, totally drunk and at full throttle, giving the speech he had prepared for the occasion. His luxurious duplex is empty but applause is heard. A machine of his own invention is giving him a hand: a contraption capable of producing applause and laughs by just pressing a button.

The fatal last words are said by one of his writers and are a sad farewell and at the same time a diagnosis of his popularity: 'Suppose I tell you exactly what's gonna happen to you. You're gonna be back in television – only it won't be quite the same as it was before. There'll be a reasonable cooling-off period, and then somebody'll say, "Why don't we try him again in an inexpensive format? People's memories aren't too long." And you know, in a way, he'll be right: some of the people'll forget and some of them won't. Oh, you'll have a show. It just won't be quite the same as it was before. Then a couple of *new* fellas'll come along, and pretty soon a lot of your fans'll be flocking around them, and then one day somebody'll ask, "What ever happened to, uh, what's his name? You know, the one was so *big* – the number-one fella a coupla years ago – he was *famous*! How can we forget a name like that? Oh – by the way – have you seen, uh, Barry Mills? I think he's the *greatest* thing since Will Rogers!" '

To sum up, Elia Kazan has made the most honest film of his career. *A Face in the Crowd* signals (or perhaps not?) a point of arrival – or of departure – for Elia Kazan. Now his films belong to him entirely. It is no accident that the hero of the film is not the demagogue but the intellectual. The poor and obscure writer for radio, movie or television (why not newspapers?) is the winner who takes all. Kazan has declared (in a prologue to the published screenplay) that it is the writer who has to save Hollywood and wrench it from the hands of the producers and the businessmen. On account of this one must take the film as an allegory, among other things. Isn't it the writer who wins the heroine at the end? This heroine could be the box office or public and critical recognition.

19 January 1958

is there some
contradiction
between the
end
questions by
cain
and the epigraph
by connolly?

Yesterday Revisited

The Naked City and *Brute Force* are two old winners from Universal. (The difference between these two strong, virile movies and the saccharine, sterile products that Universal Pictures now makes, could explain why this company, one of the greats of Hollywood, now finds itself on the brink of bankruptcy and has announced that it will not produce any movies this year.) Both are directed by Jules Dassin (the director of *Rififi*, an American of Armenian origin: so none of that Frenchified 'Da-san') and produced by the late Mark Hellinger. (If he hadn't died soon after, this fifth columnist–producer would have turned out to be a Marx Hellinger for the Committee on Un-American Activities, since Dassin left the United States under duress and *The Naked City* has a story and script by Albert Maltz, one of the 'Hollywood Ten' who was imprisoned as a communist along with nine other American writers, directors and producers who refused to declare their political affiliation before the House Committee.) So that the programme is not so badly put together. Even more so when one knows that it was not the programme for an informed film club, but was put together by a commercial brain for a second-rate theatre. The appearance of these two films over the weekend allowed the *cronista* to visit the yesterday (that's still alive) of the movies. Both movies belong to a vanishing Hollywood.

The Naked City was considered a masterwork on its release. The *cronista*, who was not the *cronista* then, also thought it was. This new viewing of the wan wonder shows how in the movies the glories of yesteryear pass by at a speed greater than 24 frames per second. *The Naked City*, seen now, has thrilling moments and a sure hand that follows the skilled script step by step. But its most important sequence (the pursuit of the killer through the approaches of the Williamsburg Bridge and on the old bridge itself) is found to be absolutely gratuitous. The reality it shows off becomes nothing more than a simple backdrop – and not a very original backdrop at that. Already earlier American movies, like *Boomerang* and *The House on 92nd Street*, used the open air in preference to the studio.

The plot is a mere police ploy, with the dependence on melodrama that this subject has. The real drama of the policeman and the criminal is yet to be made, without the crude and dangerous glorification of one or the other: something like the Italian *Cops and Robbers* sanely attempted. The subplots that are later shown to be essential pieces in the criminal puzzle lead well to the deadly climax: the discovery of the killer. But this is not enough: any American B-movie has those ingredients in a similar dosage. The photography that earlier was revealed as revolutionary is limited to successfully balancing the interior scenes in the studio with the exterior shots on the street: something that any Hollywood cameraman does with his eyes closed, something that *even* Chaplin knows how to do. The director could not dispose of the excessive narration by Mark Hellinger, which has only nostalgic value: a dead man who speaks from the grave. The brief sketches among the crowd, which the trick dubbing does not match in order to make them appear true to life, are simply abominable in their pretended spontaneity. Dassin moved the actors as they always move them in a police movie, like marionettes. Yesterday's much-commented-on appearance by Barry Fitzgerald is no more than his customary grumble-murmur-whistle-intra-external monologue in brogue: an unbearable derivation from the magic realism of the Abbey Players. Ergo: a masterwork which is considerably less than masterly.

Brute Force seemed a disproportionate, hysterical and false film – compared with another Hellinger movie made almost immediately before, *The Killers*. Today it maintains many of its qualities and gains some unsuspected ones. First, here Dassin did not try to play at realism, rather he made a totally symbolic work. A little belated, it is true: all its prisonhouse atmosphere was no more than a prefiguration – if one can use this word with a posterior sense – of Nazism, of fascism, or whatever it may be called in any country that may suffer from this pseudo-philosophy of brutal force and terror.

The weak warden is no more than the reactionary who cedes the helm to fascism faced with the fear that the boys – that is: the people – will stop behaving themselves, only because parole, the pardon – which they are owed or they have asked for – has been arbitrarily denied them by the powers that be. Then the 'hard' methods – and this criminal euphemism must be banished one day from the earth since by it nothing more is meant than savage, cold-blooded, inhuman punishment – that the chief guard administered on his own authority, without the warden's finding out, of course (as he is shut up in his complaint-proof office), become the policy of the prison. That is: of the nation. Naturally this is not a straight allegory like *1984*, but the same unreal setting, the prison building whose very architecture is evil, the isolation from the outer world – what is it: an island? – the loneliness of the inmates, the divisions that work imposes on them, reinforce, by their very evident absurdity, the sensation that they are symbolic.

The bits of plot that link the men to the outside and that at first seemed a mere gimmick to let in the women – Yvonne de Carlo, Ella Raines and Ann Blyth – in a movie with an all-male cast, appear now so unreal that their interpolation must not be taken in any other sense than that of sweetening the bitterness of a tragic fable. The tardy symbolism can also be understood as a certain premonition of a McCarthy: that grand inquisitor who interrogates with beatings and mental tortures. Might it not be an earlier image of McCarthy? Even his homosexual connotations tie him in. (Here one must make a pertinent parenthesis. Every time Hollywood wants to indicate that a character is a sexual pervert, it makes him listen to 'classical' music. Now it's Wagner, with his erotic waves flooding the torture scene. In *Tea and Sympathy* it was revealed that the true pederast of the picture was the professor and that he had recognized his deviation because he was seen listening to – Chopin?, Schumann? – desolate and alone in his house.)

And in the second place, this is a stupendous action film. Burt Lancaster – it was his second or third appearance – has never been better, with his dynamic despair. The rest of the cast was superior, even in the smallest roles – it is a real pleasure to see Jay C. Flippen in an ordinary cop role. And the climax has a glorious *Götterdämmerung* which is – why not say it? – Wagnerian. In short, one must withdraw all the bad feelings there were against *Brute Force*: today it is for the *cronista* the best film of Jules Dassin – if it is agreed that the career of Dassin really matters.

Is the reader saddened by these masterworks that are demoted in less than ten years? Don't be, please. Such is the cinema. Besides, consider the spiritual aspect: if one has lost a daughter, one has gained a son.

The Naked City is not as good as it seemed, *Brute Force* is much better than it ever seemed. But a disquieting question remains: What of a new viewing of both, tomorrow?

2 February 1958

the love of cain
for africa,
for asia,
for america
always seemed
to me like
his need
for a return
to paradise

Concocted Continent

Lost Continent (Ideal) is: one, a film false from titles to credits, two, a dandy documentary. How is that apparent dichotomy to be explained, if in fact the documentary is the exact contrary of the invented? In two ways, too: pointing out the falsehoods and showing its authentic beauty.

Falsehoods

The movie invents a continent called *The Happy Isles* and on a voyage that starts in Hong Kong to cross the South China Sea in a southerly direction and then goes south-east by south-west, easterly, and finally aims for the north-east, on a visit to Borneo, the Sunda Islands, Java, Malaysia (Singapore), Bangkok, to visit Thailand. This *tournée* is not told in its true sequence, because the documentary on the *dayaks* in Borneo, for example, appears only at the end of the movie. The narrator describes the voyage as crammed with hazards and dangers, when in reality the expedition of Count Bonzi (main maker of the film, which has four other directors) has followed frequented and familiar tourist routes.

The path of the 'explorers' is followed on an antique of a map of the archipelago of the East Indies (to use a term as obsolete as the map) and describes the inhabitants as 'Malays', indiscriminately, although the spectator may think that he isn't straying far from Indonesia. The inhabitants of the Buddhist Siam, the Muslim Java and the Hindu Bali are mixed in an *olla podrida* of diverse religions, presented in this filmic carte as a single one: Buddhism. Buddhism has ceased to be the most important religion in this part of the world (the target as well of Christian missionaries, both Catholic and Protestant) since . . . the thirteenth century!

A procession of villagers goes to throw live animals and viands into a volcano to placate its fury. Even if one knows that Buddhism strictly prohibits all killing (applied not only to men and higher animals, but also to a creature as deadly as the cobra).

The volcanoes contain temples dug in the lava where colossal statues of Buddha are adored. The volcano is in the Tengger region (East Java) and it may be the case that there are statues in the caves surrounding it, but chance has it that this corner of the world is furiously Islamic and was nothing less than the last redoubt of an old pre-Islamic religion, the cult of Shiva in the Mataram empire. For another thing, Islam prohibits the adoration of images.

The film affirms that bull races make up part of a ritual dedicated to the rice harvest. In the past, cattle ran in the flooded rice paddies of Bali, but the race had more to do with ploughing the earth than with gathering the harvest, and the animals that ran were not bulls but – oxen! Actually, the bull runs were set up by the Bonzi expedition in Madura, where rice doesn't grow and the 'natives crazed by the inebriating *amok*' are in reality tame shepherds, more preoccupied with the right breed of their flocks than with the 'frenzy of the full moon'.

The young dancers who perform in front of the Balinese temples are not priestesses, nor do their dances have anything to do (one more time) with the rice harvest. The dances make up part and art of the religious ceremonies of Bali, but the dances of the film are secular and quite different from those dedicated to the gods and, of course, impossible to photograph. As much so as the consecration ceremony of a maiden, which though realistically staged, is still staged.

The ceremony in celebration of the dead (in which the 'natives' show such delight in leading the coffin, rather than the funeral cortège of a poor fisherman of the village, seems the joyous burial of a little local dictator, dead, but not from natural causes) is utterly falsified and is nothing more than the repetition of an old Balinese dance called *Keyak*, which uses the art of pantomime to recount a Ramayana theme (intended for tourist consumption today, when it has been rechristened the *Dance of the Monkey*), without the least connection with fishermen, living or dead.*

* Facts taken from *Sight and Sound*.

These 'liberties' with reality would not be pointed out so fully by the *cronista*, if the film did not have the pretensions it has. Apart from constantly praising the courage, the skill and the luck of the expeditionaries venturing into a savage land, cruel and full of untold (here told) dangers, the movie declares pompously that 'for the first time a group of film-makers has triumphed in the task of penetrating so deeply into the life of communities so remotely strange, that they can show the European (sic) spectators what it is to live as a member of a culture where work and play, prayers and sacrifices, births, procreation and death form part of a tight unity.' This, clearly, is a lie. Why didn't this obsolete 'South Seas' movie mention that in that very place, almost at the time that the documentary was being filmed, the important Conference of Bandung was being held? Why hasn't a photo, a word by the unfortunate narrator been dedicated to praising the tremendous work of these peoples, who with no other native weapon than courage, with no tools other than their hands, have rescued Asia from a sleep of centuries and are trying to put it on a par with the Western world? Why hasn't the titanic task, aided by Unesco, of the Malay, resolving the vast problems of health, education and agriculture, been mentioned? Why not declare that these 'forgotten' towns have been deeply engaged in enormous projects for irrigation, for scientific investigation, for engineering, for combating endemic disease, and in satisfying their thirst for culture? Did not President Sukarno of Indonesia unleash, soon after the 'documentary' was finished, in these same lands 'of legend and enchantment' a necessary war of liberation from Dutch imperialism?

Count Bonzi went to look for some ideal East Indies, possibly read about in the novels of his compatriot Emilio Salgari (who by the way boasted of never having known any other world than the four walls of his Italian study), and when he didn't find it, he invented it. It is also important to call attention to the falsity of this film because the surviving members of the Bonzi Expedition are now shooting a similar documentary in the Caribbean. As is perhaps known, Cuba is in the Caribbean.

Authentic beauty

With Bonzi went Enrico Gras, one of the most scrupulous and careful makers of 'art cinema' (*film d'art*) in the world. Perhaps the partial successes of this 'documentary' are due to him.

The phrase *Tanah air kita* is the motto, the philosophy of life, of the old Malays: 'Our land is the water'. They are the 'farmers of the sea'.

They live a landless, liquid life among the stagnant waters of the rice paddies, the sweet illusion of the rivers, the unconquered sea. The camera accompanies them on fishing trips which, though staged, yet have a primitive, transparent beauty, like a Chinese watercolour. A feet and fist fight in which the arms and the legs have equal value, without losing the rhythm, the elegance of true boxing, possesses a sporting, kinetic beauty. The volcanoes roar forth lava and fire, and out of the smoke and the ash rises a terrible, beautiful image, like the voyages of Dante to the inferno. Dante also was Italian and his sense of pure plastic poetry did not come by chance from the land of painting: nor did this film's plastic sense happen by chance.

The voyage to the country of the *dayaks*, though invented, is still thrilling and shows us the women who felled Gauguin, with their fragile Asiatic build and their brutal Polynesian features. (Fortunately the spectator will see these scenes without the censorship that affected them in other countries.) From the paddies and on the wind comes the noise of rattles, firecrackers, maracas (at times, too many times, smothered by the Westernized and insufferable score), and the Balinese dancers dance their millennial dance, delicate, filled with subtle suggestions, and the spectator knows in an instant that he has in front of him an old and supremely wise people. The Balinese, Javanese and *dayak* damsels dance, kneel before a temple, bathe in a pleasant river and show a kind of eternal beauty, primitive and sophisticated at the same time. In short: here is the daily life, created from an immortal earth, of some men less mortal than the rivers, the beaches, the mountains, the infinite savannahs of rice, the trembling palms; here are the numerous terraces where the rice is sown, the ingenious systems of irrigation, the indefatigable work of man shoulder to shoulder with the beasts and the indomitable need to live, to endure all calamities, which made Orwell guess, much before English political reason understood it, that Asia was – a curious thing – for the Asians.

16 February 1958

the phrase
'not as many
years as he
(cain
is referring
to cooper)
needs,'

is a vile
phrase

Liebe

Love in the Afternoon (United Artists). The spectator should rejoice at the return of the sophisticated comedy (which had disappeared from the cinema), its tender intimism, its decadent elegance, its adorable uselessness, all frightened away by the booming of stereo and the horizontal vertigo of panoramic screens. The sentimental comedy was a gift that Vienna gave to the cinema, as appreciable as the waltz. One of its grand masters was Ernst Lubitsch, who transplanted it to Hollywood and fertilized it with his talent and sprinkled it with the grace and the bonhomie of a Continental – a gentle man, not a breakfast. Two of his greatest successes were *Bluebeard's Eighth Wife* and *Ninotchka*. The screenwriter for both films was named Billy Wilder. Soon afterward Wilder became a colleague of Lubitsch without ceasing to be his disciple. Today Wilder could be Lubitsch's teacher, if it hadn't occurred to Lubitsch to die years ago. Billy Wilder is the director of *Love in the Afternoon*.

Based on a novel by the Frenchman Claude Ault of 1924, *Ariane*, which had already been brought to the screen by the German Paul Czinner, in 1931, with the forgotten Elisabeth Bergner in the central part, *Love in the Afternoon* has strayed more from the French original (although the film is shot in Paris and Paris is its setting) than from the German accent of the translation by Czinner – fortunately, or paradoxically, this time the German accent does not have the Teutonic hardness, but rather the almost Mediterranean softness of Austria. What has caused an old cynic to make this movie in which cynicism dressed in wolf's clothes is conquered by candour disguised as worldliness? One of the dichotomies of Wilder (*The Spirit of St Louis* must be considered as a compromise) is how from the brutality and the sadism of *Ace in the Hole* he is able to turn to the sophistication of *Sabrina* and at times to join both tendencies of his ambivalent character in movies like *Sunset Boulevard*.

Samuel (alias Billy) Wilder was born in Vienna in 1906. He was a journalist, law student and professional dancer before exerting himself to write stories for the cinema. He began in Berlin with Robert Siodmak in 1929. When the Nazi storm began to blow, Wilder, with very good judgement, emigrated to France first and the United States later. His experience as a screenwriter got him work, or so he claimed, although,

'When I arrived I only knew one word of English: Film.' So he wrote. He got his first opportunity as a director on *Ball of Fire*,* in which Gary Cooper, no less, was the half-bumbling, half-romantic hero.

To comprehend the manner that Wilder has of seeing the cinema, it is a good idea to listen to his comments – cynical and romantic at the same time – on *Love in the Afternoon*: 'It is my homage to Lubitsch.' But he adds: 'The mode of the film is established by an exterior aspect, the set. For the room of the virginal and innocent Ariane, the art director copied a picture from a famous *maison de rendezvous* before the war.' For those who don't know what it means one must translate that particular *maison de rendezvous*. In English it means, plain and simple: cathouse. 'It becomes her very well,' concludes Wilder, 'because as we know, life is one thing and art another.'

The story is told with a pensiveness that recalls the deliberately retarded restrained movement of some elegant women or, better still, the slow grace of the peacock. Photographed in a low key, tenuous, as if life were being seen through a gauze (a good trick by Wilder, which while it sets the intimate, impressionist and lightly muffled tone of the story, takes years away from Gary Cooper, although not as many as he needs, and confers on la Hepburn, on her wan and only elegance, an enchanting fragility) or with the eyes of a nearsighted romantic looking at the world through a glass of champagne, the film is directed by Wilder with an exemplary astuteness. A good example of this, which is a bad example, is in the gag of the four gypsy musicians who accompany Cooper on all his amorous sallies. There is also the conspiratorial intimacy of the Ritz, the humid seclusion of a Turkish bath, the drunkenness of the mortified lover (in which a drinks trolley travels between the musicians and Cooper with a squeaky noise full of shamelessness: the inanimate go-between), an excursion along the Seine, and every *single* moment that the millionaire needs that old recourse of bad movies and bad lovers: background music.

Love in the Afternoon is set on an equipoise of perfect acting. Gary Cooper, as the roué Don Juan who refuses to age, is not as good as this dean of the American comedy and, without doubt, one of the true creators of the Hollywood School of Acting, can be: but his craft is enough. Audrey Hepburn does her best acting since the spectators learned to love her in *Roman Holiday*: svelte, delicate, warm and graceful she is the exact image of what the film wants to be: the fading romance of the bittersweet love of a dirty old man and an immature

* What a howler!

young girl. Maurice Chevalier is surprisingly good: the man who for once in his life left off being a clown to be an actor in *Silence is Golden* is at it again. As for John McGiver, the fourth leg of the equipoise (as the cuckolded husband), his constant cold in the head, his vigilant somnolence and his bewildered air of a *con* are so perfect that the *cronista* can do nothing less than think that this is something more than a character in search of an actor.

In Paris everyone does it. Single girls, couples, lost lovers, servants, dogs . . . even generals – and we see two generals kissing each other on the cheek, in Swann's way. M. Chavasse, a private detective, spies down on a suite in the Ritz Hotel from the height of the Vendôme column. There, on the distant balcony, a woman in veils and a tall man are also doing it.

The detective runs to his house, to French comfort (the French didn't invent the bourgeoisie for *nothing*) and to his daughter, Ariane, who has a superficial interest in the cello and some profound jealousy of the profession of her father: she would like to be surrounded by all the crimes (of passion, of course) that Papa has filed away in his dresser. In a little while the cuckolded husband appears, calling adenoidally for the desired information on his doubly desired wife. She is cheating on him. The man decides to kill the lover and marches off to the Ritz.

But the daughter has heard everything and departs to warn off that Galahad of love for whom each female mouth is his Holy Grail. She does so, and when the deceived husband charges into the room of Flannagan, the American Casanova, he (the husband) is doubly deceived: his wife is not there, Ariane now occupies her place. 'Sorry, Mr Flannagan,' says the husband, 'but that'll be all for tonight . . . Kindly disconnect yourself from my wife.' 'I beg your pardon . . .' says the aloof Flannagan. 'Do we know each other?' And the cuckolded husband says: 'Only by proxy . . .' The husband sees that the one who is now connected to Flannagan is not his wife, so he searches everywhere for her. Under the bed too, naturally. Flannagan seeing this asks him: 'While you're looking, if you happen to find my left slipper . . .' When the husband definitely finds out that his wife is not deceiving him (what he doesn't know is that there is a vast conspiracy to deceive him: everyone is doing it), he excuses himself: 'I'm terribly sorry to cause you all this trouble. My wife is . . . very beautiful. Matter of fact, I think she's one of the most beautiful women in the world . . . I do wish you could meet her.' Flannagan, biting his lip, says, very courteously: 'Well, maybe some other time.'

When the husband leaves, Flannagan asks Ariane the reasons that led her to save his life. 'Why? Oh, it's simple, really! I – I'm against violence. In my opinion, there's too much shooting in the world – and not enough love.' 'How's that again?' 'I mean if people loved each other more, they'd shoot each other less.' Then Flannagan remembers that he is an American and decides to reduce it all to militant proportions: 'Are you a – a religious fanatic, or – ?' While they are chatting Flannagan talks the girl into seeing him again: 'We'll have lots of champagne and lots of gypsies when you come here to dinner tomorrow evening.' 'When I come to dinner? That's out of the question . . . I really must go.' 'Eight o'clock?' 'Impossible.' 'Nine o'clock?' 'No – that's much too late.' 'Five o'clock. *Four* o'clock?' Ariane, finally: 'In the afternoon? When do you work?'

Thus begins one of the most graceful and sunny and at the same time moving screen romances in recent years. Ariane really falls in love with Flannagan, who goes away and almost forgets about her. When they meet again, she decides to make herself a woman of the world and since she knows her father's files by heart, she invents for herself a thrilling, unique and depraved life: the veritable vapid vamp. Marriages with social climbers, divorces, escapes to the Alps with alpine climbers, encounters in Stockholm with old flames, and money and furs and jewels: all embroidered in a tall tale that only Flannagan fails to notice is pure invention: he has begun to fall in love.

One day, all steamed up, he meets up with the deceived husband in a Turkish bath. The old cuckold is now a happy man and he jots down for the former roué a formula for happiness: 'You need *help*! and I know just the man who can help you . . .' and gives him a card to see the 'very best man in Paris . . . Believe me, monsieur, I am putting you into very good hands.' Has the spectator guessed who yet? Ariane's father, who takes no time in realizing the truth when he matches the deliciously tall tales that Flannagan tells him, describing the lies of his beloved, with the cases of deception that he has in his files. The father – what else could he do? – tells him the truth. 'Give her a chance, monsieur. She's so helpless. Such a *little* fish. Throw her back in the water.'

Flannagan, like a good man (the cynical bias of the film keeps one from seeing if he really goes away to do a good deed or to avoid the evil of marriage), goes away to leave the city. But he and Ariane meet for the last time at the station. The scene is like a burlesque of all the dramatic moments of the movies and the romantic novel. The spectator almost thinks he's seeing Anna Karenina deciding between life and death, or Clelia of *The Friends*, in a similar spot, less tragic and therefore that much more dramatic. But Wilder is a cynic and he doesn't believe in the tragedy of love either: Flannagan literally carries the light, amorous Ariane off with him.

The happy ending has been a *cause célèbre* of reproach for *Love in the Afternoon* (in addition, badly understood and quite mistreated), but it is the *raison d'être* of the movie, after all is said and done a comedy: all's well that ends well. Isn't this the essence of the comedy, the momentary happiness of the spectators by means of the eternal happiness of the characters?

23 February 1958

the new wave
drags
cain
in its
wake

Eve 58

And God Created Woman (Columbia) could be the masterwork of the erotic cinema, but it is obvious that the intention of Roger Vadim* goes beyond pornography. The title of the movie is lightly ironic rather than pretentious. But it attacks the fact, until now thought to be a natural mandate, that the woman has come to be for the man little less than a painful appendage and one worthy only to appear as always rupturing: a complement capable not only of calling attention but also of occasioning pain. Although her participation in the paradise plot always pictures her as perilously desirable: sin is actually the bonus of temptation.

Brigitte is Juliet, Héloïse, Eve: woman as always. Or to say it with an ambiguous phrase: the eternal feminine. Now the eternal is disturbed by the times: it is 1958. Eve is an orphan girl, taken in by a married couple, who seem more like a bachelor and a spinster associated in a mute partnership. She is independent – in a sense that more than one hypocrite classifies as unhuman – and therefore amoral: morality is no

* Roger Vadim is the director of the film and, at the time when he filmed it, was also the husband of Brigitte Bardot. It is something more than a happenstance that la Bardot is lively and kissing in the middle of marrying Jean-Louis Trintignant, her companion in the cast, and that Vadim has had a son with another woman before divorcing Brigitte. Trintignant was godfather for this new marriage and Brigitte Bardot was godmother to the child. While Vadim has promised to baptize the future son of Bardot–Trintignant.

more than a necessity of the gregarious man: the law of the group. She sunbathes naked by the side of the highway because she has no notion of her body. She works selling newspapers and goes to the job barefoot, because she lives on a beach. Her needs are limited, her only unusual wish is to possess a big car and not because of a need of ownership but because she loves speed. But she is not happy.

In this caricature of earthly paradise (the movie is filmed in one of the most beautiful spots in the Mediterranean, St Tropez, on the French Riviera) which is a wasteland for her, she seeks her complement, love, Adam. Juliette believes that she has him but she does not have him: Adam is more interested in money. She makes a loveless marriage with his brother but makes him happy (generosity, thy name is woman), although it may well cost her own happiness. Everyone opposes the wedding: actually they envy this free and kind girl. At the wedding she leaves the guests – who have come to eat – at the big table and goes to her room to help her husband who was hurt in a fight he was shy of. She takes her time. When she comes down after carrying a piece of cake up to him, his mother asks how her son is. Juliette's answer: 'Not bad.'

The days of love succeed the nights of love and the beach becomes Eden. But the brother returns. The family comes into money, thanks to a mad millionaire – film millionaires are always mad and the spectator gets the notion that they must have made their money by osmosis. He buys their old dry dock from them to modernize it. Actually it is a labour of love by proxy from the brother: the millionaire has only one boat in mind to dock in his shipyard: the svelte sloop Juliette. But she cannot resist her old flame and gives herself to the brother. When her husband, who had left on a trip, returns to meet this little cosy *liaison* he decides to kill his wife. She offers no resistance: rather she seems to be courting suicide by taking a really toxic step – dancing a cross between *mucho* mambo and a cha-cha-chá. The millionaire intervenes. A cardboard Cupid, he takes the shot and gives a lesson in turn: 'Fool,' he says to the husband, 'can't you see that she loves you?' The husband had not seen a thing and there is no need to reproach him for it: the signs that his wife chose to let him know that she loved him are obscure, difficult and generally lead in another direction. The film ends with the eternal happiness of the couple.

The movie will encounter some moral opposition. And if the Legion of Decency had not killed mosquitoes with an elephant gun when they put on the show about *The Woman Who Invented Love*, now it would have target enough. Brigitte takes her clothes off through half the movie and spends the other half getting dressed: she is naked to the full length of the Cinemascope screen and in colour. Never did the warm hues of Eastmancolor seem so sensually justified: she wears tight pullovers *sans brassières*, she jumps in the water with only a thin dress on, she goes outside with intimate underwear on, rejecting the most intimate ones, she dances semi-nude, she wraps herself in a sheet and not content with this, she also wraps her husband in an erotic pupa.

Moreover, Vadim puts in her pouting lips lines full of *doubles entendres* with a one-track mindedness. She walks barefoot along the highway, her bicycle beside her and asks a passing bus to take her on. She explains: 'I have a flat.' The driver replies: 'You don't look like it.' A man asks her to dance, she stands him up for another guy, he reproaches her: 'You've left me rooted.' She says: 'I'll come back to water you.' A woman comes to view this monster girl to decide on the possibilities of confining her sensuality to the walls of a reformatory, sees her and admonishes her for her naughty nature: 'You should go see a doctor,' implying that she must get a certificate of virginity. She responds: 'I didn't know love was an illness,' and looking closely at the spinster sphinx: 'But don't worry: you're vaccinated.'

Without alluding to Wilde on ethics and aesthetics (in art the immoral or the moral does not exist: there only exist the beautiful or the ugly, the bad work of art and the good work of art) one must declare from the outset that *And God Created Woman* is a moral film. Vadim has tried to paraphrase modern life in plain terms. His heroine only has one religion: love. As in children, she is all love and love is in all. She rejects money, the only thing that really prostitutes. Clothes bother her as much as conventional behaviour and her desire is to find a partner, without having to lose herself in the meanderings of hypocrisy and luxury. When she marries, she thanks her husband (he has kept them from sending her to the lay cloisters of a reformatory) in the only way she knows: giving him love. Her only sin is to have been born too late, something suffered by another form of French philosophy: surrealism.

To appear on the scene in the century of the brain, science and the conquest of the universe, with primitive and naturalist philosophies, wanting to return to nature, to simplicity and to love, is an anachronism, a retarded form of romanticism. In reality, Lawrence (another advocate of the return to nature) did not really understand the time he had been born in – which is his fault – and tried to evade it, seeking out primitive societies, wanting to install a naturist colony in the heart of Europe and of the United States: to graft the earthly paradise, a gathering stage, onto the threshold of cybernetics: in other words, a counter-revolution. It is on account of this that Orwell conceives the men and woman of

1984 as asexual or rather unsexed: sex now has a function which is as much related to feelings as nourishment by pills is to the sense of taste. The value of Lawrence, of the surrealists and of Vadim is in undermining the remnants of the old world with the primitive tugs of another, vanishing world.

To compare *And God Created Woman* with other French films which externally resemble it: *Adorable Creatures*, *Rage in the Body* or with the recent *Liana*, in which pornography reaches the point of obscenity (and it was quite deliberately put on a circuit that evaded the most important first-run houses), is not to understand that underneath the smooth skin of Brigitte Bardot, beyond her beautiful breasts, in the almost palpable sensuality of her body, there is a message. In a certain sense, *And God Created Woman* is a film as ascetic and pure as *The Diary of a Country Priest* was concerning the way of catechism. With this movie Roger Vadim is placed among the most promising young European directors.

It matters little that formally the film has faults, that the direction is unsteady and that the story and the script abound in more clichés and bad writing than is desirable. Perfections in this sense are offered by Hollywood every day and they haven't saved it from crisis. It is evident that Vadim has something to say and says it. At times the *cronista* even thinks that the babblings are Brigitte Bardot's and not Vadim's and that this is more a Bardot movie than a Vadim film. When she cannot dramatically resolve a situation and the director makes her leave the frame to save her, when her sensual face can project no more than sensuality and what is needed is drama, when loneliness can only be communicated by pictorially isolating her is when one perceives how much to the measure of Brigitte Bardot – of her talent and of the shortcomings of her talent – the film is made. Because what *Rebel without a Cause* meant for the James Dean myth (and one knows to what extent James Dean was a reflection of the myth rather than the myth itself) *And God Created Woman* will definitely be for the Bardot myth. More than the myth itself Brigitte Bardot is nothing but the mask of the myth. For the true rebels with a cause of this amorality in search of an ethic one must look in the audience.

2 March 1958

What's Rotten Smells Sweet

I love this dirty town!

J. J. Hunsecker in the film

Sweet Smell of Success (UA) is an unpleasant movie. True it is at times. But the taste left by this otherwise excellent film is not of the whole truth told, but of the stirred-up manure that finally comes to rest. Then the sweet smell of decomposition stays floating in the air.

It is all about success and its protagonist refers to it as: 'the most heady of perfumes . . . For it, let's toast . . .' The title in Spanish (*La mentira maldita* – the damning lie) has taken away its light ironic touch, leaving everything in danger of what the film threatens to become by the end: a domestic melodrama. The deadly race in search of success, like mad greyhounds after a golden, elusive, uncertain, all stops pulled, inconstant, fickle hare, in whose attainment Browning said that one could chalk up years of failure, is the theme of the movie: the struggle for success – 'that rare paint that always covers all ugliness'.

It is the story of a stray dog, a mongrel who knows that the bone of success will confer all the blue ribbons upon him. He has an Italian surname and many of the mannerisms of the New York Jews. For example he says 'stoopid' instead of 'styupid' and he repeats it: so that there be no original doubt. On one occasion a policeman speaks to him first in Italian and then in Spanish, as if to keep him from forgetting his native *barrio*. He is ready to do anything to become the leader of the pack and the fact that the film piles up shovelfuls of mud on his shiny and well-groomed Ivy-League suit in the mere space of two nights – or is it three? – doesn't make it any less believable. Sidney Falco stoops to rise. He is one of the dirty righthand men through whom a burdened and slimy columnist of Broadway and of off-Broadway shows operates. He uses him at autopsies, to scrutinize the stains of garbage from the grimy alleys, to root around in fetid entrails: for everything dirty: he is his second gravedigger. In addition he is a pop culture vulture and his will be the spoils, carrion is his meat.

The columnist – the other – is a personage, possibly a 'self-made man', his column, a fifth column. He makes and unmakes names. One mention by him is equal to an Oscar, his silence, to death. This megalomaniac who feels the whole city at his feet of clay is taken from several real models. One could mention Walter Winchell (whose famous WW the film repeats with JJ), Westbrook Pegler, Drew Pearson. From Winchell, the most exacting model, he gets his taste for archaic neologisms, and he boasts of his invented jargon, from Pegler, his hasty reactionary stance and his fake patriotism, from Pearson, his famed connections with the big politicos. But JJ is an Achilles' heel: he loves his sister too much. And the film uncovers one of the most incestuous situations that Hollywood has concocted since Paul Muni squeezed one of the squalid arms of Ann Dvorak in *Scarface* – with brotherly love.

The sister has fallen in love with the lead guitar of a little jazz combo and JJ wants to destroy this relationship at any cost. Sidney will be the sweet thing with which he will trap the pride of the suitor. A rotten smear is invented (Sidney, with an anonymous tip, declares the jazzman a dope addict and a communist to boot) and the boyfriend is destroyed. The smear is effective and it is good that the film places it right in the centre, because it struggles with two perverse myths, very feared in the United States: communism and vice. Communism as bird of prey in intellectual circles, vice as atmosphere in the closed world of jazz. Fortunately the musician is the most decent character in the story and his lines are truly democratic. Thus from his mouth it sounds like an accurate accusation when he hurls at the journalist: 'To – to you, you're some kind of a – of a national glory. But to me and a lot of people, your slimy scandal and your phony patriotics, to me, Mr Hunsecker, you're a national disgrace.'

The story doesn't pause for long to explain how this disgrace got to be national and the ending, as luck would have it, doesn't leave him beaten but rather temporarily sidetracked – and on a strictly private level. Almost the whole film focuses on the little machinations and great treacheries of the malign Falco to get up the steep ladder of success. It is he who lies, steals, flatters, corrupts, creeps and crawls to try to get ahead. He drags himself before JJ to beg from him a newsworthy notice about a client, he prostitutes a cigarette girl to suborn a columnist, he plays a chaperone Celestina and brother Iago rolled into one for his boss's sister, he plants a packet of marijuana in the young musician's pocket, so the police will beat him up and throw him in jail but finally his character serves to lend a certain air of morality screenplay to the story. The moral can be nothing other than the old French proverb: 'Nothing succeeds like success.' It is odd that it was first said by Dumas.

The film is written, in equal parts, it must be supposed, by Ernest Lehman (author of the novella on which the story is based) and Clifford Odets (a playwright among whose plays is *The Big Knife*). The plot shows a profound knowledge of the New York milieu (never has the city shown up as so ambivalent, nocturnal and dangerous as here, and photographer James Wong Howe should get almost all the credit for it: his photography is all atmosphere) and the dialogues are sprinkled with the jive talk that has its time and space between Broadway, Seventh Avenue and 42nd to 52nd Streets from eleven at night to five in the morning: the impregnable fort of limelight: Times Square. Odets, nevertheless, has arranged things to give it all a light touch somewhere between grandiloquent and playful, tragic but grotesque, that in its best moments recalls Shakespeare and still more his play of usurpation: *Macbeth*. The corrupt policeman who approaches sin with insouciance is, in the eyes and mouth of Falco, a 'crass friend'. He listens to the cigarette girl 'avidly, avidly', and when he advises JJ's sister on how not to commit suicide ('start thinking with your head instead of your hips . . . that body of yours deserves a better fate than tumbling off some terrace') one almost hears one of those corrupt courtiers that Shakespeare places just before some crucial exit.

Unfortunately, the authors have not been able to place themselves before their central character (and thus before the whole movie) with clarity. This intellectual fascist seems beaten down by the final flight of his sister with her musician lover, but his success will continue for sure and the last vision that the spectator has of him (standing up on the balcony of his high-rise apartment looking out at the world with a certain nostalgic pride: very similar, besides, to the ending of *A Face in the Crowd*, with which this movie has so many tangential connections) is that of the Frankenstein monster: a bit perplexed at the temporary defeat but ready to return to his job the next morning. While Falco, the truly interesting and exemplary character, takes a beating that is not deserved, considering from whom it comes: the two cop pals of JJ. Why obscure then the intent, starting the film with the well-known and hypocritical saying of Lord Acton, 'Power corrupts, absolute power corrupts absolutely'?

Perhaps the filming of three different endings, so that the Code Office would choose this one, explains the dark corners of a picture so illuminating at its rotten core. That well deserves an evaluation by an outside surveyor. Says the English critic Lindsay Anderson: 'The good thing about these films is that those responsible for them have made choices; and this seems to imply the determination to reject the spurious and the prostituted, to return to the true sources of emotion and respect for principles.'

As *Sweet Smell* is a film of characters, it is a film of actors: they give the measure of their characters. In his first American film English director Sandy MacKendrick (born in the United States but English by vocation and citizenship) has succeeded in offering different versions of that typically Hollywood phenomenon: the matinée idol. Burt Lancaster, a former ladies' man, composes his character with a stiff artificiality that contributes to making it more than incredible, in fact non-human. One does not have here an everyday columnist but the Sphinx proposing riddles, scrutinizing the person in question, devouring always. The truths that are the clothing of his character seem ingenuous lies by contrast. Emile Meyer, such a good supporting actor, projects an almost sporting sadism in his plainclothes policeman, an accomplice of every turbid turn. Susan Harrison makes a marvellous début. With her bewitching face, her voice, her subdued and catatonic gestures she is the living portrait of a neurotic girl ill with claustrophobia. But all the palms go to that actor who was already an ambiguous and unpleasant figure for the *cronista*: Tony Curtis. Always the glamour-boy with his curly locks and too-easy smile, Curtis gave signs of life as an actor in *Trapeze*. Here he leads the movie by its hand. Cynical, depraved, juvenile, spirited, optimistic, amoral, his character, in spite of its criminal connotations, is *simpatico* due to its sincerity and its force. The spectator leaves the theatre convinced that if success belongs to someone, it belongs to him. Such convincing quality plus an acting job sincere and at the same time removed from the facile mannerisms of the Actor's Studio encourage one to see the film more than once for the sole pleasure of the uncovering of this dramatic card. For as Shakespeare said:

Have you ever heard that badly done things have poor fortune?

13 April 1958

Argentine Necrophilia

Más allá del olvido (Argentina Sono Films) is a thrilling film – and almost for the wrong reasons. If you heard the story told you wouldn't be able to stop laughing at so much cheap necrophilia and an almost vulgar romanticism. The film is based on a mysterious minor novel that nobody knows, *Brujas, la inolvidable* (*Unforgettable Bruges*), but as made by Hugo del Carril with so much visual flair and a virile drive (also the characteristics of del Carril as a tango singer), the plot disappears in the *Sturm und Drang* of this gothic Argentine romance in which a man is in love with his wife with a stubborn monogamy. Because she dies he goes abroad in search of oblivion, to find in Europe an empty facsimile which he proceeds to fill with his dead love's ectoplasm of memories – hence the meaning of the Spanish title: *Beyond Oblivion*.

At first the film, with its grand prepotent master, its marvellous mistress and passion weaving around them a depraved and eternal cocoon vaguely calls to mind a novel by Unamuno, in which Don Miguel messed up a love story with the worst narrative talent: *Nada menos que todo un hombre*. Then there are the relationships with *The Great Game* (so many that at first the *cronista* got to the point of hearing another voice in the other face of the protagonist, as if the old Feyder trick were back in business, as in *The Great Game*: with the second appearance of the woman in the desert her voice is dubbed over); the resemblances to *Rebecca*: which would mean a hundred years of forgiveness: a thief robbing a thief: *Rebecca* has been traced, precisely, back to a Brazilian novel; and, finally, all the Pirandellian connotations. This hardly matters. What matters is the élan and the conviction that the movie leaves in the spectator once it is over. When the second Blanca assimilates the personality of the dead Blanca and assumes her new personality and dies, a second dead woman, the *cronista* felt that he was inhabiting a romantic tragedy, that he was transferred to one of the dolorous Arcadias that Jean Cocteau crystallized in *The Two-Headed Eagle*. And the film leaves a disquieting question in the air: why has a cinema like the Argentine disappeared with these traces, when it had all the necessary ingredients to make our best Spanish-speaking movies?

20 April 1958

cain does justice
to manuel barbachano,
felicitous producer
of dreams and nightmares

Mano a Mano

Torero (Producciones Barbachano Ponce) is the masterwork of bullfight films. The cinema has put up with almost all the bad writing (*Blood and Sand*, for example) generated by the *fiesta brava* and has missed the scarce good writing (for example *Death in the Afternoon*) by the few aficionados who happened to be good writers as well. Now, Mexico revindicates bullfighting on the screen. But a masterwork is more interesting for its breeding than for its breath. So it would be well to tell how the idea of making *Torero* came about, which is how this film in embryo became a canned cocoon to complete its metamorphosis into a perfect movie.

Manuel Barbachano is a strong aficionado. In an interview with the *cronista*, Barbachano declared: 'I have three passions: the theatre, music and the bulls.' His Mexican weekly newsreel shoots the fights every Sunday. Some two years ago they shot the *corrida* with which the matador Luis Procuna returned to the ring. Procuna retired after a very grave goring and now was trying to win back his standing as the idol of the Mexican aficionados. He was taking turns with a Portuguese bullfighter, Alonzo, and with another idol of Mexico, the skilled Carlos Arruza. Arruza and Alonzo had brilliant afternoons, but Procuna ended up with a bad bull from Tecatepec and gave such a bad show that he had to be fined five thousand pesos by 'the (bullfight) authorities'. With the ring full of flying cushions and the air charged with insults, Procuna asked for the grace of giving away a bull. (At the bullfights any bullfighter has the right to fight a seventh bull for the afternoon, as long as he pays for it.)

Into the arena came a tall, black, brave bull which at the first charged against the *burladeros*, jumped the *barrera* and slipped into the alley. It was Polvorito, a bull marked for immortality: he would die famous. Procuna presented his cape to wait for the charge. Polvorito charged and the bullfighter executed some almost perfect passes. In the *suerte de picas* (spearing) Polvorito killed one of the horses and unhorsed the other picador. When the work with the *muleta* began, Polvorito and Procuna had already won over the public, who watched them fascinated by their game of death. At the end, with a clean and sure thrust, Procuna crowned the afternoon (the bugle had already played three hails for him) with tail and ears. While the bull slowly died his violent death, Procuna was carried to his house on the public's shoulders: he had returned, fought the bull and won. Now *Torero* could begin.

When they saw that unusual shot on the newsreel in which the bull was falling to the ground dead, defeated, while his conqueror was raised up and transformed into a living statue (the symbol of the victory of man over beast and death) they understood that they had an irritated oyster in their hands: the pearl was beginning to take shape. (The idea further found its match when some American writers and a director, among those proscribed from Hollywood by the Un-American Activities Committee, confided a similar idea to Barbachano. Barbachano bought from them what they had written and consulted them once or twice.) Barbachano then went to see Procuna and persuaded him to appear in a film that would be the story of his life. In principle Procuna accepted that his life story would be adapted for the screen, but he rejected the idea of appearing as Procuna. 'I couldn't be myself,' he said. 'Besides, I'm very old.' Barbachano modified the original plans and told him that his youth would be played by another actor and the rest would be done with newsreels. Procuna had a small film library of his most important bullfights and Barbachano as well as other Mexican news programmes had in their archives enough material on bulls and especially on Procuna, one of the most beloved bullfighters in all Mexico.

Carlos Velo, technical director of the newsreel, took on the fiction filming, and he and Barbachano chose the newsreel shots that they would be assembling later. The project was carried out with precise care. The photographer of the movie was the photographer who shoots the bullfights each Sunday afternoon, the same who had caught the *faena* with Polvorito. The photography accentuated the documentary texture and the film gained an atmosphere of decisive authenticity. Procuna, with an obvious personal charm and a certain resemblance to Montgomery Clift (at times, in the confused and shy glances, in the indecision that fear obtains when it clashes with the watchful will, he was the exact Indian facsimile of the American actor), plus the clear notion that he indeed moves like a fish in the water, gives his performance the tinge of truth. If at times (in the narration, for example) he strikes a false note, it is not his fault: Procuna was dubbed. Barbachano explained why. 'It isn't that his voice was not good enough, but that it was a disagreeable shrill. Procuna, who is very macho, has a voice that could strike the spectator as ridiculous, effeminate.' But with all its shortcomings, the film goes as Procuna goes. It all lends a certain truth to the neorealist aphorism: 'The best actor to play a shoeshine boy is a shoeshine boy.' The best Procuna is Luis Procuna.

Barbachano knows as much as Hemingway. *Torero* resembles *Death in the Afternoon* and not by chance. Hemingway knew that bullfights won't make a novel. So that apart from *Death in the Afternoon* (which is a book *sui generis*) he has not written more than one or two short stories about bulls and one long short story. One of the short stories, 'The Capital of the World', which is one of his most successful stories, has to do more with bull-drunkness than with the bullfight. His long narrative 'The Undefeated' has a plot resembling *Torero*: the struggle of fear when facing the bull and the need to conquer the two beasts – but it is a pessimistic story. For its part, *Blood and Sand*, prototype of the bullfight novels, blurred its scanty documentary stuff with a torrent of tears. It was little more or less than what all the bullfight movies had done, until *Torero*. Barbachano was able to fill the story with the same type of truth with which the bullfight papers are filled: the moment of truth when the bullfighter faces the bull. Although its theme is almost the same as *The Brave Bulls* ('The bullfighter has two enemies: the bull and fear'), here there was no melodrama, but drama, and not threadbare parody but unadorned, true documentary. *Torero* would be a movie *sui generis*.

Torero, which is a *mano a mano* (hand to hand) between the bullfighter and fear, opens with the skilled Luis Procuna on the way to the plaza, preoccupied with his comeback, done more out of *amor propio* than for love of money. Before him his life unreels like a movie and the show begins. Procuna is brought to the bulls by the same bare necessities that bring our black youths to boxing: he is an Indian and his economic horizon almost ends with his flat nose: the bulls mean social advance. From an aficionado he becomes a *peón* and then a *novillero*: later he fights in small plazas and in *novilladas* in El Toreo. Finally – the billing with Luis Castro alias The Soldier. Triumph. Money. Love. Then the dazzling comet of modern bullfighting that passes noisily and leaves the other bullfighters blind: Manolete comes to Mexico. That thin long man, with an eternally mournful face, who moves before the bulls with the ungainly elegance of a praying mantis, is El Monstruo. After him, as after Belmonte, the bullfight is an anticlimax and a perilous profession.

Procuna's star begins to decline. One day, fighting *mano a mano* with Luis Briones, he is frightened by a goring suffered by Briones and his hands tremble before the sword. A series of little fears starts and after the death of Manolete, the great fear, the insuperable fear. The gorings begin: in an arm, in the belly, in the calf, in the thigh, one after another, until the worst one comes: right next to the femoral artery, almost deadly. Procuna shuts himself up to convalesce and refuses to fight. The bulls are more beautiful from the *barrera*. Nevertheless, the fans and the bullfight journalists won't leave him alone. Finally he decides to return. That afternoon of his comeback is the afternoon of his greatest failure and greatest triumph. The Mexican aficionados don't recall a more contradictory fight. (Although they remember the fight as the greatest that a Mexican bullfighter has ever achieved.) The Spanish aficionados do indeed know of this: they remember El Gallo. The movie ends with Procuna conquering fear and at the same time vanquished by fear. His last thought is: 'But . . . what about next Sunday?'

The *cronista*'s first encounter with *Torero* was on Mexican television. They were interviewing Barbachano and a *novillero* who that afternoon (it was Sunday night) had brought off an impressive *faena*. The *cronista* had thought of going to the bullfights but he decided to see *Othello*. Not that the movies were more thrilling than the bulls, even movies by

Shakespeare. It was that he had read that the first time that one goes to see the bulls one must go to a real fight or not at all, and that was a *novillada* with small bulls and novel bullfighters. He regrets it today. *Torero* has convinced him not only of the talent of its makers and of the personality of its actor, but that the bullfight, with all its ugly facets, is an art and not a savage spectacle. Contrary to the opinion that deems it barbaric, it seems to him just the opposite: sophisticated and of a desperate and unique beauty.

27 April 1958

i believe that
cain
loved neorealism
more than
he admitted:
it was his
ossessione

The Neorealist Swan Song

Due Soldi di Speranza (*Two Pennyworth of Hope*, Cofram) is one of the masterworks of neorealism with a sad destiny: it is the swan song of the neorealist cinema. Premièred at the Cannes Film Festival of 1952, hand in hand with *Umberto D* (at times the most desolate of the bitter chronicles of post-war Italy), *Due Soldi di Speranza* is a laughing, optimistic movie – although peeking out through the laughter one might see the lips stripped of flesh by pellagra and the filed teeth of hunger. Still of an exemplary loyalty to its ethic – the neorealists have had more collisions with ethics than with aesthetics – its appearance has served none the less to raise a mob of imitators and admirers, delighted more with the sweet noise of laughter (and the coins at the box office too, since *Due Soldi* left more than two pennies in the hands of the ticket-seller) than with the bitter satire that provided the opportunity for its jokes and obstreperousness.

There are works of art and artists and writers who do great good with their appearance, but who leave a depraved, harmful legacy. Such is the case of Ortega y Gasset, who has inspired several generations of *apprentis sorciers* of philosophy, critics and essayists (in Spain and also abroad: the undertow has been felt in Cuba), people who would never have had an idea, much less the nefarious idea of putting their ideas in a book. Such is the case of Igor Stravinsky: his *Rite of Spring* is one of the milestones in the history of music but the chain reaction of cacophonies, dissonances and musical show-off that it unleashed still drills our eardrums. *Due Soldi di Speranza* is a felicitous film but the sequel of rosy and facile neorealism that followed its release has not dissipated yet – remember the series of *Bread, Love and . . .* that in Spain will have its *Bread, Love and Andalusia*, soon to be filmed, and a whole flock of bucolic and humble comedies, in which Vittorio de Sica the actor, Tina Pica and all the Filippos of Filmdom have thrived spontaneously.

In 1949 Renato Castellani found himself one day (he was preparing a film with a theme similar to his two earlier successes, in which he mixed humour and love) with a *contadino* who told him the story of his life. This made him totally change the plot (and the meaning) of the film. As Castellani tells it:

> The first intention for the subject had a more picaresque tone; we gave a greater role to the little squabbles, to the 'genial' imbroglios of the city ambience of Naples. A thing of the *E Primavera* type. In the course of the construction of the script, the tone became more serious, reflecting the spirit of my principal collaborator and the protagonist of the film, Antonio. Using a stenographer, I collected, first, everything that Antonio (whom I had insisted came to Rome) told me about himself and about his town, in his fresh and intuitive language, which was very 'literary', that is to say full of metaphors, worthy of a popular poet.
>
> Episodes, characters, old and new tales from Boscotrecase came out of his mouth, which he recounted with a profound and yet ironic sadness. Stories and characters from which I took the humorous side from amid the pain. Moreover, Antonio was already, by his account, one of these characters. The first time I met him and I asked him how he was, he answered me: 'One keeps oneself', that is, it isn't going well or badly for me: he was alive, up to now he had weathered the storm and he was expecting to live tomorrow. On another occasion when I asked him why he wasn't having breakfast, he answered me that, working as a highwayman, he had 'gotten out of the habit' of eating in the morning for fear that nothing would be left for noon. So, with no preconceived programme, but through successive decantation, collecting Antonio's words and using whatever material that seemed most useful of what he gave us, the script for the film was developed, the characters took shape and the *dialogue* was

born.*

But the script, written in collaboration with Ettore Margadonna, also screenwriter of the first, second and third *Bread, Love and . . .*, was written four or five times (always in the narrative form that Castellani favours so much), adding new episodes, like the ending, and changing others. Castellani took almost two years on these tasks, because the most perfected version was written totally in some bedevilled thing that the Italians call *dialetto teano*, and though it had a great freshness and originality, there was no one who could understand it. Then they called on Titina de Filippo for her help (naturally, since she was also the dialogue-writer for *Bread, Love and Fantasy*), who seems to have an exact ear for daily dialogue and who was the one who gave it that masterly final touch of popular savour and aged savvy – the film is spoken almost totally in a curious mixture of Italian and Neapolitan dialect, which gives it a flavour very much its own. (One has to note here an acute observation of Guido Aristarco, the critic from *Cinema Nuovo*: all the great successes of the Italian cinema are spoken in dialect: *Bicycle Thieves* in Roman dialect, *Miracle in Milan* in Milanese, *The Earth Trembles* in Sicilian. In Italy, as Visconti says, 'Italian is not the language of the poor.')

With his team, Castellani went off to Boscotrecase, in the lap of Vesuvius: grey, poor, hostile land, in which the only amiable note is the undercurrent of the words of its peasants and the sallow beauty of the women. There the inhabitants of the village were its actors. 'They have worked on the film,' says Castellani, 'without understanding exactly what it was about . . . Some – the drivers and the sacristan – have played themselves; and it is unlikely that I would have been able to find more *real* players than these.'

With a tedious care, Castellani took six months on the shooting of the exteriors. 'At times,' he tells, 'a single scene took me an entire day.' He had to struggle not only against the weather and against the ignorance of the country people, but against his own sense of acting. Someone has said that Italy is a peninsula peopled exclusively by actors and opera singers. This stay in Boscotrecase has ended up contaminating the film and some daily incidents have ended up in the plot while the shooting was going on. The final scene, in which Antonio strips Carmela and throws her clothes in front of her father who is refusing to give his daughter's hand to an unemployed man, was suggested to Castellani by an almost identical incident which happened in the town while the

*From an interview published in the Italian journal *Cinema* in May 1952.

film team was waiting for the sun to come out so they could continue with the film.

Castellani's assistant director, Marie-Claire Solleville, caught many of these situations with her French eye and related them in *Cahiers du Cinéma*. The 'actors' from the town (all the women were from Boscotrecase, except the protagonist Maria Fiore, brought from Naples) learned their bits listening to them, since almost none of them knew how to read. Donna Filomena (Antonio's mother in the movie) took advantage of this illiterate condition, while she boasted to her neighbours about the important role that she had in this game for grown-ups. At times she wanted to play a scene her way and when Castellani called her over, brandishing the script, furious now, upbraiding her and telling her that that was not in the role, the good lady limited herself to responding: 'Oh, but I don't know how to read,' and her eyes shone with intelligence and contentment. The priest in the film is in real life a butcher who is always drunk. He spent his mornings in the town's only café and didn't want to work in the film. They put a cassock and metal-rimmed glasses on him and shut him up in a cramped confessional where, growling profanities, he became a perfect priest. Antonio's sister, raped in the film, was the town beauty: and though in the movie she is a girl crushed by life, in life she is an alert girl, who got a crush on Castellani, constantly inviting him to an impossible tea.

The most pathetic of Mme Solleville's records doesn't refer to the film, but to the misery of these *contadini* of Vesuvius country. There women of twenty-five seem to be fifty and have more kids than years. It is common to see couples with twenty or thirty children and those who have the least money can count ten or twelve little heads. A woman, still young, came up to Mme Solleville and asked her if she were married. 'Yes,' she responded. 'And do you have children?' 'No,' she responded. 'Ah, it's because of that that we admire Frenchwomen. Tell me how you manage it.' 'Are you joking?' she asked, taken aback, but on seeing from the girl's intense and very fixed eyes that she wasn't joking, said: 'What will the priest say if he finds out? Better ask a doctor about it.' The country woman didn't insist, but when she went she left in Madame's hands a pencil and a sheet of paper. The Frenchwoman adds forcefully: '*Bon* . . . I couldn't refuse.' But the next day the woman returned with an alarming piece of news, begging: 'My husband says he doesn't understand it very well. Could you be so kind as to go and explain it to him?'

Due Soldi di Speranza is the story of an almost impossible love. Precisely the two pennies of hope with which the protagonists seem to content themselves are what keeps the movie from becoming a tragedy of 'star-crossed lovers', as Shakespeare said of his lovers further north. The difficulties with which the path of these two kids bristle are not the familiar quarrels of 'what's in a name', but human misery and stupidity. When Antonio meets Carmela (and there is something definitively Renaissance in this encounter between the lovers in the piazza, next to the church; one thinks of Romeo's encounter with Juliet, and more fittingly, of Dante casting his first glance on Beatrice) love grows like a high-yield rice and ripens under the noonday sun.

Carmela is impetuous, full of fire, rash. One of the finest characters that the Italian cinema has created, she is the whole film. If her father threatens to beat her on account of her love affair, she offers her cheek and breaks out singing; if they tie her to the bed with a leash (because she has run off after Antonio to Naples), she, when her mother comes to scold her, answers her by barking; if Antonio refuses to love her 'because love is forbidden to the poor', she pursues him, chases him, urges him on and, finally, makes him take her when they are the poorest. Antonio, come back from military service, his only pair of pants comically patched in the seat, with an enormous desire to work (in the most beautiful scene of the film, Antonio, one more beast, helps the coaches up the bank, pulling with the coach mules) and the need to live (in one scene, he tells Carmela: 'I'm already married. Four times. To my mother, to my two sisters and to hunger'), tries the most varied jobs: he is assistant sacristan, blood donor in Naples, in show business (he runs from one movie theatre to the next carrying the reels of the same film), projectionist and, finally, poster-paster for the communist party. This work he does at night, in hiding, because by day he is sacristan of the church; but the Vesuvian temper of Carmela discovers it for her, first, and later for all her neighbours.

He doesn't know that he has committed a double heresy. He doesn't know that he has been a simultaneous servant of two antagonistic causes: he rings the bells in the town (a heraldic form of announcing that the grand spectacle of the Mass is about to begin) and sticks up posters for the communist party in the city with the dedication of a member of the Agitprop. But the Vatican and the Kremlin do not get along, for sure. And the priest throws him out of the church, without the least Christian mercy: 'So you're a sacristan in Cusano and a communist in Naples. Get out!' It matters little that Antonio answers him, with complete innocence: 'If I'd done it in town. But it was in Naples and Naples is almost at the end of the world.'

So the misadventures of these lovers continue, the daughter of the fireworks-maker (her father has an implacable motto for his perilous profession: 'Match and extreme unction') and the son of the old witch (when her elder daughter is raped by a landlord – or his equivalent in the misery of Cusano – she upbraids her son for not doing anything against *questo infame scellerà*, as if he were a character from Sade), with the rash boisterousness of the old *commedia dell'arte* (for one Italian critic this is not a neorealist film, but a sample, and a very intellectual one, of the Italian Renaissance popular comedy). The film runs along with an originality, a vitality and a fragrance that makes it seem new although it has been premièred in Havana after almost ten years' delay. This sounds like an apology for the film and is almost a diatribe against the cinema, this art which has masterworks that are no longer so only five years later.

18 May 1958

cain,
catholic
– or communist?

McCarthyism in New England

The Witches of Salem (Cofram) is the French version of *The Crucible*. This is already alarming, much as if Hollywood dared to try *The Diary of a Country Priest*. But this play by Arthur Miller is so powerful that the film still attains some of the pity and the horror that are the first fruits of the Aristotelian catharsis and also the pillars of tragedy. *The Crucible*, of course, consists of more than catharsis and historical reconstruction.

Around 1626 there was founded a town ('but we today would hardly call it a village,' as Miller explains) in a primitive Indian outpost of the Massachusetts chieftaincy. Settled by descendants of the pilgrims of the *Mayflower*, the settlers turned out to be little less than a degenerate bunch and devoted themselves to persecuting the Quakers with considerable fury. One night in 1692 a pastor named Samuel Parris found his daughter and his niece in a saturnalia in the forest, dancing naked to the sound of the drum that a female slave from Barbados, Tituba, was playing. This man, who 'believed he was being persecuted wherever he went, despite his best effort to win people and God to his side', experienced what today we would call shock. For this people who forbade themselves everything that could be the least occasion for joy (they did not even celebrate Christmas, and the holidays were no more than dates to leave off the crushing week's work and concentrate more on prayers), that little pilgrim orgy was the infiltration of the Devil in a community dedicated to God. The girls, since the eldest was barely sixteen years old, invented a good excuse to escape punishment: they had been possessed by Lucifer and two respectable lady neighbours were the authors of the spell.

In another society not so barbarous and unthinking, this would have gone no further than a good spanking and more vigilance from then on, but the pilgrims had been expelled from England for their fanaticism and in the New World they found a sharp spur. Here, regrettably, one has to confront Catholicism with Protestantism and although the *cronista* may not wish to, cast a vote for the former. The Reformation, an almost justified political and social movement, takes on a primitive and savage character in the ethical area. At the end of the Middle Ages Catholicism was a generous and liberal force compared with the obscurantism and the regression of the Protestants, who brought Christianity back to the vengeance and the fury and the sense of sin of the Old Testament: to its Judaic sources, to the Bible (which taken in a strict sense is a book full of depraved confessions and vengeance and madness), to the insanity of the prophets.

These readers of the Bible who could not wash away their sins with confession nor with any other mechanical means (for Miller the sense of responsibility of the American comes from this, but so does his hypocrisy) threw themselves with a patriotic fervour into the witch hunt. Miller says in a kind of exegesis of each character of *The Crucible*, which makes the book, more than the script of a play, a pamphlet in dialogue:

> The witch-hunt was not, however, a mere repression. It was also, and as importantly, a long overdue opportunity for everyone so inclined to express publicly his guilt and sins, under the cover of accusations against the victims. It suddenly became possible – and patriotic and holy – for a man to say that Martha Corey had come into his bedroom at night, and that, while his wife was sleeping at his side, Martha laid herself down on his chest and 'nearly suffocated him'. Of course it was her spirit only, but his satisfaction at confessing himself was no lighter than if it had been Martha herself. One could not ordinarily speak such things in public.

A long list of neighbours fell between the madness of Parris and the primitive sense of justice of the governor's deputy, Danforth. Nineteen persons were hanged and an old man killed in a torture chamber constructed ad hoc. Not very far from Torquemada and his Inquisition, as one can see. Nor very far from McCarthy and the House Un-American Activities Committee. But this belongs to the next paragraph. Or better: to another occasion.

Arthur Miller premièred *The Crucible* in January of 1953, in the midst of the din and anger of the anti-communist investigations of the Senate. The tentacles of the FBI and of the special investigative bodies reached Broadway and Hollywood almost in a single embrace. Groups of actors visited the president and other groups served as witnesses against their colleagues. Elia Kazan remade a whole career at full speed backwards and filmed an anti-communist film; Ginger Rogers, Adolphe Menjou, Robert Taylor accused actors right and left: John Garfield died of a heart attack, the careers of Larry Parks, Morris Carnovsky and others, those of screenwriters and directors, ended abruptly. But it happened not only in Hollywood. Alger Hiss was accused and tried and convicted and the Rosenberg couple were electrocuted. (Some have seen in the stoicism of Elizabeth and John Proctor, in the play, a figuration of the final refusal of Ethel and Julius Rosenberg – and the similarity of the capital letters in their names has even been pointed out – to confess their guilt and name names. This is not so. The play was already written when the hearings began. But this is not pertinent, because it makes no difference whether the witch-hunt prefigured the play or if the opposite happened.)

In his discussions of the characters, Miller makes an observation that clarifies the political meaning of the work, its message of humanism and democracy, its unlimited faith in the truth. He refers to the demonologist Hale of the play. After commenting that the audience at the première did not laugh at his logical method for detecting the presence of the Devil in Salem, he compares the audience to the students of a professor at his university who used to close up the classroom and carry on lively discussions with the spectre of Erasmus – without being dismissed from the faculty or jeered at by his students. The reason for both attitudes: '. . . that the university officials, like most of us, are the children of a history which still sucks at the Devil's teats . . .'

It is not strange that a play with such connotations would attract the interest of an awake, alert, militant intelligence like Jean-Paul Sartre. But it is Sartre's screenplay which has destroyed the political message of the film, reducing it to a merely local issue. The prologue presents John Proctor as the dweller of a dirty hut, a repellent man himself, more like the miserable French villagers of *Jeux Interdits* than the prim puritans of New England; or at least, the embodiment of pulchritude that history has bequeathed. His promiscuity with his maids and his wife, his brutality, separate him definitively from the man 'powerful of body, even-tempered, and not easily led', who made 'a fool [feel] his foolishness instantly' – the portrait Miller draws of him. And now from here on the rest of the film seems to go astray in the ideological justification of a being primaeval, immediate, with no historical life: little less than an animal with conceits of transcendence.

The attempt at a witches' sabbath in the woods, now visualized, loses the power of evocation that it had in the play each time that gathering of girls – almost children – naked in the midst of the sycamores was mentioned, and becomes a cheap reconstruction, almost laughable. The trial destroys the interplay of unreality–reality, of fiction within fiction, and the repetition by the girls of every word that one of them, Mary, says, pretending they are all possessed, loses its echo of a Greek chorus. Finally, the confession by Proctor, and his ulterior denial – which in the play were not only the major key, but which sustained the edifice of ideas built by Miller (it has been said that this attitude of the character obliged the author to adopt another, identical one when the Senate called him to testify five years later) – and all the leftist tinge of the work evaporate and therefore its message of democracy is suspended; for the *cronista* the concepts of democracy and leftism do not eliminate but necessarily complement each other. At the end, with its aggregate of Christian charity, the spectator does not leave with the feeling that theocracy has eliminated itself from Salem, but that by a curious mechanism, which is provincial and at the same time universal, the characters have resolved a family quarrel and set up the foundations of a collective farm.

Nevertheless, it would not be fair to say that the catharsis has not completed its circle. To say it is to recognize the complete catharsis: *The Witches of Salem* leaves the spectator thinking of many things. One of them is that man stops being man when he is a fanatic and that the true human condition is that of the constant revision of his conduct.

1 June 1958

cain
declares himself
a pacifist
one more time

The Purple Testament

Paths of Glory (United Artists) could very easily have been an indictment against war as effective as the novel *All Quiet on the Western Front*. It isn't that anything is lacking, rather there's too much restraint. Faced with such a powerful enemy, whispers are useless and one must shout out from the rooftops. Despite all that it is a useful, necessary film. Shown in 1938 (as was *Grand Illusion*, for example) it would have been an instrument of appeasement, in 1958 it is a weapon for peace. Back then there was no solution other than war or absolute destruction. (There is no doubt that this was what the perverse alliance of fascism and Nazism meant.) Today the dilemma is peace or absolute destruction – and the word 'absolute' barely manages to suggest the total destruction that an atomic war conveys.

There are two generals. One with two stars and another with one star more. The three-star general conceives a petty plan to nourish his reputation as a warrior. The two-star general seconds it, in order to earn one more star and out of personal vanity. The scheme: to offer the general staff a war show by taking an enemy position which is evidently impregnable. The preparations for the assault begin and the general, to liven up those soldiers who are going to die (it has been calculated that eighty per cent of the attackers will fall), announces that he too will be on the firing line – that is: in his armoured trench.

The assault begins at dawn. The men come out like ants from the trenches and die like insects, mown down before getting to the barbed wire on their own lines. 'It's magnificent, but it isn't war,' the general almost thinks now, in the phrase of another general, his compatriot Pierre Bosquet, when watching a light cavalry charge. Or better: 'It's war, but it isn't magnificent yet.' The dead soldiers still advance and fall and get up and fall again further on. A few begin the retreat. The first battalion is annihilated and the second battalion is still in the trenches unable to come out.

The two-star general rises in anger before his fleeting star. 'Order the artillery to fire on our positions,' he instructs the communications captain. The officer protests but the general repeats the order. The artillery captain rejects the order: 'An order in writing is required for me to do that.' The two-star general, definitively demented, shouts: 'Carry out the order or I'll have you shot.' He had decided to send his soldiers to the glory of death with a kick in the pants if necessary, as Mussolini wanted. Now he reacts with a fascist dementia. 'I will shoot the whole regiment.'

But it does not come to that. Military honour will be preserved in an almost symbolic manner: one soldier is taken from each company and they are subjected to a summary court martial. The men have been selected by the system of derision. One of them is chosen because he is considered a 'social undesirable' – without further explanation –; the second soldier because it fell to him by lot, although he has been decorated earlier 'for extraordinary valour on the field of battle'; the third one is singled out by a lieutenant who fears the secrets of his cowardice and debasement that this man keeps.

Their colonel will defend them, a man who in civilian life was a famed lawyer. But no true defence is allowed: the trial is another farce. The charges are not specified nor is it permitted that the defence present witnesses nor is a stenographic record of the trial kept. The men are condemned beforehand and the colonel knows it. This leads him to say to the courtroom: 'At this moment I'm ashamed to belong to the human race.' The general's response? 'There are few things more stimulating for a soldier than seeing someone die.' Can we top that one? 'Troops are like children. They need discipline. For example, shooting someone once in a while.'

While the men spend their last night awake (there is a Heideggerian dialogue in which the soldier who has been falsely accused by his lieutenant sees a cockroach dragging itself along the wall and says: 'In a few hours that cockroach will have more contact with my wife and children than I do'), the generals make war in their fashion in an ample ballroom: martial to the rhythms of a waltz, veterans attacking impregnable busts, showing off the cheap patriotic bric-à-brac of their decorations, chatting about their favourite topic: valour in the face of death, which is always someone else's death, perhaps citing the corrupt saying of General Sherman: 'War is inevitably cruel and impossible to refine.' But this amiable armistice is broken by the arrival of the colonel for the defence, who communicates to the three-star general what he has just found out about the two-star general: that man asked that his own troops be fired upon. He is the real traitor. But there are still other traitors and the three-star general limits himself to holding onto the evidence against the two-star general and announces that he believes in discipline: 'One must give examples.'

The soldiers are put before a firing-squad and the generals are there, dressed as for a gala occasion, almost transforming the execution into a parade's ending. The men are shot with a martial, competent and refined show of force. One of them had suffered an accident the night before and was in a comatose state. They carry him on a stretcher and tie the handles to the post. At the moment of shooting him, the sergeant of the squad pinches his cheeks to obtain a fleeting consciousness before *nada*. From the violent deaths, the camera goes to a portentous breakfast with which the generals regale themselves early in the morning. Here, the colonel, called in by the three-star general, is witness to the accusation that the latter makes against the two-star general, who first denies the charges and then complains that he has been stabbed in the back and takes refuge in the extant excuse of the war criminal: 'Before anything I am a soldier,' the worn-out reference to his caste, and withdraws, presumably to shoot himself in the temple. But not to worry: generals die in bed.

The three-star general asks the colonel: 'Are you satisfied?' And then he offers him the post of the disgraced general. When the colonel rejects it, the three-star general, genuinely surprised, says confused: 'I don't understand you. Justice has been done and any way you're not agreeable.' To which the colonel answers: 'If you don't understand, I feel sorry for you.' The general believed that all was reduced to a mere opportunism, to chasing stars any way possible. At the end the colonel comes upon his company enjoying themselves by making fun of a female prisoner in the tavern. Bitterness and disillusionment flood him: the soldiers have already forgotten their dead companions. But in a startlingly laconic twist, the film shows its preference for cordiality, affection and love of men, of peoples, of humanity, above that game of generals: war.

Stanley Kubrick (his work on *Killer's Kiss* and, especially, on *The Killing*, cannot be forgotten) has made his film in Munich, although this story of filth as fertilizer for decorations has the French army as its butt. It might seem craven or gratuitous that the French army has been chosen, since the American army has its history too, but the fact is that the happening that was the basis for the Humphrey Cobb novel took place in France, at the beginning of the First World War. The incidents occurred in Sovain on 17 March 1915 and it was not three men who were 'shot to provide an example', but four: corporals Maupas, Girard, Lefoulon and Lechat. The unforgettable name of that example-giving general: Reveilhac. The executed men were rehabilitated, posthumously of course, twenty years later, in 1934. The movie has been banned in France and Kubrick was denied permission to shoot. With good cause. The Dreyfus affair first and then the matter of the 'exemplary shootings' have placed the prestige of the French army in the sights of the vigilant criticism that still remains in Hollywood. Not for nothing that their most prestigious generals of the hour are called Massu, Salan, etc.

Photographed with exact care, as appropriate as the period reproduction, *Paths of Glory* is an austere, serious movie. Kubrick puts away his technical brilliance to stick to the story with the dry passion of a document. Moving the camera with as much precision as boldness, he offers (the overwhelming trenches and the scorched, implacable battlefield that recalls the narrative of Remarque) a vision of war to the extent of showing its filth and its uselessness and its savagery: the fate of the hero is not to die clean, face to the sun, with a pretty and rapid rabbit shot in the temple or the chest, as the recruitment posters show, but to drag himself along the ground with his guts spilled out to die cursing among blood and mud.

Kubrick was also served by an effective, coherent script by Calder Willingham and was able to contain Kirk Douglas (Colonel Dax) to the point of bringing him back to what he seemed to be on his début: the prospect of an actor. While he obtained from George Macready (the two-star general) his best performance since his real scar in a Nordic face appeared in *Gilda*, a long time ago, and used with much effectiveness Adolphe Menjou (the three-star general), and Ralph Meeker, Joseph Turkel and Timothy Carey as the soldiers. Nevertheless the mugging grimaces of Timothy Carey almost ruined the dry, emotive pathos of the shooting. Kubrick edited the material with the nervous, reiterative and arbitrary punctuation that Orson Welles taught all the American directors who came after him, denuding the drama to the point of leaving it as the mere statement of a terrible and shaming denunciation.

In sum, Kubrick has made the ideal war film: the one that helps to show wars as what they always should have been: not a vision but a bad dream, a nightmare to be forgotten, a movie.

8 June 1958

the wind
of criticism,
alas!
doesn't blow
where it wants

The Diary of a Condemned Man

A Man Escaped (*Un Condamné à Mort s'est échappé*, Cofram) won for its director, Robert Bresson, the prize for best direction in the Cannes Festival of 1957. The prize was awarded unanimously. This fourth film by Bresson has taken for its script (almost scripture) the memoirs of the Commander in the Resistance André Devigny, published in *Le Figaro Littéraire* with the same title. Bresson makes it clear in the film that he has only limited himself to transforming the text into lights and shadows, 'without embellishing it'. But this movie, like its precursor *Le Journal d'un Curé de Campagne* (*The Diary of a Country Priest*), has taken a notion and has elevated it to God by an almost mystic devotion, and it is surprising how it has changed in appearance. So much so that Commander Devigny (who was present at the shooting, vigilant and ubiquitous) has refused to recognize himself.

One day in 1943, in Lyon, a lieutenant with the Resistance named André Devigny was taken prisoner by the Gestapo. On the way by car to the prison of Montluc, Devigny attempted to escape, but he was picked up not far away and beaten brutally. By mysterious designs (is it his faked lameness, his head covered with clotted blood, his shirt torn to tatters?) he is not shot at once. Despite his failure, he still thinks of escaping. Nevertheless he now knows that caution and cunning must prevail. He proves that isolation can be overcome and from down below, from the yard where they walk sometimes, other prisoners get him a safety pin with which to free himself from his manacles. Little by little he discovers a new sense of solidarity, in which gestures or a half-spoken word effectively substitute for effusiveness.

Slowly, in the hundred days his arrest lasted, he develops the escape plan. With a spoon stolen on the sly and filed on the slabs of the floor, Devigny begins to widen the joints of the wooden door of his cell. With an insect's patience, he manages to displace three planks and goes out into the corridor to start exploring the possible escape routes. Not far away there is some tubing that will help him to climb up to the glass roof which lets light into the building, and from there to go over to the adjoining roof. To test his strength and firm up the solidarity, he whispers words of encouragement to a man condemned to death and erases the chalk signs on his door that prohibit giving food to him.

Now to weave a rope. He extracts the transverse wires from the bed springs and weaves them with shreds from one of his blankets. His labour is meticulous and delicate, and he carries it out with a devotion urged on by a force superior to the need to escape, as if one were dealing here with the transcendence of the soul rather than with the flight of the body.

In prison he has met a pastor who in the brief wash recess comforts and inspires and, at times, warns him. There are some prisoners who fear that the flight will be discovered and they will all be shot as accomplices. In the cell beside him an old man has arrived, who at first does not respond to his knocks and who then shows himself to be fastidious and pessimistic, embittered by the loneliness and the bother of life. He meets another prisoner, with scurvy and a twisted and angular face: he has been squealed on by his wife and now trusts no one. These knots in the escape rope are no more than spurs for Devigny.

Soon he learns that the prisoner with the fugitive face intends to make his whole body fugitive. His plan is to hide himself above the watertank of the washroom and escape by night. One day he tries it, but desperation and hysteria betray him and he is condemned to death. Before he dies he passes a message that is very useful to Devigny: two metal hooks and a lot of rope are necessary. He tells him how to make the hooks. Luck the puppet master begins to move the strings and Devigny discovers in this incident the signs of a grander scheme: God's will.

He works with eagerness and, later, with skill. He has learned to make the ropes and now he has the hooks ready. There also has come to him – fallen from heaven, which is something more than a coined phrase for the prisoner – a package of clothes from home, which he instantly makes into strips for more ropes. One day he finds that all is about ready. But still he holds up. An internal weakness has replaced the old urgency and he feels incapable of anything. His companions are starting to be afraid. The pastor urges him to escape: a collaborator in the prison reveals that Devigny is condemned to death. But he doesn't react.

It is necessary for them to take him to the warden's office and tell him of his sentence for him to get moving. That same day they put a soldier in his cell who is wearing part of a German uniform. He is a boy from Alsace, who calls himself a deserter from the German army. Is he a deserter or a spy? Might they not have put him next to him with the hope that softened by the news of his sentence he may confess? Devigny wavers between killing him or trying to convince him that they should escape together. Finally he decides on this course of action and the boy follows him in the escape.

The prison is surrounded by three concentric walls and during the flight Devigny has to kill one of the guards. While scaling the third wall he understands that the deserter is the last rung of the ladder: he never would have escaped alone. At the end both flee towards a city in shadows and full of hidden menaces. Nevertheless they go happily, because they carry in their talons the wings of freedom.

It is not frivolous for Bresson to have titled his film *A Man Escaped*. His intention is as far from suspense as is *The Diary of a Country Priest* from village gossiping. Exterior action or adventure is of almost no interest to him. He has deliberately confined the prisoner in a bare, tiny cell and shoots him almost always in medium shots and in close-ups. The noises from outside, the changes in the surroundings are the threads of threats. His captors remain remote although always premonitory, present only in menace. The prisoner (Fontaine, as he is called in the film) executes the parts of the plan for escape with the devotion of the medieval artisan who is working on a cathedral. His steps are taken in the direction of the flight, but a grander intent is latent.

Everything is told with a crushing factuality: the data are like the diverse propositions of a greater engima. The prisoner will escape: in that respect there is no doubt. As a matter of fact, the three walls of the prison, with their layout like a labyrinth (which, after all, is a structure built not for its exit to be found but for one to get lost looking for it) effectively surround Montluc, but learning about them makes them no less mysterious. The postponements of Fontaine's flight do not occur to make the spectator despair: they are real, they come from an older desperation, from a nature for which life is an eternal postponing.

Bresson does not want mysticism to be spoken of in connection with his films but nevertheless it is necessary. This is most evident in *A Man Escaped*, because its hero is not a priest who transforms neglect by the hierarchy, the hostility of the flock and his mortal illness into successive steps towards an intimate sanctity. He is a prisoner for whom the will to escape, the preparing of the flight, the flight itself, are moments in learning about his existence and at the same time the proof that chance can be an article of faith.

The subtitle of the film – *The Wind Bloweth Where it Listeth* – taken from the gospel of St John, converts the finger which directs Fontaine's way, the chance that facilitates his flight, into a divine hand. Of course, this almost amounts to heresy: chance is a pagan god. But this beautiful sentence that St John the Apostle puts in the mouth of Christ when he confronts the sophistical Pharisee Nicodemus, ends thus: 'and thou hearest the sound thereof, but canst not tell whence it cometh, and whither it goeth: so is every one that is born of the spirit.' Who knows if Orsini rather than the pastor, the young deserter rather than the old neighbour, the mysterious package from home, might not come from where the wind blows, the wind that is born of the spirit?*

The movie has been made with a realistic ardour that has implications beyond the documentary. Bresson has used the text by Devigny as he used the Bernanos novel and the narration almost seems like the spoken titles for a silent film. All the movements, the most minimal action have a liturgical inflection, evocative of an inner life. The fervour with which Fontaine gathers the little bits of wood which have fallen to the floor, the meticulous and passionless care with which he disguises the door panel he has broken, the infinite patience with which he weaves the ropes and makes the hooks, the decision to kill the guard received almost by infusion, are all part of a plot which is religious, theological.

'The reconstruction of reality with dispersed, incomplete objects,' says a theorist of cinema when speaking of Bresson, 'has nothing to do with abstraction, but is constructed with a dialectic of the concrete and the abstract by the reciprocal, internal action of the contradictory elements of the image, the sound and their interrelation.' The result is a style which is hard-surfaced, difficult and absolutely unusual. Seeing a film by Bresson is a unique experience and if all the French film-makers were to disappear and it were necessary to choose only one as survivor, the *cronista* would choose Robert Bresson. Even though the reflections to which *The Diary of a Country Priest* and *A Man Escaped* lead may have very little to do with the metaphysical destiny of the reflections of the *cronista*, to whom the transcendence of the soul, divine grace and the hand of God matter quite little. It happens that Bresson works with such a fervour, a dedication so evident and a seriousness such as to make the rest of the cinema seem by contrast the work of frivolous but costly craftsmen who, holding in their hands a magic wand, waste it by asking that it rain money, that they be happy for an hour and a half or that a pigeon come out of a top hat: silly things really.

15 June 1958

* It is due to this that in the harsh environment of the prison, in the midst of the agony of the condemned men, in the misery of men reducing men to confinement and animality, in the thundering silence of the desolate life of the prisoner, the painfully beautiful and fervent notes of the great Mass in C Minor by Mozart do not sound out of context, but rather seem the only commentary possible.

The Unquiet Englishman

The Quiet American (United Artists) shows how each time Hollywood buys fish it gets worried about the bones. The film is based on a novel of the same title by Graham Greene, who has filled it with a serious discussion about the validity of Western politics in Asia. The dilemma of the hero (a cynical English journalist who smokes opium, doesn't believe in God and has a Vietnamese lover) is how to replace the worn-out European imperialism without the communists rushing in. One of the characters says, referring to the quiet American: 'He was talking about the old colonial powers – England and France, and how you two couldn't expect to win the confidence of the Asians. That was where America came in now with clean hands.' To which the Englishman answers: 'Hawaii, Puerto Rico . . . New Mexico.' With lines like this it was very unlikely that the novel would keep its integrity in Hollywood. Why make it then? The book offered some of the natural ingredients that Hollywood blends in its plastic recipes: sex, violence, intrigue. Besides, there always remains the first recourse of rewriting it and improving on the author's work. This is more or less what the writer–producer–director Joseph L. Mankiewicz (*All About Eve*, *The Barefoot Contessa*, *Letter to Three Wives* and a two-time Oscar winner) has done.

The American of the story comes to Saigon sent by one of those American foreign aid organizations with all-purpose acronyms. There he gets truly involved, beginning with driving a wedge between the English journalist and his lover, always in good faith and with a clean purpose as evident as his crew cut and his youthful demeanour but not any less harmful. If he falls in love with Phuong, the Vietnamese kept woman, it is because he has visited the place where she worked before as an elegant prostitute. If he proposes marriage to her, it is because every woman has a right to the security of matrimony. If he tries to take the girl away from the Englishman he does not steal her but tells him about it first, and then saves him from dying at the hands of the communists. If he wishes to help the natives, he doesn't stick around to look at their poverty and then complain, but backs one of the groups opposing the communists and the French. But here he commits his first blunder: the 'third force' is a band of outlaws, led by one General The, who use the plastic explosives that he gave them to start a series of explosions in downtown Saigon that will kill women and children.*

* One ploy that gives the plot its particular force is that General The as well as the Saigon bombings are sheer fact. The anti-Americanism of the book comes through when Greene brings American responsibility in these incidents to a documentary level.

It is characteristic of Greene that the Englishman delivers the American to the communists from an ambivalence that gives the measure of the ambiguity of this character. The Saigon bombings follow immediately after the flight of the Vietnamese girl, after she has found out that the Englishman cannot marry her because his wife will not give him a divorce. But the ambiguity continues when the author ends the book with this sentence by Fowler, the Englishman, who is also the narrator: '. . . how I wished there existed someone to whom I could say that I was sorry.' This means that no one is interested in knowing that Fowler regrets the death of the American, as much for one man's sake as for the other's. Neither Phuong, the lover, nor Vigot, the police chief, nor Phuong's sister, nor the compatriots of Pyle, the American, seem saddened or even bothered. Rather they seem satisfied.

The Englishman returns to his opium, his wife gives him the divorce, they no longer decide to move him to London and Phuong has come back to him. The American catalyst has disappeared and life once again takes its old and new course in Vietnam. Because, as Fowler says, this people only wants to live in peace, to be born, die, work, eat, procreate and die in peace. 'They want enough rice . . . They don't want to be shot at. They want one day to be much the same as another. They don't want our white skins around telling them what they want.'

This anti-imperialist credo has been written by Greene with a beauty on a par with its political lucidity. Among many polemical barbs ('. . . I haven't noticed much regard for truth in our papers either . . . here in the East – well, I don't like Ike.' (Liberty) 'Why have we only just discovered it?' I said. 'Forty years ago no one talked that way') the novelist has found the road that leads to the Asiatic ideal – Asia for the Asians – and gives the clue as to why England (and it is an Englishman who is speaking) is abandoning her colonies in Asia with the cleanness and the grace which is the philosophy of old nations: 'I know that record. Siam goes. Malaya goes. Indonesia goes. What does "go" mean? If I believed in your God and another life, I'd bet my future harp against your golden crown that in five hundred years there may be no New York or London, but they'll be growing paddy in these fields, they'll be carrying their produce to market on long poles wearing their pointed hats. The small boys will be sitting on the buffaloes. I like the buffaloes, they don't like our smell, the smell of Europeans. And remember – from a buffalo's point of view you are a European too.'

Mankiewicz asserts that in *The Quiet American* there is more Graham Greene than in any other movie based on his novels. Maybe he is right, because in the first one hundred minutes the film follows the novel with enough fidelity (the opium has been suppressed along with one or two interesting conversations, but these are bare necessities of the movies, and one must recognize that the need of suppressing the excessive dialogue has allowed the director to make a movie which is entertaining, true, and full of interest), but in the last thirty minutes, with the death of the American, everything falls apart.

'I like films with happy endings best,' says Phuong in the book, but this time the cinema has refused to please her. Phuong does not go back to the Englishman, but acquires a sudden sense of Western honour and although she has quickly learned what the word 'future' means she appears to forget it with equal speed: now she prefers earning a living in the cabaret to being the Englishman's lover again, despite his offer of marriage. Fowler, scorned by everyone, haunted by the idea that he has killed the American, repents, and what was the last line in the book, here provides a pretext for the police chief, doubling as a missionary, to tell him, when he says that he would like to tell someone his feelings: 'There's a church on your way.'

But the most curious change is undergone by the quiet American. His character in the book is the incarnation of that sly enemy, slimy evil disguised as innocence. Or even better: evil innocence. Fowler says: 'Innocence is like a dumb leper who has lost his bell, wandering through the world, meaning no harm.' Except that in the film Pyle is not a guilty innocent, but an innocent innocent. Fowler has been deceived: the communists planted the bombs and they invented the conspiracy with General The so they could kill the American, who not only was innocent but a true lay saint. And since every opus by Graham Greene has a lot of the crime novel, doesn't the reader guess whom they're going to put the blame on? Characteristically – or is it an evil innocence on Mankiewicz' part? – on the only character in the book who echoes the kindness of Gandhi, an Indian–Spanish mestizo named Domínguez!

29 June 1958

Mourning Becomes Lambetti

The Girl in Black (*To Koritsi me ta Mavra*, Columbia) is the second Greek movie to come to shore in Cuba and it is no freak accident that it is by the same director as the first import: Michael Cacoyannis. Filmed in only eight weeks on the Greek island of Hydra, at the laughable cost of $60,000, *The Girl in Black* is such a well-made film that it has made *Time* magazine exclaim: 'It is just possibly the best full-length talking picture ever made for $60,000.'

To the island come two rich Athenian young men on summer vacation. They stay in an old mansion that's come down in the world in the same calamitous fashion as its owners have gone down in the esteem of the town: the house had belonged to a wealthy merchant who died broke. Now his widow, a son and a daughter live in it.

The widow is still young, and need and loneliness have made her clutch at sex with the desperation that reaches women when they are near to the death of sex that is the menopause. Frequently, the boys of the town discover her in the thicket that surrounds the nearby ruins with her occasional lover: a fisherman, a salesman, any hooligan of the plaza. When the son finds out, he upbraids his mother and even strikes her in public, in a scene of brutal frankness.

Life has become difficult in the extreme for the son, chased by the laggards of the town, who pursue him with their taunts, their knowing looks, their infinite cruelty. One day he will decide to go off to Athens. The girl, Marina, holds on to a pride that is a stockade with which to defend her modesty, the dike for holding back the pain of being the daughter of that woman, the sister of her brother, a local girl: of being still alive. Dressed in black, always, with a fierce independence and a serene haughtiness, Marina suffers her own ordeal. In her mind is the terrible memory of her younger sister, a monster of ugliness with the heart of a child. Her kid sister was in love with one of the town rascals. One day (she was alone in the house) the suitor tried to kiss her in her room. She rejected him and told him that her sister's boyfriend shouldn't behave like that. 'Me that monster's boyfriend?' the guy told her. 'I've courted her to get close to you.' But the whole time the conversation lasted the kid sister had been in the next room, listening. Three days later she threw herself into the sea.

Now the same character, Christos, chases her, organizes groups of friends to sing winking serenades to her, to needle her every time she goes down to the town, to pass by in front of her house and say things to her at the top of their voices: to make life intolerable for her. One day they chase her down to town and they only stop when Marina sees her brother on the ground, brutally beaten by another in the group. Then she speaks for the first time, shouting: 'What have we done to you?'

One of the guests, Pavlos, is a young novelist and rich boy from Athens society. He makes love to Marina, more to have a good time on his holiday than out of real love. But little by little, the (Greek) tragedy of Marina wins him over. One day he tells his friend that he is marrying Marina. The latter ticks off an inventory of the difficulties he'll meet on the way to the altar: his social position, Marina's breeding, his life in Athens, the mother – especially the mother. Pavlos tries to break down these hurdles and calls his mother to tell her that he's getting married. But the telephone line shows itself as one more extension of the umbilical cord: Pavlos decides to leave. At the last moment, though, he will change his mind and will live out a nightmare.

Mirto, Marina's brother, has gone away, and she and Pavlos make a date in the old monastery, in the little bay that washes its feet. Pavlos rents a boat and Christos decides to play one more joke on them . . . for the pure pleasure of seeing him swimming in ridicule he scuttles the boat. But Pavlos invites some boys from the town to go for a ride in the bay. The ride is an excursion with death. The boat sinks and three boys die. Pavlos himself almost drowns and when they bring him to land the whole town looks at him like an assassin. Marina, who has been waiting in the monastery, comes down and finds out about everything. It is she who uncovers the true authors of the killing. Now she decides to give herself to Pavlos and to face the comments of the town.

This could have been the true and tragic ending of this Lorcan conflict (and the characters and the town and the people of Hydra are so reminiscent of Spain, Andalusia, of Lorca's territory), but the producers have stuck on a happy ending that almost ruins the loving, patient and wise labour of Cacoyannis. As a Greek wag said: 'In search of drachmas they have run smack into melodrachma.'

Cacoyannis, born on the island of Cyprus, son of a well-known lawyer, studied theatre in London and has directed plays in Nicosia and Athens. In 1953 he won the Edinburgh Festival Prize with his first movie, *Windfall in Athens*. Now, at thirty-six, he has just relased his fourth film, also starring Ellie Lambetti, *A Matter of Dignity*, which was received coldly at Cannes. Cacoyannis is an intimate director, who owes much to Michelangelo Antonioni, whom he admires. He has mastered the theme of love as few young directors have these days and his tragic sensuality leads him to approach modern emotionally charged subjects with a taste for tragedy that is very Greek. Discoverer of Melina Mercouri (now an international star) and of Ellie Lambetti, Cacoyannis is the true father of the future Greek cinema. With his customary modesty, when an American producer asked him in Cannes, last year, how he had been able to film *The Girl in Black* with only $60,000, he responded: 'That's seven and a quarter million drachmas.'

As in *Stella*, in *The Girl in Black* Cacoyannis has proved to be skilled in managing the passions behind a woman's face. If Stella was passion with the eyes of a woman and the heart of a man, Marina is one of the most introvertedly feminine characters in the cinema of the last few years. Everything in her is withdrawal and love is like the cement with which to reconstruct the walls of her inner castle. She is there, longing, trembling from a fever of the spirit, lifting her lashes with a measured modesty, uncovering her Hellenic eyes; her profile out of a Greek vase leans over at a noise and when she discovers that it is love going up the stairs that she is going down, she stops, now she doesn't hear the steps because her heart is beating bravely, loudly, deafening, fugitive, and she almost gives a half turn to disappear. But no: she turns around and is lost down a nearby alley and when the man finds her hiding in the generous whitewashed doorframe, longing, fevered, and she lets herself be kissed and she kisses back and surrounds him with her eternally feminine timidity, as old as those houses, like this air that comes from Asia Minor loaded with odours, in the golden, amber sunset, and he extracts the promise from her that he will see her in the same places where they surprised her mother, and she knows that she will sin like her, and when she at last understands her mother, when she finally knows what love is, she half-opens her lips and whispers: 'I would like to die.'

To film this scene Cacoyannis took half a day and managed it thanks to his actress, Ellie Lambetti. With her nose of the purest Greek, her eyes which recall the neoclassical drawings of Picasso, her raven mane and her long, graceful neck, la Lambetti is a memorable figure for the cinema: all in black against the whiteness of the Mediterranean sun. Now, with no more adjectives, recognizing how difficult it is in the cinema to project a wounded interior, unarmed and at the same time valiant, and to awaken in the spectator the portrait of love that is afraid to acknowledge its own force, the *cronista* announces Ellie Lambetti, from Crete, to be one of the most suggestive actresses to have come out of Europe recently: from now on he declares that her work in *The Girl in Black* is the slender spine of the film.

13 July 1958

Hello, Nostalgia

Bonjour tristesse (Columbia) is a masterly adaptation of a novel. In this case, the famous novel of the same title by Françoise Sagan. Its director, Otto Preminger, has not only achieved his best film since *Laura*, but has almost made a masterpiece. He has not quite managed it because the material – the flimsy novella by la Sagan – did not measure up.

One day in 1954 the French woke up to a piece of good news at their bedside: they had a new literary hero. Or better: a heroine. A girl of eighteen (small, fragile, with a common and homely face) had grown up overnight into that French beast: the sacred monster. She was called Françoise Sagan and seemed to unite in her diminutive figure Rimbaud, Colette and Sartre. Her first book – a novelette of barely a hundred pages – sold in a short time 600,000 French copies and a million more American ones. Her publisher Juilliard was helped in his persuasion by the most unlikely collaborators – even by the enemy. The Catholic François Mauriac said of his namesake: 'She is a little demon.' Soon afterward the praises crossed the ocean, innumerable as literary salmon who came to spawn dithyrambs in their native land.

La Sagan became a legend. Her striped pullovers, her numerous sports cars and her successive novels added up to a 'new' personality. But the subsequent novels showed that la Sagan had only one chord. Sometimes she played it in one key, other times in another, but always the sound was suspiciously similar. Today la Sagan is back where she belongs. The ballet *The Broken Date* has brought scandal around her once again, but no one thinks now that she is a literary phenomenon, a Radiguet of the fifties. It is no more no less than M. Delly bound in a suntan: the romance novel with spines of cynicism, the dime novel reduced to a pamphlet of euphe-mystic sexology.

Nevertheless, it is right to acknowledge that the book is highly readable, that it is written with a literary savvy that very few great authors attain not at eighteen but at eighty-one, that from among the newly coined commonplaces (the book at times almost seems to be prey to a self-destructive complex that sprouts caricatures of its own style, for example: 'I did not know sadness but I did know boredom'; '. . . I felt decadent and this gave me pleasure'; '. . . the gap between my gestures and me, the weight of Ann's glance, and this void around me, this intensity of the void . . .') there are certain revelations about the nature of feminine adolescent conduct and for many people the book is a kind of sentimental Baedeker of France between de Gaulle and de Gaulle: 1947–57.

The movie, in spite of its originality, which goes beyond the use of colour (it starts in black and white and when Cécile recalls her Mediterranean vacations, the greys of Paris vanish and brilliant, luxuriant, very Côte d'Azur hues appear), cannot escape the allure of a recipe. How is it possible for a film that has Georges Auric as composer, Georges Perinal as a photographer, Roger Furse as a production designer, David Niven and Deborah Kerr as acting supports, and Mylène Demongeot and Jean Seberg bringing up the rear with their young charms, as well as a famous novel and all the Riviera sunshine, to be a flop? From the moment the beautiful, startling title credits designed by Saul Bass open, the spectator knows that he is in front of a film that will be original, sensual and highly intellectual. When the movie opens with its grey and green tones, its vertiginous flight over Paris at night and the inexpressive, stiff, pained face of Jean Seberg, one knows that Preminger has put in more than Sagan intended and that the *Bonjour tristesse* of Hollywood will be more a *Bonjour tristesse* than the *Bonjour tristesse* of Paris.

In the novel there was a relationship between the widower father and the orphan girl that bordered on incest, but a sentimental incest, with the daughter in love with the easy, carefree life of the father who trusted in love, in sexual relations to socialize with his peers. 'Sin is the only note of living colour that still exists in modern life,' the narrator quoted Wilde, and she kept herself at the level of that certain paradox. Cécile loves her father and can get along with the multiple lovers that he has. The two have money and can permit themselves everything. Their long leisure is rose-tinted by that glamour which money brings to human relations.

One day, Anne arrives, the friend of her mother, the modern professional woman who has within her an egalitarian feminist: that is to say, the last remnant of Victorian puritanism exported to the Continent; and Cécile is amused with the situation. But then alarm takes her over: this woman will introduce bourgeois respectability into that bohemian house and will try to transform it into a home: the leisure of vertigo and sun and sea will end, and responsibility, adulthood will arrive: Cécile is actually afraid of losing her independence, her rebelliousness, her moral apathy: her adolescence. If she loves her father tenderly it is because she understands that he has all the irresponsibility of an adolescent.

In the book the narrator could step back from herself and contemplate her life. She loves her father, because he is what she could not be: an innocent. It is not for nothing that Raymond's youth was spent in the 'roaring twenties' and that he retains an irresponsibility impossible in 1956. Even in leisure and the easy life. Sartre has said that existentialism is first and foremost responsibility, and Cécile is a monstrously responsible character, a Sartrean being. She quotes Bergson and Pascal and has the same lucid ability to observe her actions and to classify them as phenomena, experiences, gratuitous acts. In the film, irresponsibility also extends to the daughter, and the infinite sadness – the sadness of the knowledge of life – is diluted and there only remains a tenuous nostalgia, very filmic, very tender and very poetic, but by the same token very different from the taste that the book leaves in the reader: there is no mischief, no everyday sadness, no rejoicing in a certain Baudelairean wickedness, but an external, almost plastic pathos.

The cover by Bass explodes in some formless bombs in vivid colours: an orange, lilac, Prussian blue spot. Then they are transformed into some fat, summer raindrops that fall slowly. The rain is succeeded by tears, unexpected ones. Finally, a single drop remains, as the memory of the rain or like the mourning that the rain of time does not manage to erase and rests on a face that is formed before the spectator: the face of a young woman. This is something more than an allegory. At the beginning, when Juliette Greco sings the song that replaces the book's epigraph by Éluard, we see the fixed face of Jean Seberg, obsessed, frozen in its pain. Then, with memory, there comes the youthful carefree life and a certain laughing wickedness. In the climax it is the composed, symmetrical face of Anne which decomposes and falls to pieces after watching Raymond making love with his former lover, destroying the love that he created in her: the foolish words that push her to suicide.

At the end, the grave voice of la Greco and her inert song return, and while Cécile covers her face with cream, over and over, in a demented daubing, of ultimate pain, it is a pathetic image, in which the adolescent face disappears and a tragic mask emerges, where the stiffness of pain, the mobility of the desperate Anne, the grimace of death are contemplated: it is Anne who has won. Her death has allowed Cécile to assume her loneliness, to recognize her profound moral misery and finally to enter the world of adults: now there will be no more holidays even if there are. The abandon, the lassitude of the primitive, animal life will be absent in the effort to be sophisticated: Cécile has grown up. This final image of the film, created, made out of pure cinema, says more than the whole book and will be, without any doubt, one of the most moving and painful endings that the cinema has produced since Chaplin in *City Lights* recognized his misery in the restored vision of the blind girl and shrank into a fleshless smile that was also the image of misery, of pain and of death: of life.

3 August 1958

cain
rated

films with dots: 5 dots was a masterwork

The Touch of Welles

Touch of Evil (Universal) is the return of the prodigal to the fold: Orson Welles, after ten years of absence (his *Macbeth* was filmed, under a storm that seems to be his particular halo, in 1948 for Republic), returns to Hollywood. He has come back, again, triumphant. Universal hired him to make a melodrama, intended at first as a B-movie, and he has turned in one dot less than a masterwork. How he has done it is the secret that has kept Orson Welles, twenty-five years after having made his first movie, *Citizen Kane*, the most original, vigorous and innovative author in the American talkies. To him we owe the careers of John Huston, Elia Kazan, Nicholas Ray, Stanley Kubrick and Robert Aldrich. As a young French critic has said, 'without Welles *Citizen Kane* would not have existed and without *Citizen Kane* the present American cinema would not exist.'

Welles has complained (wherever there has been someone who would listen) that Universal, like Republic with *Macbeth* earlier, Columbia with *The Lady from Shanghai*, RKO with *Journey into Fear* and *The Magnificent Ambersons*, the producer of his latest film, had not let him finish *Touch of Evil*. 'There are scenes in the film,' he declared to the English journal the *New Statesman*, 'I neither wrote nor directed, about which I know absolutely nothing.' And he added that 'the executive producer has done a major re-editing' of the film. Welles considers that a movie is made neither in the script nor in the shooting, but in the cutting room. In cutting and editing. 'The only "direction" of any importance is exercised in the process of editing,' he says. 'Well, in the editing room I work very slowly, which has the effect of arousing the ire of the producers, who then take the film away from me. I don't know why it takes me so much time: I could work forever on the editing of a film.' Chaplin knew why: he usually shot 200,000 metres of film to end up with 2500, and that is a labour that is not done in a day: the important thing in a film is not what to put in, but what *not* to put in.

Touch of Evil is based on a terrible crime novelette called *Badge of Evil* in which some shifty smugglers cross and re-cross the Mexico–United States border. Welles has taken this banal story to tell one of those Gothic tales that so thrill him. This time it is not a mighty millionaire who goes in search of his turbid, torpid lost past, as in *Mr Arkadin*. Nor a quiet American who finds himself wrapped up in a muddle (it takes two to tangle) of depraved millionaires, killings and infinite mirrors, as in *The Lady from Shanghai*. Nor a Nazi spy discovered in the heart of the American democracy: a little town in New England, as in *The Stranger*. He is – lame, filthy and disagreeable – a policeman now: that type liked so much by American hard-boiled fiction that it seems to be a faithful portrait: the cop who tells more and better lies, the cop who does not hesitate to make a fall guy out of his own mother, the cop who is judge, jury and executioner all at once: the ideal policeman of the police state. Not for nothing, at one point in the film the hero says to the anti-hero: 'It's supposed to be. It has to be tough. The policeman's job is only easy in a police state.'

There has been a criminal outrage and a Texan multi-millionaire is blown to bits by a time bomb in his car. The bomb was planted on the Mexican side of the border, and Quinlan (the name of the policeman) is not slow in catching a Mexican and in 'finding' all the evidence on him. But Vargas, a customs agent who is at the same time a big shot in Mexico, intervenes. The rest of the film is the struggle of decency and justice against the law and deceit. Justice, for once, is represented by the Mexican.

That is the whole story. But Welles has poured those dreary elements into a nightmare and at the same time shown how he constructs his films. The immediate artifact would be that of the concave and convex mirrors. The real image is virtually reflected but it comes back like a monster, amorphous, recognizable only with difficulty. At the beginning, we see some ominous hands carrying a crude time bomb. The hands place the device (the 'infernal machine', as journalists like to say, with an emphasis that would delight Gaston Leroux) in the car. At this point a drumming of bongos starts and doesn't leave the car until it blows up. A moment before the explosion its other occupant, a dumb blonde, pretty as only dumb blondes are, says to the customs officer: 'I've got . . . this ticking noise in my head!' The officer and the millionaire beside the blonde laugh but the audience recoils in dread. As soon as the bomb goes off there is a masterly mayhem: the fire engines join in, the police cars arrive, people mill around, the district attorney appears and whispers something, his assistant comes up and shouts something that is not heard louder than the whisper, people go to and fro and to, say things in half-sentences and move around in hyper-hysteria. It is then that the spectator realizes that this scene, as it is filmed, could only be done by Welles. Or by one of his imitators. Robert Aldrich, for example.

Vargas is trapped in a conspiracy against his life. In the street his American wife receives mysterious messages and goes to depraved dates. If she is in her hotel at night, they shine flashlights on her from neighbouring buildings. If she walks through the town, ominous footsteps follow her. Vargas goes to phone his wife and has to do it in a hardware store watched by a menacing and sombre blind woman. Vargas's wife returns to the United States, to stay in an empty motel, whose only occupant is an hysterical night watchman. When the watchman disappears with sunrise, some mysterious cars full of boys, rock'n'roll and drugs arrive. Through a wall they whisper to Mrs Vargas: 'You know what the boys are tryin' to do, don't you? They are tryin' to get in there.' Vargas is called by another hissing voice and when he turns around he receives a sprinkling of acid that corrodes a poster on the wall behind him.

Parallel to this twisted story runs another twisting story. Quinlan, the policeman, is an old drunk, who takes refuge in a whorehouse. The madam doesn't recognize him and when at last she succeeds in locating him in a corner of her mind, it is to tell him: 'You're a mess, honey.' The longing for and the memory of his wife murdered by a mobster haunt Quinlan . . . in the form of a player piano which plays and plays by itself. At the end, Quinlan and Vargas, the two sides of the coin of law, cross and criss-cross each other's path, pursued and pursuer: Vargas with a portable tape recorder, Quinlan with his old bloodhound's nose. The film ends with the peace and the restoration of law which is the final feature of all Shakespearean tragedies. Quinlan is defeated by technology, by the truth, by justice. His old flame bids everyone farewell with a mysterious '*Adiós!*' in Spanish. But he is vanquished and victor: he was right. The man he falsely accused turned out to be the killer after all.

Welles has again looked head-on at his favourite character: the powerful man who has a big crack in his make-up: the man with a terrible but empty secret. He already said it himself in *Mr Arkadin*, in the fable of the scorpion who gets a frog to carry him to the other side of the river. The frog was afraid of the scorpion and got a promise out of him that he would not sting her. The scorpion gave his word. But just in the middle of the river the scorpion stung and killed the frog. Sinking, the frog said to him: 'Logic! . . . There is no logic in this!' And the scorpion responded, sinking: 'I know . . . but I can't help it. It's my character!' Quinlan's character destroys him and destroys everyone around his viscous and pathetic figure but he cannot avoid it. The powerful end up falling victim to their abuse of power, corrupted as Lord Acton foresaw: 'Absolute power corrupts absolutely.'

Welles has directed the film with his usual technical wizardry and his Shakespearean passion. He has collected several of his former actors from the Mercury Theatre, recognizable in their curious cameos: Ray Collins, Joseph Cotten. He has attracted Zsa Zsa Gabor, Mercedes McCambridge and Marlene Dietrich with his personal magnetism. He has succeeded once again in demonstrating that Akim Tamiroff is one of the most versatile actors ever. And among them, those two normally so mediocre actors Charlton Heston and Janet Leigh move like sane people in a madhouse. But above all he has given a lesson in characterization and mastery of the role in his policeman. So dirty one can almost smell his filth, lame, enormous, racist, nasty, the policeman Quinlan is a vision as powerful as was Kane in *Citizen Kane* and infinitely more believable than Arkadin in *Mr Arkadin*: thanks to this character, from among the violent paraphernalia of a cheap melodrama, Welles shows what his true talent is. With an old pianola tune, Marlene smoking a cheroot and he himself contemplating his own ruin, in the midst of the alcohol and the smoke, he composes one of the most depressing and disagreeable images in the cinema, while at the same time preserving the aura of longing, of a certain nobility among the ruins, of Dante: 'There is no greater sorrow than remembering happy times in disgrace.' And the fact is, definitively, that Orson Welles has always had an enormous talent for the pathetic.

17 August 1958

a careful
reading
shows that
cain
was also 'a poor
vainglorious
ant'

And Vadim Created Taste

Sait-on jamais? (*No Sun in Venice*, Columbia), if movies were measured by the quantity of good visual taste that they contain, would be the film of the year. Rarely has the horizontal Cinemascope screen served to bring together so much sensuality which is visual . . . and auditory, because *Sait-on jamais?* has what can be considered the best score of the year up to now. Composed especially for the film, the well-known jazz group The Modern Jazz Quartet runs through its slippery melodies in a counterpoint with the action, masterful and suggestive. John Lewis makes the vibes of Milt Jackson, the bass of Percy Heath and the drums of Connie Kay, and his own piano – all so American – become this decadent French plot as the ubiquitous pigeons, graceful and numerous, become Piazza San Marco.

At first, *Sait-on jamais?* was going to be the drama of human abjection. There still remains in the movie something of what was originally a novel by its director, Roger Vadim. Then the producer Raoul Levy wanted to add on part of a detective novel, to which he had the rights. The result is a not very felicitous plot symbiosis, but Vadim has handled things so that the sensuality of its realization makes the spectator forget the gratuitous absurdity of the plot.

The love conflict doesn't offer anything new. It is the same French triangle as always, with one of the sides cruelly imprisoned in the mysterious seduction of the hypotenuse. Sophie meets Michel in a theatre. This allows the beginning of the film to surprise the spectator: the actors are as much spectators as the spectators: the film begins with a UPA cartoon. Soon one discovers that the protagonists are inside a theatre. She is the lover of a rich Nazi forger, now hiding out in Venice, surrounded by antiques and famous paintings in a house charged with implications, as if Daedalus had brought the blueprint of the labyrinth from Crete to near the Lido. In the house there is an amateur pianist, an oligophrenic and that fish out of water in all French movies, the *maquereau*.*

Sophie falls in love with Michel because she feels that she must bring something clean into her life, which is as stagnant as the canal that passes by her house. Von Bergen, the Nazi, loves this woman but in his twisted fashion, that of an erotic fascist: he permits her to have her adventures so as not to lose her. When he senses that he is about to lose her he sends Sforzi, the pimp, the man who has put Sophie in his hands for money, to retrieve her for more money. It is here that the amalgam of elements is shown to be the happiest. Among the sordidness of the house, its ominous architecture and the love of Sophie and Michel plus the intrusion of Sforzi, who wins her anew, are said the most important things that Vadim wants to say.

Sait-on jamais? is not *And God Created Woman*. In the first place,

* Here there is a play on words untranslatable from Cainite: *maquereau*, in dictionary French, means mackerel; and in popular French, simply, pimp.

because *Et Dieu créa la femme* is a key film. By means of it many actual attitudes are explained and understood. Vadim says that he did not intend to portray The 1957 Woman in his film, but that he did intend to give an idea of the relations between parents and children, of the gap that has opened in family relations, not only with the emancipation of woman, with her awakening to sex (and to life), but with the total corrosion of the old moral codes, dated, antiquated. He says, very aptly: 'The daughters have an unrestrained sensuality. The sons hide their romantic soul with a deft cynicism.' These two sentences not only say why *And God Created Woman* is an important movie: they explain, besides, modern life. The rebels without a cause are really children of conformists without a cause. It happens that *Sait-on jamais?* disappointingly, doesn't deal with adolescents, but with men and women who have left youth behind, mostly because they have associated themselves with the corrupt and the old.

A Tennessee Williams character, the Val Xavier of *Orpheus Descending*, also manages to explain it: '. . . there's just two kinds of people, the ones that are bought and the buyers!' Soon he will correct himself and will say that there are also those who are never conquered, but this is almost a ratification because those who are never conquered, are those who have never fought, those who have remained at the margin of society, the Quixotes without a lance or a shield or a nag or a Sancho worth anything.

Sophie lies, because she cannot face her own life. She has not been reared from childhood by von Bergen, she has prostituted herself to him by the time she was beginning to become a woman (and the most effective move in the film is the choice of Françoise Arnoul for this role, because she conveys perfectly that sickly adultness of certain women who have never been girls, who knew evil and lived with it when they had still not begun to live, and their look is that of a filled tooth: it works, it seems healthy, but one knows that inside is the decay, working hard, lurking underneath the brilliant porcelain exterior), and it is now that she really knows love, the generosity of love, not the slightly soiled, mean facsimile that she always got before.

Michel has the indolence of one who knows that the age of chivalry has ended for ever. At one point he says: 'Fight over a woman? That's *been* out of fashion.' Of course he doesn't say that the struggle for the lady went out of fashion a long time ago, that it was all a medieval invention. For him the implication is greater: the struggle for life has also gone out of fashion. Don't we live for death? Why bother? In the end, one will always be defeated. Sforzi is the most complex character in the film and thus the most credible. There is in his moral misery something that makes him like the Raskolnikov of *Crime and Punishment*. Except that Sforzi doesn't want any kind of redemption. He wants to live, and living in these times only means to him one thing: living well. That is, having money, that gold key to happiness, because happiness is also a prostitute. As far as von Bergen, his henchmen, the inspector from Interpol are concerned they are characters as three-dimensional as the heroes of Mickey Spillane. Only a miracle has let Vadim manage to make them coexist in the same story: the miracle of that marriage of commerce and art that is the cinema.

The external beauty of *Sait-on jamais?* succeeds in piercing the plot to find a place in it. Vadim rejected the easy lure of a golden and luminous Venice, with the Byzantine yellows of Titian, and chose a Venice closer to Veronese and Tintoretto. All is leaden and grey in the film; nevertheless, seldom has Eastmancolor been used with more sense of colour. As a matter of fact, only once: in *Gate of Hell*, that masterpiece of the Japanese colour cinema. But the beauty is not only on the outside, which would just be a matter of photographing a canal, a bridge, a façade: it is also on the inside. If the characters go to a cabaret, they go in through red felts, green velvets, marbles that are almost palpable in their livid texture. In the background, almost unnoticed, there might be a reproduction of the portrait of Gabrielle d'Estrées and her *petite amie*, the Duchess of Villars, making this *chef d'œuvre* of the Fontainebleau School seem like a Venetian *capolavoro*, and at the same time implying the *corsi e ricorsi* of times and customs, of the amorality that goes and comes while the world turns and turns: now the privilege of castle-dwellers, tomorrow the everyday practice of commoners.

If Michel kisses Sophie he does it through a tenuous brocade. If Sophie wants to demonstrate how love makes one return to an umbilical nirvana, she wraps him in a bed-sheet that is like a protective chrysalis, the maternal bosom: the woman being also the eternal mother: Adam really grown from one of Eve's ribs. Incidentally, this gesture is repeated in *And God Created Woman*, when Brigitte draws Trintignant towards the sheet that wraps her and wraps him in a cocoon too. When Sforzi is going to meet the lovers in Piazza San Marco, he feeds the pigeons, and the startling noise of their flapping and its innumerable echo fills the screen with pigeons, the symbol of love and peace, but which on this occasion take on the appearance of a bad omen.

Sforzi's words are also premonitory: 'If they asked that pigeon on top of the *campanile* what he thinks of men, he would respond: *Poor vainglorious ants.*' Von Bergen's exit is followed by a beautiful cortège of black gondolas that navigate with the rhythm of a funeral march, imposing in their leaden mourning. The ending gathers together two speedy motorboats that are running towards the Grand Canal, leaving a wake of luminous foam, going towards a purple, amber, charcoal grey sky, while the music and the voice of Sforzi, dead, repeat: 'Poor vainglorious ants.' Love does not exist. It is another mirage. Like that sky.

21 September 1958

The Passion According to Marx

An injustice is always preferable to disorder

FRANÇOIS-RENÉ, Viscount of Chateaubriand, in his *Historical, Political and Moral Essay on Ancient and Modern Revolutions in Their Relation with the French Revolution*

He Who Must Die (*Celui Qui Doit Mourir*, Cofram) seems to be the last Gospel . . . as Marx would have written it. This French film, directed by an exiled American – of Turkish origin – and based on a novel by the greatest modern Greek writer, has as its theme a tragic parody of the Passion. But this time what is Caesar's competes with what is God's and vice versa, and the kingdom of the followers of this new Christ is on the Earth: in a little Mediterranean country called Greece. The novel by Nikos Kazantzakis – properly titled *Christ Crucified Again* – recounts a real episode and it seems that the author was more interested in the mere study of the worst human bondage, egoism. Now Jules Dassin (*Rififi*) has brought it to the screen with a passion that at times is too schematic, but which evokes some histrionic hysteria that is always moving and cruelly honest.

It is the year 1921. The Turks have thrown the Greeks out of Smyrna and now occupy the whole province of Anatolia. As always, there are those who oppose tyrannies, those who collaborate and those who are indifferent. One group has fought the Turks and are condemned to a forced pilgrimage from town to town. They are led by Pope Fotys, a kind of Archbishop Makarios of his time, who encourages and comforts them: more a hero of the resistance than a shepherd of souls. One day they arrive at Lycovrissi. There everything is peaceful. There is an agha who is a complete oriental lord. He has Asiatic patience and certain refined tastes. A young boy with long hair in ringlets, curly sideburns, a full mouth and big eyes veiled by thick lashes, sings him sweet songs at dusk and lets the rude soldier drop figs in his mouth. The local landlord, the village pope and the merchant are in cahoots with the enemy and now they have time for other recreations.

The whole town, given over to abulia and inaction, has no other concern than that of celebrating a type of Greek Oberammergau. Every seven years they produce their own facsimile of the Passion, with different town dwellers playing Peter, James, John, Judas, Mary Magdalene, and, of course, Christ. The casting hangs on the word of the agha, who amuses himself with his consort on the balcony that looks out on the plaza. When the bell announces that the celebration will be permitted, the town does not know that soon it will have to face the same problem that ancient Judaea confronted almost two thousand years ago . . . and not on the stage: the son of God – or his problem – will return to the present century.

The choice of the townspeople who will play the sacred figures brings surprises. Peter will be a porter, a general factotum; James, a bartender scorned by his wife; the landlord's son will be John; Mary Magdalene, accordingly, will be the merry widow of the town; and of course, Christ will be a shepherd of a bleating flock and a stutterer to boot; as far as Judas, that unknown one, is concerned, he will be played in accord with the tradition of treason: by the most turbid and bellicose townsman. It is customary that the chosen ones feel themselves anointed. There is a rumour in the town to the effect that one Christ from years ago went crazy from thinking so much about the true Messiah: overwhelmed by a role superior to his acting talent. This seventh anniversary the actors will undergo a harder test.

Along the rough and dusty road advances the column of Pope Fotys. Many have died, others are walking dead: urged on by that strange form of inertia that is faith. Fotys has his champion in a character strong in the extreme and almost a challenge to the selection of the cast for the plot: how is it possible that this Hercules could bloom so in the midst of misery, fatigue, and starvation?

The caravan of hunger draws near to the town and there is something of the entrance of Jesus into Galilee, except that the ancient joy has been replaced by affliction: the recent arrivals are poor, are hungry and what is worse: they have fought against the Turks: they doubly represent the enemy: they are the walking conscience and the opponents of an invader who has come to be tolerated on account of the convenience that accrues to each one. It is not by accident that it is the

Church* which first sniffs out the danger: these people mean defection and the disaffected are a threat to all order: the Pharisees are again face to face with an extension of the Anointed. When the two popes meet, one knows that one of the two is a heretic and most probably it is the less powerful. Fotys and Gregoris bottle themselves up in a discussion not in the least theological: hunger and Christian love and human duty are spoken of. The noise barely disturbs the nap and the voluptuous waking of the agha: 'These Christians are always the same,' he says. 'They will end up killing each other.' In his Muslim manner, he is a prophet.

Gregoris, his mind activated by a good meal, wins out over Fotys, although he has to resort to a dirty trick. A pilgrim woman falls dead and he cries: 'Look at it! It is a message from God! It is the cholera!' The word still has, in 1921, in Greece, a medieval resonance. The whole town flees and the pilgrims must continue their journey. But Fotys has returned, like all Christian heretics, to the primitive source: now he is almost a Biblical prophet: he hears voices, has visions and one of them counsels him to found his city on the skirts of the Sarakina. The bonfires that light up the night from the mountain are metaphorical votive lamps for the few Christians – or better, for the few human beings – who remain in the village. Pope Gregoris has won a battle, but he is not sure that it is a victory.

Meanwhile, the characters in the Passion play feel that, in a religious sense, something is taking possession of them. Stanislavsky pointed it out as the first principle of every actor: fiction begins to supplant reality and fictional life is more real than lived life. Katerina, the widow, 'Mary Magdalene', presents her milk goat to the pilgrims. Yannakis, the salesman, gets the dirty job of deceiving them, but he joins them instead. Manolios, the shepherd, 'Christ', sees them with love. 'Christ' and his 'apostles' join the cause of the pilgrims and Manolios sees that soon he will have occasion to put into practice his hypothesis concerning the divinity of Jesus. 'He was a man like us,' he has said. 'And what was it that he did? Simply what was necessary.' Fotys now tells him: 'Manolios, we need you.'

In an almost pagan procession in which they drink and eat and dance, Manolios says that he wishes to speak. Gregoris gives him permission,

* The film got a 'very honourable mention' from the International Catholic Office of Cinema and this is in itself a contradiction, because the ICOC is an official organ of the Church and precisely by being Christian, *He Who Must Die* harshly attacks the official Church. Doubling the contradiction, this movie split the prize with *The Nights of Cabiria*, which, from the Catholic point of view, is a heresy.

because he is confident that this character will be put in his place: in the ridiculous. Manolios tries and stutters. Someone shouts at him: 'Let your heart talk.' And now Manolios is no longer the town stutterer, now he speaks and tells the sufferings of the pilgrims. They don't have cholera, what they have is a worse plague: hunger. Gregoris cuts him off, but it is much too late: Manolios is now the Messiah, in a local and obscure way. But, wasn't Christ that way too?

Manolios is the new voice of the pilgrims and little by little all the characters begin falling into this new Passion that is no longer a play. Judas betrays him; Peter denies him; Mary Magdalene is with him, always; the merchants fill up the temples and Gregoris, the new Pharisee, makes a deal with the invaders. The power of the agha is required to restore order, because this is preferable to justice. The rebelling and almost triumphant pilgrims are besieged by the Turkish troops and Manolios has to undergo an interview with the agha. The latter shows a wisdom that almost originates in Islam. 'I am an old soldier and a politician,' he advises Manolios. 'Tell your followers that you have been mistaken, that the others are right, and you will save your life. Otherwise I will turn you over to Gregoris.'

Manolios is at the point of no return; he is now Jesus: he also needs his sacrifice. He refuses and tries to revolt. But he is captured and taken to the church, where they punish him in a roughshod and rancorous manner: they cut his throat before the altar, as in a pagan sacrifice.

At the end, nevertheless, there is an encouraging note, one of hope, that seems to emerge more from Dassin's convictions than from Kazantzakis's imaginings: it is the drum roll of the troops of the agha who are advancing, ready to die, believing that Manolios still lives: or better still, that his spirit of redemption of the meek, of the rights of the common man, of faith in an attainable better life, is immortal, unfading, that 'government of the people, for the people, by the people shall never perish from the earth'.

What has prevented Dassin from making a masterwork of this beautiful, symbolic story, in which slaves seek an earthly redemption? Several things, which in spite of everything do not weigh heavily enough to leave in the spectator any other feeling than that of seeing a movie which is brave, honest, capable of posing current, eternal, but not insoluble problems. One of them: the excessive staginess of the situations, in which the spectator finds out what is happening because someone comes on stage and relates the news, as if the movie came from the theatre and not from a novel. The false dramatics and the lack of imagination in the photography, in the direction of actors, in the progress of the action, which have always been the ballasts of any cinema that wishes to carry a clear message. (In a certain way this relates *He Who Must Die* to *The Witches of Salem*. A relationship that is still more evident in the combative and belligerent ending, as per the recommendations of socialist realism. Although it must be admitted that the ending of this present release is truly moving.) And how is it that these faults do not result in *He Who Must Die*'s being a mediocre film and transform it, despite itself actually, into one of the most important releases of the year? Because *He Who Must Die* is an *engagé*, dedicated film and has a moral message that is so important, so contemporary and so old that it has been repeated by men as different as Jesus, Lincoln and Marx.

16 November 1958

Arsène Lupin and Old Lace

Les Aventures d'Arsène Lupin (*The Adventures of Arsène Lupin*, Metro) is one of the most delicious movies of the year. In it Jacques Becker (a director who tackles the social themes of the present or of the past – as in *Rendezvous de Juillet* or in *Goupi Mains Rouges* – as easily as he does difficult social reconstructions – *The Golden Helmet* – or light and sentimental comedy – *Edouard et Caroline* and *Rue de l'Estrapade*) has welded many of these virtues and placed them at the disposal of a subject that always was a compromise. But – just a minute! – a willing compromise, as he has declared in an interview with the French newspaper *Arts*.

Becker has begun by rejecting the original by Maurice Leblanc and has concocted a Lupin to his liking. 'I did it,' he confesses, 'to avoid any temptation of pastiche.' There is not the slightest trace of criminal adventures like those of *The Hollow Needle* (actually a novel as thrilling and amusing as this movie, although the *cronista* prefers Becker to Leblanc, any day) but nevertheless Lupin is still quite the gallant safecracker, Raffles on the banks of the Seine. Lupin robs almost for sport, but he also lives a millionaire sportsman's life: the proceeds of his thieving don't go to any asylum or charity; we have a thief here, not a social worker.

The movie is really a pretext to link up three almost droll stories. In the first Lupin goes to a gala. The President of the Republic is there, the First Lady is there, the first mistress is there too plus *le tout Paris*. What is worthy and shines in Paris – including diamonds and pearls. A preposterous Italian ambassador shows up and takes the First Lady to the dance floor. The First Lady dances and flies and flirts like a French lady should, but the Italian has something better to do than steal kisses. In the house there is a fabulous collection of paintings: Botticelli, Leonardo, Michelangelo. The lights go out. The Italian moves quickly, eagerly. In a moment all the paintings have disappeared – except one. Beneath there is a note that says: 'I regret the inconvenience. But the Michelangelo is a fake. Arsène Lupin.'

The other two stories also involve love and humour mixed with Gaulish guile. The crimes are committed by Robert Lamoureux, who has always been a very unpleasant actor but who puts his Slavic features here to the service of the best comedy: comedy that seeks, rather than a laugh, a mild Mona Lisa smile. There is also an epilogue which is the logical ending to a chain of stories that could be without end.

Nevertheless, the most notable thing about the film is not the acting, nor the plot, nor the pleasant colour photography, nor the music, but the sets by Rino Modellini, erected under the direct vigilance of Becker. In this film the sets are precious: seldom has an historical reconstruction so painstakingly perfect been seen. Not even under von Stroheim during his period of reconstructive furor, nor with René Clair in his most prolix longing for the past, nor around Max Ophüls with his crushing Teutonic inventories. Because the character of the reconstruction in *The Adventures of Arsène Lupin*, rather than sentimental (which it is on occasion, as when an ancient bus goes by drawn by three horses), rather than minute (which it is to the extreme that even the gloves are made in the typical fashion of the turn of the century), is decidedly humorous. Thus, when Lupin gets into an ancient Model T or bathes in a period bathtub or discovers the obstreperous trap of the Kaiser, everything is in the service of humour. It is as if Jacques Becker were thinking: 'Arsène Lupin, had he lived, had to have done this in his time. Because he was ingenuous, carefree, profoundly lighthearted and not at all grave.'

14 December 1958

Portrait of the Artist Naked

The Goddess (Columbia) is a painful picture. For two hours it shows an audience accustomed to adoring a deity that she is in reality the obscene version of Janus Bifrons: at the front the golden façade of success, at the back where all the sordid life now hides. Except that there are degrees: little lives hide little filthy things, in sprawling lives what is rotten can smell across the sea of time: the state of Denmark is often the only human condition.

People don't like the truth much. This reluctance to take in disagreeable things has always been taken advantage of by merchants, religious men and politicians. Hollywood has been transformed into a gigantic factory of gilded pills. The sacred monsters have been sponsored by the cinema with a fervour manufactured by a laborious technique. When not long ago, Harry Cohn, the late president of Columbia Pictures, said to Kim Novak: 'Baby, we *made* you', 'we' meant the whole Columbia Pictures studio, but he could just as well have been speaking of Hollywood, of the entire star system. What he was saying was that Kim Novak (who was called Marilyn before) had been literally invented, and from a daughter of immigrants from the sticks there had been born a Venus, a myth but also a box-office lure.

In *The Goddess* the life of a star is told, but departing from the opposite point of view from which a fan magazine would start. (At a given moment, the star gets married for the second time and is returning from her honeymoon, when asked, 'Do you think marriage will interfere with your career?' She says, 'Oh, no! Dutch and I are both intelligent people. We see no reason why I can't have a career and be a wife too.' This is a caricature almost as incisive as having the star say: 'Now I've really found true love.')

By the special construction of the story, the movie is divided into three parts:

Part one: portrait of a young girl

The girl is travelling with her mother. It is 1930, Year Two of the Depression. They travel through hunger and squalor. They arrive at an aunt's and uncle's house. That night the mother argues with the aunt and uncle. She hasn't come to stay, she isn't looking for money. What can she want? There is a man who has proposed to her, but he detests children. Now everything is clear: she wants to leave the girl behind. There is a heated discussion. The mother shouts: 'I'm only twenty-six years old! I still got my figure! I wanna have a little fun! I can't support her! I don't have any money! . . . I don't want her! . . . I didn't want her when she was born, and I don't want her now!' All this time the girl had been sitting on the stairs, listening.

The girl has now grown up and she comes home from school. She has passed to grade five, but she doesn't have anyone to tell it to: her mother doesn't want to listen to her, one of her little friends isn't at home. Finally she has to tell her cat about it – in one of the most moving and poetically bitter scenes in the recent American cinema.

The little girl is now a young woman. She works in a department store. The boys from the school all want to go out with her, since she's so attractive. She goes out with them but with supreme disgust. They kiss her and touch her and she lets them because she knows that if she doesn't she will never be able to mingle with these boys who are not of her (social) class. 'I'm goin' to Hollywood someday,' she says, and she isn't far from the truth. 'I *am!* I *am!*'

One day the girl meets a drunken soldier. He is the son of a famous actor. His buddies take him to a nearby hotel and she stays to take care of him, in part from curiosity and in part from sensing that in some way this may be her ticket into the movies. But the soldier is a desperate man: a failed suicide.

Now, when he wakes up, he has a message for her which is also addressed to the spectator: 'What are *you* living for? . . . Be honest, tell me. One of these days you'll be necking in the back of the car with one of the boys from town and because all your friends are getting married, you'll get married. You'll put on weight, your husband will take up with a waitress in a hotel in Chattanooga. And you'll have babies, you'll fret about rent, and your hair will go grey. Suddenly you'll look back and say: "What happened? It's all over." Your friends will die and you'll sink into melancholic hours sitting by a window, peering with unseeing eyes through white chintz curtains. And finally they'll drop your long wooden box into the mouldering grave, and what was it all about except – slings and arrows?'

The girl marries him and her husband continues drinking. One day he goes off to war and in one of the most despairing scenes, in a film that has that quality of anguished, bothersome and humdrum life which the best films of Italian neorealism had, she has a daughter and her piercing cries pursue her and chase her and finally she also cries: 'I'm only nineteen years old! I've got a good figure! I still turn men's heads when I walk down the street! I wanna have some fun!' 'What about the baby?' asks her mother. 'I don't want her. I don't want her! I didn't want her when she was born and I don't want her now!' And it is the mother who remembers that it is she who has brought this confused girl 'into this sick century'.

Part two: portrait of a young woman

Now the girl strolls her svelte body through the false architecture of Hollywood, indiscernible from its cardboard sets, false herself and with the trappings of the trade: sportswear, sandals, sunglasses and a script under her arm. To get publicity, she invents a romance with a retired boxer. But the romance turns out real and she marries for the second time. The marriage is a long night of boredom and fights, and the boxer, with more intelligence than the rest, understands that his wife has never loved anyone, that she is emotionally a cripple. The punch-drunk mind is the one which uncovers the message of the film: loneliness is the absence of love.

Part three: portrait of a goddess
Now she is a star. She has a spectacularly ugly mansion, servants of all shades, a secretary, a hairdresser, a swimming pool and a nervous breakdown. She doesn't have friends and in her loneliness she grabs at everything, including the alien religion that her mother brings her. She believes she is saved, but when her mother leaves and the loneliness returns, emptiness occupies the place of faith and she turns to drink.

When her mother dies, the star is so drunk that her wobbling gait and her awkward look can pass for grief. There is a last suicide attempt by the actress, a failed one, but her secretary dictates her epitaph: 'We got her to a psychiatrist for four months. Then he said to me: "She will never really respond to treatment. She will always be the same" . . . I'll take her back to California and she'll go on making movies, because that's all she knows to do . . .'

The Goddess is an original story for the screen. The script – done with the same painstaking care with which the plot pokes into human lives – is one of the most brilliant pieces that has been specially written for the cinema. Paddy Chayefsky – *Marty* and *The Bachelor Party* – continues to demonstrate that he is the leading chronicler of his generation. His stories formerly concerned themselves with the little man and his problems. Now he tackles the Gordian knot of the little woman overwhelmed by fame. Fame – that is the goddess the title refers to – is also a whore: she exacts a price in exchange for possessing her. This poor woman envied, pushed and pulled is actually a prisoner.

Chayefsky has been able to suggest this claustrophobic existence with an art borrowed from Clifford Odets in *The Big Knife*. There is the same neurosis, the same catatonic abulia. But there is also a confluence of his dry and sparse art with the baroque paraphernalia of Tennessee Williams. Not only in the fugitive Southern mother and in the lonely and unhappy daughter, but in the unusual poetic language that Chayefsky now puts on the lips of his characters, carrying them beyond the narrow limits of his previous naturalism. In the review of *The Bachelor Party* the *cronista* regretted that Chayefsky did not lard his chronicle of manners in poetry. Now he has done it and in good measure: it is because of this that *The Goddess* is the masterwork of a new kind of literature made of images.

1 February 1959

cain
launches himself
in full sail
in search of the
lost masterwork
– and is shipwrecked

Old and Seasick

The Old Man and the Sea (Warner) is, fundamentally, a mistake. The *cronista* cannot forget that they had attempted art: an enormous effort has been wasted on one of the noblest intentions that any producer in Hollywood has had in the last ten years. But the road to hell is paved with good intentions – and apparently the one to Hollywood too. That is the reason that where there should be the worst sign that *Cine* can make – a thumbs down: worse than mediocre –, there is an asterisk to salvage for the spectator what he can. *The Old Man and the Sea* is not a bad movie: simply, it is not a movie.

The first mistake and the one that led to the path to hell (or high water) is having made the film at all. *The Old Man and the Sea*, the book, is a masterpiece and it will remain among the classics of American literature, more outstanding than more pretentious and grander works, although the *cronista* prefers, among all the novels of Hemingway, *The Sun Also Rises*. Why? Because the talent of Ernest Hemingway is merely the talent of a storyteller, of a short story writer who was able to find a different style and combined it with a strange ability to make the most false and unreal conversations in all literature – by a miracle of graphics, because typography is still an obscure craft – be read with an easiness and a sense of immediacy that left a sensation of natural ease and randomness, when they were really the work of tenacity and artifice.

The Old Man and the Sea joined together too many recognizably Hemingwayan virtues for it not to be a masterpiece: the economy of means, the exaltation of human courage in the struggle against loneliness and man's lot, and the tenacity that overcomes bad luck. Although at the outset it seemed that the *fatum* – or it would be better to say the *ananké*, because on occasions the book has a load of tragedy, of inevitability which is purely Greek – would crush the will of the fisherman. When the old man says: 'I should have some luck. No . . . You violated your luck when you went too far outside', he is calling by its name the hand that unleashes the tragedy: hubris, boasting, the step of pride that leads to perdition. But he also says: 'But man is not made for defeat. A man can be destroyed but not defeated,' which is the recurrent theme in Hemingway, his philosophy – if there is one.

Jake Barnes, the protagonist of *The Sun Also Rises*, loves and fights for love, although he is incapable, physically, of loving and is loved by the woman to whom he would like to give everything, everything that he can give, although he cannot, and that other men cannot give, although they can, because she does not accept it: love. Harry Morgan, he with the surname of a freebooter, himself a freebooter in *To Have and Have Not* (which is a novel, from the Cuban revolutionary point of view, precisely, to which one must make many objections), struggles against bad luck, his 'not having' and even though he dies, he wins: his unbroken spirit is present in the final monologue of his wife. Colonel Cantwell, in *Across the River and into the Trees* (the other book by Hemingway that the *cronista* prefers), has been disgraced because he is superior to his superiors. He is wounded and mortally ill and nevertheless he enjoys Venice and the beautiful Venetian countess, his two loves, with the intensity of a sudden sybarite. In 'The Undefeated', a long short story, there is a bullfighter who passes over bad luck and death with his old Cordoban smile and the dignity of a taurine Seneca.

When, again in *The Old Man and the Sea*, the old man asks himself what has defeated him, he can answer, with a sense that is at once profoundly Greek and profoundly Hemingway (some day there will be some thesis, an exegesis that will explain that Hemingway is not an American writer at all and that will make it clear that if his work already has that durable and eternal air of the classics it is because he is not a regional writer, like the rest of the American writers of his generation, but a man who is deeply concerned with eternal values because they are ecumenical: courage, fighting, defeat, death and the struggle for life and the courage of the struggle and defeat in the face of death), he says: 'Nothing. I went out too far.' Perhaps to die – and not only for Hemingway – is to live out too far.

As every work of art has multiple interpretations – the Mona Lisa, to cite no more than a commonplace of painting, has been described by someone as 'the sweet smile of the mystery of eternity', and by someone else as a woman who actually suffered from asthma – *The Old Man and the Sea* has been described successively as: 1. a book on fishing, 2. a Greek tragedy in colloquial language, 3. a sophisticated primitive fable, 4. an allegory of the literary battles of Hemingway: the old man is the author, the fish is success or a great book, the sharks are the critics, 5. a petty-bourgeois diversion in one of the outposts of capitalism – the latter was said by a Soviet critic, in the *Litteraturnaya Gazeta*, and he further made it clear that Hemingway should have written a page on the tragedy of the Cuban fishermen oppressed during the uncertain struggle against their oppressors, but that he did not have the courage and limited himself to praising the hero, in order to bait the personality cult.

It cannot be denied that all the interpretations are valid and that from the Marxist point of view (and even from the point of view of the fishermen of Cojímar) the latter is not the most preposterous. So, Hollywood, which does not believe in exegesis, decided to take the allegories like whisky: straight, the fable at face value and to discard the equivalences, while it totally emptied (and this is no metaphor!) the book on to the screen. The result was to be expected: *The Old Man and the Sea* as an adaptation of the book is perverse, as an interpretation is a nullity and as cinema, useless. Here everything has been done as if instead of the best intention, there were a malicious porpoise – *purpose*.

'It is the most botched movie I've ever made in my life,' said John Sturges and he spoke well. If the script was amateur – in the worst sense of the word – even more amateur is the realization. Cinematographer Howe has done a passable job at times, but there are so many variations of tinting and of light that the movie looks as if it were made thirty years ago, when colour was more a headache than a technique. It can easily be seen that the marlin fishing scenes take place not only in separate shots and in another movie but also in another ocean – in fact, the beast was caught off the coast of Peru! At several moments another line crosses the screen and the sensation of loneliness, of struggle, of the fisherman's courage is totally lost, if it was ever achieved. (At one point, the quality of the film is so poor that it causes the narrator to say that the old man had cloudy vision, in the hope of justifying the blurred scene. (Cataracts anyone?) Asked about this, the second unit photographer Tutwiler said: 'That business about the line was terrible. But there was nothing we could do. We'd been in Peru a month and we hadn't caught anything but sardines. It was quite a large marlin. But then, when we ran the rushes, we saw the other line. It was terrible.' And it's true: it is terrible.) In this way, the movie that needed a first-class technical support is a lamentable spectacle – if one excepts one brilliant moment, the underwater photos of the sharks devouring the marlin. But this has as much to do with *The Old Man and the Sea* as the shots of the lions have with any Tarzan movie.

If the book should never have been brought to the screen, on account of its original form as an intimate epic (although they have tried to give it the tone of a ballad, of a filmed poem that has nothing to do with the cinema or with the story or with the meaning of *The Old Man and the Sea*), if it should never have been shot except in black and white and if its protagonist should have been no one other than Bogart or Walter Huston or even Walter Brennan, the fact that they have brought it to the screen, that they have filmed it in Warnercolor and on wide screen, and that Spencer Tracy has been chosen to play the fisherman, gives the measure of this tragedy of errors.

Tracy is the worst of actors for this folly, with his flabby face, his cynical mouth and his mocking air. The nobility, the simplicity, even the poverty of old Santiago have vanished. When Tracy says, 'Hand,' calling to his wounded hand, in the melancholic and despairing and virile tone of Hemingway, 'come on, hand. Hand!' Or when he laments: 'Ah – I went out too far, fish. No good for you, nor for me.' Or when he addresses a shark: 'Come on, *galano*. Come on! Come on!' the dialogue, instead of becoming poetry, turns into pure silly sally: the babblings of an old man and not the heroic monologue of a man with bad luck and defeated, but with his 'eyes unconquered'. Tracy's girth, his urban, New York look, even his voice, make him incredible and there is not one moment when the spectator feels empathy, let alone the age-old sympathy of the spectator for the hero. Not to speak of the pain, the profound sadness of watching a struggle which is useless and destined for failure.

What remains of the movie? Practically as much as there remained of the marlin when the fisherman arrived on shore. Perhaps the *cronista* is a *galano*, a dark shark. Probably so. What will never be possible is for *The Old Man and the Sea* to be a marlin, a formidable fish of the cinema.

8 March 1959

The Artist's Mouth

The Horse's Mouth (UA). At the end of the novel by Joyce Cary that gives its title and story to this movie, its narrator, dying, would like to laugh at life if his shirt weren't so tight. 'It would be better for you to pray,' says the nun who is taking care of him. To which the painter responds: 'Same thing, mother.' It is this death, it is this sense of tragedy, the knowledge that although one may be a buffoon, although one may treat life as a joke and be one of those among whom Eça de Queiroz counted himself – '. . . the strong ones, those of us who go through life with a laugh . . .' – the river of life always flows into death, that we exist for *nada* and that life is essentially tragic.

On the other hand, the painter in the movie travels down the Thames in his floating house, measuring the hull dimensions of all the boats, longing for an ever bigger barge, searching for the immense wall where his enormous pictures, the expansive pictorial energy that he has in his head, will find room: at the end he will wind up at the sea, but not to die, rather to paint an infinite fresco upon the horizon. Or, at least, this is what the movie suggests. The *cronista* believes that if Gulley Jimson had died, miserable, forgotten, justly deserted by the humanity which he always detested and to which he leaves his pictures – not out of love for culture, but because for a painter a finished canvas weighs as much as would a corpse tied to his ankle for a killer – *The Horse's Mouth* would be a significant movie and possibly the most complete interpretation made by the industry of that eternal walking challenge which it respects and scorns at the same time: the artist.

Out of jail walks a small, raggedy man, sick from filth. Immediately a sidekick appears. They talk. The pal is respectful to the point of adulation. An underworld boss? No, a famous painter. A little later it will become clear why this well-known artist is treated like a criminal: he is a criminal. He steals, lies, slanders, ruins, fights, insults: but he does it all for the sake of his art. He could say: 'Painting, how many crimes I have committed in your name!' But he does not say it, because he is a perfectly amoral being, for whom reality only exists as a composite of colours, planes, lights: his true reality is painting.

The man is a dirty and obscene and lying *poseur*: he considerably resembles old man Karamazov, although his interest is not women. At least not three-dimensional women, though on two planes they interest him greatly; especially their feet. 'You are a painter of feet,' a sculptor tells him. 'Too many feet!' This man gets lost in a blank wall and to fill it with his nightmares he would give up heaven and hell. In one of the most comic scenes in the English cinema of the last five years, Jimson visits some rich art patrons, makes love to the woman, insults the man, treats their secretary familiarly, gets drunk, stays over in their house to sleep it off and, taking advantage of the sudden absence of the owners in Jamaica, installs himself in it. Reason? To paint the living-room wall. To pull it off he sells porcelains, antique clocks, tapestries, everything he finds lying about in the house, and buys pots of paint and crates of champagne. Into this pictorial nirvana bursts a sculptor who quickly installs himself, but on the upper floor. Then a block of marble falls by accident on to the lower floor and opens a six-foot hole. Through that same hole the astonished owners of the house will fall six weeks later, mute witnesses of this masterwork of English art.

Leaving aside two or three implausibilities – English painters of genius, having to consider really great the paintings that are seen in the movie, believing that a painter of the stature of the film's Jimson can live quietly without the *marchands* besieging him – *The Horse's Mouth* is short by a brush's bristle of being the only movie that reflects in some measure the onerous private life of the painter. This portrait of the artist as a senile delinquent reveals in jest what neither *Lust for Life* (the biography of Van Gogh) nor *Moulin Rouge* (the biography of Lautrec) nor *The Moon and Sixpence* (the alleged biography of Gauguin) have been able to do seriously and what, apparently, *Montparnasse 19* (the biography of Modigliani) hasn't succeeded in doing either.

When the painter confesses, late at night, late in life, the way in which he came to art, the spectator senses that mysterious world where the artist lives and perhaps comes to create, without knowing it, a blurry image of what the Greeks called *daimon*, the Promethean fire, the creative urge. It is only in this way that the spectator can understand something of the respect that this man inspires in his socially 'superiors'. If someone doubts that the portrait, at its best, is serious, let him try to approach the real equivalent of Gulley Jimson, Francis Bacon, and he will see to what extent the movie has hit the mark with a character who is almost a mythological man: the furiously independent artist, strangely alienated and perfectly conscious of his importance: a man who knows that he exists because he is necessary, because he has an interpretation of reality many times more accurate than the thesis of the philosopher or the hypothesis of the scientist: the vision of the poet.

14 June 1959

Male, Female – Who Cares?

Some Like It Hot (UA) is a parody of sexual relations. But the satire on sex must be taken seriously, because no less than Marilyn Monroe is charged with making fun of all that she represents – as if being 'the sexual dream of the American male' were a thing to joke about. But all things considered it is one of the funniest movies that Hollywood has made in a long time. Thanks to whom? To Tony Curtis and Jack Lemmon, that's who. To get a laugh they can hold a rose between the lips and for a guffaw they even wear a corset. We must make it clear that laugh and guffaw come in skirts and on high heels.

Tony and Jack have witnessed the infamous St Valentine's Day Massacre. They go on the run. Wait a moment, Tony has an idea. '. . . we're gonna shave', he says. '*Shave*? . . . At a time like this? Those guys got machine guns ready to blast our heads off, you wanna shave!' complains Jack. Tony looks at him: 'Shave our legs, stupid.' Those uncertain steps in stiletto heels are the first in one of the most amusing female impersonations since Homer had Achilles in drag in the court of Lycomedes. Jack complains: 'How *do* they walk in these things, hah? How do they keep their balance?' Tony's answer: 'Must be the way the weight is distributed.' Jack again: 'It is *so* drafty. They must be catching cold all the time, hah? . . . I feel naked! Feel like everybody's starin' at me!' Tony, looking at Jack's limbs: 'With those legs? Are you crazy? Now come on.' From here on there is a succession of sentences with double meanings, especially an exchange occurring between Tony – dressed as a woman – and a bellboy – pushy and on heat – that the *cronista* declines to reproduce here, in case the page might be read by someone who was so scandalized by the movie she left the theatre. Who was that, your wife? No, that was a lady.

Tony and Jack go, as members of a female orchestra, to Florida, where they meet a double row of millionaires, like lizards in the sun. One of them – superbly played by Joe E. Brown – falls in love with Jack, the one with those tempting curves on his bent high heels. Jack loses a slipper and Joe E. Brown eagerly recovers it. 'I'm – Osgood Fielding the Third,' says Brown. 'Ah – I'm Cinderella the Second,' is Jack's answer. But this is enough for Osgood to fall in love *madly* with Daphne, Jack's alter eager. He pursues her, he chases her, he pinches her and finally he wins her. (Should we say him or put some inverted commas around her?) The scene in which Joe E. Brown gets Jack to give him a yes is a marvel of script construction and of film synthesis.

Joe and Jack go to dance at a cabaret where there's a rumba band that plays tangos. Jack dances with a rose between his lips, in grand style, then, doing a turn, Joe takes the rose with his big mouth and marks the steps of the tango: rigid, ceremonious, fatal. Joe to Jack: 'You're leading again, Daphne.' The dance continues, now the orchestra plays blindfolded and Jack and Joe are alone on the dance floor and on the way to a skit of grand buffoonery, with Joe baiting Jack, like a bull, with a tablecloth. *Toro!* At the end, we see Jack in his room, still playing the maracas that Joe gave him as a present, humming '*La cumparsita*', a tango for two.

Dialogue between Joe and Jerry:
(Joe is Tony, Jerry is Jack.)
JOE: Hi, Jerry! Everything under control?
JERRY: Have I got things to tell you!
JOE: What happened?
JERRY: I'm engaged.
JOE: Congratulations! Who's the lucky girl?
JERRY: I am.
JOE: What!?
JERRY: Osgood proposed to me. We're planning a June wedding.
JOE: What are you talking about? You can't marry Osgood.
JERRY: You think he's too old for me?
JOE: Jerry, you can't be serious.
JERRY: Why not? He keeps marryin' girls all the time!
JOE: But – but you're not a girl, you're a guy! And why would a guy wanna marry a guy?
JERRY: Security.
JOE: Jerry, you better lie down. You're not well.
JERRY: Willya stop treatin' me like a child? I'm not stupid! I know there's a problem!
JOE: *I'll* say there is!
JERRY: His mother. We need her approval. But I'm not worried, because *I don't smoke.*
JOE: Jerry – there's another problem. What are you gonna do on your honeymoon?
JERRY: We've been discussing that. He wants to go to the Riviera, but I kinda lean towards Niagara Falls.
JOE: Jerry, you're outta your mind! How are you gonna get *away* with this?
JERRY: I don't expect it to last, Joe! I'll tell him the truth when the time comes.

JOE: Like when?
JERRY: After the ceremony.
JOE: Oh.
JERRY: Then – we get a quick annulment, he makes a nice settlement on me and I keep gettin' those alimony checks *every* month!
JOE: Je-Jerry – hold . . . – Jerry, Jerry, listen to me . . .
JERRY: Wha – ?
JOE: . . . listen to me – there are laws – conventions – it's just not being done!
JERRY: Shhh – Joe! This may be my last chance to marry a millionaire!

The whole movie is full of these crossed lines that owe so much to vaudeville. Better still: to burlesque. *Some Like It Hot* feels nostalgia for the orgiastic (an orgy of slapstick) movies of Mack Sennett – and this is something that every critic has said: but one must see it with his own popping eyes: the initial pursuit of the hearse by the old patrol car, the peripatetic policemen, the surprise birthday cake, the true running gags of Lemmon and Curtis – but equally it has been able to dole out tricks that the camera of the silent cinema wore out, with sure verbal derring-do borrowed from the stand-up comedians: the sentences with a double meaning – which almost always have only one – the puns, the crossed-up quodlibets and the five o'clock shadow of sex and its close shaves come from that corner. To this the director Billy Wilder has added the send-up of the old gangster epics (*Scarface* for example), of the erotic comedy (*How to Marry a Millionaire*) and of his own romantic movies (*Love in the Afternoon* is side-splittingly parodied by Lemmon and Brown, with the old Hungarian quartet now transformed into a Cuban orchestra that plays tangos until dawn or midday, whichever comes first).

The movie was made with something of the old spirit of adventure of the silent films and so its depraved dialogue, its ambiguous quid pro quos and its almost obscene shticks are softened by the sporting sense that gives the tonic and the dominant. Tony and Jack are not gay but sad: two musicians, a sexophonist and a bull fiddler on the hoof, whom the gods – as they did to Achilles or Changó – transform into fleeting females, despite their permanent virility. Like Ulysses, they are to journey and navigate from mishap to mishap, before coming home, among them, every night, Marilyn, a too frequent Penelope, weaves her web of erotic dreams *ad perpetuum*.

It is this that places *Some Like It Hot* above and beyond the call of the wild vaudeville and gives it a certain tragic sense among the roar of the laughter. This bitter role is provided by Jack Lemmon; Joe E. Brown has a supporting role that is one of the best of the year; Marilyn Monroe shows, besides her charms, the gifts of the great comedienne that she now is, the definitive substitute for Carole Lombard in the American comedy; Tony Curtis doubly delights in his role of a man not badly dressed as a woman and of the perfect imitation of Cary Grant, in a movie that he has declared his favourite, 'Because it's the one I had the most fun making'.

But Jack Lemmon does something more: he creates a character. His fake, precarious woman in perennial flirtation with ridicule, lanky, ungraceful, with false eyelashes refusing to stay in place, with make-up – like that of ugly or old women – that transforms her face into a grotesque mask, and among the wig and all that fakery the job of staying alive and the camaraderie, breaks, painfully, the real predicament of the female inpersonators who have made of their perversion an art and a way of earning a living. Like them, Jack Lemmon is a pathetic caricature of a woman, also like them he has to remember, alternately: 'I'm a girl, I'm a girl, I'm a girl,' or 'I'm a guy, I'm a guy, I'm a guy.'

16 August 1959

Rebels of a Feather

Wind across the Everglades (Warner) is going to turn out to be the movie *maudit* of the year. Shown last year with more pain than paeans in a gala première in Miami, *Wind across* attracted the attention of the American critics – only it was a perverse attention. All joined forces to use against it the whole defamatory spectrum: they heaped insults of every hue on it. Shown this year in Havana, it served as a programmer for movies of the ilk of *Auntie Mame* and the few critics that saw it have not exactly fallen in love with it. Nevertheless, the French critics – those of *Cahiers du Cinéma* – are putting it in its place: they have ranked it as almost a masterwork. We shall see what we shall see.

Walt Murdock is a naturalist who arrives in Miami. We are at the end of the last century and there are no grand avenues nor sumptuous hotels, but barracks, huts, some bathhouses for local use and primitive walks along the boundaries. Walt sees with horror how the beautiful birds of the swamps disappear and end up as decoration for the hats of fashionable women. This repulsion wins him a magnificent opportunity: they make him guardian of the swamps. Salary: none. Obligations: plenty. Risks: all. The greatest of all: Cottonmouth, an always furtive hunter who lives off feathers, and his gang, whom they call the Swamp Rats. But Cottonmouth has some of the grandeur of the Old Testament and his power over the tribe yields nothing to that of Moses. But he is a prophet for profit. He also has a moral code and in his primitive life there is a certain stoical sternness. On one occasion – and Burl Ives gives a pathetic connotation to this moment – the smuggler eats a melon on the seashore, on his face a feral and at the same time sybaritic satisfaction when he exclaims, like a Biblical character: 'Ah, the sweet-tastin' joys of this world!' The character is moving for anyone who does not live in his element: sad, limited and poor indeed is the life of a man whose grand feast and greatest gluttony is eating a melon.

Murdock (much of the effectiveness of the character and that of Christopher Plummer as an actor is the novelty of his recent arrival's face, welcome to the cinema, which always has the spectator weary of the same faces with the same gestures movie after movie) tries two or three times to stop the killing by stopping the smuggling and fails. In his stubborn courage there is something of the self-denial of the characters of Hemingway, who fight because fighting is what they know best, and who fight against death, against men and against that evil entity, bad luck. The men of the swamp have made fun of him, have wounded him and left him for dead, and under his nose they continue killing herons and selling the feathers. But Murdock always returns to the swamp to try to punish the wrongdoers. Their crime is minor and the deeds of Murdock are not great accomplishments, but he takes on the enterprise with the fervour of a crusader.

When he finally meets Cottonmouth face to face, the movie takes on a tone of delirium that the *cronista* had only seen in the nightmares of Buñuel. Plummer has been sick with fever, when he gets a boat that will take him to the smugglers' hideaway. There he is disarmed by Cottonmouth and invited to a feast: they will drink moonshine and will eat roast alligator. They spend all night drinking and making merry and Cottonmouth thinks he sees one of his own kind in the warden and challenges him to a singular duel: they will drink to see who passes out first. In the morning, when he comes to, Plummer sees Ives already up and ready to make the duel of the night a formal one: both will leave for Miami: for Plummer it can mean death, for Ives, jail. Together they try to get out of the green labyrinth and when Ives thinks that Plummer is trying to kill him and discovers that the swamp fever has actually made Murdock mistake a branch for a snake, he decides to carry him to Miami, because he has left him crippled from blows. Ives' hat has fallen in the shallows and he stoops to pick it up. There is a brusque flapping and Ives takes out his arm with a cottonmouth, like his favourite pet, hanging from his wrist. 'Bite deep, brother! Bite deep!', he shouts at it, crestfallen when he realizes that it is not the law of man that conquers him but the law of the jungle, his own law: 'Eat and be eaten'.

The movie ends with the warden downcast, embittered, knowing that the law was too strict with that primitive man and with Ives who recognizes before dying that Plummer was right: the birds are prettier than their feathers, alive they are a spectacle not for women's hats but for the man who truly loves nature. Both men experience a double recognition that has the grandeur of human brotherhood and that gives the movie its stature. It is in this exaltation of friendship between men – the reconciliation between the warden and the hunter is identical to the reconciliation of the Colonel played by Curt Jürgens with Lieutenant Richard Burton in *Bitter Victory*, and his gesture of hanging his decoration on the dummy, faced with the memory of the gallant death of Burton, relates Jürgens to Plummer in his defeated, contrite gesture, one of bitter victory when Ives' corpse fades into the distance – that the spectator can recognize in *Wind across the Everglades* the sure, sentient hand of Nicholas Ray.

Apart from its intellectual connotations, there is much cinematic sensuality in *Wind across the Everglades*. Plummer is seen for the first time through the dusty window of a railroad car and the movie unveils an impressionistic, fin de siècle aura, which distinctly recalls the best Renoir, on the beach; Berthe Morisot, with its women; in intimacy Toulouse-Lautrec, at the Southern whorehouse; Monet, in its country picnics; although it is definitively American and decidedly original. (For some the photography, like the movie, is a failure. For the *cronista*, the movie is among the best of the year, without any doubt, and the photography perhaps the best colour photography of 1959.)

One love scene, under a boardwalk, furtive, interrupted by the band that comes to play, is Ray at his most tender and affective, very similar to the famous scene with James Dean and Natalie Wood in the abandoned house of *Rebel without a Cause*: decadence and ruin witnessing the love that is being born. The prostitutes' boat that sails by the beach and the picnic by the seaside and the boys shooting off rockets and enticing Chana Eden, who returns from bathing and carries Christopher Plummer away towards intimacy, with *Dixie* playing happily on the 4th of July, are moments to recall, along with the savage tragicomedy of the film. Example of tragicomedy: Ives longs for his youth, some fierce cathouse lost in his memory, and asks one of his band: 'One Note! Play me a nice, sad song about kissin' n' killin'.' 'One Note' accommodates him:

Her lily-white hand held a dagger as she
Gave him her kisses
One, two, by three . . .

23 August 1959

when
harpo marx
discovered that the
oldest profession
was not mime

Of Love and Money

Cabiria (*Le Notti di Cabiria*, Ponti) could also be called *Of Love*. But in Fellini love is always a relation between human beings that is more like a mystic state of grace than of erotic play. Lovers in Fellini never kiss – except the supporting characters, with whom they develop a relationship which is always onerous, one of dependence on testimony, of being there to see the communion of others and to feel one's own loneliness in the soul rather than in the flesh – and never do we see them in bed nor in the least amorous intimacy. In *Cabiria* the subject is the search for love by someone who should know the most about love, since this is her stock in trade: a prostitute.

Cabiria is a Roman streetwalker – and this word in Fellini is quickly revealed to be quite absurd, quite gratuitous and comically cruel, although at the same time it acquires a reality that the French cinema, for example, skilled in this profession (*Dedée d'Anvers*, *Golden Helmet*, *The Respectful Prostitute*), has never achieved. Reality and sordid life don't mean the same thing, even though Yves Allegret, Yves Ciampi or Luis Saslavsky may believe otherwise. Cabiria dreams always of leaving the profession, not for a comfortable retirement but for harassing love. Her engagements always lead her to failure but never to defeat. One day one of her lovers pushes her in the river to steal her purse. On another occasion a movie actor takes her as a shield from despair and Cabiria lives for a moment the golden dreams of every teenage girl. So much so that she makes the actor sign an autograph for her: Cabiria was here. This time Cabiria hopes for a miracle. She goes on a pilgrimage in the most harrowing scene of the film and one of the greatest examples of cruelty produced by a cinema that, on the pretext of kindness, has offered the public doses of that spectacle which good souls reject and which always elicits an exclamation from the robed bourgeois in slippers: 'There are enough misfortunes in life. One goes to the movies to enjoy oneself.'

Finally the miracle arrives one day. Cabiria reveals herself before the audience of a theatre in one of the most moving strip-teases ever seen: the soul that bares all in public. There she meets her last love. He is a timid, garrulous and hesitating man. He loves her. Cabiria believes it and the audience does too. But there is a slight fluttering in his gaze, a toothpick carried somewhat carelessly, a phrase that sounds false because under the apparent humility there is the hardness of city life. The boyfriend is a scoundrel. He also tries to kill her and rob her afterwards. Cabiria wants to die but Fellini does not let her: he has another end in store for her.

This ending has been what has disappointed the *cronista* with the whole movie and in part with Fellini. His observation of the world of prostitution and his comprehension of loneliness make a memorable experience of the first part of the movie. But the ending is lacking in the impossible courage of a Rossellini, who can leave his characters in despair because he understands that life is a tragedy. Fellini has needed the happy ending and the Christian piety – astutely disguised as human solidarity – in order to attempt a commercial compromise. It wasn't there in *La Strada*, much less so in *Il bidone*. It is here in *Cabiria* – as also is some wretched photography that reveals the same intentions as those of Chaplin – because Fellini is paving the road to the cinema in a big way and because to have left Cabiria without her little miracle would have given his work other, quite different, connotations.

But in the end it is Giulietta Masina who most works against the wholeness of the film. The sketches that Fellini makes before the shooting, the care with which he photographs each gesture and amplifies it to an absurd level, the loving management of the situations are dedicated to la Masina, who is his wife. But this time la Masina comes up short, to coin a phrase, and makes the whole film fail – and in the process Fellini fails. She is a prostitute not to be believed. At times she is a clown who is a whore, at others she is Gelsomina on the Via Flaminia, but most of the time she is (the *cronista* regrets it but he has to say it: there is no way around it) Harpo Marx walking the streets.

30 August 1959

sometimes,
the sureness of
cain
scares me:
did
von bismarck
really say
that?

Cowboy Cop

Rio Bravo (Warner) poses a posse of problems. A critic should instantly recognize a masterwork but everywhere the film has gotten a thumbs down at sundown.

In the United States it has been considered boring, slow and pretentious. Come on, fellas. *Rio Bravo* is a masterwork and something more: one of the most original films of the year.

Formally the movie is a Western, but it could just as well have been called *Lost Weekend on the Range*, because the central problem here is the means that the town drunk chooses for his rehabilitation – with a little help from John Wayne. At the same time it is a cop movie. For the first time the sheriff is a real policeman and the plot has all the astute legerdemain that Dashiell Hammett made his trademark in a novel that is at the antipodes, *The Maltese Falcon*. From another viewpoint – the formal – it is a study in what could be called the Frozen da Vincian Geometry of the movies. Howard Hawks, the director, has achieved a total mastery of that apparently easy game of chess, as if they were elements in a triangle in which the besieged hypotenuse always finds itself in danger of being crushed by the villainous Anglos.

Dude is the town drunk. The action takes place in Rio Bravo where Spanish is still the dominant language: everyone calls him 'Borrachón'. 'Borrachón' will do anything for a drink, even retrieve a coin that they throw in the saloon spittoon for him. This is what Joe Burdette does in the first scene of the movie, and when Dude masters his disgust and his shame for the sake of his thirst and tries to recover the coin, John T. Chance, the sheriff, kicks it away. Joe Burdette laughs. Dude comprehends, from within the haze of alcohol, his ruin, his total degradation, his vile self. Furious, he hits Chance with a club and leaves him unconscious. He goes after Burdette, who smiles like the villain he is. Dude tries to hit him. Two of Burdette's men pin him down and reduce him to a punching bag and the beast beats him mercilessly. A stranger, repelled, tries to stop the beating, Joe turns around, looks at the man who is holding his arm and, still smiling, draws and kills him. The stranger, unarmed, dies with a look of astonishment. Burdette is now a killer.

This is the first sequence of *Rio Bravo* and the one which engenders not only the movie, but also a new style in Howard Hawks. The whole scene is set up as if it were a pantomime, without words but with the maximum of movement, and only when the sheriff Chance meets up with Burdette in a cantina and tells him, 'Joe, you're under arrest', is the first word said and the movie really begins. The sequence is intended an an ironic response by Hawks to the movies that open with a prologue before the credits or with the credits that are printed over the prologue. This time the prologue is within the context of the film and not only explains the future behaviour of the characters but sets the melodramatic, cop-like and slow-moving tone of this frozen film.

The plot is mainly concerned with the rehabilitation of Dude – played in his now idiosyncratic vein, somewhere between humorous and lightly sarcastic, by Dean Martin, whom the separation from Jerry Lewis has benefited more than one thought. Who, from being a drunken good-for-nothing on account of a woman, goes up step by step in our estimation, thanks to the friendship of a man: Dude helps the sheriff Chance to guard the prisoner while the county marshall is coming for him from abroad. It is this wait – long, enriched by the least expected incidents – that is the subject of *Rio Bravo*. For some it is a stay in the dentist's waiting room. For the *cronista* it is a memorable experience, worthy of remembering: this is what makes masterworks.

Dude's anxiety for alcohol, his courage, his legendary marksmanship, the dry humour of Sheriff Chance – John Wayne is now the great actor of these epics in the dust, whom John Ford discovered in *Stagecoach*. He is the cowboy *par excellence* and aside from Gary Cooper there is no one who can outdo him with his slow drawl, his mincing walk and his aloofness towards life. In *Rio Bravo* Wayne has acted with an ease that the *cronista* has not seen in him for years. The explanation: Wayne was irritated because Dean Martin had all the breaks in his role and because they had put him in between two singers, one almost retired, the other a teenage idol, and he considered himself demeaned and his reputation diminished. Thus he engaged himself to do with a pencil point what it cost the other two God and a proud posse to do. They say that on one occasion Martin and Nelson had to repeat their takes fifteen times while Wayne did his fine on the first.

Then there is the griping bravura of Stumpy – which Walter Brennan has brought off with a competence very much his own: stereotyped but stealing all the scenes like candy from a papoose – the wait in the jail and the growing tension; the rounds of the town, charged with humour and fear; the arrival of Lou Burdette, dashing on his white horse, the unpolluted villain; the song played by the mariachis, Spanish and terrific, that one of the characters explains is 'El degüello', the tune that Santa Anna ordered played day and night before crushing the American resistance at the Alamo: its wailing sound in the night, its repeated macabre insolence; the fatal glass of beer in which the blood of the fugitive killer falls, when Dude is just about to let himself give in to the alcohol and the exacting death of the outlaw in the old style, updated here by that geometry of suspense that one thought Hitchcock had cornered for himself and that is now seen transplanted with easy success to the country of the six-shooter and the stagecoach; the inventive stratagems of the bad guys and the ingenuous, ingenious nature of the good guys, who dispatch their enemies one after another like square dancing without missing a step; the final killing, sportive and so dynamic; and the humorous note with which the movie ends, so like Hollywood and so like Hawks: so like the movies.

Howard Hawks declared once that he did not want to make any more Westerns, as if he thought that *Red River* was a masterwork and there was nothing more to say. Now, with *Rio Bravo* – and the choice of the title leaves nothing to chance: not even the chance in John T. – he has made another masterwork, and in passing he offers a retrospective review of his career: the parody of the genre and of his own work jumps into view. Note that:

Scarface opens with five minutes in which nothing is said and everything happens as in a pantomime: the first killing by Tony Camonte will set the tone for the whole film – and for a whole genre. *Rio Bravo* has the technique of a detective novel and precisely of those written by Dashiell Hammett and Raymond Chandler, who were Hawks's favourites in the past. As in *The Big Sleep*, *Farewell, My Lovely* or *The Maltese Falcon*, the spectator does not know what will happen next: at times, it is a silly thing, full of whimsy, at others a killing catastrophe, when a murderous bullet pierces the night.

One of Hawks's jerky jokes, noted this time by an English critic, is to have chosen Ward Bond for the character of a wagonmaster and to have killed him off in the first twenty minutes of the film: Bond, surprise, is an indestructible wagonmaster in a long-running television programme. Walter Brennan is in the film as a friendly recall of *To Have and Have Not*, since there he was also an old man, grumpy and lame, and the ending was entrusted to his jerky walk, while Lauren Bacall and Humphrey Bogart were kissing. Also Angie Dickinson – a discovery of Hawks, like Bacall – recalls something of Betty Bacall's role: one of the famous lines of the latter ('It's better when you help,' she said after Bogart showed himself cold to her kisses), is parodied blow by blow by the former: she says, after she has kissed Wayne and he returns the kiss: 'It's better when two people do it.'

The presence of the woman as the disgrace and the grace of a man and the femininely cynical lines of la Dickinson appear in the work of Hawks very frequently, especially in *Gentlemen Prefer Blondes*. The relationship between John Wayne and Rick Nelson – who is not as bad as the reviewers say nor as good as the teenagers wish – is very similar to the relationship between the same Wayne and Montgomery Clift in *Red River*. Throughout the film there are clues that relate to moments in the movie history of Hawks and to very precise moments in his work, which one must know well to be able to detect them.

In sum, *Rio Bravo* is a masterpiece of the genre and one of the most important and richest movies that Howard Hawks, a master, has made. A movie that the *cronista* has enjoyed enormously and that he recommends highly. Although beyond the humour and the sporting chance and the purely filmic he has been able to detect that bad seed of Hollywood, an element which is regrettably always present in Westerns: fascism. *Rio Bravo* shows it clearly in one single sentence. The powerful rancher Lou Burdette says when he sees some of the feats performed by Dude, considered until then an irredeemable derelict: 'Every man should have a little taste of power before he's through.' It happens that that sentence was pronounced some 100 years ago by Otto von Bismarck.

11 October 1959

cain
didn't understand
that the ending of
north by northwest
was the best thing
in the film:
a fun for all

Hitch Hitches Hitch

North by Northwest (MGM) is the return of Alfred Hitchcock to the world of the game for which he can be game, of free fantasy and intrigue, of sheer entertainment. After *The Wrong Man* and *Vertigo*, Hitch does a sleight of hand and for two hours he makes it possible for Cary Grant to escape from one of those traps for the falsely guilty man which is one of the constants of his work.

The movie begins with the logo of MGM – the lion with a pallor of chalk – enveloped in a jungle-green shroud. According to a particular cryptology this is the colour signifying the past for Hitch. (Please note that in *To Catch a Thief* Jessie Royce Landis put out her cigarette in a freshly fried egg: Hitchcock was the son of a hen coop owner and detests eggs: 'I never eat them,' he says. 'Eggs are sinister.') And this is already a warning that the lady who vanished on a train is on the road again – another of the constants in Hitch: the man taken for someone he is not. This loss of identity is one of his watermarks and vertigo – one of the ancestral fears that Hitchcock exploits to the point of nausea – besides that generatrix idea that in the past gave birth to *Foreign Correspondent* (a windmill that refuses to turn while the others whir around it), *Strangers on a Train* (a spectator at a tennis match whose head is (trans)fixed, while the rest of the crowd move to the rhythm of the ball) and *The Man Who Knew Too Much* (the musical accomplice, who reads the score to check when the cymbals will crash so that the assassin can fire his weapon).

It was some time ago that Hitchcock had the idea of putting a hunted man on the nose of the Jefferson on Mount Rushmore (in *Saboteur* the guilty man hid in the torch of the Statue of Liberty and fell from its arm to the sea). Now, Ernest Lehman, with a script which is exacting, painstaking and full of humour has enabled Hitch to put Cary Grant – and Eva-Marie Saint – almost on the buzzard's beak, and to make him suffer the most dangerous running gag of falls and pratfalls since James Stewart couldn't master his *Vertigo*.

There are moments of sheer humour which almost recall the civilized smile of Stanley Donen or the sophisticated tongue in cheek of Vincente Minnelli. Grant tries to escape from the hospital but he must do it through the adjoining room. The female patient there puts on the light and cries 'Stop!', threateningly, but when she sees it's Cary, she pleads: 'Stop!' There is the admixture of the humour with some drops of ominous black. Cary and his mother go down in the elevator along with the killers: Cary shows them to his mother, she, half nervous and half incredulous, asks the thugs: 'You gentlemen aren't *really* trying to kill my son, are you?' One of the hit men smiles, chuckles and finally bursts out laughing, the whole elevator shakes with laughter, even the mother. In the middle of this conspiracy of cretins, Cary feels the cold air of death breathing down his back: the breath of one of the killers falls on his neck.

On occasions the old Hitch comes back too: the master of suspense, as the publicity likes to call him, is at it again. Then, within an innocent phone call which is made from one cabin to the neighbouring one, in the careless flight of a cropduster, in a furtive note sent by the hospitable lady passenger to some anonymous hands on the train, is hidden all the terror in the world.

Alfred Hitchcock has directed *North by Northwest* (almost a masterwork, if it were not for the ungainly, improbable, drawn-out ending) with a fluidity, a delicacy of accent, a lightness of touch: like the product of a well-oiled machine. But in the mechanical play of the images, in the pure analysis of a terse and individual style, it is possible to detect the essence of things, their hidden individuality. One has only to review, airily, the best sequence in the film.

The desolate red prairie. A bus arriving in the distance. The bus stops: a man gets down from it. Diving from an extreme long shot the camera zooms to a close-up of the man. It is Cary Grant coming to meet Mr George Kaplan, spy. Long shot of Cary Grant, waiting. Shot of the desolate prairie. Medium shot of Cary. Shot of a fence that is lost in the horizon. Medium shot of Cary, looking from one side to the other. Shot of the empty highway. Medium shot of Cary, listening . . . Shot of a car that is approaching rapidly. Medium shot of Cary, who sees it pass. Shot of the car that fades away. Medium shot of Cary, impatient. Shot of the empty highway. Medium shot of Cary, attentive. Shot of the highway where a black and ominous Cadillac approaches slow, hermetic. Shot of Cary, watching. Shot of the car, approaching. Medium shot of Cary, waiting. Shot of the car, passing. Medium shot of Cary, now despairing. Shot of car fading away. Medium shot of Cary, more impatient. Shot of a truck that approaches, draws nearer, almost seems to run over Cary but passes him, covering him with dust. Medium shot of Cary, tired and full of red dirt. Shot of a dusty green car that emerges from behind a cornfield, until it reaches the highway and drops off a man. Medium shot of Cary. Long shot of the two men.

Their being placed one on each side of the highway and at each side of the screen adds a touch of humour to the scene. Cary goes up to the man: 'Hi. Hot day,' he says. The man's answer: 'Seen worse.' 'Are you supposed to be meeting someone here?' asks Cary. 'Waitin' for the bus,' answers the man. 'Due any minute.' 'Oh.' Medium shot of the man who is looking at the sky. He is watching a cropduster. 'Some of them cropduster pilots get rich, if they live long enough,' observes the man. Cary says: 'Then . . . your name isn't Kaplan?' 'Can't say it is,' says the man, ''cause it ain't. Here she comes, right on time. That's funny.' 'What?' asks Cary. 'That plane's dustin' crops where there ain't no crops,' says the man before he gets onto the bus and leaves Cary Grant at the mercy of the killer cropduster, of Mother Nature and of luck.

This is badly told of course. Seeing how Hitchcock has done it on the screen is the difference between a rough sketch and the delicate art of pictures.

25 October 1959

cain
put this movie
among
'the ten best films
he had seen'

In Search of Long Lost Love

'You have acquired the rights to a French novel by Boileau-Narcejac: *Cold Sweats*?'

'Yes. Oh, it will be very interesting to make.'

'Indeed, it's a subject well suited to you. One would think it was written with you in mind!'

'It may yield some good things. The bit of the story I like best is when the man recreates the woman from the dead.'

From an interview done in France in 1955

Vertigo (Paramount) is for the *cronista* the best movie by Alfred Hitchcock that he has ever seen. *Vertigo* partakes of all the Hitchcockian keys – the passionate green that makes the past return, the double, the terror of heights – but it is finally given to searching for a long lost love with an intensity unknown in this veteran director of sixty-five years who, with time, is becoming the most persistent genius of the English-speaking cinema after Orson Welles. What has pushed the *cronista* to go and see the movie on three successive, obsessive nights like a date with fate is not its absolute novelty, nor its obvious avant-garde allure, nor its terseness of manufacture, but its complete immersion in the sea of magic. Seeing it one thinks immediately of the *Aurelia* by Nerval, of *The Monk* by Monk Lewis, of *Nadja* by André Breton: *Vertigo* is the first great surrealist film.

The keys

When John Ferguson accedes to the entreaties of his old classmate Gavin Elster that he watch Gavin's wife (a rare creature who suffers fits of forgetfulness, mutism and crises of alienation) he is shown her in a restaurant with fire-red carpets. She is a livid, remote waif who moves with the slowness of one wandering among dreams. She is dressed in black and green and when she stops as if by chance next to Ferguson, he knows that he will live and die forever in love with this sweet silent Sphinx. (The green of memory, the red of passion, *l'amour fou*!)

John and Madeleine discover their passion in front of the bright ocean, over an abyss of rocks – the setting of *Suspicion* and of *Rebecca*, the movies with the theme of love and death and mystery that Hitchcock made in his distant past, departing for a moment from entertainment and suspense for suspense's sake.

The creature is ghostly and lingers over the contemplation of an old portrait, before a mouldering grave, in front of the deep mystery of the sea. In 'The Oval Portrait' by Poe the painter's beloved is dying before his eyes, while he feverishly paints the portrait that will capture the fading beauty now escaping through death's door: soon nothing more will remain of the woman than the memory and the painting.

The down to earth and practical girlfriend of Ferguson – the only rational character in the movie – comes directly from the woman analyst of *Spellbound*, from the girlfriend of *Rear Window*: her world is the pragmatic world of advertising and Coke, her ultimate goal is homely happiness. By annulling it, Hitchcock has chosen the grand romantic passion, the possession and the irrational as future features of his cinema.*

The death of Madeleine is prefigured in a dream and has the atrocious unreality of nightmares. As in Shakespeare ('We are such stuff / As dreams are made on . . .'), as Eliphas Levi foretold ('Dreams are the voyage of the past towards the future'), her death follows the diagram of the dream and now it is no more than a dream which Ferguson will try to reconstruct, in a process inverse to that carried out by the painter

* Cain seemed to have the gift of prescience: his words anticipate *Psycho* and, especially, *The Birds*.

of the oval portrait: memory is a victory over death: to gather memories, to recover the past is to conquer tragic human destiny.

The woman reappears in daily life, vulgar. But she is dressed in green: it is not her resemblance to the dead woman which opens the door of the future for us, but her direct link to the past. The identical profile is no greater pointer than the simple green suit.

Like the shy substitute in *Rebecca*, Judy has to fill the empty mould of Madeleine. Ferguson reconstructs her step by step from the grave. The everyday dress gives way to the fine grey tailor-made, the black dressing gown returns and the visits to the restaurant where he met her are renewed. The mouth and the slant of the eyes recover their past model. Her reddish hair is transformed once again into the ash blonde – and in one of the most beautiful, most memorable scenes that the *cronista* can recall (the sensual and mysterious, evanescent music, the diffused and tenuous image, the eternal Mona Lisa smile of the woman when she returns from the bathroom): Judy is Madeleine who has come back from the dead.

The antecedents

In *Aurelia* life unrolls at the slow and smothering pace of dreams. De Nerval called Aurelia 'the most fascinating incarnation of the ghost of a woman'. Here, according to Gautier, 'reason is the stenographer of madness'.

A desperate lover waits next to the gate of a castle. The dark is deep. His beloved will escape with him. She will resort to the trick of making herself pass for the ghost that each anniversary crosses through the castle bleeding from a dagger that it carries in its hand. The lover waits. When it strikes twelve his beloved passes through the gate and flees with him. The coach takes off violently. A little further on an accident happens. But when the lover awakens he is two hundred leagues away from the castle. Almost dead, delirious, each night he receives a visit from his beloved and by day he lies dying. Nobody else witnesses the apparition of this nocturnal creature – with which he has escaped towards death. The purloined bride is the Bleeding Nun, the ghost of the castle whom the real beloved made fun of and scoffed at! This passage is from *The Monk*.

Nadja is a mystery consecrated to mad love. Breton recalls the mysterious woman whom he met once: her remote past, her deep secrets, the indefinable aura that envelops her: the strange drawings, the sweet harmony of the encounter. One day the woman is lost and there only remain the memory and the love. The book is one of the sacred texts of surrealism.

An eternal myth

Vertigo is a masterwork and with the years its importance will become clear. Not only is it the only great surrealist film, but the first romantic work of the twentieth century. Its elements are from everyday and its material is what one sees around the corner, any corner. Nevertheless there is in it a mystery that seemed exclusive to the romantic dramas. He is a detective who pursues a trail armed with logic and reason; she drives a flashy Jaguar. The scene is present-day San Francisco and modern in such a way that one of the characters must lament the flight of the old days of the founding of the city. But when Ferguson searches for her ghost, he clings to the romantic symbols: the bouquet of roses, the golden locks and all the old familiar places.

In a way, *Vertigo* is an American vision of the myth of Orpheus. Ferguson and Madeleine have been born to love each other and the encounter seems arranged by the gods. She is a creature marked for destruction and the tragic signs are everywhere: in a persistent dream, in a family curse, in a chance encounter. Ferguson refuses to see the signs with a stupidity that Orpheus had already paid dearly for many centuries before Socrates: reason can never conquer fatal destiny. Madeleine is recalled and disappears. Some time later, Ferguson begins a search through the infernal regions and goes down to the heart of the nightmare, to the world of the mad, to daily life. He meets Madeleine and tries to rescue her from the grip of death. But he must not look back, ever. He disobeys, looks the past in the face and Madeleine – like Eurydice – disappears again. This time forever.

The first part of the film makes the spectator believe in the supernatural. The second part, in the natural world of the detective mystery. Nevertheless, the first part is ruled by dreams and it ends with the nightmare which is now famous (making an avant-garde movie, Hitchcock tints a landscape red and blue and the cemetery through which Ferguson is walking is seen alternately red and blue in contrast with the drafts of reality that drift through the cracks; there are composites, superimpositions, disintegrations of the image and that world of concrete reality which hides a disturbing magic truth, as in the surreal paintings of Magritte), while in the second part madness is the love that lasts beyond death or necrophilia.

There is an important revelation almost half-way through the movie, but this same revelation – which the *cronista* did not understand the first time – makes more evident the intention of getting rid of the detective topic and staying with the passion. From here on one senses that the true mystery is not to find out who killed whom, but who is who, and the detective hit the mark point blank from the start: the identity of Madeleine is the heart of the matter. But the very ending shows that Ferguson was always in love with a dead woman and when he is seen suspended from the double chasm of his phobia and the ledge, there is the certainty that he will carry on with the search for Madeleine: for him the important thing is recovering the past, that mad moment when he truly knew love which returns in a magical and strange and fearful form: when he kisses the replica of Madeleine and the room and the present dissolve and the coach from the past returns and also the first kiss. The *cronista* confesses that this resurrection of time is the scene shot by Hitchcock which has most frightened him, by being precisely the one that has least to do with that mechanical and external fear which is called *suspense* – and much to do with the ancestral fear of the loss of the present time by the total recuperation of the past.

The elements

The movie begins with the masterwork of Saul Bass, the extraordinary designer of credit titles of whom *Cine* has spoken more than once. There is an enormous eye, in black and white. The eye is tinted red and from its mysterious depth rises a visual vortex, a spiral in motion that suggests the unfathomable abyss of the dream and of death and the fatal appeal of empty spaces, creating the metaphysical fear that Pascal felt when he looked closely at the stars and sensed instantly the mystery in which time and space are fused. The credits are accompanied by the background music of Bernard Herrmann, superior here even to that of *North by Northwest* and which, at times, has that quality somewhere between hypnotic and filled with expectation, and at others, is evanescent, enveloping and sinuous like a theme by Wagner: a great part of the success of the film – like the photography by Robert Burks, who continues in his psychological use of colour – is due to the obsessive score by Herrmann, to his depraved habaneras, to the fateful castanets that cast a net in the nightmare, to the fainting theme of love.

James Stewart has never been better, because never has he seemed more a human being than now. Before he was a Hitchcock puppet who projected a very durable American innocence before the onslaughts of evil. In *Vertigo* he is a man in love whom passion leads time and again to disaster, madness and death. *Cine* has never truly liked Stewart, but it thanks him for the final scene on the staircase, which technically is very difficult and which is dramatically perfect thanks to his conviction. Barbara Bel Geddes has a beautifully written part that is beautifully acted and in one of the two or three close-ups she enacts her attractive American homeliness with a wisdom that goes beyond the technique of the Actor's Studio.

But the best thing Hitchcock did was to choose Kim Novak for the double role of Madeleine and Judy: she projects a morbid sensuality, decadent and at the same time highly attractive, as if underneath the frozen surface there were hidden fire: the iceberg whose submerged part is all lava. Nevertheless, her pallor, her bovine air and her hermetic smile confer on her exactly the quality of a creature in danger of death that *Vertigo* needed, and never would scenes like the possession of the past among the age-old sequoias, like her exit from the bath transformed into Madeleine again, like the pathetic ending, have been obtained with another actress who was perhaps more talented but less beautiful, less refulgent and distant, less patently attacked by an eternal and incurable disease.

Cine said when *Pushover* was released that Kim Novak in her début seemed ready to go a long way. Now it says that if she abandoned her career or died or disappeared, she would be transformed into one of the great myths of the land of myths: the cinema.

The master

What would have become of *Cold Sweats* (a literal translation of its title) if this necrophiliac novel had fallen, for example, into the hands of Henri-Georges Clouzot? It would have suffered the same funereal fate as *Les diaboliques*. Or worse still, Luis Saslavsky would have transformed it into another *Démoniaque*. Boileau and Narcejac (two ordinary psychiatrists who write ordinary novels together) should be happy because Hitchcock has made their little novel for them into a great movie, into a lesson in film-making.

Hitchcock is looked upon (and sometimes looked down on) as a humorist and on many occasions he is one. But as the critic Jean Douchet says, apparently his realm is suspense, not in the physical sense in which Clouzot, for example, understands it but in an almost metaphysical context. The keys of fear, the almost superstitious phobia of unleashing the mechanisms of evil, the coincidence and the changing identities permit one to recognize in Hitchcock a mind much richer than the religious one: the magical temperament. A man who proposes characteristics – all macabre ones – beyond reality for an everyday object like an egg, is a pre-Socratic. For Hitchcock all is mystery and daily life – the worn-out wide world – hides as much arcana as the Gothic past.

In *Vertigo* he has abandoned humour – when it surfaces it is transformed into a bitter smile which is crushed by the unknown – and given full rein to all our modern mysteries. The wonder is not at the coincidences of the real world but at the insistence of unreality. The fact that a minor divertimento like *North by Northwest* comes after *Vertigo* means nothing more than that Hitchcock, for another thing, knows very well that his art is a cyst in the talon of the Philistines.

It has been said that Hitchcock is an innovator, that he is twenty years ahead with respect to the other film-makers. *Vertigo* proves it. Here the moviegoer finds himself before cinematic concepts radically different from the ones in vogue twenty years ago. But the fact is that in *Shadow of a Doubt* (1943) Hitchcock was already posing and resolving his problems in a coherent manner, in frank opposition to the fragmentary world that the silent cinema, Eisenstein and the Russian school of montage had left as a legacy.

Now, fifteen years later, Hitchcock in total mastery of his flow of images can show off his style in *Vertigo* without disturbing the story. There are numerous tracking shots in the movie but only three cut-off close-ups. When the camera moves from one object to another to place them in relation to each other – the hair-do of Kim Novak as identical to the hair-do of the woman in the painting, the bouquet of the woman in the painting as the same bouquet recently bought by la Novak – the camera moves slowly from one to the other and by creating a time of its own space, leaves a trail of doubt on the road which is the refinement of suspense. It is this manner of storytelling – copied by all the young French film-makers – which permits Alfred Hitchcock to give to *Vertigo* that flowing and re-flowing rhythm, of tide and undertow, of the swinging of time over space, of ethereal stream, that is the exact sensual and magical vocabulary for this movie which is as obsessive as the eye that looks at the chasm down below.

That sensation of being up there on the ledge and feeling oneself drawn by the bottom, of wanting to sink oneself into the pit and sensing terrified that those dour desires are about to be realized in an imminent, abrupt manner, that voyage of space through time and the exact sensation that the bottom is rising towards us at the same speed that we are descending towards the bottom, curiously, is called vertigo.

15 November 1959

cain,
sedulous sawdust,
said to me:
'one must defend
this film,
even from one's
friends'

A Love Story

Les Amants (*The Lovers*, Cofram). The critic Lionel Trilling said that *Lolita* was a book 'about love'. And he clarified that. 'Perhaps I shall be better understood if I put the statement in this form: *Lolita* is not about sex, but about love.' It seems a paradox but *The Lovers* has nothing to do with sex either. It is true that the publicity has made a lot of the 'famous scene of twenty-two minutes', which is promised to be juicy for the salacious spectator, 'without a single cut'. But the abominable samples of the worst taste, the worst vulgarity and the worst spectators ever seen by the *cronista* – who confesses having gone to the *Pacífico* once and to the *Shanghai** more than once – have to do more with the disappointment of the person who buys an erotic novel for the lurid cover to find inside the wordy essay by Stendhal, *On Love*. (And this audience that has filled the La Rampa and Arenal theatres for two or three weeks, always avid, always impudent, shows the *cronista* how far the Havana public is from a true maturity: the clapping, the shouts and the shrieks – because it must be said that both were there: men and women – seemed more like the work of Cuban kids who daub obscenities on the walls with a hidden delight than of the adult faces which one saw on the way out: and the *cronista* is sure that a young, new public would seize upon this adult and beautiful film with the silence of one who witnesses a fundamental mystery. It is to them that this review is addressed.)

One has spoken of love – or rather of *On Love* – and this is in order to say that *The Lovers* must be understood as an essay on love. The director Louis Malle did not want to attract the spectator with a lure of entertainment and has made one of the most deliberately boring movies of the year. The sickness of this bourgeoisie which he portrays is tedium and the tedium is caused by *vita*: everyday existence, days piled upon days, the home weighing down like a dome of tin, the

* Theatres in Havana where porno films, called in Cuba *de relajo* were shown.

boredom of the old rich of the provinces and their daring adventures: polo, a trip to Paris, an occasional adultery.

She is married to an elderly man. She has a daughter, a Peugeot and a sporting lover. She is bored and does not know it. One day she awakens to the idea that her days are slipping through her hands that are stifling a yawn: she knows that her daughter is a shadow, her husband a minor sadist and her lover a social idiot. Her life is over. But on the night of that day, surprisingly, in an uninvited guest, she finds love and goes off with both: with love and lover. The ending is the complete opposite of an erotic excursion for middle-class wives. In real life she would go off with her husband on the planned fishing trip and he would take up the old ways again. The real fact – on the real stage of the movie – that both escape towards an uncertain future is illustrated as a definitive decision in favour of love which Malle makes. It is for this that *The Lovers* is an important film.

Malle chose a story from the eighteenth century titled 'Without Tomorrow' and adapted by Louise de Vilmorin, a kind of Colette who grew up reading Heine and not Emile Zola. (One must note the interest that the whole New Wave has in the French literature of the two past centuries. Vadim has just finished *Dangerous Liaisons*, a film based on the famous, infamous book by Choderlos de Laclos; Alexandre Astruc – the eldest of the young tide – became famous adapting for the screen the well-known novella by Barbey d'Aurevilly, 'The Crimson Curtain'; *The Cousins*, by Chabrol, is an old folktale: as Cocteau did with Greek literature and Norman legends, the New Wave is seeking a private mythology in French literature.)

The story is no more than the tryst of two lovers in the moonlight and the certainty that the dawn will carry away their love with the shadows of the night. But the ending is inscribed somewhat with the amiable cynicism of rococo literature (and the movie begins very appropriately with one of those old maps of the passions, which were in vogue in France in the mid-eighteenth century, with their Lake of Indifference, River of Vanity, Valley of the Futile Passion, etc.) and Malle transformed it because, as he has declared, he believes that the only possible communion between two human beings is realized through love and that one cannot know a person well until one has loved her or him.

His choice of night for the great love scene was not only due to the tenets of French censorship, but because physical love is a defined act and the moonlight, the play of the shadows, the guessing of gestures and words, lent it an unreality not only poetic but also practical. In an obscene novel the reader is led from lewd liaison to lascivious lasso and as Nabokov says – and the author of *Lolita* should know something about this – one proceeds by accretion, always adding one more fornicator in each episode. (In the canonical texts the chain always ends in the curious gardener or in the chauffeur with haemorrhoids.) In *The Lovers* there is a single great scene of love and it is realized with the least possible elements. A horizontal body, a growing sigh, two hands that clasp with tension and a whisper: 'Give me your hand, love' – and nothing more.

Of course the disappointment of the voyeurists is extreme, but the scene (on the second, on the third viewing, when the effect of 'terrible sexual suspense', which the publicity talks about, has passed) gains with time. And nevertheless, this is not because of the beautiful Brahms quintet, or the extraordinarily handsome images of Henri Decae, or because the whole movie is sustained by this great moment of courage (on the part of Malle, of actor Jean-Marc Bory and above all of Jeanne Moreau, the most capable of the French actresses of the present day and the most courageous, because one must know how a scene is filmed in order to feel part of the stress that Jeanne Moreau must have felt re-creating a coitus in front of the impudent eye of the camera and under the always scrutinizing Klieg lights) but because without it one would not understand the reason for making or for seeing *The Lovers*.

The memory of a notorious and abominable film, *Ecstasy*, by Gustav Machaty, is never far away: a single allusion, the same omissions, identical insinuations and an almost identical result. But here they are preceded by scenes which are the most mature and best directed – in terms of actors and of camera – that a director twenty-eight years old and after a single previous movie has ever brought off in the French cinema. If *The Lovers* had no more than the one achievement – without counting its defence of love, its faith in love, its actualizing of love – of being the only accurate portrait of the bourgeoisie of France, this would still make it memorable.

13 December 1959

cain
dust in love

Love and Loneliness

Middle of the Night (Columbia) is a study of that evil of big cities: the loneliness of anonymous lives. But it also concerns itself – and not marginally – with what *The Lovers* makes its *raison d'être*: love. The film is essentially a script-dominated film, because behind the director the true authority is that of the author, in this case Paddy Chayefsky (the author as well of *Marty*, of *The Catered Affair*, of *The Bachelor Party* and of *The Goddess*, and the chronicler of the pathology of American civilization). In all his movies Chayefsky is more than the author of the script (which has come from a play first seen on television – it must not be forgotten that Chayefsky is originally a television author) since his watchful will is always looking over the shoulder of the director, a position (which can be very comfortable or very uncomfortable, depending where one is looking from) which allowed him to take the unexpected and sudden success of *Marty* four years ago with the stride of one who knows himself to be chosen.

Of *Middle of the Night* it can be said that the success belongs totally to Chayefsky but the partial defeats, since the success does not manage to be complete, are of Delbert Mann, who time after time demonstrates why the skill, the sure application of an understanding of surface realism, the direct accounts of everyday life are not enough to make a true creator: a film author also has to be – and most of all – a poet.

The stage play (which was *Cine*'s first contact with this chronicle full of neurosis and urban poetry) is almost always moving. The movie is rarely painful. The *cronista* was asking himself while he was reading what depraved civilization, what mistaken destiny of the human race could put a man in complete desperation and on the brink of death, while blaming the mere fact that in the middle of the road of his life there came to save him from confusion a Margaret of the skyscrapers. (One tried to think in terms of a perversion of society, of capitalism, hoping they would provide a solution, but a more accurate answer hit at the heart of the family: man, alienated from the society which has created him, is also a stranger to its primary institution: the family. The conception is bourgeois, it is true, but none of the new societies created this century has dared to revise the family concept, which is essentially corrupt.)

This Faust of the stores (Chayefsky's play is set in New York's Garment Center but not the Garment Center of the big bosses or of the giant firms but of the small retailers who enjoy an obscure and unknown prosperity) has become a widower and feels age arriving escorted by loneliness. He has a daughter – or two, there are slight changes from the play to the screenplay – and lives in comfort: he works, eats, sleeps and knows that he is not happy. He must listen to the same droll stories of old men that these old men told when they were kids: unheard-of sexual feats, quick kills, traces of unforgettable passions: sexaggerations.

One day he meets a girl whom he describes as a total woman enveloping the heart of a confused little girl. She is getting a divorce and suffers repeated crises of crying and mutism (in the play one is allowed to understand the double confusion of the distant husband, a libidinous monster who is essentially a latent homosexual), not only before the memory of the lost love, but because of the present torment of her mother's house, of the world of double recriminations and the onerous dome of gossip. She and her boss go out two or three times and suffer a situation that in truth is not very far from the jokes about the secretary who doesn't know typing or shorthand but can surely give you a hand.

Nevertheless, he knows that this is the thing they call love and she senses that the respect, trust and affection are transformed into a sentiment which is greater, all-encompassing. Now, in the heart of the film, they have to suffer the torment of Romeo and Juliet. Montague is the passing of time and his sister's house and a daughter. The development of the dialogue reveals these two as substantially identical: both have an erotic fixation. The sister disguises it as filial love, as the care of a housewife who can cook kosher, the daughter can handle pseudo-psychiatric jargon but she is not free of the complexes that her projections cast right and left. Montague is also the job. Capulet is the adolescent and turbid, disturbed sister, the mother degenerated by a motherhood cut in half, and a totally frustrated life, the nosy neighbours, her friends, tender and wicked counsellors. They both suffer this well-worn ordeal and at the end, after the suicide attempt by the man's closest friend, the woman and the man reach a state of understanding and accept the joining of their destiny, come what may.

The moral may be that even among retails and through fear, the average American can aspire to life (sexual, that is) beginning after fifty. But this is too cynical and the intention of the film becomes pathetic in its description of cant and customs. It would be better to say that the happy ending is no more (as in *The Lovers*) than a reaffirmation of love: Chayefsky – like the romantics, like the surrealists, like Louis Malle, like the *cronista*, or more modestly like Virgil two thousand years ago – believes only in one motto: *Omnia vincit amor*.

But – alas! this is the most detested word and, nevertheless, the one that the critic always has most at hand – *Middle of the Night* is a failure as a film: its triumph is the triumph of the script. The few good things in the movie, curiouser and curiouser, come from Kim Novak. She with her fragile, evanescent beauty and her eyes of an endearingly neurotic cow creates all the poetry that there is in the film by the simple means of letting it grow around her, like an orchid that climbs along the frigid fogged-up wall of a greenhouse: her appearance is always the opposite of the unmoving.

3 January 1960

cain,
in analysis,
arrived
at the threshold
of dementia praecox

The Force of Evil

Les Cousins (Cofram). Néstor Almendros said (Almendros is a young Cuban film-maker who may occasion much talk: in fact his short *1958–1959* is the best experimental film made up to now by a Cuban: which does not fail to be amusing if one specifies that it was made in New York), he said that it was curious that several different reviewers had mentioned the word fable when speaking of *Les Cousins*. He used to say: 'Jordán spoke of the locust and the ant. This kid from *Time* talked about the city mouse and the country mouse. And you,' he said and pointed at the *cronista*, 'you spoke of Cain and Abel.' Almendros had read the review in which the strictly moral terms of the director Claude Chabrol were spoken of. Of course Almendros is not a Catholic nor does he belong to one of the 666 Protestant sects, much less is he a reader of the Talmud. Otherwise, he would not have spoken of Cain and Abel as a fable.

And as one has arrived at the equipoise, it is time to talk about the film. Or to speak rather of its antecedent.

'To put face to face, in the minutely described frame . . . two types of young men who are strongly opposite and yet friends,' this was said by Chabrol, exactly describing his first film, *Le Beau Serge* (*Bitter Reunion*). It is clear that Chabrol is very interested in what he himself has called 'the traverse of appearances'. Chabrol also says: 'In fact, beyond appearances a truth must be culled by the spectator: the unstable, the complex, the crazy one is not Serge but François. Serge knows himself . . . François, on the contrary, knows himself only at the level of appearances.'

If the name of Serge is replaced by that of Paul, the city cousin, and François by Charles, the country cousin, one will have a precise analysis of what takes place in *Les Cousins*. It is a pity that in Cuba *Les Cousins* has been released before *Bitter Reunion*, just as it is a nuisance that the *cronista* has seen *A Double Tour* (*Web of Passion*) before any other film by Chabrol, and with this brilliant exercise in direction still in one's mind (*A Double Tour* is one of the most beautiful and most perfect, coolest films that the French cinema has produced in the last decade: the vision that it gives of the kind of talent that Chabrol has is quite different from that of *Les Cousins*: Chabrol appears in *A Double Tour* as a lurid, lucid disciple of Hitchcock, with much more taste than his master for colour, but much less sense of entertainment) to have to consider a film in which the issues are radically moral and in which beauty, humour and the romantic aura are functions of the analytic will of the author: 'To sum up, in *Bitter Reunion* two films are juxtaposed: one in which François is the object and Serge the subject, another in which François is the subject and Serge the object. By definition the first film is the one which appears at the beginning. My ideal is that one be sensitive to the other film.' The first film in *Bitter Reunion* is that of the return of François to his hometown and the shock that it produces in him to find his good friend out of the past, famous for his beauty, transformed into an alcoholic ruin. François tries to lead the lost sheep back to the good path with mixed success. The second film reflects the intrinsic kindness of Serge, the knowledge that he has of his tortured soul and the sheer hypocrisy of François, much less deserving than Serge of his present destiny.

In *Les Cousins*, in the second part of the fable, the country man, supposedly healthy and serious, tries by example to reform his city cousin (cynical, drunken, a swindler) and manages nothing more than to allow himself to be destroyed by chance when he discovers that his whole life is founded upon failure. Charles suffers from an obvious Oedipus complex, asphyxiated by an entangling mother, who from afar stretches out her umbilical tentacles in letters, advice, references.

Jaime Soriano, in *Revolución Recommends*, has tagged *Les Cousins* thus: 'The good go to hell.' It is clear that Charles has let himself be guided by the thread that does not lead to Ariadne but to the labyrinth of Dante: Charles is innocent, simple, he falls in love with Florence without noticing that she is a nymphomaniac with all the lesbian connotations of nymphomania: the worst woman for his primitive morality. Paul is a cynic and makes himself into the great scoundrel so that his cousin will forget this woman; Charles must suffer the triangle at face value and pass through the test of seeing his cousin triumph in everything, including in the exams for which he prepared so much and in which he himself fails miserably. When he tries to kill his cousin, aided and abetted by luck, he ends up dead in turn, because luck is a weapon which, like all deadly weapons, one must know how to handle. This is the first film: Paul is the subject, Charles the object. But there is another film underneath, less apparent but more real.

Chabrol has Hitchcock for a master but it is not suspense that most interests him – in fact, he considers the greatest film by Hitchcock to be that old admitted failure, *Under Capricorn*. Why? Here Hitchcock has used his world of banal gestures that enclose an always atrocious and compromising reality, not to amuse the spectator with the mousy mystery of who put arsenic in Lady Agatha's tea, but to specify a relationship which is complex and covered by false appearances, as in *The Wrong Man*, as in *North by Northwest*, as in *The Man Who Knew Too Much*, as in *Vertigo*.

The *cronista* would like to insist on the importance of understanding *Vertigo* in order to understand the cinema of now and of tomorrow. A cinema that will return to romanticism in frank opposition to neorealism, a cinema that will be served by magic, the subconscious, the sound and the pictures of passion, rather than by conflicts between poverty and wealth, rather than by the subject that seems concerned with the social destiny of man and is almost always condescending, and whose great false gesture – because it thought of itself as throwing off a hypocritical mask – is, for example, *Gold of Naples* or *Due Soldi di Speranza*; the opposition to which is as varied as *The White Nights (Le Notti Bianche)* by Visconti, the French New Wave and Alfred Hitchcock, in *Vertigo*. It is not an ideal cinema, but a real one: the cinema that is there, in front of one's eyes. The critic who does not see this simply does not see – or does not go to – the movies.

Chabrol has wished to pose the conflict of the false identity, of the overwhelming presence of appearances, of the true face under any mask: whether it be the disguise imposed by society, class or even by a nest of naïve spies. In one scene in the film – the now famous scene of the monologue by François that has Wagner as its despairing background – Paul comes along with his idiotic chitchat, a chatter that pretends to be transcendental, to where Charles and Florence are in the grip of love. He says: '*Im Liebe*' and when he understands that he has spoken of love in falsetto in front of real love, he turns pale and hangs his head. The movement is slight but it is enough. Now then, does he mean this exactly or is it another quite different thing, the other film that lies underneath and to which Chabrol was alluding?

When under the auspices of 'The Ride of the Valkyries', Paul attempts to go back to Florence and only manages to push her into the room where Charles is studying desperately, there is in Paul another guilty or innocent look: which one it is, is left up to the spectator to decide exactly. If the spectator is intelligent – or better still: if he paid attention to the film not as simple entertainment but as a chess game of passions – he will be able to decipher this glance of Paul's. On the surface and separated from its context it could belong to *To Catch a Thief*, but that intrinsically tries to say something quite different.

On another occasion it is Florence who, after being rejected by Charles, runs into his gaze, fixed on the window of the café like an indictment, to which she responds – at the same time that she responds to a cynical question from her old friend, 'Do you have another lover now?' – with a look that might be one of distaste, of approval of the question-cum-answer of Clovis, of a useless farewell to love and to the new life – and of total identification with the condemnation that the death of Charles will impose on Paul.

It is possible that all this may sound complicated but *Les Cousins* is a complex film. Chabrol said, making fun of the grand subjects of the cinema: 'Virile brotherhood: I am my brother's keeper and I save him from the Fall.' He was joking but equally so when he says further on: 'God: and I defrock myself, you defrock yourself, he defrocks himself. Why do we defrock ourselves?', one knows that that mockery of God comes from nothing but a religious spirit and that contrary to his subjects (and when fable was spoken of in the films of Chabrol it was to point out that the fable is a truth subject to interpretations) in which there abound corruption, cynicism and falsehood, his spirit is immediately recognized as profoundly religious. And if one adds the proof that someone has said that the New Wave takes the cinema as a new religion, the spectator will have the key to the latest Chabrol, *A Double Tour*, in which the theme of the film is the murder of beauty and the whole plot is nothing more than searching out the criminal.

Somewhere Chabrol has said that he can compare a movie with a symphony. In *Les Cousins* the interrelation of the music with the story is too evident not to be noted. Wagner is not here for nothing and those who have seen homosexual connotations between Charles and Paul, from the simple fact that the music which is heard in the instant that Paul kills Charles is the 'Liebestod' from *Tristan and Isolde*, have done nothing more than let themselves be guided by the evidence. The movie is in its cocoon and now Paul is not the object, but the subject: if Wagner is heard by chance in the moment of death, it is like a joke on his own joke on Wagner and on realities as frightful as Nazism and the persecution of the Jews: his toy revolver, because it was not loaded, is now a deadly weapon with a simple cartridge inserted and chance intruding. His cynicism that covers up a flayed sensitivity has turned out to be a true cynicism: the excessive protectiveness that he extended towards Charles (he will not be able to say, 'I am not my brother's keeper', rather he will have to admit that he has been his cousin's guard all along) has ended up annihilating this precious object of primitive purity in the midst of civilized corruption. Evil is also a force of nature and one cannot play with it.

But there is a final ambivalence in this film full of contradictions that confers on it a richness superior to its realization (which is excellent) and to its strength as entertainment (which is considerable) and that must be noted. With his death Charles has destroyed them all: Paul will never be the same again: his lust for life, his Nietzschean philosophy of living dangerously is no longer a jest, his pulp Nazism has become real. Florence will not be the same either: the love that entered through her every pore and that utterly distanced her from real love will now be like anything else and there will remain nothing but the skin of the man-eating she-shark, which grows older every day and which tomorrow will be reclaimed by death. The faraway mother, if she has the intelligence to see past her egoism, will know by the death of Charles to what extent she is guilty – although the most probable thing is that she will never find that out. But Charles – Abel, the innocent, the dead one, Abel the intruder, the guilty innocent, the dead good man – is still declared the definitive guilty one. They have wished only to save him and he with his depraved innocence, with his killing ingenuousness has ended up sinking them all in the true hell, reality: not the hell that is others but the hell that is I.

7 February 1960

The Soviet Cinema Rides Again (I)

Potemkin versus *Chapayev*

Two weeks of Soviet cinema (*The Forty-First*, *Mother*, *Chapayev*, *The Idiot*, *Don Quixote*, *The Battleship Potemkin*) in the Estrada Palma theatre. A sniper (*Othello*) over at La Rampa. The threat of a continuity in the cinema which up to now was considered the most fraudulent in the world and amazement before an important discovery: the new romanticism is also reaching the new Soviet cinema, making the month of February a month dominated by the liquid sonority of the Russian language, by the Soviet cinematic rhetoric and by a nostalgic recall of past glories – at the same time that a mantle of pious silence has been thrown over the academicism, the silliness and the ordinariness of the cinema under the man who invented socialist realism: Josef Vissarionovich Djugashvilii, the supreme beacon or deacon of the Soviet cinema between 1929 and 1953. He at times used the more familiar alias of Stalin.

Everyone already knows what the Soviet cinema was transformed into under Stalin. It has been said here and everywhere (and the *cronista* has also seen, alas, *Glinka*, *The Fall of Berlin*, *Skanderbeg*, etc.). But it is fitting to repeat a testimonial. 'In 1930,' says the American critic Dwight MacDonald (and one has here a left-wing writer), 'the plan was extended to the cinema . . . and the bureaucracy swept all branches of the industry under the control of a single "All-Union Soviet Film Trust" . . . But this decline has set in not after the possibilities of the new approach had been exhausted, but . . . at the moment when the introduction of sound seemed to open up vast new fields for development. It came also with peculiar swiftness – as abruptly as an electric light is switched off.'

The *cronista* not long ago attended a round table on the new Soviet cinema. There he said: 'I would not be here if a very interesting phenomenon had not happened in the Soviet cinema, one which is called Nikita Khrushchev.' It seemed a pedantic remark at the time and up to a certain point it was, but like every pedantry it had an essential base of truth. It is very possible that this review would not be being written if there did not exist a cinéaste called Nikita Khrushchev who has permitted the Soviet Union to return not only to the theme of love but for this love to allow itself the luxury of conquering ideology. That happens in *The Last Shot*. But before getting to *The Last Shot* it is better to begin with the first one.

The Battleship Potemkin has achieved a rare unanimity in the cinema: everyone considers it a masterwork. From MacDonald (who declares that Eisenstein is 'without question the greatest master the movies have yet produced', a judgement that is partially revised nowadays, but which was the word of God in the days when *The Battleship Potemkin* was released), an anarchist, even Georges Sadoul, a party hack, and, in passing, the Catholic Henri Agel, all celebrated the appearance of this short silent film, shot under precarious conditions by a young unknown Soviet theatre director and without any experienced actor in the cast.

Now, thirty-five years later, the film can be seen with the same eager emotion as on its release. *Potemkin* emerged at a moment when the cinema – dominated by the ever-present American factory – was living through the apogee of the star-system and Rudolph Valentino was making the ladies sigh with his vaseline gestures and was throwing gentlemen into a demented wave of imitation of his vaselined hair-do. It is true that this is the time of *Un Chien Andalou*, of *The Gold Rush*, of *Tol'able David* but in some way *Potemkin* brought to the cinema a new message with a different content: a revolutionary cinema expressed in revolutionary terms: and it is this which MacDonald was reproaching in his essay 'The Soviet Cinema: 1930–38': saying that Stalinism – that socialist realism would finish off the new form to the point of making the content intolerable which now was not new either.

What is *Potemkin*? In the first place a movie that achieves emotion and true poetry by strictly intellectual means. Eisenstein himself was not able to repeat his *tour de force* (if one excepts certain moments of *¡Que viva México!* and as a whole *Ivan the Terrible* (first part), which apparently had a notable antecedent in *Strike*, Eisenstein's real first film, in 1924) and the Soviet cinema literally mistook the celluloid for the film to become lost in montage. Later but swiftly came the political errors, ideological crimes and punishment and the never-to-be-postponed self-criticism to go back to Red Square one. As far as montage (the film technique that became a poetic device of placing one frame next to another and extracting from the analogous or counterpoised propinquity a dialectic of images) is concerned, it only worked while the cinema was not the master of its mechanical means.

Today, with techniques perfected to the maximum, what with wide-angle, deep-focus lenses and the camera achieving total mobility* there is no need to juxtapose before the spectator a terrified face and the ominous revolver: the camera simply can take them both into its field or travel from the pupil dilated from fear to the impassivity of the weapon with the fluidity (and the natural ease and beauty and mobility) of sight. Eisenstein could not foresee this precisely because he had seen that a happenstance (the scarce film stock that forced director Lev V. Kuleshov to place short snippets of film one after another in a 1924 documentary) had now provided the different, dynamic, revolutionary accent because it was absolutely new (and it must be noted that any art

* Cain predicted the steady-cam invention.

which may wish to carry a revolutionary message must do it in new terms: the rest – and the rest is what happened to the Soviet cinema between 1935 and 1955 – is academic vision, scholastics and truly empty rhetoric).

Potemkin is put in first place in a well-worn list of the *Ten Best Films of All Time*. The list is delirious in itself: to presume, Dr Eisenstein, that someone can say which are the ten best films of the short history of the cinema is to generate the most alarming generalities: for example the old critics, those who are over fifty years of age, will take refuge in the contemplation of the silent cinema navel – which in reality was a trap of equivocations softened by time – and instead of doing criticism they will sing of the good old times, to nostalgia, to longing for the past. The young critics and among them the *cronista* can for their part declare that they consider that the cinema has begun with the talkies and that the silent cinema belongs to the museums, to the cinema clubs, to the pre-history of the movies and this would be terrible. But if it occurred to anyone to offer the opinion that *Vertigo*, for example, is among the ten greatest masterworks, now the matter would arouse scandal, hubbub and tumult. And actually this doesn't seem bad to the *cronista*, because *Potemkin* (which until the arrival of this version sonorized with vacillation, musicalized with a nice touch and synchronized without pain or glory) is a true masterwork. A single sequence proves it.

Everyone has talked about the 'famous sequences' of *Potemkin*. Some have spoken of the 'famous sequence of the shooting' of the sailors covered by a tarpaulin. Others have spoken of the 'famous sequence of the Odessa steps'. Still others have spoken of the 'famous sequence of the stone lions that move with the roar of the cannons'. Others have spoken of the 'famous final sequence' (which is really a small study of a certain primitive technique of suspense) in which the loyal battleships come out to meet the rebel *Potemkin*. One must, thus, arrive at the conclusion that *Potemkin* has – more famous sequences than real sequences! But the sequence – not terribly famous – that best reveals the new character of the film, the talent of Eisenstein to manage non-professional actors and crowds and his great poetic sense, is that of the arrival of the body of the marine murdered in the mutiny on the Odessa docks. There is in it an exemplary simplicity and a capacity for true emotion.

The launch leaves the battleship. On the deck is the dead man. In his crossed hands he carries a candle that burns in the wind of the bay. The launch ties up to the dock. The body is laid in state on the esplanade.

The word spreads through Odessa: 'Vakalinchuk, a hero of the *Potemkin*, is laid out on the dock!' The people go down to the dock. The crowd fills streets, avenues, squares, bridges. It soldiers on. To the long file are joined new groups. The crowd arrives at the dock. They surround the body. A woman puts a new candle in the hands of the murdered marine. She lights it. Someone protests. Others protest. One – presumably a bon bourgeois – laughs. The throng presses, threatening. The laughing man turns pale. The fury of the crowd grows. A woman tears her hair. Other women weep. The men shout, threaten. A woman gestures, shouts, wails. Little by little the hostile feeling towards authority grows and bursts out in a rebellion.

The sequence is managed with faces, halves of half-bodies, general views (a long line of people on the march crossing the screen prefigures a similar scene in *Ivan*) and the effect of repetition and accretion. The spectator knows that he is almost faced with stills, that the arrangement is knowing but also full of tricks, that the figure of speech that most leads to emotion is the *crescendo* and nevertheless he cannot keep from being moved by these naked, primitive and at the same time highly sophisticated elements. The *cronista* – who confesses to a soul as hard as nails or at least as hard as the jawbone that his namesake carried in his hand – confesses as well that he was touched to the point of tears by this sample of an art that though anachronistic, past and lost is no less moving and full of poetry. It is here that Eisenstein reveals the great dictator* he could have been if his formal pretensions, the personal contradictions and the political intrigues which extended into art, had not led him first into an artistic dead end, and finally to sterility and to death.

Chapayev is also a masterwork of the Soviet cinema but only after a fashion. This movie, which had an enormous public success in the Soviet Union (contrary to what happened with *Potemkin* and especially with *The General Line*) and which it is said wrenched applause and tears from Stalin, has the primitive freshness of a Western (in fact, the Vassiliev 'Brothers', who directed it, started from the affection that Eisenstein and Pudovkin had for the American cinema, especially for Ince and for Griffith) and the political responsibility of a pamphlet and

* What mortal or immortal hand could be
that with such tragic irony
produced this unerring error?
Or is it the obliterating judgement
of the exterminating angel?

nevertheless in its ending, in the real and not at all 'heroic' death of Chapayev it grows to the level of true poetry.

There is the single little bell (the Soviet cinema is in 1934 on the dawn of the talkies, above all because the exigencies of heavy industry and the refusal of Eisenstein and Pudovkin to understand sound, had delayed the arrival of the Vitaphone (reg. mark) to Soviet screens) that echoes insistently while a certain sleigh approaches, that serves to announce the arrival of Chapayev even before his famous vehicle appears, and it is this little bell that produces different effects on the different armies: courage, anger, expectation, fear and much trembling. And there are the repressed desires of an orderly (who hates the general because he has ordered the flogging of his brother, killed in the beating) and the concern of the general (who now is not very sure about turning his back on the orderly) which transform the fall of a broom into a shot.

These scenes are recounted in almost all the cinema books that talk: 1. about the cinema in general, 2. about the Soviet cinema, 3. about the beginnings of sound, 4. about the use of sound in the cinema and 5. in general about the use of sound in the beginnings of the Soviet cinema. The surprising thing and what speaks much better of *Chapayev* than all these books is to meet these talked-about scenes with surprise and newness.

It is certain that *Chapayev*, with its popularity, its facileness, its obvious plot and the tremor of poetry that it brought set the stage for the whole Soviet cinema (advised by the political commissars, decided by Boris Shumiavsky and his General Directorate of Cinematography or thought out by the timorous directors) to embroil itself in a contest to see who could dechapayize *Chapayev*. The example of the Vassiliev brothers was recommended to Eisenstein himself as a sure path for his future art after his return from the trip to the United States and the world.

But no less certain is that if the film has been able to maintain its rank for almost thirty years and that the *cronista* can see it and overcome the old hatred that it had inspired in him and enjoy it and believe that it is among the best that the Soviet cinema has done in its history, is because the film reaches the same heights (although the planes may not totally coincide) as *Potemkin* or *Arsenal* or *Dura Lex*. Also because the *cronista* may prefer, when choosing between a highfalutin Western and a simple little Western, the simple little Western – which will always be a better movie. It is because of these feelings that between *Alexander Nevsky* and *Chapayev* he will always choose *Chapayev*.

6 March 1960

The Soviet Cinema Rides Again (II)

Shakespeare, Dostoevsky and Co.

It is curious to note that a cinema to watch closely in the last five years has been the Soviet cinema. Like the French New Wave in its beginnings of three years ago (Vadim: *And God Created Woman*) the signs are barely tracings: the death of a character resolved by a piano, a storm and a weeping willow, the rape of a girl in the midst of a fiery bombing, a lover killed by his lover among the roaring of the waves: Shakespeare, Dostoevsky and Co. Of course they are two completely different movie waves but like the young French directors, the young Soviet directors represent the only nascent phenomenon of present-day cinema. Some of the signs are among us.

It was to be expected that after twenty-five years of lethargy, silence and high academicism, the Soviet cinema would awaken from its long winter with too much strength. But soon an artist will appear with enough control to tame the nascent state and try to catch up with the immortal stride of Eisenstein or of Dovzhenko. Some – less wise because older – have taken the metaphor literally and have tried to step on the toes of the masters. For example Mark Donskoi in his *Mother*, which is that sometime thing that seemed to be the monster invention of Hollywood: the remake or the movie that is made at least twice.

Everyone knows that Donskoi has employed more technical know-how than Pudovkin in bringing the novel by Gorky to the screen. Not because Donskoi is an artist (a thing that despite *The Youth of Gorky* he is not) capable of equalling Pudovkin (who despite his latest years and *The Return of Vassili Vornikoff*, certainly is one), but because the *talking* cinema is a cinema with all the elements necessary to tell a story and this time the Soviet cinema demonstrates that what it has in abundance is precisely those elements. It is thus that Donskoi, who has not been able to alter Gorky as did Pudovkin (if memory does not betray the *cronista* the first *Mother* gave the sensation that the tumults, the revolutionary mutinies occurred in the middle of St Petersburg) makes a film that is everything but revolutionary. In it there is technical perfection (in the mechanical manner of the majority of Hollywood movies), the colour system is more successful than in any of the other Soviet films seen in Havana and the movie runs through its time without tripping up. But it also has an academic taint that reveals at once that Donskoi belongs to the old Stalinist school of thought: from that quarter comes the bad aftertaste that *The Mother* leaves.

Another old Stalinist is Grigorii M. Kosintzev, director of a version of *Don Quixote*. In the first place, it is quite senseless for the Soviet cinema to engage itself in making a costly, long and always risky version of the Cervantes novel when they keep virgo intacta Gogol, Lermontov, Turgenev, Tolstoy, Dostoevsky, Chekhov and the numberless minor figures of Russian literature. But no, the Soviet cinema had to take on the colossal task of coming up with a cinematic equivalent for the first and greatest novel, which is at once a jolly good book, the first social novel, a chronicle of customs, a treatise on the spiritual conflict of man, a satire and an interpretation of the Spanish character. Everyone knows that the *Quixote* – separated from the two or three novels interpolated in the action – is one of the funniest books that has ever been written. Well then, the Soviet *Quixote* is one of the slowest, most ponderous and boring movies that has ever been filmed.

There is an attempt to get to the externals of the book – a rocky plain that recalls Castile, a whitewashed village, people in black and a Court all dressed as if the dress designer were named Velázquez, which is a successful stab at reconstructing a period and a country through its painting. But nothing of the peripatetic plot, of the punishing and laughable trek, of the tragicomedy of Alonso Quijano appears in the film. Besides, so many alterations have been made that on leaving the theatre it is necessary to return to the pages of Cervantes to find out who the hell is who: Aldonza Lorenzo is a maid in the Quijanos' household, Don Quixote is not an eager intellectual but an importuning and meddlesome old man, Sancho recalls the buffooneries of Lou Costello. (The Knight of the Sad Countenance himself always looks as if attacked by a tenacious cold in the head.) To top it all the whole book has been turned upside down and Don Quixote returns home to die – after having been defeated by the windmills! The *cronista* does not know what the Russians have meant to say with this Soviet *Don Quixote*, but it is evident that anything that may have been said has been said badly. Unquiet flows the don.

Another useless film but a truly beautiful one is the version of the *Othello* of Shakespeare. One must not reproach the director Yutkevich – another old champion of socialist realism – for having given himself the pleasure of recreating the Moor of Venice because the spectator receives in his turn one of the handsomest films that the Soviet cinema has made in at least twenty years. The *cronista* sees here the sign of love in an old man won over by the passion of the young and *Othello* has the impudent zing that Shakespeare must have had on the Romantic stage and much of the first furore of the Elizabethan theatre.

The movie is as calculating as any film by Laurence Olivier but the absence of fear of that perennial enemy of Shakespeare, the ridiculous, makes it approach the vision in the grip of delirium that Orson Welles has achieved in his *Othello*. There are people who are betting that Yutkevich saw the Welles film at least once because there are too many coincidences: the passions are taken out to the open air, set free in all their force, Iago is transposed into the heart of the matter, Desdemona is a mere pretext for the tragedy, the betraying handkerchief takes on the singularity of a character: actually the fact is that Shakespeare suggests all that and more, much more.

Yutkevich besides drops in that something extra: he has not loaded up his hand with a Stalinist *obbligato* for every Communist cinéaste: explaining the social and economic causes that make Othello strangle Desdemona. At the same time he has singularized the Moor, allowing Sergei Bondarchuk to play him with an unbridled unbalance, with a lugubrious and baroque theatrical play, with a primary and sombre fatality which in some way suggest that Othello is a person quite different from the contained courtiers who surround him: the passion of the jungle, the madness of the sun, primitive life are behind every gesture of Othello. Thus the tangled web that the *chestny* Iago weaves around him like a busy spider envelops him with a violent ease: a courtier would have toyed more with the truth and amused himself with the Venetian project of trapping the unfaithful lady in the arms of her lover.

The *cronista* suggests that one should notice the sad poetry that there is at the end, when the handkerchief that started a tragedy remains in the hands of Cassio, so that the spectator may know with certainty that the subject of Yutkevich is love – or jealousy, that monstrous fellow traveller with green eyes that accompanies suspicious love on every trip – and that Shakespeare is a worthy pretext. The *cronista* also recommends that in order to appreciate how the Soviet cinema is changing and is moving away from the orbit of what has been known as 'Russian montage', the spectator be attentive to the arrival of Othello to Cyprus, when he discovers that Desdemona has preceded him to the island and he murmurs an oath of love and breaks out in a run along the steps that leads him to the esplanade and to the love of his wife: the camera, a faithful Desdemona, also precedes Othello up the stairs, waits for him and finally follows him in a single flowing movement.

This is not only a technical feat but a signal that the old fearing foe of Stalinist art, that thing they were bent on calling 'formalism' and which is no more than the search for a happy expression to go together with the content, is, along with love, back in the Soviet cinema.

The Idiot allows the viewing in the Soviet Union of an old faithful leper: Fyodor Mikhailovich Dostoevsky, accused more than once of being a rotten sample of the decadent Tsarist literature. Dostoevsky comes back triumphant because he comes letter for letter and word for word – but he does not return transformed into film. *The Idiot* now makes Dostoevsky into a dramatic author and his situations are resolved as Kazan, for example, resolves the dissimilarity that there is between Williams, Steinbeck and Schulberg: by dividing the action into little dramatic situations that always seem designed and written for these bits of the film that seem to happen on a stage.

Here there is no more than the first part of *The Idiot* and although many await the second, it is not probable that it will turn out that way. Then there will be no one who will be able to avoid letting the hairy Dostoevskian ear show: the struggle between good and evil, the seeming superman confronting other men whom he makes inferior with his pity and his piety plus his cruelty and a mixture of all these things – and also the parable of the life of Christ in terms that if they seem anti-Christian are never anti-religious. Now Prince Myshkin is an aristocrat irresolute between love for all men and love for one woman, between generosity with money and the show-off use of an inheritance, between intellectual distance and mad passion. The actors – from the theatre just like the movie – are all so able that it is worthwhile seeing *The Idiot* to be able to read, for once, without knowing Russian, Dostoevsky in his original language.

OK, ladies and gentlemen, here comes the star! The movie that *did* return the theme of love to the Moscow Soviet. *The Last Shot*. Or better, *The Forty-First*. The subject is the same old love but the contingencies are new: politics put between the lips that kiss each other like a necessary intruder. Someone has said sometime – and if someone hasn't said it the *cronista* claims at once the dubious paternity – that the twentieth century is the century of politics and that the great conflicts, the great tragedies, the great problems of our time, are the political problems. Does someone think that Romeo cannot love Juliet because the Montagues are partisans of private property while the Capulets believe firmly in the socialization of capital? Could Madame Bovary have cheated on her husband because she detested the surplus values of the bourgeoisie? Did Anna Karenina imitate the French adulteress because she was affiliated with the Nihilists, while her husband advocated a passive resistance to the Tsar? Surely no. Well now, all that and more can happen in the century capable of defining the old Tsarist despotism as a totalitarian state. In this film (and this is its great originality) the subject is brought as an object for the first time to the cinema.

Isolde (a woman with eyes so deadly that where she aims she strikes the bull's-eye) is entrusted with watching over a captured Tsarist officer. This weak and stubborn, irresolute and valiant young man knows some crucial enemy orders by heart. Isolde is very primitive and very courageous and at the same time as frank about, as she is proud of, the firm pulse that has gotten her forty dead enemies in the latest skirmishes. After countless wanderings through a hostile desert, they arrive at the promised ocean and later to an idyllic islet. This time by themselves. Since whenever a woman knows she is alone with a man she is capable of betraying the firmest love, Isolde gives the lie to her marksmanship, her passion for the Bolshevik cause and her revolutionary firmness: she falls in love with the Tsarist officer. He is the prototype of the class that she detests: indolent, superior, aristocratic and not without certain feminine manners. But he is another kind of love, real love.

On the island, Robinson has found an unforgettable Friday and together she and Oleg spend happy days in the Soviet version of a taboo for two. Little by little the primitive life, the love and the passage of time change them. Now Isolde does not have so much integrity, now Oleg is not so lacking in understanding. One day, a boat appears. Isolde believes that they are friendly fishermen or perhaps her companions. Oleg recognizes the sailors as Tsarist forces looking for him. Oleg takes a gun and makes signs. Isolde discovers her error and when Oleg takes off to meet his companions, she seizes the weapon and orders him to stop. But he keeps on running and she fells him with an insult, 'Damned cadet!', and a last shot. She has just made her number forty-one. For a moment she knows triumph and then defeat: she has killed love. Her decision was between the new duty and the eternal love, and the Communist duty has won out. Nevertheless, she can still mourn her lost love and this is how *The Forty-First* ends.

The movie contains sufficient ambiguity (and already this is a great triumph for the new Soviet cinema: that the heroes are not good from head to toe and the villains wicked from waxed moustache to dancing feet: the Soviet Western from the East has been left behind with Eisenstein, with Stalin, with Shumiavsky and his censors) so that there may be more than one interpretation. Does Isolde really not survive the death of her love which is her own death? Is not the Tsarist officer, that man who doubts, painted with too much sympathy? Is not the triumph of pure love the defeat of ideology? The *cronista* declares expressly that it does not interest him to answer these questions – as he rejects the imputation that there is a double meaning in every situation and that the film wishes to say between the lines that the Communists, like Isolde with her last shot, killed in Russia all that was fine and subtle, something that someone or other has suggested: to admit this for one moment is to do an irreparable harm to the new Soviet cinema and to confess that only by betraying the revolution can there be made in the Soviet Union a film that may replace the pompous triviality and academic ponderousness of the Stalin days (besides the fact that in Cuba there is the need to make a cinema that while being revolutionary in its content will be new in form, that will make for itself a thesis that is even, at first sight, profoundly reactionary). The *cronista* confesses that he prefers to believe that it is the old consumptive love of the Romantics that is returning now in present-day terms: politics can separate two people who love each other, like any divine force, only this time fate has probably read Karl Marx.

13 March 1960

The Illusion Called Renoir

In the memory of the *cronista*, *Grand Illusion* was an odious film. Released everywhere in 1938, it had, among a story of escapes (failed and successful) from a German prisoner-of-war camp during the First World War, a last pacifist message. The ideology of Jean Renoir the director was not very clear, but it *was* specific: the barriers between men are more horizontal than vertical: the caste differences (and Renoir does not ever say 'classes', but 'castes': his interest in India when filming *The River* comes from this) and not important, because the castes are being eliminated (in wars and in other annihilating activities) in tandem with the elimination of their members: the true problem of man is borders – and the customs house philosophy of Renoir is related here to the famous saying of Toscanini: 'The times have changed – and not for the better. Once trips took months, but you didn't need passports. Now trips only last hours but you have to wait months to get a visa.' This foolish and slightly reactionary ideology is also shared by the poor man's Wagner called Gian Carlo Menotti, when in his opera *The Consul* he subjects his hero to the legal labyrinth of the consulates and the embassies: it must not be forgotten that in a certain way Kafka is in the air.

For Renoir it was the frontiers which were the ones guilty of the wars, of the racial hatreds and all types of human calamities. It is not for nothing that at the end of *Grand Illusion* salvation comes in the form of a white and not very distinct frontier, capable of stopping the hounding fury of the German soldiers: this is a paradox *à la* Renoir.

So in 1938, in the middle of the Spanish Civil War, when Guernica had been destroyed totally, when the Abyssinians were massacred by the troops of Mussolini, when Kaltenbrunner was ordering the methodical killing of five million Jews in three or four concentration camps, when the greater state ruled by Hitler was preparing for the invasion of France itself, Renoir was showing (with great success, one must admit) a strangely pacifist film.

When the *cronista* saw the film the first time he didn't think much about it, because he was six or seven years old. But some years later, in a cinema-club, the film revealed itself to him in all its cowardly pacifism and definitely as quite overrated. It was then that the news arrived one day that *Grand Illusion* had been placed second or third on a mythical list of the ten or twelve best films of all time. The list was made by critics and cinéastes recognized everywhere. For another thing all the film books were talking wonders of this film that has turned out to be the most well-known by Renoir, so much so that to speak of one is to speak of the other. It is true that there were dissidents. A young Spanish critic considered *Grand Illusion* an academic and falsely respected experience. François Truffaut of *Cahiers du Cinéma* and a friend of Renoir opined for his part: 'Its immense success rests if not on a misunderstanding, at least on appearances . . . One must know that another reason for the success of *Grand Illusion* is that in it psychology takes precedence over poetry, which is rare in the author of *Paris Does Strange Things* (*Eléna et les hommes*). This is the least "mad" of the French films of Renoir.' The antipathies of the *cronista* balanced other antipathetic sympathies: Roosevelt, Louis Ferdinand Céline, Marshal Goering – even Goebbels loved this movie that so conveniently came to them from Paris: all that he did to allow it into Germany was to eliminate the name of the Jewish character who is likeable in some sequences. But it also had some antipathetic antipathies: Spaak, brother of the screenwriter and at the time Minister of the Interior in Belgium, prohibited its showing on Belgian screens, Mussolini boycotted it in the Venice Festival of that year and a famous French critic tagged it as anti-Semitic.

Some years had passed. Ricardo Vigón was collaborating with the *cronista* on the entertainment pages of the newspaper *Revolución*. Frequently the topic of conversation was Renoir, whom the *cronista* execrated for his latest films (especially *Paris Does Strange Things*) and whom Vigón always exalted: 'He is a modern,' he would say. 'He was doing in the thirties everything that has been done later by the *Nouvelle Vague*. You have to see *Grand Illusion*, you have to see it now,' Vigón repeated with his usual vehemence. One day Jaime Soriano came to confer about what to say in his *Revolución Recommends* box about *Grand Illusion*. The *cronista* told him: 'Say that it was a pacifist film – in 1938.' That was what Soriano did. Of course the *cronista* had not then seen *Grand Illusion* in at least ten years and he did not know – the *cronista* is ignorant of more things than one thinks – that Jean Renoir had the plan of *Grand Illusion* in his head since 1934, when Hitler and the future war were not even a cloudy threat and the last war was fresh in the heart and the mind of every Frenchman. Renoir, like any other artist, had suspended time around his idea and when he came to complete the working plan he did not realize that time had passed and his film turned out to be compromising, contrary to any idea of pacifism, namely peacemaking. It is very probable that the success, the continued permanence of *Grand Illusion* throughout the world have impeded Renoir from understanding exactly what *Grand Illusion* meant in all the theatres in the world in 1938, 1939 and 1940 – even including what it meant for France.

When a year or two ago the *cronista* was talking about another present-day pacifist film, *Paths of Glory*, he said that if a pacifist film was criminal in 1938, in 1958 it was of a necessary human urgency. Then the *cronista* came to think that the origin of *Grand Illusion* was the Communist sympathies of Renoir in that period coinciding with the stupid political necessity that led Stalin to underestimate Hitler first and to conclude with him later a devious non-aggression pact with the same myopic historical vision based on the contrary logic that still, weeks before the Nazi invasion of the Soviet Union, made Stalin think that Germany would never attack. But when one knows what Renoir thought and thinks in matters of art, his rudimentary ideology, his political innocence one realizes at once that rather than part of a grander scheme *Grand Illusion* is an individualist work, a paean to 'human solidarity across all frontiers', that it is exclusive to Renoir as was exclusive to Erich Maria Remarque his neurotic pacifism or to Henri Barbusse his abstract pacifism: if *The People of France* or *La Marseillaise* are Communist in some measure *Grand Illusion* is simply an isolated case full of a humanitarianism that can lead in many directions: to vegetarianism, to nudism, to this film.

Seen today *Grand Illusion* surprises one more than anything with its modernity, as Vigón said. It begins to surprise from the start when the montage principles of the end of the silent era and the beginnings of sound disappear so that Renoir may attempt that harmonious linkage which is the daily bread of the modern French cinema, of Hitchcock, of Rossellini: a record spins, the camera moves away and takes in the whole phonograph and the bar-room in which it is playing. There is a man beside it. Someone enters and the camera moves laterally towards the door and follows the man while he walks up to the phonograph. They talk. The man goes off with another man and the camera goes after them. On arriving at the door one of the men turns around and waves farewell to everyone. The camera returns to the imperturbable waiter who tells a timely joke. It goes down along the bar and stops in front of a sign that says: 'The daring demons of the air' or something similar. With just a simple movement the place, the situation of the characters, their individual psychology and their group mentality have been determined and in passing it has been possible to say that they are war pilots who are waiting for their turn to fly to face the enemy and to face death or victory, whichever comes first. This time the speeches are also simple, direct, free of all the rhetoric *à la* Carné–Prévert of the films of the period and so communicative that between the lines one can almost read the intent, the culture and the station in life of those who talk. (Here the translator has done an enemy job but those who can understand a little French know the difference, the social abyss – of 'caste', Renoir would say – that there is between Jean Gabin and Pierre Fresnay, who for once is good in his role, from their diverse dispositions before an identical contingency.)

Famous are the scenes in which Gabin tries to communicate to the prisoner who is just arriving that they have left behind a half-dug tunnel, only to discover that all communication is impossible because the prisoner – is English. Famous is the exchange between von Stroheim – in white gloves, correct, chivalrous – and Fresnay who seem to say in their speeches: 'Aristocrats of the world, unite'. Famous is the moment in which the prisoners remain silent before their companion disguised as a woman in the burlesque show. Famous the moment when everyone hums *The Marseillaise* in front of the Germans on learning that their people have won a battle. Famous are these scenes and amazingly they preserve their original impact.

But more than these, more than the extraordinary moment when

Carette sings his vaudeville song with amateurish charm, more than the ending so beautiful to look at, the *cronista* will remember the moment in which Gabin is put in solitary confinement and shouts to demand to speak with someone. The guard enters. Gabin wants to hear French spoken and shows his desperation. The guard can only think of giving him his harmonica, which he leaves quietly in a corner. When he goes out, another guard asks him, almost bellicose, what has happened and the first guard, a poor man whom the war has put in a position of being another man's enemy, simply says: 'Nothing, this war is lasting too long.'

He will remember as well the death of Fresnay. Not because it is any marvel of dramatic conception but because it brings a very simple surprise: Fresnay dies, von Stroheim regrets it because he has killed him and he appreciated him. He steps away from the body and goes to the window. One believes that he will look outside, that this is no more than a pretext to make the spectator see the snow and then jump to the prisoners who are fleeing under the snowfall. But all that von Stroheim does is go up to the vase which has the only flower that there is in the whole inhospitable castle, takes some scissors and cuts it, in a gesture of last, respectful grief.

He will also remember the prodigious level of acting when Jean Gabin and Erich von Stroheim barely show their dramatic bag of tricks and, nevertheless, offer the spectator one of the most subtly acted scenes of the French cinema in these twenty years that have gone by. Von Stroheim asks Gabin why he was punished in his former prison, Gabin says that what he did was try to escape in the garbage that was leaving the prison and what he managed to do was to be snatched stinking, but that he tried it out of a spirit of solidarity with the garbage. He says it with indignation, in order to annoy the German but von Stroheim accepts the slight. He cannot fail to laugh at the joke and at the same time he knows that his job is extremely grave and all that he does is trace the least perceptible smile with the edge of his lips, furtively, fleetingly. It is this scene which made von Stroheim say that that role in *Grand Illusion* was his favourite. It is the *cronista*'s too and also a favourite of the *cronista*'s is this film which is long, at times tedious, but always sincere, new and yet so perfect that it only permits one to give in to the evidence, to the evidence that Ricardo Vigón pointed out: Jean Renoir is a master, *Grand Illusion* is the work of a master, *Grand Illusion* is a masterwork.

17 April 1960

cain
said, at the end
and so suddenly,
that 'suddenly'
was a
masterwork:
i have absolved him
for this last
exultation:
i took out the line

Williams Served by Mankiewicz

Somewhere, someone, an analyst, a philosopher, a mixture of both things, said that Romanticism was the arrival of neurosis in art. This statement is simplistic but, like all simplistic statements, it is based on a primary truth. Romanticism – as a summation, as an attitude towards life not as a literary school nor as an artistic movement – never worried that life ends up copying the monuments of the past, that man lived in profile waiting for a useless medallion: equilibrium, eternity, contention were his natural enemies: his preferences were in despair, in impulse, in fury, in what has been called since then *Sturm und Drang*. Into this line of descent fit the plays of Tennessee Williams, from *The Glass Menagerie* to *Suddenly, Last Summer* – and the plays of Tennessee Williams have brought to the cinema a Romanticism (no one is arguing whether it is genuine or not) derived from a milieu in deadly decadence, from the perfume of the memory of this past in which 'the moon always shone bright', usually expressed by a desperate lyricism, by a rhetoric rich in verbal felicities, by a joy in exhibiting his private teratology. In a certain way *Suddenly, Last Summer* is the apotheosis of Tennessee Williams. If not in the theatre at least in the cinema.

In *Suddenly, Last Summer*, there are: sex galore, incest, rapes, homosexuality, cannibalism, the mere symbols of the expressions of decadence. 'Symbols, when one uses them with respect, are the purest language of the theatre,' Williams has said somewhere, and as the symbols grow, they become evident too. Sebastian Venable is the invisible catalyst: because of him occur all the cataclysms of the private cosmos of the Venable family, on account of him Doctor Crukowitz is dragged to the brink of love and murder, through him we discover an underworld of outsized horrors. Sebastian has a refined taste: imported silk suits, voyages around the world, a primaeval jungle transplanted to his garden, a book of private poems published each summer: 'The life of the poet is the work of the poet.' What does Sebastian write in his summer booklet? No one will ever know: all is secret in Sebastian: 'The work of the poet is the life of the poet.'

But some truths – thanks to analysis, practised here with an inductive genius that has nothing to envy Sherlock Holmes – slip through: the secret poetry does not manage to reveal the miseries of the secret life. He has grafted the botanical garden into his backyard because he loves the violence of feral life. Among the plants in the garden there is a carnivore fed with costly flies (imported as well) and here the first secret is revealed: it is money that permits Sebastian to adore and do violence. Not everyone, fortunately, can permit themselves the luxury of sadism. This axiom was first formulated by Sade himself: the castle in the Black Forest, the complacent eunuchs, the innumerable concubines are the privilege only of princes, of royalty or of the church. In the modern world sadism and its derivations become privileges of the big bourgeois, of capitalists. Is it not an extravagance that Sebastian launches a yacht to go in search of the blue bird of primitive violence when he always has had it in his own backyard – that is to say in his family?

The fact is that he has refused to see his mother as a grown carnivorous plant, it is that he does not recognize in his relatives the vultures which he will discover in the Pacific, it is that he does not want to see himself as a sadist, as a sick man who hides his deformed body under silk and his degraded soul in poetry. Sebastian writes a brief secret poem every summer in order to say nothing: it is his foolish cousin who will reveal his secret. To avoid this his aged mother is prepared to use her millions. That is to say to practise charity. Can some big bourgeois be horrified now? They must have forgotten that the charity of the Rockefeller Foundation hides the Rockefeller crimes, that the Mellon museums cover up the Mellon crimes, that the indigenist investigations paid for by the United Fruit Company throw a blanket over the crimes of United Fruit against the descendants of such civilization. Violet Venable will build a new hospital only if the famous surgeon Crukowitz performs a lobotomy on her niece and makes her forget her deep secret: the death of Sebastian, who must have died as he lived. To become acquainted with his death will thus be to reveal the secret of his life. But the physician is an honest man, a very dangerous animal: it will not be possible to buy him. In fact he will become the investigator: through his science it will be learned exactly what – not who – Sebastian Venable was.

Sebastian was a homosexual and this does not explain anything. The world is full of homosexuals but not all of them use their mother as bait, only to replace her with a pretty cousin when the mother has aged. Not all can build themselves a *garçonnière* in the middle of an Albigensian jungle. Not all have yachts in which to sail to the Encantadas, where the flocks of cormorants devour the little tortoises by the thousand and there, on contemplating this monotonous act of nature and struggle for life, to acknowledge God. But Sebastian has wanted to be a singular man, to lead a singular life and he only manages to have a singular death. One day abroad, in one of his criminal forays, he meets the most horrible death: he is torn to pieces by a mob of hungry boys and practically devoured by them. The play (and almost the movie) ends with an exemplary speech: 'I think we ought at least to consider the possibility that the girl's story could be true . . .'

Not long ago the critic Alfred Kazin asked himself how it was possible that no one who was not homosexual could be interested in the plays of Tennessee Williams. Joseph L. Mankiewicz, who is not homosexual, seems to be disposed to answer him. The theatre of Williams is a diagnosis in which homosexuality (like nymphomania, frigidity, neurosis and even cancer) is no more than another symptom of a greater sickness: the decadence, the end if not of a civilization, of a way of seeing life, of the 'American way of life'. If it is the Southern United States which is chosen as a model, it is because the contradictions which will finish off the capitalist civilization are more evident now in its feudal predecessor.

Mankiewicz – who has a long record as an anti-fascist film-maker, from *All About Eve* to *The Quiet American*, passing through *No Way Out* – has been able to see that the violence of the theatre of Williams, its struggling passions, its morbid fits, are the clear expression of fascism. What else is Violet Venable, disposed to use her money to kill the soul of her niece, the only real intimate of a truth that everyone senses, but a fascist? Her ways of obtaining silence are not far from the Nazi ways of making people talk. What else is Sebastian himself but a fascist poet, who believes that 'love is being able to use others' and 'hate is not being able to use them'? One almost thinks of D'Annunzio, of Ezra Pound. Except that Sebastian is the caricature of a poet. Rescuing the play from this aura of caricature, of a joke between pederasts, has been the true labour of Mankiewicz.

Williams perhaps had intended to write a play in which at last he would exterminate the glamour of sodomy, in which the world of pederasty would be brought out into the open, with its horror of the open air, 'like a bouquet of roses wrapped in white paper', in which all those pseudo-artists, pseudo-writers and pseudo-intellectuals that everyone has known – and who in the past were called 'decadents' – would be unmasked once and for all. Mankiewicz has shown the original intentions of Williams but also he has revealed much of the hidden world from which Williams takes his creatures. In *A Streetcar Named Desire* it was the struggle of a primitive world, basically honest, against a world in decadence, in which there were not yet discernible the elements of destruction, of self-destruction, which appear more clearly in *Cat on a Hot Tin Roof* and that now in *Suddenly, Last Summer* emerge with full frankness.

Here is the primitive world, not now opposed to decadence, but rather serving as a future model. Strength is not entrusted to a rude and almost brutal man but to a scientist, to a man of tomorrow, who believes that 'one must be useful' and possibly thinks, without saying so, that love is letting oneself be utilized and hate is refusing to be utilized. It is not for nothing that Williams – who has always seen the so-called primitive countries, Latin America, for example, as the forces that must be observed closely from the United States, as the world of the future – makes his hidden hero, the summer poet, end up being devoured by a gang of famished boys who previously have shouted at him 'Bread, bread!' in Spanish and to whom he has thrown a handful of bills useless for hunger. These boys – Spanish, Latin American, Asiatic – have devoured the rich capitalist, who before used them in his degradation – the *cronista* thinks he sees an image of the final act in which the world where Sebastian Venable represents refinement, culture and power will be destroyed by the primitive world, not in search of essential truths, nor writing a poem every summer, nor trying to find God in the violence of Nature but shouting in despair: 'Bread, Bread!'

26 June 1960

ricardo vigón
once
said
to cain:
'otto preminger
doesn't make
anything but
masterworks'

Poetic Justice

Anatomy of a Murder (Columbia). Parnell says at the end of the movie, when the actors (and the spectator) have been fooled by their Frankenstein: 'This is called poetic justice.' The film is also called poetic justice. Essentially it is no more than an exercise in what Otto Preminger has called 'my passion for that American chess game: the trial by jury'.

One of his old masterworks (*Angel Face*, which contrary to the general incomprehension one must point out is the first modern film: in the same way that *Citizen Kane* is the first modern-day classic of the cinema and *Shadow of a Doubt* is a sketch of what was to come, *Angel Face* is a movie that also has all the elements of the modern European cinema, the newest of the present-day cinemas: the passion for speed, which transforms into an axiom the surrealist proverb: 'Rape is love plus speed': a tragic design in the most everyday facts of life: the definitive decadence of the bourgeoisie: the conduct of a younger generation that spends its vacations in a moral inferno: in Europe they say that *Bonjour tristesse* is nothing more than Françoise Sagan after having seen *Angel Face*) revolved around a trial in which the innocence of a guilty man was proven by means of legal tricks. There the woman was the catalysing agent and the man appeared as the plaything of some circumstances in which his primitive masculine brain failed against slight feminine stealth.

In *Anatomy* there is a feminine character – the man about whom in her confession the woman tells the lawyer that he likes her to dress in a provocative manner – who paradoxically plots a killing starting from a rape. The woman, on the other hand, is a masculine character what with her happy manizing – and traps her lawyer in her nets and confounds the pretext of the murder and even justice itself in an act of desperate guile that amounts to individual fascism.

In a certain way *Anatomy of a Murder* is a complement to *Angel Face*, except that here Preminger has allowed himself the luxury of wrapping the problem in the sugar-coated crust of the dialogued satire, of the farce that shares with the melodrama the taste for Grand Guignol. Curiously, when one of the characters cries: 'God bless juries!', almost at the end of the film, the spectator knows that the sentence, with all due respect, implies a direct mockery by Preminger. The entire trial has been a false debate between a guileful lawyer and a cunning prosecutor. No one is really interested in justice but rather in the force of arguments, directly proportional to an essentially sporting virtue: timing. At moments the wittiness (not the witness) takes on that search for truth which hides underneath every euphemism and which is the visible basis of humour, from Aristophanes to Harpomarx.

The judge calls the lawyers and the district attorney to the bench because the moment for unveiling truth is approaching. (The woman has been 'raped', remember?) 'I'm calling you in about an important matter,' says the judge. 'Are you going to bring up the matter of the torn panties?' he asks the defence attorney. 'Yes,' he answers. 'Isn't there any way to call them something else?' 'That's what my wife calls them,' says the district attorney. 'I'm a bachelor,' says the defence lawyer. 'I know another word,' says the assistant district attorney, 'but I'm afraid it's indecent: it's a French word.' Debate ended by the judge: 'Most French words are.'

The movie is highly amusing, a masterwork of entertainment in fact, because Preminger (who has not taken the book by John Travers too literally) has permitted himself the cynicism of not seeming to be a reformer from the outside but of being one from the inside. One must not forget that he is talking about 'American justice' and that along with the trial by jury (a folly similar to performing an operation by relying on the first man who passes by the hospital) it is also an American tradition to hold an occasional mock trial: the most recent, the most terrible one has been the espionage trial of the Rosenbergs. The whole movie is a gigantic mock trial and Preminger has loaded his hand with the word 'mock' knowing, like the expert showman he is, that the cinema is first and foremost entertainment. If one can hardly see the threads with which the necklace has been put together, it is because Preminger has arrived at an incredible perfection in that difficult art that was once called the cinematograph and that now is called cinema for short – and for ever.

17 July 1960

a
    roll
        of the drums
will
    never
        abolish
cain:
    he will attack (the movies
                as well

as the r
e
a
d
er)
again

Buñuel, Charity and The Christ Who Laughs

A certain ad, on its première, reduced the prospects of *Nazarín* to the trivial discussion of whether the film was Catholic or anti-Catholic. The *cronista* says trivial because the gazetteer thought, without a ghost of a doubt, that he was faced with *The Fugitive*, *God Needs Men* or with any other movie whose interests are immediate: the permanency of the priestly oath, all God's chillum got soul, God is with Donald Meek, etc., etc. The *cronista* also said trivial because the career of Luis Buñuel flatly denies that what is at stake is the agreement of any of his works with Catholicism: actually Catholicism concerns Buñuel as much as the Seventh-Day Adventists do: one may not believe too much in the fury of Buñuel when together with Philippe Soupault he used to slap priests on the street, but one must believe in the ending of *El* in which Arturo de Córdova hypocritically takes refuge in a monastery and confesses himself cured of his intractable jealousy, but on leaving he goes off making a criss-cross pattern, showing his old paranoia to be still there. Or one must believe in the ending of *The Golden Age* where someone announces the appearance of the most depraved, dissolute, unwholesome creature in the whole universe and after a beating of drums there appears the image of the Sacred Heart. This ending, the rolling drums, the anti-Christian message strongly relate *Nazarín* to *The Golden Age* – except that Buñuel is not twenty-five years old but sixty and he has left behind a joker's violence for the slim declaration of principles.

If *Nazarín* carries a message it is an anti-Christian message. It is in fact another film director, born and educated in Catholic Spain, Juan Antonio Bardem, who reveals this: 'At each step, with each roll of those drums, there will be buried more deeply in the heart of Nazarín the frightening anguish of understanding Christian futility.' This message (fortunately for the film its ambiguity transforms *Nazarín* into a masterwork: it is the interpretations that will maintain its integrity) is never explicit.

In the Mexico of Porfirio Díaz, don Nazario is a singular priest. A land-hungry society, backed by the army and the clergy, has to create an ideology that will sustain the economic scaffolding and that will hold firm everywhere that the leaders (landowners, soldiers, ecclesiastics) may send their minions. It is not strange therefore to see that the dispossessed live in a total indifference (when not in hostility) towards the values upheld by the very man who resists their degradation. Such values are commonly designated with a label that betrays its original intentions, 'values of the spirit'. It is on account of this that Nazarín is a rara avis: he possesses almost all the true values of the spirit intact – he is good, generous, humble.

He has in addition another trait (and here the *cronista*, along with Buñuel, does not care to say if it is a vice or a virtue) which is quite pronounced: he lives outside reality. From it he can only interpret correctly that greed is a cardinal sin, and the disobedience of the sixth commandment a mortal one. Thus, in the midst of the disdain of his superiors and the incomprehension (which prefers to present itself as mockery) of his neighbours, Nazarín is seen wandering along the dusty roads of Mexico, without a cassock and with two women for his only company. One of the women is a criminal, a fugitive from justice. The other is a hysteric, haunted by the erotic imaginings of a boyfriend whom she desires and rejects. As at other times these associations of Nazarín's are perfectly involuntary. Here Benito Pérez Galdós (*Nazarín*, the film, is based on the novel with the same title by Galdós) sets up a parallel between Nazarín and Don Quixote, in which the holy scriptures seem to have replaced the books of chivalry and Sancho is made into a reduced court of women. Actually Galdós used satire and parody to denounce the vile clergy of his time.

It is a brilliant touch of Buñuel's to have transformed the Spanish anti-clericalism of the nineteenth century into a real problem of doubt and negation of all Christian values, moving the original that Galdós confined to mere casuistry to the plane of theology. But before this revelation, that makes *Nazarín* into the first philosophical film, Buñuel transforms the rovings of the peasant priest into a season in the hell of faith: Nazarín believes so much, believes so fervently, that he manages to sow in his path death, wickedness and hatred. If he tries to ask for work on the construction of a highway he unleashes a quarrel between the foreman and the workers, which ends with the good Nazarín hearing shots in the distance and learning about the fray just by guessing. If he agrees to cure a dying little girl, he creates a group of women adorers who venerate the new saint, while they shout: 'Miracle! Miracle!' If he sits next to the bed of a dying plague sufferer, it is to hear instead of the simple act of contrition an ardent cry of love: the dying woman does not want to be with God in spirit, she wants to die with her husband between her legs. Thus Nazarín believes he is sowing good everywhere and he only reaps a harvest of sheer disasters. Finally, the people know more than he does and they recognize the two women as two more-or-less platonic lovers of the priest and all three land in gaol, first, and on a chain gang later.

In gaol, like Don Quixote on his deathbed, Nazarín learns the truth. A prisoner has mistreated and beaten him and another prisoner defends him. Nazarín, moved, gives him his blessing and tries to return that black sheep with white spots to the flock. But the prisoner opposes this and when Nazarín tells him: 'You are good', he responds: 'No, I am bad, father. I'm a good for nothing. You on the good side and I on the bad side, no one is good for anything. Your life, what is it good for?' Nazarín understands and his whole world of grace and eternal life is cast down: he had left in search of an absolute and finally he has found that the only possible absolute is *nada*.

Overwhelmed by his discovery, a changed man, Nazarín is on the road again. On the way, a woman fruit vendor offers him charity in the form of a pineapple and he, who always had sought alms, refuses it. But he turns. The priest who was a rebel due to his acceptance of a lie as total truth and a practitioner of some virtues that have merely been imagined as moral models, turns to take the pineapple. This simple act transforms him into a true rebel: alms and charity do not exist and when he practises them knowingly, he is demonstrating their non-existence. Buñuel surrounds this last scene with the racket, thunder and rumbling of the drums of Calanda (the only 'music' in the whole film) and thus he has achieved one of the most memorable endings brought off in the most recent cinema. The transformation and the true rebellion are given by the vigorous, repeated rattle of the drums and also by the dramatic intensity: the exact atmosphere of the moment, which elevates the film over and above a personal document and converts it into a work of art and also into a moment of philosophical import.

But Buñuel does not forget having said that 'the cinema seems to have been invented to express subconscious life', and while he gives a mortal blow to the double Christian and bourgeois concept of charity, he shows Nazarín as a simple sick man: his messianic mood is a sublimated form of compulsive neurosis. Of course Nazarín would always be able to answer that, after all, the apostles were also made from this cloth. Luis Buñuel could add, putting an end to the argument: 'Precisely.'

17 July 1960

Revolución
1959–60

It seems inescapable that the mirror image, the other nightingale that Cain was, would be the man himself: Cain, for a year, was the Sosia of Cain. In a Marx Brothers movie Groucho and Chico simulate a mirror. But the servitude becomes rebellion: one of the brothers scares his facsimile with the unexpected: an odd mimicry. Cain – prudent, cautious, pliant – never risked the rebellion of his Ersatz and continued being in Revolución *the Cain of* Carteles *– what is more, he was doing this double act at the same time. Only there was a slight change – that hand raised out of sync with the double in the mirror – in which the apparently just* cronista, *the objective, distant third person, the impersonal and prepotent* Cine, *were transformed into a personal and accessible I and under these lights that much more human: for me this was an improvement in what is known in critical circles as* Cain's disease. *Others, more certain or more cruel, say that it was nothing more than a writer's trick.*

it is evident
that the first
column by
cain
in revolución
was much better
than the first one of
carteles*:*
five years on the job can make
a sorcerer out of an apprentice

Frantic

Frantic is going to be a memory as pleasing in my mind, or so it seems, as *Kiss Me Deadly* is. Both look like a star (or a light bulb) seen from a distance. I don't mean to say that either of the two is a light bulb in the distance (or a star) for the other for that matter. Come to think of it they don't resemble each other at all. *Kiss Me Deadly* is one of the ten best *films noirs* of all time – and the best film by Robert Aldrich. But *Frantic* is also one of the ten best *films noirs* . . . from France. There ends the resemblance and begins one of the most refreshing, most original and at the same time most deceiving movies of the French cinema of today.

Among the young French critics there is a love for the American cinema that leads them to say that only in Hollywood can one find a cinema *d'auteur* – that is to say, that American directors are the sole authors of their films, as is the writer of this book. This is contrary to the old American notion (from North, Central and South America) that it is in France where a cinema director is a director indeed. But in France everything that seems made in the United States is celebrated – from *And God Created Woman* to *La Parisienne* passing through *No Sun in Venice* – as the most salutary thing that could happen in a cinema, the French, that, for them, is made up by the bad imitator of Hitchcock (H.-G. Clouzot), the worst craftsman of them all (Duvivier), the anti-movie men (Christian–Jaque) or the Law considered as the Tenth Muse (André Cayatte). If a Renoir and a Guitry are salvaged it is because they impose on their films a personal Gallic mark – good visual taste in Renoir, caustic *esprit* in Guitry.

The new critics are suddenly transformed into new directors. Louis Malle is twenty-four and *Frantic* is his first movie. He could not have done it better – for the new French critics and for me. There is a clearly perceptible influence by Orson Welles (for example, the frequent change of backgrounds upon which the action floats or is sunk, with a rare symbolism, from image to image, from scene to scene) and from Welles through Aldrich and the American cinema from the fringe (through Stanley Kubrick because *Frantic* greatly resembles *Killer's Kiss*), influences that are soon forgotten, because the spectator feels himself submerged in a plot in which violence is foreshadowed, is seen coming and is discharged like the storm that floods the soundtrack of half the film.

Visually the film has a perverse, ominous beauty. The cars that run along the freeway: speedy, blinding, diffuse. The sinister Mercedes like a depraved insect. The itinerary from bar to bar of a woman searching for her lover, unavailing, unceasing, accentuating the murky, enclosed atmosphere of the bars and of the film: its title, in the original French, heralds a double torture for claustrophobics only. The scene of the failed suicide of the juvenile delinquent lovers is very beautiful indeed. Its plastic beauty has the sound equivalent of the duo for violin and piano that the girl plays to accompany their rendezvous with death. The whole setting – the office, the bars, the motel – has a decadent aura and nevertheless the style of the film is new and vigorous.

The movie has made me spend an hour and a half in frank and rank entertainment but – in spite of the double surprise of the ending, of the thriller tone – it seems to me that Malle's intention has been that of a moralist. A modern moralist (like Vadim in *And God Created Woman* or in *No Sun in Venice*), who only visits a precinct to say that the

French police are as brutal with delinquents as they are servile with the powerful. He knows that it is a police force which is there to preserve order, social order that is, and which actually functions as a corps of bailiffs for the rich. A moralist who makes the killer a hero of the war in Indochina and a man who believes in no values except for money. His only personal solution is to kill. (Are his binges just the expression of a guilty conscience?) A moralist who says that the dead man is an arms dealer who is now becoming rich from Algiers as he did before from Indochina. A moralist who knows that in a bourgeois society that has silenced the class struggle (France, England, the United States) the outlaw is the only rebel.

18 March 1959

The Cranes Are Flying

Sometimes they talk to you so much about a movie that by the time you go to see it it doesn't work for you. Other times there's something like a contrary little man inside you that by opposing ends the others and a bad movie is transformed into a good one. Or from just numbering its faults you find virtues. Or which makes you, faced with a great film, wield a microscope to find minute defects, barely scratches on the negative. I hope that none of these viruses that attack the attentive spectator and the critic equally has made a habitat of my circulatory system because I have not liked *The Cranes Are Flying*. I think that it is a good film and nothing more. Everything else that has been said about it has been either very well-staged propaganda or eagerness to witness a resurrection devoutly to be wished: the hope that the Soviet cinema will once again be what it was thirty years ago.

The film has a slight, almost trivial plot in which the grandiloquent emotions that moved Eisenstein or the lyrical heroism preferred by Pudovkin or the personal expressionism of Dovzhenko have been replaced by something that the Western critics, for lack of a better adjective, have called human content. I've seen this 'human content of *The Cranes Are Flying*' mentioned everywhere – even by the critics who had the worst political sense or the best film sense.

This human content does not go beyond being, at the level of the plot, what must be the first enemy of proletarian literature: the petty-bourgeois play. On the level of the realization, it is just what has most been attacked in Soviet Russia: formalism. *The Cranes Are Flying* is a model of what the Soviet cinema should not be, almost better than *Chapayev*.

After five years of successes like *Potemkin*, *The Mother*, *Arsenal* and after having recovered the elements that D. W. Griffith and the primitive Westerns had invented as the language of film, the Soviet cinema created – by deed and decree of Stalin – a sphinx without secrets which would devour all: *Chapayev*, the champion of socialist realism. If one reviews the history of the Soviet cinema, one will see that from 1932 to date the thematics have been steadily less militant, that the style has been increasingly less revolutionary and that the cinema has become little more than mere scholasticism. Is there anyone who has seen more than two or three movies who thinks, leaving aside the addicts and the adepts, that *Glinka*, that *The Fall of Berlin*, that *Sadko*, that *The Stone Flower* have something to do with the cinema? I would extend this list as far as *Alexander Nevsky*, which seems to me a failed attempt at creating a hybrid: the film opera.

In this panorama solely inhabited by the historical reconstruction and the clever biography – where Glinka seems a Bolshevik and Stalin wins the Second World War single-handed – a film that dared to move the tripod to break into the isolationism of the Soviet cinema with the externals of *The Cranes Are Flying* was bound to start a scandal: the camera that flies like a crane.

Tatiana Samoilova is a happy girl with a happy boyfriend. War comes. The boyfriend goes off to war. Tatiana's parents – in a gesture that anybody has to judge as sheer suicide – remain chatting calmly at home while the bombs are being dropped everywhere around them. When Tatiana returns from the bomb refuge there is no house nor father nor mother nor Marx who built the house. Tatiana goes to live with her boyfriend's parents. But there dwells the big bad Russian wolf of the story: a pianist. In this fable without a moral the good guy is an engineer, the ingénue is Tatiana and the bad guy the artist. The pianist pursues her, chases her and finally rapes her (with the aid of some sound paraphernalia that annul one another successively) with more guile than guilt. Tatiana, as in the best bourgeois tradition, becomes an untouchable and has to marry the evil pianist. Meanwhile her boyfriend is killed in the war, soon after a fist fight in which he was arguing that Tatiana was not the same as all women who cheated on the soldiers with the scum that stayed behind. The rest of the film is seeing how Tatiana learns what the spectator already knows – her boyfriend is dead – and the boyfriend's parents find out what the spectator also knows – Tatiana is as innocent as the lamb, the wolf sits on four legs at the piano.

With this story that Wagner* might have made in 1944, the director Kalatazov has cooked a potboiler that will put those friends of mine in a big quandary, all those who said those nasty things about Orson Welles – while they looked wide-eyed at Zavattini. Kalatazov has done nothing more than blind those Soviet black eyes with a formal brilliance we have been accustomed to over here since nineteen hundred and forty-two. Since we saw *Citizen Kane*, to be precise. The result is new bottles for old Soviet vodka: *The Cranes Are Flying* reminds me of a new copy of an old German movie. Even its naïve and urbane opening recalls some Pabst, some Rüttman long forgotten. On occasions – the rape scene, for example – I can think of nothing but the worst English psychology films, let's say *The Seventh Veil*. Here the double, triple images, the sound crescendo in an echo chamber, the skin-deep expressionism are in the worst taste. At other times – like the death of the boyfriend, in a puddle, suddenly – a moment that seems to be very knowing, is made merely naïve, and when the sun fades away before the now dead eyes of the soldier and the shot is replaced by the false wedding in slow motion, one already knows that Kalatazov's case is hopeless – except to find out where his photographer is going to lead him.

The photographer carries him at breathtaking speed on a vexing voyage of vertigo. So much so that it seems that he only knows how to doodle dollies (this is what moving the camera is called technically but pedantically in cinema circles) and that at the least provocation Tatiana will come out running: before her boyfriend who is chasing her, after the train that is carrying her boyfriend away, one step ahead of the werewolf, towards the train under which she will attempt suicide, before the marriage cortège. Thus Tatiana becomes famous for her quick step on the steppes – and Urusevskii, the cinematographer, turns into the Gabriel Figueroa of the Soviets: many claim that Figueroa was the one who directed the films of El Indio Fernández.

What have I liked about *The Cranes Are Flying* that allows me to say that it is a good film? Some things. Among them the scene in which Tatiana learns of the death of the boyfriend and refuses to believe it, in which for the first time the sense of coldness coming from the film left me. Also the final scene – except for the inevitable Soviet speech – in which Tatiana acknowledges that her boyfriend is dead, in which over the PA system they are shouting 'This is a grand day for the Soviet Union' and she cries in silence, in which an old man asks her to be happy

* Wagner Bros, not Richard Wagner Inc.

and she decides to scatter flowers among the crowd. Unfortunately these moments are few.

But there is also the extraordinary performance and the extraordinary beauty of Tatiana Samoilova, who carries the movie all by herself, with her slanted eyes, her straight black hair and her passive resistance to adversity: if there is something memorable in the film, it is her without any doubt.

27 July 1959

No Name on the Bullet

A catalyst is an element that changes the real conditions of the medium that surrounds it but those conditions return to the former state as soon as its action ceases. A catalyst in literary terms is a dramatic element that alters a given situation with its presence. Hamlet is a catalyst. The Chaplin tramp is another. The American hack writer who arrives in Vienna, in *The Third Man*, is also another. John Gant is a perfect catalyst in *No Name on the Bullet*.

The little town in the West is peaceful and puritanical. There are its latent passions but they are controlled by a kind of imported sense of order. One day a young man dressed in black appears, arrives at the hotel and whispers a name: 'I'm John Gant.' Immediately a poker game comes to an abrupt end. A shopkeeper becomes bellicose. A salesman lets it be known that he has taken his adulterous wife from his best friend. A miner finds out that they want to steal his mine from him. The respectable manager of a bank is revealed as a swindler and a coward and finally commits suicide. An old judge turns out to be the grey eminence of a criminal gang. Why all these turns of events?

Gant is the forerunner of Crime Inc. They pay him – people he doesn't know – to kill – people he doesn't know either. When he arrives in the town he is a kind of unleashed conscience. Everyone who has something to fear begins to tremble. It is Gant's custom to call out the man he is going to kill and he always ends up the victor. But this time Gant doesn't have to fire a shot: all his victims die by their own guilt: it is fear, the man within who defeats them.

With this simple plot of a rare richness Jack Arnold – one of the few men in Hollywood who can make a B-movie that is seen with more pleasure than many an epic – has made a little frozen Western that is the most interesting movie of the week. Audie Murphy impeccably gives the vicious image of the gunman who is too young for all the cold evil that he brings with him not to have a hint of the supernatural.

When he appears early in the movie and the dog of a quiet farmer barks at him we all know who he is: the avenging angel of death.

29 July 1959

Passional Obsession

First of all one must not confuse this film that is called *A Woman Obsessed* with *Magnificent Obsession* (twice) nor with *Fatal Obsession* nor with *Sinister Obsession* nor with *The Obsession to Kill* nor with *Obsession*. Here Susan Hayward runs that gauntlet of outrages to which she is accustomed. Other forms of former outrages: she has been gassed, beaten, soused, burned, a tree struck by lightning has fallen on top of her and on a certain occasion the shooting was stopped on *Tap Roots* because she had suffered serious contusions that were not, for once, intended. Susan, between spasms, shouted: 'Go on shooting. We're going to need those bruises tomorrow!' All of which makes her the leading masochist of the movies – after Joan Crawford of course.

Poor Susan has a husband who lasts her through three feet of film before he kicks the bucket or falls in flames. The husband just goes off to the nearby woods which are on fire. To die. She is left alone with her little boy. The bucket is on the floor, Susan cannot even lift it. But help arrives in the shape of Stephen Boyd who now is called, curious coincidence, Mr Helps. And does he help. He cuts wood, ploughs, sows, harvests and lifts the bucket. But between chores he has time to smack Susan's son. Here conflict comes to visit the characters. A very necessary thing because between the promenade of Siegfried – this is what Susan's son should have been called – through the forest and all the little animals that people the environs it was enough to make Walt Disney cry. Hathaway (yes, the same Henry Hathaway of *Kiss of Death*, the man who was once considered one of the most able hands at violence in Hollywood) takes his little exercise of violent action and after the fire in the woods there are: a family quarrel (Susan beaten by Stephen), a brawl on the mountain (Stephen's car almost runs over Theodore Bikel, that excellent European actor wasted in Hollywood), a fight in the town store (Boyd hits someone and someone hits him), a storm, an abortion (Susan's naturally), a rise in the river-level, a lost boy, a tower of strength (Boyd who carries Susan twelve kilometres upriver), a whirlpool (Boyd falls in it but is saved by the boy) and the final reconciliation of everybody with everybody else, like a happy end to end all happy ends. What remains of this endlessly boring movie?

Only one question for Hathaway. How did Stephen and the kid clean the mud off themselves?

7 August 1959

Three Examples with Three Documentaries

(The documentary is dead but three survivors remain)

A première, a pursued old film and a hazardous encounter have let me know of three extraordinary documentaries among us. The first is *The War in the Pacific*, a Japanese documentary that shows a new vision of the war in the Pacific, because it is the vision of the 'enemy'. Made with Japanese documentaries and some American footage when the Japanese did not have their own material available, the film in a certain way pays tribute to war correspondents. On one occasion a battle is spoken of and we are told, very simply, how seven correspondents died. There are moments in which lamentably an almost laughable naïveté drags down the ultimate effect of a documentary in which the Japanese are seen as a humble people, unprepared for the ferocious face of the propaganda at the time. At the same time the film has a poor grain quality that makes it beautiful, with that beauty that documents worm-eaten by time can have.

I remember being moved by Niki, the young suicide pilot, with his fast and decided step at dawn, walking towards the first kamikaze, his hermetic face through which there can nevertheless be seen a certain fear, not the fear of death, but what for a Japanese is still worse: the fear of failure. I see his aircraft battered, broken down, almost a relic of war, its paint peeling away, next to the other planes ready, steady in the early morning, in a row, as if waiting for death and I think of the infamy of the war propaganda, in an article in *Reader's Digest* that denied to these heroic warriors their futile death, the fine desperate gesture and said that the kamikaze went off locked into their cockpits and that the landing gear was designed to fall off as the plane took off so as to discourage any last-minute quitters. I remember the sombre Japanese narrator counting the calamities of his people with a bitter nostalgia. I remember as well the hungry children in camps beyond the reach of the bombs, learning to write correctly, letters to their parents. But beyond the memory, beyond the beauty of an almost masterful documentary, is the clean anti-war, pacifist sentiment which is the underlying message of the film.

Lu tempu di li pisci spata, by Vittorio de Seta, an Italian and a recent arrival, was released a year and a half ago and mutilated, though even with its Feraniacolor almost waterlogged and beached it still has the beauty of the great fish that Santiago caught. De Seta has achieved a masterwork among the pure documentaries by means of its movement, the beauty of the movement, the pure movement, the movement that brings with it the sound: the voices, the guttural noises of the fishermen and the reiterated movement towards the fish, towards the beautiful elongated form that moves: a quicksilver blue slipping fast in the still bluer water to create the most intense fifteen minutes that the Italian cinema has achieved in this genre in decline.

The last documentary is one whose title I don't even know. It is a compilation of sequence after sequence of all types of cars racing along all kinds of tracks: the old wooden track of Altuna, the new earthen track in Altuna, the asphalt of Indianapolis, the sands of Salinas, the concrete of Sebring are the looping reels to run on which the running reels recreate a lost, sporting, unceasing and very American movement. The documentary is dead. Long live the documentary!

25 August 1959

Green Mansions

Once Hemingway said that *Green Mansions* was a book that should not be read after one reaches twenty. He was referring to the fact that its romantic impulse, its primitive and unreal aura, its sentimental exuberance were impossible for a mature reader to accept and thus the famous novel by William Henry Hudson came to be a fairy tale for adolescents.

This could very well be a moving tale for three generations of English adolescents. I confess to having come to it ten years too late for the book and, unfortunately, an hour and a half too early for the movie.

2 September 1959

My Uncle Jacinto

What Ladislao Vajda lacks in order to be Chaplin is what prevents Charlot from being Ladislao: the distance that stretches between both. In his previous film Vajda (and, please, don't confuse him with Andrejz Wajda, the author of *Kanal*, a truly important film, of a dry and honest realism) had locked up his favourite star (Pablito Calvo, a child actor with all the disadvantages and some of the virtues of child actors) in a convent, in a kind of novitiate for minors under ten years old or in a greenhouse for minor saints – there is not even a minor doubt that in *Marcelino, pan y vino* Pablito Calvo goes to heaven like a rocket – and there is not the most minor irreverence in the metaphor. Now Pablito is loose upon the world revealing the true goal of Vajda: the boy is not an innocent but a Lazarillo, the *pícaro* in a minor key.

17 October 1959

Fantasia

Leopold Stokowski shakes Mickey's hand and whispers: 'Goodbye, Mickey'. The most visible expression of the Disney–Beethoven collision – an amorous and swift embrace under the *dolce far niente* of the Pastoral Symphony – is a Cupid whose rolypoly fat ass is transformed into a Tchaikovsky fantasy heart and the erotic saccharine of the *Nutcracker* converts the dragonflies into predictably asexual nymphets, insipid Lolitas. A majestic and pompous – why not say it? – Toccata and Fugue by Bach is transformed not into a forerunner of Norman McLaren (the Canadian wizard with the scratched film and the abstract moving visions) but into the dregs of Fischinger and Schillinger or Lewis Jacobs. Or worse still with Mary Ellen Butte or Ted Nemeth come to nought. *Night on the Bare Mountain* engenders a vision like the rosy dream of a Bosch who has read too many comics . . . and it melts into – of all things! – the 'Ave Maria' by Schubert: Ave Maria! For the *Rite of Spring* there is a line that they say Stravinsky said to a journalist when he asked him his opinion: 'Mr Disney, in view of having paid the royalties, is perfectly within his rights to use my music. The fact that he has given it to Mr Stokowski to play is indifferent to me.' Only Ponchielli with his *Dance of the Hours* and the surrealism which is at the same time pink and beastly (in *Fantasia* Disney not only animates the animated but even the vegetable world comes out dancing) and gross has one or two moments of humour – even though it be at the ballet's expense and with an utterly American attitude: that of considering any manifestation of culture as a laughable thing – with the greatest respect.

And here is the key to Disney – he is an artist – he is? – who is utterly American. His taste for fuchsia red and chartreuse green as 'synthetic' colours is not a happenstance. The languor, the Coca-Cola sensuality, the cheap sentimentality correspond more to majority needs than to individual preferences: hence their success. But in *Fantasia* there is, due to the dance itself, a *faux pas*. Disney was quite good in his early cartoons, with the creation of Mickey – or even better, of Donald Duck who is a universal and unforgettable cartoon character – with moments as in *The Dance of the Skeletons*, with his 'silly symphonies', with a certain naïveté which is also very American, with his facile, sporting and lightweight genius. But in *Fantasia* the man got transcendent and latched on to the 'great' music. Quite a leap. From McKinney's Cotton Pickers to Dukas, from late twenties jazz to the symphony and the symphonic poem, from Sausalito to Salzburg. The leap became a somersault and *Fantasia* is a great failure by Disney: a fiasco cut to the measure of his ambitions and the first great flaw in his character, the fissure that let in all the criticism that has come afterward: an arty artless movie.

But all in all twenty years later *Fantasia* maintains its mighty myth. Coming out of the twin theatre I saw an enormous and eager line next door. If I had kept at it for an hour and a quarter like most of the one-liners I too would have come to think that it is a work of art.

21 October 1959

Floods of Fear

A stentorian announcer (with an English accent) praised hell and high water in the trailers (with an American accent) for *Floods of Fear* (without an accent). He said: 'Howard Keel, for the first time does not sing, he fights.' Back there a wag shouted: 'And why doesn't he sing while he's fighting?' Faced with such a Rank promise, I went to see *Floods of Fear* and I was almost drowned in that flood of waveless action, of still movie-making. It is an English movie but so American that the powers that be had to set it in Canada.

I don't know if Charles Crichton will take into account much of what I'm going to say but after making *The Lavender Hill Mob* signing *Floods of Fear* is coining a counterfeit penny. If *Lavender* was a marvel of mirth, *Floods of Fear* is so serious that it seems as if they wanted to make us believe that the whole hullabaloo of the floods were a true account. Neither the newsreels of the floods in Council Bluffs in 1952 nor the well-made sets nor the studio tank full of churning water manage to erase the Keel's wooden mien. As far as Cyril Cusack is concerned (he has the reputation of being a great Irish actor) his whole effort concentrates on looking like an Alec Guinness who believes himself to be a dangerous jailbird. In Keel's face there is only one graved grimace as he dives, comes back to surface, survives waves, the cruel currents, rapids, goes back in the white water, comes out, swims some, drowns some and finally stares at the terrible torrent – to submerge himself in it one more time. Wouldn't it have been easier to provide Esther Williams with a moustache?

23 October 1959

Richard III

One will never thank the snobs enough for their interest in art cinema (or if we follow Koestler, their interest in art *tout court*), since they have permitted the avant-garde to infiltrate the ranks of the Philistines to plant the standard of an always better cinema. (Though this declaration may not be very far from the soul of Hollywood, 'Movies are better than ever'.) But the agitprop mob has taken the cinema down some of its blindest alleys. For example? The English cinema, whose highest *gloria in excelsis* is the rendering of Shakespeare every five years. (To whom did it occur that this hallucinatory poet, this wizard of words, this pre-romantic baroque bard was ideal for the screen?) Now the snob hosts are crowning *Richard III* again.

Not that I'm accusing the admired Rine Leal of being a snob, because I know that his interest in *Richard III* is his interest in Shakespeare: his interest in the theatre. That is what led to his enthusiasm for the film, which is more precisely an enthusiasm for the Old Vic, for a theatrical tradition and for the actor who is its present-day culmination: Laurence Olivier. But I cannot accept Rine's rejoicing in Shakespeare as the best story-man the English have. That is in fact the capital sin of the English cinema: that a dramatic author who lived four hundred years ago and wrote for the theatre with a verbal vitality only equal to the fire that he transmitted to his characters turns out to be the most up-to-date author for Rank, Balcon and Co., does not demonstrate anything but the early decrepitude of the cinema in England.

Richard III is a furious diatribe against the last of the Plantagenets and the fruit of Shakespeare's youth. Badly planned and written without even the beauty of some of the speeches of *Henry V*, and very far from the perfection of *Richard II*, the best of his dramatic creations,* *Richard III*, nevertheless, has an internal force that the reader will only find in a tragedy: *Julius Caesar*. Perhaps the fact is explained by the liberties that Shakespeare took as much with the chronicles of the War of the Roses as with Plutarch's *Twelve Lives*. Here Richard is a creature of

* Cain must have meant to say historical. A Freudian slip, no doubt.

perfidy, a wicked man from head to toe, and if Shakespeare had had the terrible taste of Lombroso he would have called him a born criminal: 'Deformed, unfinished, sent before my time / Into this breathing world scarce half made up, / And that so lamely and unfashionable / That dogs bark at me as I halt by them; / . . . And therefore, since I cannot prove a lover / To entertain these fair well-spoken days, / I am determined to prove a villain . . .'

Richard has a galloping success in his villainies and successively sickens his brother King Edward with rumours of misfortunes, sends to prison and then murders his brother the Duke of Clarence, decapitates Lord Hastings, assassinates his nephews, the Prince of Wales and the Duke of York, marries the widow of Edward of Wales, whom he himself had killed 'in my angry mood'. Richard murders more: he seizes and beheads his old comrade and cousin, the Duke of Buckingham, holds as a hostage the son of Lord Stanley, and fills the stage with so many villainies that from the time he intones his first sentence ('Now is the winter of our discontent') until he cries, 'A horse! A horse! My kingdom for a horse!', Richard is the most perfect embodiment of a villain since the times of Caligula. Of course we are talking about Richard, the creature of Shakespeare, because the historical figure has been redeemed in part (as much as any of these medieval monarchs can be redeemed) and the 'poisonous hunch-backed toad' has been redressed with the truss (though not the truth) of an historical orthopaedics. According to a present-day revision, Richard was a righteous creature who gave his life to keep the realm for his nephews and ended up torn to pieces by the pushing dynasty of the Tudor – who wrote the history. But none of this interests us – I mean, at least not me – but rather the pathetic, laughable and grotesque figure of Shakespeare's Richard. It is with him that *Richard III* is concerned, the third Shakespearean film by Laurence Olivier – and the worst of the three.

Much more simple than the elaborate, rhetorical and false *Hamlet*, less lyrical and surprising than the pleasant *Henry V*, *Richard III* (through the battered copy that has been shown disgracefully in Havana: streaked, scratched and censored by bad treatment, as if it were destined for a dump in the outskirts and not to a première theatre) is a slow and monotonous movie, with its principal cinematic recourse in the grossly visual approximation of one of the first images of the play: 'I . . . Have no delight to pass away the time, / Unless to spy my shadow in the sun.' Richard passes from felony to felony by the deleterious transit of his shadow and the shadows come and go, at times opportune and apt, at others brought in forcibly but always seen as a solution to the script. This time the charm of the medieval illuminations of *Henry V* has been lost in what appears to be an imitation of the *tableaux* by Jean Clouet: an effort to arrive at the plot of spies and counterspies, palace intrigues and family squabbles. At one moment in the film the royal marriages, the schematic stage directions by Shakespeare and the assumption by Olivier that every spectator has a degree in English history make Richard seem to be his own father. All done with realism – assuming that Shakespeare allows for reality.

There are also the perennial transmutations, the usual changes in the text and even the unusual interpolation of scenes, incidents and characters that do not even appear in the Elizabethan play – plus a few important suppressions. But if what Olivier was looking for was simplicity, a direct point of view, *Julius Caesar* has him beaten by a mile. Since it was not seeking a poetic parallel expressed in images, *Macbeth* continues to be the most cinematic of the versions of Shakespeare until now. A curious thing this, that in the transferring of the plays of Shakespeare to the screen it is the American cinema with *Julius Caesar* by Joseph L. Mankiewicz and *Macbeth* by Orson Welles that offers the best buys.

Not that there are not in *Richard III* some glimpses of intelligent direction and a display of exact equivalences. For example the scene in which Hastings discovers that he is going to be sacrificed to the hunger for power of Richard (from whom he has just received palpable samples of sympathy) is told with an accurate eye for the mammoth intrigues and the little royal cowardices – and this time the alteration of the text is welcome. When Lord Stanley informs Richmond of his plans to betray Richard the next day on the field of battle, the scene permits an exchange of direct affection between the stepson and the old soldier by making Stanley visit Richmond before dusk. In the play the message was logically brought by a messenger. Making Richard slip down by the rope of a bell after he has first rejected popular acclaim and accepted the crown with false modesty shows in visual terms the abject histrionics of the demagogue, the servility of the clergy and the cowardice of the feudal lords – in one single image.

But the greatest merit of the film is its array of actors. Here are all the authorities on Shakespeare as Shakespeare wished them: on the stage. Seeing them together is a privilege for which one has to thank Laurence Olivier and Arthur Rank. It does not matter that some (like John Gielgud) slant their character falsely towards saintliness. It does not matter that others (like Claire Bloom) have to struggle against badly written parts. It does not matter that someone else (Sir Ralph Richardson) transforms a duke into a bumpkin bordering on a moron, when in the original he was a skilled manipulator. It does not matter. All is forgotten when Laurence Olivier is on stage – and Sir Laurence is on stage all the time, as Richard is the eye of the storm of infamies that is the play. From the time he pronounces his 'Now is the winter of our discontent', until he cries, 'My kingdom for a horse!' and lifts his sword between his deformed digits, his work is little short of masterly and his Richard III is one of the most brilliant, coherent and . . . amusing conceptions of an evil man that the theatre has known. This time he has made one forget the false, Douglasfairbankian Hamlet and has lent more veracity to this king than to the other Plantagenet, Henry V. Rarely has the cinema seen a performance so lucid, so complete – and so theatrical. It alone is worth the price of admission and if one could isolate it from the faults and the flaws that the others bring to *Richard III*, this would be a masterwork of the stage on the screen. But with all the cornucopia of diction, psychological precision, conception of the character, movement on stage, I can only remind the reader that the long monologues, the tirades before the spectator, the hissing asides scarcely have to do with the movies. And declare, before the bravura speech of Sir Laurence Olivier, that I *prefer* the sparing *yep* of Gary Cooper.

13 November 1959

cain,
soldier of the cinema,
goes off to the war
of the festivals:
and comes back
more wounding
than wounded

Fortitude in the Fortress

The scene is the fort of San Diego. Here they will show *The Hidden Fortress*, the first film of the Second World Mostra of Cinema Art of Acapulco. *The Hidden Fortress* won the prize for best direction at the Berlin Festival. Its director is Kurosawa Akira. Its lead actor Mifune Toshiro. The action is set in the Japan of the imperial struggles of the seventeenth century.

It is necessary to climb the cliff where the fort is to reach its ramparts.

The fort of San Diego was a wonder of Spanish military architecture and was built in the sixteenth century. Now it is not even a shadow of what it was: it has been destroyed in the twentieth century. In 1959, just a few weeks ago to be exact. The fort was washed, scraped clean and burnished, they built a theatre on its esplanade and a helicopter pad on one of its bastions. On the outer wall shine dozens of torches, obviously taken from a cheap staging of *Othello* or from the concept that Spyros P. Skouras has of Samarkand. The torches take light away from the dim stars that adorn the *World Review* etc.

The inauguration is at 21:00, as the Mexicans call nine at night. At 22:00 no one has arrived. At 22:30 a band emerges. At 23:00 the stars begin to arrive. The band plays – quite visible on one of the lateral bastions – Mexican music. There are heard the rhythmic chords of the Mexican *danzón Almendra*, composed by the late and celebrated Mexican composer Abelardito Valdés, no relation of the late Cuban composer Aberlardito Valdés, author of the *danzón Almendra*. The Soviet stars arrive. Occasional music is heard: the Mexican bullfighting *paso doble Gallito*, which is hardly a relation of *Gallito*, a Spanish bullfighting *paso doble*. The Swedish star Ingrid Thulin and her husband arrive. Occasional music is heard. It is the Mexican waltz *Der Blaue Danube*, by Juan Estraus.

The curtains open. Title credits in Japanese: very sombre – white on a black background – and very simple and very beautiful. *The Hidden Fortress*. Surprise! We will see two-thirds of a fort, because the screen is six feet too short on each side and much of the play of lights and shadows in Cinemascope escapes through the corners of the frame, on the way out to oblivion. Kurosawa is the first film-maker of outer space. Will this be the cinema of the future? It seems that Mexico has hit by chance – happenstance is the mother of the sciences – on a greater invention than the waltz.

The Hidden Fortress is a story full of violence and humour that takes place in that golden and black age of Japanese history and literature, which was peopled with brave samurais, with noblemen loyal to a dethroned house, with implacable political persecutions, with sudden and laborious restorations of the defeated house to power. Apparently it is the time of Lady Murasaki – the mythical authoress of *The Tale of Genji* –, of the deadly passion of Kesa and Morito, of the infernal Jikogu Mon or Great Gate of Hell. The movie is perhaps a little long and full of the brilliant and fatiguing art of the Kabuki theatre, but it has the mobility of a Western. In the past Kurosawa has not attempted to erase the evident influence of John Ford and on this occasion –

without the metaphysical anguish of *Rashomon* or the socialist touches of *Seven Samurai* – one sees quite clearly that *The Hidden Fortress* is a perfect Eastern. Here are the ineradicable bulwarks of Ford – *Fort Apache* –, the hair-raising action in perilous passages – *Stagecoach* – and even part of his Irish humour transferred to some sort of Japanese vernacular.

Three things are evident in *The Hidden Fortress*:

1. Kurosawa Akira is one of the greatest directors in the world. His use of Cinemascope is perfect and novel.
2. In East and West good cinema always means good entertainment.
3. Mifune Toshiro is the most powerful presence in Asian cinema.

12 December 1959

Chabrolissimo

A Double Tour (which is French for 'double locked') is the third film by Claude Chabrol and the most costly. Here there are brilliant colour, much professional savvy and famous actors. (Madeleine Robinson won a prize in Venice from it.) The movie is unlikely to be seen in Cuba, since in Mexico it got the coldest possible shoulder under a *sarape*. Nevertheless, it is the most interesting *double tour de force* of the Festival. It is everything bad that they have said about it: false, artificial, decadent and cold. Because of that it is full of virtues: never has a French camera been moved with such calculated precision and at the same time managed to bring to the spectator the surprise of new, original shots. The plot is a little mystery of passions – and Chabrol has declared that he chose the mediocre little pulp novel to demonstrate that the plot is not necessary to a movie when there is imagination: a thought that, like many of the ideas of Chabrol, comes from Hitchcock. A French actress, sitting beside me, told me that a *charade à la Chabrol* in France is asking what frame from what movie of Hitch begins with the camera moving around a table. If nobody answers one can ask Chabrol for the answer. He will say, 'First sequence of *Shadow of a Doubt*. At the end the camera goes to a window and follows the man through a deserted summer house.' Chabrol has, at least, a taste for colour very superior to that of Alfred Hitchcock and Henri Decae, the photographer of *Les Quatre Cents Coups*, demonstrates that in colour as in black and white he is, in scarcely a half-dozen films, the best photographer in France.

Someone pronounced the unintended eulogy of *A Double Tour*. He said about the film: *Chabrolissimo. A Double Tour* is *Chabrolissimo*. I wish that one could say the same of all films: then it would mean good taste, sense of rhythm, eye for the cinema. That, unfortunately, is not seen every day.

14 December 1959

cain
travelled to acapulco
to wait for
the boat from
*acapulco**

The Eye and The Face

Acapulco is expensive and not for the pensive. There is no modest (or immodest for that matter) hotel available. There remain two saving graces, the Pierre Marqués, solitary branch of the Pierre hotels on Marqués Road, 38 kilometres from the site of the Festival and El Presidente, the most expensive hotel in all of Mexico. There is nothing else to do but to seek asylum in that Aztec temple to the dollar called after the once and future president. Headache? An Alka-Seltzer please. *Ahoritita señor*. Instantly they send a bell-boy with a briefcase, another with the key, one more with a bottle of mineral water, another with the remedy and finally a fifth Mexican with a glass. They all want their tip. When they see that I only offer thanks, they leave me alone. But still the incredible luxury and the genuflections that the dollar gets are bothersome in this present from an ex-President to his little dear son when he came of age. Mexicans are doting fathers.

The Face was the film for tonight. It is the second film by Ingmar Bergman that I've seen and neither this one nor *Secrets of Women* justifies the fame as a Scandinavian magician Bergman has. *The Face* is an extraordinarily well-made film – more than anything else because Bergman is a wizard with actors – and amusing. But its metaphysical pretensions are hardly justified.

Fugitives from justice, Professor Vogler – played by Max von Sydow with a Pirandellian mimicry and one must consider von Sydow one of

* In the history of piracy a coveted ship that used to travel between Mexico and the Philippines loaded with treasures was called 'the boat from Acapulco'.

the great actors of the world cinema – and his troupe are heading for a vain village where the hamlet dwellers all want to test their own firm convictions. The chief of police is known to be astute and powerful, the old doctor believes himself an eminence of rationalism, a husband who is burdened with a wife full of spirits wants to disillusion his spouse. Herr Vogler will perform the play with which they will unveil the unconscious of each other.

Vogler is pursued by the nasty accusation of being a mesmerite and dons a disguise that makes him a cross between Christ and Svengali. He is deaf and dumb. On the road he sees a drunk die and before his eyes the evident mystery of death escapes him. He travels with his grandmother, a witch of the old school, all crosses of ashes, dark prayers, spells, inconjurable curses and love philters. With him travel also a boy too pretty to be a man, a phony and astute assistant and the young coach driver. Vogler believes sincerely in his occult powers and feels himself at times chosen by a redeeming mysticism. But soon the game of transmutations begins.

The chief of police is a filthy and incompetent wretch. The husband endures the deceit that is wife attempts with Vogler: he has discovered that he loved her more than he thought. The doctor feels that his security in rationalism and science shakes with a mere glance from Vogler. But it is not only the hosts who change. Their guests do too. The pretty dark-haired young man is Vogler's blonde wife, disguised to flee from justice. The love potions of the witch are mere filthy philters. Vogler himself is a fake, the worst kind of fake: the one who tries to believe in his own fakery. He is not of the school of Mesmer but a poor magician who has taken up the fake beard, the wig and the top hat with the same devotion as his pretended muteness. Defeated, all his magic exposed as mere sleight of hand and found out, Vogler attempts a last gambit to frighten the doctor, who now tries to carry his wife away: he stages a magnificent panoply of substitutions, pretends to be dead, changes places with a dead body and, when the doctor thinks he has just finished the autopsy on the vanishing magician, Vogler rises from the grave in a seance of terror that has nothing to learn from the best horror shows of Universal Pictures.

But Vogler ends up vanquished forever: he has proved nothing, except that he is a skilled prestidigitator. Now he bums a few cents and watches his company dissolve before his eyes. When he seems already finished, an announcement from the Palace arrives: the king has heard of a priceless magician named Vogler, holds him in great esteem, wants to see him at the Palace, tonight. Vogler smiles and one does not know if his smile is from professional pride – or that of the man who knows that he knows a secret.

What has Ingmar Bergman meant to say in *The Face*? It is known that he is a cinéaste who takes the cinema as a theatre of thesis. But here, has he put into pictures the old phrase of Shakespeare, 'all the world's a stage . . .'? Or is he saying that a man is only accepted as genuine when it has been proven that he is a fraud? If Christ returned to the world, would he have to do sleights of hand to prove that he was the Messiah? Mere miracles would not be enough? Faith in the evident is less worthy than a belief in deceit? It is difficult to say. Bergman seems to have performed a masquerade, a *tour de force* in the old Scandinavian manner of mixing fiords and fantasy. He has given us a good show, too. Here, as in Kafka, as in Dostoevsky, as in Shakespeare, metaphysics can also be enjoyed as a tale told by a sage signifying something.

21 December 1959

A Taste of Trnka

A Midsummer Night's Dream is a fragrant, beautiful and poetic pantomime in which Jirí Trnka (pronounced Trenka) has taken Shakespeare's text as a pretext for animating the irresistible world of his marionettes. Trnka – now at the midpoint of his life and with the look of a busy Norman *patron* or better still: a good-humoured Stalin – is one of the few natural poets of the cinema and some day it will be seen if he must envy Walt Disney his art. For me, Trnka is almost a magician, and I lovingly recall his version of *The Nightingale and the Emperor*, the toy tale by Andersen, narrated by Boris Karloff with something that can only be described as unheard-of mastery.

In *A Midsummer Night's Dream*, Trnka has worked with gusto, for he has found three incentives: 1. Shakespeare, first of all an old idol of Trnka and of Czechoslovakia; 2. a new material to make the dolls with (a special gum, which gives them an enormous mobility and allows them to be a more manageable size); and 3. the panoramic screen. Here (in the film) is Shakespeare without Shakespeare: that is without words. *A Midsummer Night's Dream* is a pantomime with music and narration. As far as the panoramic screen goes, Trnka spent a year studying the complexity of the new dimensions and totally altered his former concept of stage space.

The result is a masterwork for Trnka, a pride for Czechoslovakia and a feast for the spectator. Here are the amiable characters of

Shakespeare, with their happy passions, their rapidly resolved messes and their theatrical vitality. The poetry of the words of Shakespeare is missing, of course, but in the cinema one must be glad of this and Trnka also shows himself to be a master in that art which does not get any easier through repetition: the adaptation of the plays of Shakespeare to the cinema. Moreover Shakespeare's verse has been replaced by the poetry of images. For instance the complex palace plot has been reduced to a minimum and the scenes in the enchanted forest have taken on a greater importance. Thus the world of gnomes, fairies, imps and goblins is now the habitat of the fabulous passions and all the amorous imbroglios.

A Midsummer Night's Dream is the most beautiful film I have seen in a long time. An exemplary job of good taste, of good humour, of good cinema.

2 January 1960

cain
trips up
two times twice:
with the cinema
of the future
and with the old
politicking
of festivals

Les Quatre Cents Coups, the 'André Bazin Prize' and the Politics of Festivals

I still recall when barely a year and a half ago François Truffaut was not invited to the Cannes Festival. They were afraid of his reviews, harsh and terrible (as in *enfant terrible*) and how he would write all about it in the newspaper *Arts*. The next year – a curious thing – Truffaut was the most important figure at Cannes and there was nothing else to do but give him a prize for *Les Quatre Cents Coups* (*The Four Hundred Blows*): his colleagues down there considered him the best director of the year. I have come to Mexico just to see three films: *The Face* by Bergman, *General della Rovere* by Rossellini, and – of course – *Les Quatre Cents Coups*.

Les Quatre Cents Coups lost out at Cannes to *Black Orpheus* but in Mexico and Acapulco it will win out not only against the shrill thrill in the film by Marcel Camus – a poor competition after all – but to two works of merit by two great masters: *The Face*, the strange, strong film by Ingmar Bergman, and *Nazarín*, the masterwork by Luis Buñuel. Why? Because *Les Quatre Cents Coups* represents the cinema of the future – and not only in France. With time it will be seen that to a certain degree it is a film as important – and please! I'm not trying to set up comparisons – as *Open City* (*Roma, Città Aperta*), *The Battleship Potemkin* and *Citizen Kane*, in the sense that as much as this one has for the French cinema, the others blazed a new trail for the Italian cinema, for the Soviet cinema and for the American cinema. And of course *Les Quatre Cents Coups* is also a masterwork.

Seeing *Les Quatre Cents Coups*, I could do no less than imagine the face that Ricardo Vigón would make watching it. We had talked a lot about Truffaut, about his reviews in *Cahiers du Cinéma*, about his adamant position on the cinema, about what we shared. He, like us, scorned the films by Duvivier, Carné, Clouzot. We, like him, believed that American movies, Hollywood and all those classics were the most important cinematography in the history of the cinema, he and we fought for all the films *maudits*, for the forgotten directors, for the new directors with talent and against the false reputations, the literary cinema and the lies of the technicians. There were of course the inevitable divergences. And here I was faced with *Les Quatre Cents Coups*, the film made by a young man of twenty-eight who had learned everything he knew about the movies at the movies (*cinemathèques*, neighbourhood cinemas, first-run cinemas), knowing that each movie one sees, old or new, is a lesson. The same guy who could repeat along with that famous German general, 'All technicians are liars', the critic who was about to show the way to all the French directors, old and new. And, of course, the author of *Les Quatre Cents Coups*.

It begins with a dedication which is moving: *Ce film est dedié à la mémoire d'André Bazin*. Bazin was the man who had met the young almost illiterate Truffaut, back from the war in Indochina and released not long before that from a reform school: Bazin was the man who had introduced Truffaut to the true cinema. The film was dedicated as a book or a poem is dedicated: to indicate that it was a work by an author, a film of which François Truffaut considered himself the sole owner of its minuses and its plusses: an author's film: the first totally autobiographical film. Then there follows a view of Paris in which one only sees the tops of the roofs, of the old houses, the high windows of the buildings, the needle at the end of the Eiffel Tower, the treetops in the Champs-Elysées. Rarely has a film begun in a form so poetic, so suggestive and so cinematic.

Les Quatre Cents Coups is the life of the director as a tyro. It could just as well have been called *Portrait of the Cinéaste as a Young Man.* Doinel is an intelligent high school student with bad grades. The explanation is in his home. He lives in squalor and in disturbing promiscuity with his father and his mother. His father is really his stepfather: a weak, good but also cowardly man. Some time ago he committed a grave mistake in recognizing the failed abortion of this blonde, pretty and indifferent woman who cheats on him at all hours of the day and also at night. She is young Doinel's mother. While playing truant from school, Doinel sees his mother kissing a man in the street. The next day they ask him at school for an excuse for having been absent. The answer he gives the teacher: 'My mother died yesterday.' When they discover the lie, Doinel is severely punished: it is the last time they will do it. He writes a letter in which he explains that he will 'give the four hundred blows'. (Literally: to go on the run.) He leaves home, lives in the street and steals. One day he tries to sell a typewriter from his father's office and is caught when he tries to return the stolen item because he could not find a fence. Doinel is thrown by his father into a reformatory which seems more like a concentration camp. One day Doinel escapes and in one of the most beautiful endings that I have ever seen in the cinema, he runs and runs and runs followed by a long flight of the camera. Finally he comes to the sea, sees that his *fuga* has ended and here the film ends too with a monstrous freeze-frame of Doinel who faces – the audience? His lost childhood? His fate?

This ending filled with poetry, with pain and with beauty has been interpreted in various ways by different critics. One American critic says that it has the feel of the photos of juvenile delinquents in the police pages of newspapers: the hunted and haunted boy is confronted finally with those responsible for his crime: his parents, his family, society. A French critic has said that in the ocean the young Doinel saw liberation, the golden dream, and on finding it he sees that his life stops and his childhood of fantasy collides with hard reality. An English critic suggests that Truffaut threatens a second part of a possible trilogy that will have these three cinematic volumes: 1. 'The critic as a child'; 2. 'The critic as a critic'; 3. 'The critic criticized by critics.' I believe – without naïveté but without cynicism – that the ending is simply the image, in which any symbols are left to the spectator's imagination, of the poetic conception of an instant. Whether this be the end of a life or the ending of a film is absolutely the same to me.

Les Quatre Cents Coups is full of poetic and cinematic subtleties that I will analyse when it is released in Cuba. Now I want to speak only of its unusual poetic language, of its painful humour, of its inexhaustible film imagination: here is an example of the cinema of the future: personal, human and unburdened by the equivocal ballast that has been called in some parts 'audiovisual counterpoint', 'the specifically cinematic' or 'film sense'. Montage – as invented by Griffith and systematized by Eisenstein – has ended. Depth of focus, the incredible mobility of the camera, the new techniques make the close-up and its scaffolding of relations, obsolete. In this sense *Les Quatre Cents Coups* is the cinema of the future. As Alfred Hitchcock, Orson Welles and Roberto Rossellini have been. As Claude Chabrol and Stanley* are.

I would like to talk about a lot of the film, to give the reader an idea of what the new concepts of montage are, of what *Les Quatre Cents Coups* is. I will try to do it by saying that the film owes a great part of its structure to Jean Vigo and to his *Zéro de Conduite* (*Zero in Conduct*), much of its humour to Jacques Tati, to *Mr Hulot's Holiday* and to *My Uncle*, part of its storytelling technique to Rossellini – and all the rest to Hitchcock. And if I wished to point out an influence foreign to the cinema and still more comprehensible, I would speak of Arthur Rimbaud, of his hallucinatory adolescent poetry and I would cite, from among the dirty things locked in my memory, that poem called 'Seven-Year-Old Poets' or something like that:

The Mother closed the copybook, and went away
Content, and very proud, and never saw
In the blue eyes, beneath the pimply forehead,
The horror and loathing in her child's soul . . .
Seven years old and he made up novels: life
In the desert, Liberty in transports gleaming,
Forests, suns, shores, swamps! Inspiration
In picture magazines: he looked, red-faced,
At Spanish and Italian girls who laughed . . .
He relieved himself†

The day after seeing *Les Quatre Cents Coups* I ran into Denis Marion, General Secretary of the IFCP or International Federation of the Cinema Press. He asked me if I would be interested in being a member of the jury that would award the only prize of the Mostra: I told him I would. He asked me if I would be staying in Acapulco. I told

* Stanley who? Kim Stanley? Stan(ley) Laurel? Stanley & Livingstone?
† *Quelle mémoire!*

him no, that it was very expensive, that I would be going back to Mexico City. Two days later I received a letter from him:

My dear colleague

The Jury of the IFCP has decided to count on you as the representative of Cuba for the prize . . . which will be given to a film presented in the course of the Mostra.

If you return to Acapulco, please arrange to contact our president, M. Vinicio Baretta, Hotel El Cano. If not, you can send your vote by mail.

In the latter case I take the liberty of informing you that in the course of a first meeting of the Jury, many of its members showed the intention of voting for *Les Quatre Cents Coups*. In case you prefer another candidate and this does not receive the majority of the votes, you can then indicate that you do not oppose this selection.

Veuillez croire . . . etc., etc.

Le Secrétaire Général
Denis Marion

What to do? I spent the whole day musing with the dilemma of the vote in my head. I thought about *Nazarín* which was a masterwork, about the fact that I still had not seen *General della Rovere*, that the terms of the letter did not please me, because they were peremptory, turbid. I thought about it for four days. I went to see *Nazarín* again, as well as *A Double Tour* by Chabrol and *The Prodigal Sons*, another strong contender. Today I saw *General della Rovere* and walked along the wide avenues of Mexico, flanked by leafless, thin trees, thinking.

When I get back to the hotel, I sit down to write:

Sig. Vinicio Baretta
Hotel El Cano,
Acapulco.
Caro Signore Baretta:
Mon vote est pour *Les Quatre Cents Coups*.

I seal the letter. But I don't mail it.

The next day I tear up the letter. And I make up another one voting for *Nazarín. Les Quatres Cents Coups* is still the newest film. But the politicking that is carried on around it, almost the work of canvassers, bothers me. Furthermore *Nazarín* is the pared-down work of a master and also deserved the prize. Perhaps an *ex aequo* will be reached. Both are worth it.

All this has allowed me to become acquainted with the interior workings of a Festival, its miseries, its flaws. I think about the film by Truffaut, how they have made into something soiled – the force of habit – a win that could have been clean and clear.

4 January 1959

The Eleventh Hour

At one time Stanley Kramer was considered a progressive producer – and the adjective progressive reaches even as far as his political fringes because Kramer produced, among others, *Home of the Brave*, a film that attacked racial discrimination with war as a bond between the races. Kramer was the totem of every new producer and the taboo of the old big companies. He made money, won fame and the applause of the critics. One fine day he began to compromise. The anti-Communist hysteria had touched him closely and one or two of his directors (Kazan, Dmytryk), many of his actors (James Edwards, Sterling Hayden, Kirk Douglas) and an occasional screenwriter (Albert Maltz, John Howard Lawson) had been accused of being Communists, fellow travellers and all the gamut of the colour red, sometimes downgraded to slightly pink. To cleanse himself he dipped into the box-office Jordan of two or three boffos which at the same time filed the rough edges off their sources. (*The Caine Mutiny* is the best example.) One day he became a director and what he had accomplished as a producer – in every sense – he put into his new career: *Not as a Stranger* was not very far from *The Caine Mutiny*. About two years ago Kramer took a new tack and got involved with a trend that seemed to want to recover its former self. *The Defiant Ones* greatly recalls *Home of the Brave*. *On the Beach* attacks an evil disease of the century: atomic war.

1964 is not very far off but a calendar at the beginning of the film makes it appear as remote as the utopia that Orwell described in *1984*. There has been an atomic war and the city of Sydney (Australia) looks like London must have done in 1864 – except for an occasional Ferrari and a too-aerodynamic tram. Everyone continues to be imperturbably English and one can almost hear the lady with the pink straw hat whisper to her guest: 'Drink your tea, dear, before any atomic ash falls in it.'

Everyone is waiting for imminent death in the shape of a lethal cloud that has finished off life on the planet – except in this Erewhon which already is vanishing in remote Oceania. As in *Ape and Essence* by

Huxley, in the novel by Nevil Shute on which the film is based, the life that is left on earth has taken refuge in the faraway Pacific. Here we will get to know the last literary characters in the world and also their last petty problems. People continue having the same conflicts as in the *ante bellum*, only now there is no Oedipus complex, nor guilt feelings nor frustration about the past to blame on someone, but rather the anxiety about an ominous future. Ava Gardner is an inebriated nymphomaniac, Fred Astaire a drunken scientist, Tony Perkins a callow, shallow officer and his wife a catatonic madwoman. Meanwhile Gregory Peck plays an absolute schizoid. Singularly he is chosen as the last leader of what is left of the American Fleet – but the blame is on Einstein not Freud.

Anyway, if the cloud that kills is coming, the spectator finds out because the characters tell him. Finally everybody dies with the suicidal passiveness of kamikazes in peacetime. After all is said and done, this is not a war movie but a post-war one.

The singular thing about this film which formally is a hybrid (Kramer alternates monstrous and dated close-ups with bold camera movements and even an obvious steal from rich Hitch, in a kiss between Ava Gardner and Gregory Peck which is identical to the famous kiss of Kim Novak and James Stewart in *Vertigo*) is that it turns out genuine at times despite the phony plot, and is moving in the midst of many a naïveté. It is not the alarming music and the vision of a deserted San Francisco which are terrifying – contrary to what Kramer might think – but the Coca-Cola bottle that is transformed into the last telegraphist on earth, or a line of citizens who are fighting to get their ration – of poison that will free them from radiation sickness. (I don't know why I remembered 'The Lottery', the wicked story by Shirley Jackson where a whole town played a lottery in which the winner was stoned but not drunk.) Or the empty streets and a sign that remains as a reminder of the warning from the Seventh-Day Adventists: 'It's later than you think.'

These moments make one forget that Fred Astaire – still with the breath of a tap-dancer – shuts himself up in his garage and commits suicide by making his Ferrari fill the room with carbon monoxide or that Tony Perkins does a bad impersonation of Gregory Peck and his grimaces are the worst in the film or that in a aristocratic club the Australian aristocrats seem to come right out of the scene of the wager in *Around the World in Eighty Days*.

I at least came out of the moviehouse with a feeling that could be called reflective anxiety: all this may be true. The film perhaps is not an announcement of the apocalypse but the apocalypse revving up.

6 January 1960

You Are The Poison

Robert Hossein is the director of this film and also its leading actor. The spectator must start guessing who gets the best acting slice. Hossein the actor did not have good luck gambling that night. He is seen walking, alone and beaten along the stony strand of Monaco. Suddenly a car stops. 'Which way to Nice?' asks a woman's voice from the car, and it seems that what she really wants to know is the way to nice. But good old Hossein heard well: 'Turn left, then right, go straight ahead and then turn again to the right of the left and . . .' 'Do you want to show me the way?' begs the voice. Hossein gets in. But they don't go into the Nice road. When Hossein is about to protest he receives a striking jolt: the lady at the wheel has not let her face, covered by a magnificent blonde mane, show, but now she becomes more revealing: under the dressing gown she has absolutely nothing on. Well, that is, nothing in the way of clothes. Hossein the actor says nothing, but acts. When he gets finished, it is the woman who is doing the acting: Hossein doesn't want to get out of the car, naturally, but this driving Lady Godiva threatens him with a pistol, a coercion as striking as the earlier two and he is let alone in a convenient forest, with no memory, other than the Cadillac's tag, 20–EV-06.

When Hossein arrives at the house of the owners of the car, he meets with a double surprise: the blonde has multiplied: there are two now. A serious, intense sister (can it be her? In two words, impossible) and the other one an invalid, romantic and eclectic. (Can it be her? Out of the question.) Hossein stays and stays on in the house because of those strange bedfellows of the French detective novel: here, homicide and adultery are twin crimes. The ardent blonde sister continues calming her furore with medicinal walks along the deserted beach at midnight and the aid of a passive pedestrian. Hossein does not know what to do: he has in his hands a great mystery perhaps but its saline solution does not demand great urgency. Here is the problem for spectators. Who is really the nymphomaniac from Cadillac 20–EV-06? The sane sister with the beautiful blonde mane, the invalid sibling with the beautiful blonde mane, the cook with the beautiful blonde mane or the gardener with the beautiful blonde mane? Here is the sole solution. Hossein will have to choose between the grand reserve of Odile Versois or the contained exuberance of Marina Vlady Versois. They are uterine sisters, aren't they? So, one must not blame Robert Hossein (the director) because it takes Robert Hossein (the actor) a good hour and three-quarters to end the tale of two sisters.

The Thirty-Nine Steps

You all know that the best English film by Alfred Hitchcock is called *The Thirty-Nine Steps*. Now you will find out that the worst English film is called *The Thirty-Nine Steps*. What has happened? Well, there is no spectator who can go up so many steps without a helping hand by Hitch. Not only for the entertainment's sake but to give the most apparently banal moments a twist and a metaphysical turn. Fear in Hitchcock is not a sensation but a state of the soul. Mistaken identity in Hitchcock is not a device to make the action go forward but a Pascalian mystery. Humour in Hitchcock is not a pleasing piece of clockwork drollery but a coherent response to the irrational.

18 May 1960

last
of the last
chronicles by
cain:
curiously,
its subject was,
one more time
for the last time,
ladies and gentlemen,
les quatre cents coups

Les Quatre Cents Coups

Doinel has escaped from the reformatory on a cold spring day. He succeeds in fooling his pursuers by hiding under a bridge. He goes out to the country and starts running for his wretched life – and does he run! The camera follows him in a lateral dolly while he runs along a road, then turns on to a path and finally makes a dash for the open country. The camera takes him in a pan, catches the cold early landscape and reveals the sea in the distance, until once again Doinel is seen in a twist of the path. Doinel is still running: now he is on the deserted beach. For the first time in his life he sees the ocean he has fled to. He runs along the beach, reaches the white and frozen waves. He runs a little more through the water, stops perplexed and sees that the ocean is still a prison. Or, simply, thinks that he has arrived at the end of the road. He stops, looks back (at the past or at the audience) and is shot into a still that immobilizes his flight, his face, his life – while the Doinel theme plays nostalgic, tender and there appears the phrase THE END.

This is the final sequence of *Les Quatre Cents Coups*. Rarely has the cinema taken less elements from its technical arsenal – a five-minute dolly plus a still – and obtained better results. 'It's terribly depressing,' said Calvert Casey on the way out. True, because the boy, the child, the adolescent who has lost forever his golden age, faces the spectator with a terrible accusation: you are the guilty one, he seems to be saying. The last photograph has the desperate gesture, the terrible nakedness of police mug shots. But it is precisely this final sequence, this violent running and this photo still in the memory which transform *Les Quatre Cents Coups* into a masterwork.

Up to the end there are truly pathetic moments, there is lyricism, there is a dry and bitter humour that the novice François Truffaut has taken from one of his masters, Jacques Tati. Nevertheless, it is here that all the poetic description of the child's world, of the vicissitudes of high school, of the double confrontation of the universe of the child and the edge of the adult, in which the infantile naughtiness seems a just response to the degradation of the adult orbit, takes on a real meaning of accusation, of unveiled denunciation. The children do not live in a closed world, penetrated at times by the insidious intrigues of the adults, but rather their life of lies, of escapes (from school, from adult life), of the movies considered as a last refuge is a response to the false values that their parents present as sole and lasting.

Thus *Les Quatre Cents Coups* is transformed into the first film that truly denounces the people guilty of creating so many rebels. Like *The Catcher in the Rye* (a great American novel which anyone who has read it considers the first cry of alarm about juvenile delinquency, though still a cry wrapped in the ether of poetic description, of a realism that is almost magic), *Les Quatre Cents Coups* prefers humour, suggestion, hints to denunication: reformatories, farm-schools, the technique of making delinquents while one is made to believe that they are being stamped out, are definitively revealed as what they really are: the torture chamber which presents itself as effective therapy. In this sense its only possible antecedents are *Zéro de Conduite* by Vigo, from which it has inherited its poetic aura, its love of childhood, its comprehension of juvenile alienation, and *Los olvidados*, which it recalls in the fierce brutality of the adult world and the absolute innocence that is shredded day by day while the child 'becomes reasonable'.

What more is there to say? What I said when I saw the film in Mexico almost a year ago, when I wrote to the late Ricardo Vigón telling him: 'It is a masterwork and curiously it doesn't seem like it.'

21 June 1960

Requiem
for an
alter egotist

Intruder in the dust of love

Cain was just dying to parody Quevedo's verse. As a matter of fact he was just dying. He was dying period. The reverse of Marion Crane he didn't die in the shower. There was no Mother Bates to give him the coup de grace under pressure, shower pressure. He wanted to die as he was born: in the shower, singing. This is a fitting death for a tenor or a crooner but for a film fan or buff or both it is ridiculous! But in one more reversal in his life he had to die dry. Quevedo also died dry. What can one do? Death must have a stop! In the meantime let's hear Cain sing the song he learned from a butler that he wanted to sing in the shower:

> *For all a reviewer's rule,*
> *Love teaches only how to be a fool*

Then he turned into dust before returning to dust. In such an erotic person dust in love not dust the intruder was his destiny. But Doubt, a mugger, assaults me while I praise Cain. Let Doubt empty the pockets of the Turk, that chess player who always checks mate for me, a Maelzel of myself, to shout out loud his whisper: 'What if he hadn't died? What if he were lurking not like a shadow in your heart but hidden in the star dust, cosmic ash his comic ashes?'

Sherlock Holmes seemed to fall into the abyss but it was Professor Moriarty, the Napoleon of crime, who had his Waterloo, prescient name, while Holmes came safely back to Baker Street, with Wat-Watson stuttering incredulous. Ulysses, on his return to Ithaca, found the solicitous pretenders all in a row to marry the smiling weaver who played her stalling game. Mattia Pascal could not resist the fatal lure of the dusty dossiers, of the old asthmatic archivist, of his woman in waiting. Can some horrendous horror movie, the missing masterpiece, the fourth dimension of the screen make the spectre of Cain, his sawdust in love, come back? Remember that all becomes dust except, naturally, dust itself.

I think, for another thing, about the faithful, obsessive Mrs Danvers waiting for the return of her mistress, unaware that she had been there all along: her dreams were Rebecca and her desires were Rebecca and even the house she set on fire was Rebecca. I see myself in the front row of a first-run theatre, looking at a still born from a magazine, before the rusty Remington: in each corner of my memory I'll be waiting for the return of the cronista, *a crony, and the image depresses me to the point of no return: I do not want the comeback of Cain if I have to pay the price of waiting for it.*

Infinite dream of Cain

Cain dreamed of being a cronista. *When he woke up he didn't know if he was Cain who was dreaming about being the* cronista *or if it was the* cronista *who was dreaming he was Cain. (That's called butterflies of the mind.) Such perplexity prefigured his end. A critic can die of strangeness, what he cannot do is live in strangeness. I knew that his term was nearing its end by his recurrent dreams: he was dreaming that the cinema would be a garden of earthly delights. The movies would supplant not only the theatre or the opera, but the novel, the short story, the poem: in the future there would only remain the art of architecture, fused with the abstract design and the concrete sculpture, to create beautiful and inhabitable objects. And the cinema, which would be at the same time art, history and spectacle: the narrative entertainment 'that instructs while it delights', a visual* Dímelo Cantando.* *He was dreaming of a free, happy life, confident that the words police, army, war, race, sex, family and, especially, death, would be abolished forever from our vocabulary and from life. He was dreaming of a future in which work would not be a miscasting and life would stop being a serial of prejudices and man would cease to live, as in a melodrama, between fear and hope. Dreams and more dreams: Cain was the stuff dreams are made of. At times, he had thrillers in the shape of nightmares and the ending could be touched with his hand: the atomic bomb was bursting out all over: a mushroom in his dreams. Life was ending thus among the smoke and the bang. This dreamer of apocalypse, near the end of his days, to be able to sleep, was opening the seventh seal of Seconal every night.*

* *To clear up an image recurrent in Cain, which seems to me too obscure, I'll explain. The* Dímelo Cantando *was a radio programme sponsored by Gravi the dentifrice or 'the queen of toothpastes', in which singer Chanito Isidrón and other* decimeros *responded to questions from the audience by playing an ur guantanamera. Model question: 'What is life?' Model answer:*

> *'Life is breath, good or bad,*
> *that we aspire to be born,*
> *to be gone*
> *when we cease as a deceased'.*

What does doubt smell of?

Goethe said once that the tragedy of Hamlet was having asked a man to do precisely what that man among all men was incapable of doing. Cain engaged himself with his double to do the only thing that it was impossible for him to do: criticize. To censure and applaud – the eternal trade of the critic – one must have a position in life and he had none. I believe that I must explain what many readers have probably already noticed: Cain is compared with Hamlet too often. It is unavoidable: both suffer from the same sickness of the self. Cain was a critic who could not make up his mind and died in an odour of doubt, which is worse than BO: brotherly offensive.

Life, passion and death of Cain

Life and death were overflowing Cain's vida. *He was also overflowing with passion, and all was in the cinema. For him the cinema was a gospel, because it contained his life and his passion and his death. The bachelor Sabuco had an idea once – and I say once, because later his daughter, Doña Oliva, would steal it from him – and he shared it with the entire Middle Ages: 'Those bitten by the tarantula are cured by dancing to good music.' Would Cain come back to life by jumping up and down 24 times per second? I don't think so: more than good cinema would be needed. He would need a miracle and then to be called by another name. But we can (I and those who may wish to follow me) make him live in our memory: no one really dies while he is not forgotten.*

I prefer him alive, because I believe with Solomon that a live dog is worth more than a dead lion, and he is a dead lion. I prefer to see him alive, even if he had to wag his critical tail grateful to be with us. Cain thought otherwise and chose a farewell, going off to 'sail other seven seas of madness', as that poor man's Seneca, Lucho Gatica, would sing.

A *cronista* vanishes

Cain went away: he vanished, he disappeared. His ashes were not scattered at sunrise with taps at reveille. Nor was his corpse cremated *on a boat in the sacred Almendares,* nor buried in a pauper's grave, which is the monument to the unknown corpse. Simply, he was lost from sight: now he accompanies Sandor Petöfi in that popular limbo of missing heroes.*

Since I do not fear an inevitable death, but voluntary oblivion, I will make him return in my totalitarian recall. I will not recall his hands moving nervously about, nor his irrelevant exabrupt at the theatre exit, nor how he always used to sit in the first row to share the melodrama with the magnified fleeting shadows, but a particular morning, an aura, the live man living, leaving, and a single sentence, said without wanting to. It was in the morning and they had invited us to a press show at the Astral moviehouse.

You know how it is there in Havana in the early morning, down there on the corner of 12 and 23 at that time, with the ticket vendors shouting the imminent departure of the last train to Chance (I don't have to tell you it was lottery Saturday) and the bus commuters that come and go and the early employees that get away just to drink a demitasse in midmorning and the occasional daughter who buys flowers for her dead mother lying there in the cemetery next door and the people with paper-slip transfers on the corner or on the opposite corner, waiting for their bus and the noise of the cars and the trucks passing by and the bustle and the black smoke that the buses release and the whistle of the policeman futilely hurrying up the traffic, trying also futilely to make the pedestrians enter the white crossings of the law, finally adding racket to racket, and the always open café on the corner that changes its human skin five times during the day: all that, you already know: La Habana en la mañana.

Cain confided to me that he liked most to go to the movies during the day and how much more he liked going to the movies in the morning, especially, and coming out to see how 'the excessive sunlight formed outer walls with the dust'. But more, much more, than that he liked to go into the house from the lively, livid light that fell like baking powder on the asphalt black from smoke to change to brown, purple,

** The expression 'sacred Almendares' is not mine, it's Cain's: I took it from his article 'A River Is a Running Gag', subtitled 'Heraclitus used to sing in the shower'. Cain begins his essay, left unfinished, with these retrospectively prophetic lines: 'No one bathes twice in the same Almendares: the turbid waters, the sewer wastes, the must from a nearby brewery, make this river sacred – for me, at least. I believe it my duty to pre-Socratically demonstrate why the Almendares must be sacred for other humans too.' Next there was a long exposition in which Cain made the history of the Almendares visible, turning to pre-history to establish as proved, scientifically, that the river was one of the oldest streams of consciousness on the globe. In fact, as Cain explained, the Almendares River is older than the island of Cuba.*

mauve, and then deep blue and smoky black again, and feeling when going in from the Chinese laundry heat of the tropical street to the humid coolness in the artificial jungle of the air conditioned dreams and changing his dark shades good for the street glare for his movie eyeglasses and stopping in the aisle to look at the red backs of the seats, deaf, blind and mute witnesses to the passions on the screen and seeing the timid lights that hardly lighted the house knowing that in a very short time, in a few seconds, now!, the monumental curtain will open and there will appear the cetacean, inhuman whiteness of the giant screen and over it there will be fired a flashing, obscene beam, which will stain the sheet with pain or joy or action or all the colours that nature did not dare to invent: the daily miracle of the movies will take place.

We cross the street in the middle, without concerning ourselves at all with the traffic lights, we push open the thick glass door, we cross the threshold of all wonders and enter the room, the theatre, the moviehouse. It was then that Cain whispered to me almost in fury, livelier than hell: 'This is the life!'

He seemed the happiest man on earth! But as the chorus warns Oedipus at the time of his demise, no man can say that he is a fortunate mortal until he sees the end.

An epitaph without a tomb

A few days after this Cain came to see me and let loose a line: 'I need an epitaph', was all he said. I wrote it, half jokingly, almost with pleasure. I didn't know then that I would also be his exegete, not to say his gravedigger. The epitaph was never published, because the gravestone that was to receive it did not materialize. A little later I found out that Cain never deserved a grave.

Here's what I wrote then.

Goodbye to Cain

I think there's no one better than me to say farewell to Cain: if I saw him born, I can certainly see him die. Cain, like the great ships, sinks down with his name. Must I make it clear that he scuttles in oblivion? I can say in his clear-cut name (and as I am familiar with his narcissism – he wore out the silvering on all mirrors – I can permit myself every immodesty in his name) that he bestirs himself to ask with a foot on the stirrup, because he knows that people will miss him. He will be missed by the reader who marvelled at the coincidences: 'This man and I think the same.' He will also be missed by the other reader, the one who never used to share his judgement: that one who always was carried by the beastly opinion – that one's cup will be overflowing with hemlock words to poison his memory. He will be missed by the greedy or lazy exhibitor. He will be missed by the badmouthing distributor, the prissing publicity man, the woman with haemorrhoids at the ticket window, the dragging usher with flat feet. He will be missed – last but not missing any missing – by the future cinéaste, who knows that in the review begins and ends his every opus. Cain, like his limbs, disappears with the end of the function (his malfunctioning) and with him will leave behind a job that he loved as much as his alter ego *hated it: the job of the critic. Job his writing, Job his reader. It is in the name of scorn that I can say that he dignified the profession at the same time that he incited a fearless few to follow in his footsteps and to find in the reviewing of movies a hole to peep at art and, in passing, at life.*

If someone wishes to say that he was a pedant, pitiless, a show-off let him speak now or forever hold his piece. No one, though, will rise to claim that he was dishonest, unjust or mean – or, worse still, boring. Some have reproached him for having allowed himself the easy rebellion, the taste for the ludic bustle, a too frequent irony. He will forget them with a smile and will say, speaking Latin with a Cuban accent: In riso veritas.

As he was the complete man, a hater of the picayune, of the mean gesture, of the whispering gossip he decided to commit suicide in silence. Cain dies to give further life to his alter ego, *who has more important things to do: mend his socks, trample old nuns, write obituaries. That is to say the labours of lust. The little that Cain did others will do better or worse, which amounts to the same: growing callouses on their ass and wearing out their eyesight and copying the old masters. The six years at* Carteles *are seen today as a time of training for the other: the ubiquitous and prepotent* cronista *disappears, but not his cross-eyed critical vision, and there will remain the poor game of summer dialectics, the scurrying verbal gymnastics to attempt to formulate vain aesthetic axioms that perhaps no one will bring into doubt – but not into practice either. The year at the newspaper* Revolución *served him to erect a watch-tower and to enlarge his spleen: there he wrote early in the morning (or late at night) and used the first person singularly. He also established a rivalry with himself: he knew the medieval legend where the nightingale dies of shame when another bird sings better and he wanted that other nightingale to be a mirror.*

And all his life was useful to him to know how to die: one day, in a last intellectual scruple that is equivalent to the pistol in the mouth or to the capsule of cyanide under the tongue, Cain declined to respond to the lively lady questioner of The Critic's Choice.

'I'm no longer a critic,' he said cryptically and disappeared, this time for good: now he lives in the province of Nada. There were demonstrations. Some shamelessly exhibited their grief: they proposed a funerary frolic. Another murmured: 'He was a strange man.' (At that time I heard name instead of man.) There was, speaking in terms of historical analogy, the same riot that there was on the listing Titanic *when they counted the lifeboats, the pain of five o'clock, sharp, the afternoon they killed Sánchez Mejía (see Lorca), the anxiety of the day that Al Capone showed off his striped suit, the final panic of the moment when General Custer realized that the Indians were shooting live arrows. I can say that I will never forget the horror, the horror of that tragic day! Cain he dead! To make sure I took notes.*

Well, back to Ithaca, UL. In the name of G. Cain I offer thanks for the futile attempts to keep him alive by offering critical plasma, puns and penicillin, television and radio isotopes: the cronista *(the name means chronicler in English and it is related to chronic, which could mean from inveterate to very bad) stubbornly decided to die, even at the cost of his own life: just like a chronic smoker. To that unknown friend (he wears a mask) in his tomb called The Spirit a handshake and a thankful murmur for what Sam Goldwyn always called the good witches. Truly to all, once more, thanks for your multiple attempts to give word of mouth resuscitation – except for those who were suffering from halitosis.*

G. CABRERA INFANTE

Taco-Taco, 1 April 1961–Havana, 29 February 1962

Index